Social Anxiety in Adolescents and Young Adults

Social Anxiety in Adolescents and Young Adults

Translating Developmental Science Into Practice

Edited by

Candice A. Alfano and Deborah C. Beidel

American Psychological Association • Washington, DC

Published by
American Psychological Association
750 First Street, NE
Washington, DC 20002
www.apa.org

To order
APA Order Department
P.O. Box 92984
Washington, DC 20090-2984
Tel: (800) 374-2721; Direct: (202) 336-5510
Fax: (202) 336-5502; TDD/TTY: (202) 336-6123
Online: www.apa.org/pubs/books
E-mail: order@apa.org

In the U.K., Europe, Africa, and the Middle East, copies may be ordered from
American Psychological Association
3 Henrietta Street
Covent Garden, London
WC2E 8LU England

Typeset in Goudy by Circle Graphics, Inc., Columbia, MD

Printer: Edwards Brothers Inc., Ann Arbor, MI
Cover Designer: Mercury Publishing Services, Rockville, MD

The opinions and statements published are the responsibility of the authors, and such opinions and statements do not necessarily represent the policies of the American Psychological Association.

Library of Congress Cataloging-in-Publication Data

Social anxiety in adolescents and young adults : translating developmental science into practice / edited by Candice A. Alfano and Deborah C. Beidel.
    p. cm.
 ISBN-13: 978-1-4338-0948-4
 ISBN-10: 1-4338-0948-6
 1. Anxiety in adolescence. 2. Social phobia in adolescence. 3. Young adults—Psychology.
I. Alfano, Candice A. II. Beidel, Deborah C.

 BF724.3.A57S63 2011
 155.5'18—dc22

                              2010038802

British Library Cataloguing-in-Publication Data

A CIP record is available from the British Library.

Printed in the United States of America
First Edition

doi: 10.1037/12315-000

CONTENTS

CONTRIBUTORS

Candice A. Alfano, PhD, Department of Psychology, Children's National Medical Center, The George Washington University, Washington, DC

Deborah C. Beidel, PhD, ABPP, Department of Psychology, University of Central Florida, Orlando

Bridget K. Biggs, PhD, LP, Division of Child and Adolescent Psychiatry and Psychology, Mayo Clinic, Rochester, MN

Ruth C. Brown, MA, Department of Psychology, Virginia Commonwealth University, Richmond

Joanne Davila, PhD, Department of Psychology, State University of New York at Stony Brook

Timothy Day, BA, Department of Psychology, University of Nevada, Las Vegas

Andres De Los Reyes, PhD, Department of Psychology, University of Maryland, College Park

Chad Ebesutani, MA, Department of Psychology, University of California, Los Angeles

Paige H. Fisher, PhD, Department of Psychology, Seton Hall University, South Orange, NJ

Marisa Gauger, BA, Department of Psychology, University of Nevada, Las Vegas

Abigail A. Goldsmith, PhD, Posttraumatic Stress Disorder and Stress-Related Disorders Research Program, Veterans Affairs, San Diego Healthcare System, San Diego, CA

Trevor A. Hart, PhD, Department of Psychology, Ryerson University and University of Toronto, Ontario, Canada

Charmaine K. Higa-McMillan, PhD, Department of Psychology, University of Hawaii at Hilo

Lindsay E. Holly, MS, Department of Psychology, Arizona State University, Tempe

Christopher A. Kearney, PhD, Department of Psychology, University of Nevada, Las Vegas

Courtney P. Keeton, PhD, Department of Psychiatry, Johns Hopkins University School of Medicine, Baltimore, MD

Kerri L. Kim, PhD, Department of Psychology, Children's National Medical Center, Washington, DC

Annette La Greca, PhD, Department of Psychology, University of Miami, Coral Gables, FL

Ryan R. Landoll, MS, Department of Psychology, University of Miami, Coral Gables, FL

Kristy A. Ludwig, PhD, Department of Child and Adolescent Psychiatry, New York University Medical Center, Child Study Center, New York

Carrie Masia-Warner, PhD, Department of Child and Adolescent Psychiatry, New York University Medical Center, Child Study Center, New York

Megan M. McFadden, MA, Clinical Child Psychology Program, University of Kansas, Lawrence

Franklin Mesa, MS, Anxiety Disorder Clinic, University of Central Florida, Orlando

Melissa M. Nieves, MA, Anxiety Disorder Clinic, University of Central Florida, Orlando

Adair F. Parr, MD, JD, Department of Psychiatry, Children's National Medical Center, Washington, DC

Armando A. Pina, PhD, Department of Psychology, Arizona State University, Tempe

L. N. Ravindran, MD, Department of Psychiatry, University of Toronto, Ontario, Canada

Rebecca Rialon, EdM, Department of Child and Adolescent Psychiatry, New York University Medical Center, Child Study Center, New York

Roxann Roberson-Nay, PhD, Department of Psychiatry, Virginia Commonwealth University, Richmond

Karen E. Roberts, MA, Department of Psychology, York University, Toronto, Ontario, Canada

Julie L. Ryan, PhD, Department of Child and Adolescent Psychiatry, New York University Medical Center, Child Study Center, New York

Marilyn L. Sampilo, MA, Clinical Child Psychology Program, University of Kansas, Lawrence

Rachel Schafer, BA, Department of Psychology, University of Nevada, Las Vegas

Amie R. Schry, BA, Department of Psychology, Virginia Polytechnic Institute and State University, Blacksburg

Danielle Schwartz, MA, Department of Psychology, Ryerson University, Toronto, Ontario, Canada

Rebecca Siegel, PhD, Department of Psychology, University of Miami, Coral Gables, FL

Lisa R. Starr, PhD, Department of Psychology, University of California, Los Angeles

M. B. Stein, MD, MPH, Department of Psychiatry, University of California, San Diego, La Jolla

Rachel D. Thompson, MA, Department of Psychology, University of Cincinnati, Cincinnati, OH

Giao Q. Tran, PhD, Department of Psychology, University of Cincinnati, Cincinnati, OH

Susan W. White, PhD, Department of Psychology, Virginia Polytechnic Institute and State University, Blacksburg

Argero A. Zerr, MA, Department of Psychology, Arizona State University, Tempe

Social Anxiety
in Adolescents and
Young Adults

INTRODUCTION

CANDICE A. ALFANO AND DEBORAH C. BEIDEL

The patients showed shyness, inhibition in thinking and of memory, and a tendency to withdraw from social activities. The physical symptoms . . . were sweating, blushing, fatigue of the voice, and shaking. One may call the condition . . . social neurosis. The fundamental mechanism . . . is an increased tendency to self-love and self-admiration based on admiration and love given by the parents. The increased demand for self-love and self-admiration can be met only through renewed admiration by others in social contacts; [however] this proves to be insufficient.
—Paul Schilder, (*The Social Neurosis*, 1937)

The concept of social fear dates back to the time of Hippocrates, and the existence of a condition characterized by excessive shyness, social withdrawal, and symptoms of autonomic arousal has long been noted in the psychiatric literature. Although the specific constellation of symptoms that defines this condition has remained largely consistent over the course of more than 100 years, current understanding of the mechanisms that underlie *social neurosis* has evolved significantly. Today, social anxiety disorder (SAD) affects up to 15% of children, adolescents, and adults (Ruscio et al, 2008; Wittchen, Stein, & Kessler, 1999). Although SAD exists across the life span, the average age of onset is during mid-adolescence; it commonly remains undiagnosed until late adolescence or early adulthood. What is it, then, about this particular developmental stage that seems to be the critical period for onset of this debilitating disorder? This question represents the central query of this book.

Although several other volumes have described the etiology, presentation, and treatment of SAD, most have limited their focus to adults, with little more than simple reference to the fact that the disorder is most likely to begin during the teenage years. Because the vast majority of research to date has been conducted among socially anxious adults, such decisions were most certainly reasonable. Within the past decade, however, research has expanded not only to include social anxiety in adolescents and young adults but in many cases to focus exclusively on this age group. The result is an ever-growing body of developmental research in need of both integration and clinical interpretation. The material in this book is, therefore, aimed at researchers and clinicians alike because both groups are confronted with the challenge of keeping abreast of these emergent findings.

WHY FOCUS ON ADOLESCENCE AND EARLY ADULTHOOD?

The term *adolescence* is derived from the Latin word *adolescere*, meaning "to grow up." Accordingly, this transitional period is characterized by a vast number of developmental changes and challenges, including hormonal and sexual maturation, expanding social networks and demands, romantic feelings, dating and sexual activity, vocational training and decisions, cognitive growth, as well as underlying neurological changes. Although puberty is traditionally used to designate the beginning of adolescence, in fact, the onset of puberty continues to shift to earlier ages—today, typically around 12 to 13 years. Thus, contemporary adolescents are required to grow up faster than ever before. Similarly, the point at which adolescence ends and adulthood begins varies considerably across cultures but is generally marked by certain societal milestones, such as the ability to serve in the armed forces, vote, consume alcohol, drive a vehicle, have legal sexual relations, and marry. Perhaps most universally, the end of adolescence and early adulthood is marked by a significant increase in independence from caregivers. This collective shift toward adulthood, incredibly, takes place over the course of just a few critical years.

On the one hand, such rapid physical, mental, and social advancements translate into a period of great excitement and opportunity for the emerging adult. On the other hand, the teenage years are a time of considerable physical and psychological risk, including increased rates of sensation-seeking behaviors, psychiatric disturbances, injury, and mortality. Indeed, Dahl (2004) rather appropriately referred to this developmental period as a time of great paradox. This observation certainly holds true for the socially anxious adolescent, now expected to navigate an expanded social network complete with complex interactions, conflict, new relationships, and budding romantic feelings. As is highlighted throughout this book, associations between anxiety and the social world are extraordinarily complex, and during the adolescent years social anxiety increases the risks of social isolation, peer rejection, and victimization. Similarly, peer relationships influence a teen's self-concept and well-being, including feelings of social anxiety. These associations differ across various subgroups (e.g., males vs. females, heterosexual vs. sexual minority youth, Western vs. Eastern cultures), rendering broad conclusions not only difficult but often inappropriate. Accordingly, the chapters selected for inclusion in this book represent vital areas of both current and future research.

Although the precise point at which adolescence ends and adulthood begins remains debatable, the research and clinical data included in this book focus exclusively on adolescents and young adults between 12 and 25 years of age. The inclusion of this somewhat broad age range is not meant to suggest that that this period is without significant developmental change. More accurately, this crucial developmental period was selected as the focus of this book on the basis of its critical differences from both childhood and adulthood, including, importantly, the formation of a social identity.

FROM DEVELOPMENTAL SCIENCE TO CLINICAL PRACTICE

At first glance, the reader will notice that the current book possesses some necessary similarities to existing texts on SAD, including comprehensive chapters covering clinical characteristics, etiology, assessment, and treatment. Other chapters, however, present content that is unique. Unlike other volumes, this book uses a developmental framework to review and integrate research and theory on the factors that give rise to, maintain, exacerbate, and/or protect against the development of SAD during the period of greatest risk. Contributors specifically limited their focus to the teenage and young adult years to provide the reader with a review of and unique perspective on the latest research exploring social anxiety during this developmental period. Although much of this research has yet to be adequately integrated into the clinical literature, these chapters demonstrate the current knowledge base regarding this transitional stage and demonstrate how such findings can (and should) inform developmentally sensitive models of SAD.

In Chapter 1, Mesa, Nieves, and Beidel review the clinical syndrome of SAD, including its prevalence, course, and negative effects. They compare and contrast the presentation of SAD in adolescents with that observed in adults and children by examining specific features and patterns of avoidance in the context of existing models of the disorder. A comprehensive review and discussion of the role of social skill is also included, guided by consideration of what specifically constitutes *social effectiveness* at different ages of development.

In Chapter 2, Higa-McMillan and Ebesutani review current theories of SAD's origins using a developmental psychopathology framework. Building from existing models, they propose a transformational model of SAD in adolescence and young adulthood, including both predisposing (e.g., neuro-biological vulnerabilities, inhibited temperament, parenting styles) and pre-cipitating (e.g., negative life events, conditioning experience) factors.

Because adolescence is a critical period for the maturation of neurobio-logical systems underlying emotion, Roberson-Nay and Brown examine the neurodevelopmental aspects of SAD in Chapter 3. As the authors point out, even though brain regions associated with attention, affect, and behavior undergo considerable reorganization during adolescence, rarely has the role of development been considered in neurobiological models of the disorder. Unique to this discussion, the authors begin with a review of "typical" brain development as a basis for understanding the pathogenesis of SAD.

In Chapter 4, Starr, Davila, La Greca, and Landoll examine the fre-quent overlap of SAD and depression. Because both disorders are associ-ated with impaired interpersonal functioning and loneliness and have a typical onset during the teenage years, the authors review shared and unique risk factors that predict SAD and depression. Toward elucidating this com-mon comorbidity, they also examine the temporal sequencing of SAD and depression.

La Greca, Davila, Landoll, and Siegel examine dating and romantic relationships among socially anxious young people in Chapter 5. Although these relationships represent a normal and important aspect of social devel-opment, they remain a largely understudied aspect of social anxiety. The authors discuss both the broad developmental and qualitative aspects of dat-ing and romantic relationships during this period.

Thompson, Goldsmith, and Tran examine the relationship between SAD and alcohol and drug use in Chapter 6. As highlighted by the authors, although these behaviors are well studied in adults with SAD, investigation in young people is limited yet critical because heavy drinking and drug use often begin during the adolescent and college years. Current theoretical mod-els accounting for this relationship are reviewed and considered in terms of their applicability to socially anxious teenagers.

In Chapter 7, Kearney, Gauger, Schafer, and Day review the literature on oppositional, defiant, and school refusal behavior in socially anxious ado-lescents. Given the often persistent and unremitting nature of school avoid-ance in this population, the authors provide a comprehensive model for both assessment and intervention that includes multiple methods, informants, and treatment goals.

Critical to the world of the adolescent are friendships. Biggs, Sampilo, and McFadden thoughtfully examine the peer relationships of socially anx-ious adolescents in Chapter 8, including friendship quantity and quality, social standing within the peer group, and peer victimization. The authors describe a conceptual model for understanding SAD and peer relational difficulties that also considers interpersonal and cognitive factors that may affect social interactions.

We are particularly delighted by the contributions of Roberts, Schwartz, and Hart in Chapter 9. Empirical examination of social anxiety and SAD among lesbian, gay, bisexual, and transgender (LGBT) individuals is woefully rare despite a documented greater risk as compared with heterosexuals. In this chapter, the authors examine specific factors that might contribute to higher rates of social anxiety in these adolescents, such as gender role nonconformity, discrimination, victimization, and decreased social support. The authors also consider the potential (negative) effects of social anxiety on the behaviors of LGBT youth, including increased alcohol and substance use, risky sexual behaviors, and suicidality. By its inclusion, it is our hope that this review and discussion will stimulate greater interest in understanding the unique challenges and aspects of social anxiety in LGBT young people.

In Chapter 10, White and Schry examine social anxiety in adolescents with autism spectrum disorders. It is noteworthy that although it is often assumed that youth with autism spectrum disorders favor social isolation, in fact, a desire for greater social interaction and connectedness is common and frequently co-occurs with considerable social anxiety. The authors describe social challenges specific to youth with autism spectrum disorders and examine how the teenage years present a particularly challenging period for this group.

Zerr, Holly, and Pina describe cross-cultural similarities and differences in the presentation of social anxiety in Chapter 11, focusing specifically on African American, Asian American, Hispanic and Latino, and Native American adolescents and young adults. Both individual and cultural factors that may help explain syndromal differences are considered. These authors provide important direction for future research, including a need for cross-cultural measurement equivalence.

De Los Reyes and Keeton focus more broadly on evidence-based measurement of SAD in Chapter 12. As clinicians well know, assessment among socially anxious teens presents unique challenges. In this chapter, the authors review existing measures of SAD for this age group, including assessment of behavioral, cognitive, and physiological symptoms, while also considering the clinical utility and predictive ability of these measures.

Readers also will find three separate chapters concerning treatment. In Chapter 13, Kim, Parr, and Alfano review the psychosocial treatment literature and consider the appropriateness of specific cognitive and behavioral treatment strategies. The authors also discuss emerging treatment innovations, including virtual reality therapy and cognitive behavioral treatment augmented with D-cycloserine. In Chapter 14, Ravindran and Stein review the existing evidence base for pharmacological interventions and consider some factors that may explain the current (underdeveloped) state of this literature, including parental fears, adolescent motivation for treatment, and culture-based stigmas. Last, in Chapter 15, Masia-Warner, Fisher, Ludwig, Rialon, and Ryan describe the development and implementation of a school-based treatment program for adolescents with SAD derived from empirically supported techniques. Both the advantages and challenges associated with school-based interventions are discussed.

As the content of the following chapters illustrates, the contributions of an outstanding group of experts have produced the reality of our initial vision for this book. It is our hope that the collective result of their research, scholarly efforts, and hard work helps to improve the lives of young people everywhere struggling with social anxiety.

REFERENCES

Dahl, R. E. (2004). Adolescent brain development: Vulnerabilities and opportunities. *Annals of the New York Academy of Sciences, 1021,* 1–22.

Ruscio, A. M., Brown, T. A., Chiu, W. T., Sareen, J., Stein, M. B., & Kessler, R. C. (2008). Social fears and social phobia in the USA: Results from the national comorbidity survey replication. *Psychological Medicine, 38,* 15–28. doi: 10.1017/S0033291707001699

Wittchen, H. U., Stein, M. B., & Kessler, R. C. (1999). Social fears and social phobia in a community sample of adolescents and young adults: Prevalence, risk factors, and co-morbidity. *Psychological Medicine, 29,* 309–323

I

OVERVIEW OF SOCIAL ANXIETY DISORDER IN ADOLESCENTS AND YOUNG ADULTS

1

CLINICAL PRESENTATION OF SOCIAL ANXIETY DISORDER IN ADOLESCENTS AND YOUNG ADULTS

FRANKLIN MESA, MELISSA M. NIEVES, AND DEBORAH C. BEIDEL

A pervasive pattern of social timidity, social anxiety disorder (SAD; American Psychiatric Association, 2000) is the third most common psychological disorder in the United States (Kashdan & Herbert, 2001). SAD exists across the life span, with an average age of onset of mid-adolescence. It is interesting to note that despite the broad acceptance of this time as a critical onset period (Liebowitz, Gorman, Fyer, & Klein, 1985; Turner, Beidel, Dancu, & Keys, 1986), there has been relatively little study of SAD specifically as it presents in adolescence and young adulthood (e.g., Beidel et al., 2007; Essau, Conradt, & Petermann, 1999). With very few exceptions, studies examining the psychopathology of SAD either restrict themselves to adult populations or to combined populations of children and adolescents (e.g., Arnold et al., 2003; Spence, Donovan, & Brechman-Toussaint, 1999). Such a combination is problematic because childhood and adolescence represent distinctly different age groups. Each period is characterized by rapid and extensive development, with unique physical, cognitive, and behavioral maturational stages. Clearly, these different developmental stages influence how the symptoms of SAD will be manifested at these distinct age periods.

In this chapter, we examine the clinical presentation of SAD and review the descriptive phenomenology; its physiological, cognitive, and behavioral elements; the course of illness and detrimental effects; as well as comorbid and related conditions. When pertinent, we highlight how the developmental stages of adolescence and young adulthood may uniquely impact any of these components. We begin with descriptive phenomenology.

PHENOMENOLOGY

Anxiety is conceptualized as a tripartite system (Lang, 1968), consisting of physical symptoms, subjective or cognitive distress, and behavioral avoidance. In the sections that follow, we examine the data pertaining to each of these dimensions, specifically as they affect adolescents and young adults diagnosed with SAD.

Physical Symptoms

The physical complaints of adolescents and young adults with SAD are similar to those reported at other ages. When in contact with, or sometimes even in anticipation of, social or performance situations, people with SAD report a myriad of possible physical reactions. However, the most commonly endorsed symptoms represent a specific subgroup of responses that are characteristic of the beta-adrenergic system (Gorman & Gorman, 1987) and consist of tachycardia, blushing, trembling, and sweating. Most of what is known about the physical responses of adolescents and young adults with SAD is based on self-report. Few investigations have directly examined physiological reactivity when individuals with SAD are engaged in social interaction. In an early investigation (Beidel, Turner, & Dancu, 1985), young adults with social anxiety had significantly larger increases in systolic blood pressure and heart rate when interacting in a role play scenario with an individual of the opposite sex than peers without social anxiety. Furthermore, individuals with high social anxiety, in comparison with nonsocially anxious peers, had a similar significant increase in systolic blood pressure when giving an impromptu speech. It is important to note that study participants were selected on the basis of their scores on a self-report measure of social anxiety, which were in the range of people who would be diagnosed with SAD. However, participants did not undergo a formal diagnostic process. Furthermore, physiological variables were assessed at 2-min intervals rather than continuously throughout the assessment.

In a more recent investigation (Anderson & Hope, 2009), there were no group differences between adolescents with SAD and no psychological disorder on measures of heart rate or blood pressure reactivity during a speech or conversation task. In this study, heart rate and blood pressure reactivity were continuously monitored. Although these results are in direct contrast to the earlier investigation (Beidel et al., 1985), differences in the age of the participants, the more sophisticated assessment equipment used in this latter study, and the frequency with which the physiological variables were sampled either individually or in combination may account for these different findings. Interestingly, in this latter investigation, the adolescents with SAD had higher scores on perceived physiological reactivity during both tasks. Thus, despite no actual difference in heart rate or blood pressure response, they perceived their physiological response as more severe when compared with a group with no disorder. This enhanced perception may have been a result of heightened anxiety sensitivity, which was present in adolescents with SAD but not in the adolescents without a disorder.

Cognitive Symptoms

SAD is characterized by unreasonable worry that the person will do or say something that will be seen by others as embarrassing or humiliating. This worry may take the form of specific negative thoughts, a general unease in social settings, or even specific beliefs that one will not behave "appropriately" in social interactions. Several different strategies have been used to examine the presence and/or frequency of the cognitive symptoms and include assessment of self-statements (specific cognitions), expectations of performance, and evaluations of actual behavior when engaged in social interactions.

In the majority of investigations, negative thoughts are assessed by self-statement inventories, which list possible positive, negative, and sometimes neutral thoughts. Assessment of the type and frequency of cognitions varies across studies. In some instances, people endorse statements on the basis of how they feel in general in social situations. In other instances, participants complete the form immediately after a social interaction, endorsing the thoughts that they had during the preceding interaction. Overall, these studies indicate that adolescents and young adults with SAD report more negative thoughts and fewer positive thoughts on self-statement inventories when engaged in social interactions or public performance situations (for a review, see Beidel & Turner, 2007).

In contrast to self-report measures, other investigators (e.g., Alfano, Beidel, & Turner, 2006) have directly assessed the presence of cognitions during structured role play scenarios and a read aloud task. In addition to describing their thoughts during these interactions, participants (both adolescents with SAD and adolescents with no psychological disorder) rated their performance expectations prior to a social interaction or a read aloud task. In anticipation of and following a social interaction, adolescents with SAD were more likely than adolescents with no psychiatric disorder to expect to perform poorly on the task and afterward and to rate their performance as inferior. Importantly, even though their evaluations were more negative than those of their peers, they accurately appraised their performance. Independent evaluators, blinded to group assignment, rated the adolescents with SAD as significantly less skilled than peers with no psychological disorder. With respect to their thoughts during the social interactions, only 20% of adolescents with SAD reported the presence of negative cognitions. These data are in contrast to assessments using global, self-report measures in which retrospective reporting consistently finds a higher frequency of negative thoughts among individuals with SAD. Yet, when assessed at the time of the interaction, this pattern of negative thinking may exist among only a subset of adolescents with SAD.

One cognitive model of SAD proposes that in social situations, the attention of adults with SAD is directed almost exclusively on the self rather than external social cues (Clark & Wells, 1995). This model posits that people with SAD are overwhelmed with negative self-images when engaged in social interactions, believing that others also perceive them in an identical negative fashion. The validity of this model for adolescents with SAD is unclear. In one investigation (Hodson, McManus, Clark, & Doll, 2008), 11- to 14-year-old adolescents who scored high on a self-report measure of social anxiety had significantly higher scores on self-report measures of negative social cognitions, self-focused attention, safety behaviors and pre- and postevent processing when compared with children with low levels of social anxiety. However, in addition to the fact that youth were not diagnosed with SAD, measures used to assess dependent variables were not validated for use in an adolescent sample. This may be particularly important because symptom expression differs at different developmental stages as a result of basic cognitive, emotional, and physical development.

In an experimental study (Alfano, Beidel, & Turner, 2008), adolescents without a psychological disorder were provided with imagery training and then instructed to engage in negative self-focused imagery while involved in social interactions (negative self-focused imagery group). Their self-ratings and observer ratings of anxiety and performance, as well as co-occurring cognitions, were compared with those of adolescents with SAD and adolescents with no history of SAD but who were not provided instructions to concentrate on negative imagery (control group). Results indicated that the negative self-focused imagery group (who successfully engaged in imagery) were no different from the control group in terms of self-ratings and observer ratings of anxiety. Furthermore, negative self-imagery was not reported by adolescents with SAD when they were engaged in social interactions. Although more studies are necessary, at this time it is not clear if spontaneously occurring negative self-imagery exists among adolescents with SAD. One possibility is that among adults, negative self-imagery may develop over time as a consequence of continued negative social experiences and performances (Alfano et al., 2008).

Behavioral Avoidance

Avoidance of social situations is the third aspect of anxiety, and its presence has been documented repeatedly among adults with SAD (Beidel & Turner, 2007). Interestingly, even after its introduction into the diagnostic nomenclature in 1980 (as social phobia), clinicians were reluctant to diagnose children and adolescents with SAD because it was assumed that they did not avoid social encounters. However, avoidance may often be subtle, consisting of strategies such as avoiding making eye contact with the teacher or requesting to be on the behind-the-scenes stage crew when the class is preparing a school play (Beidel, Neal, & Lederer, 1991; Beidel & Turner, 2007). At young ages, children may not recognize their behaviors as deliberate avoidance of social interactions, yet in other instances children may specifically downplay their behavioral avoidance. In fact, parents and children and adolescents are consistent in their estimation of the severity of social fears, but parents endorse significantly higher rates of avoidant behavior than do youth (DiBartolo, Albano, Barlow, & Heimberg, 1998). Children's reports of avoidance were significantly correlated with a measure of social desirability, suggesting that they may underreport their avoidant behaviors. Therefore, best-estimate procedures, which consider parent and child report, provide the most accurate depiction of avoidant behaviors.

On the basis of diagnostic interview data from the Anxiety Disorders Interview Schedule for *DSM–IV: Child and Parent Versions* (Silverman & Albano, 1996), it is clear that youth with SAD endorse behavioral avoidance across a range of social settings. As with other aspects of this disorder, developmental factors may influence the extent and severity of social avoidance. As depicted in Table 1.1, in comparison with younger children, adolescents report greater avoidance of a broad range of social interactions (Rao et al., 2007).

The typical developmental trajectory of friendships and social engagement may provide one explanation for this more extensive pattern of avoidance among adolescents. During childhood, parents exert significant control over their child's participation in social activities (e.g., arranging play dates, enrolling children in extracurricular activities, ensuring attendance at scheduled activities). During adolescence, the increase in behavioral independence and pressure to participate in peer interaction includes the responsibility for initiating and maintaining social engagement (Hartup, 1989; Hartup & Stevens, 1999). Decreasing parental control may provide more opportunities for adolescents to avoid distressing social situations, establishing a pattern of

TABLE 1.1
Percentage of Subjects Endorsing Avoidance of Social Situations

Situation	Children ($n = 74$)	Adolescents ($n = 76$)	X^2
Speaking to unfamiliar people	71.6	73.7	.08
Initiating/joining conversations	66.2	75.0	1.40
Asking teacher a question	55.4	73.7	5.48**
Giving oral reports or presentations	59.5	71.1	2.23
Speaking to adults	59.5	67.0	.94
Attending parties/dances or other social activities	35.1	65.8	14.10***
Answering questions in class	56.8	63.2	.64
Musical or athletic performance	48.6	55.3	.66
Inviting a friend to a get together	32.4	53.9	7.07***
Writing on chalkboard/in front of others	33.8	50.0	4.05*
Attending meetings	33.8	44.7	1.89
Working/playing with a group	27.0	42.1	3.76*
Dating	5.4	35.5	20.75***
Answering/talking on telephone	29.7	32.9	.18
Participating in gym class	18.9	31.6	3.17
Eating in front of others	6.8	28.9	12.51***
Walking in hallways	5.4	27.6	13.34***
Having a picture taken	21.6	22.4	.01
Using public bathrooms	12.2	21.1	2.13
Taking tests	13.5	19.7	1.05

Note. From "Social Anxiety Disorder in Childhood and Adolescence: Descriptive Psychopathology," by P. A. Rao, D. C. Beidel, S. M. Turner, R. T. Ammerman, L. E, Crosby, and F. R. Sallee, 2007, *Behaviour Research and Therapy, 45,* pp. 1181–1191. Copyright 2007 by Elsevier. Reprinted with permission.
*$p < .05$. **$p < .02$. ***$p < .001$.

impaired social relationships. Thus, the increasingly pervasive pattern of distress and avoidance that characterizes adolescents with SAD, coupled with increased opportunities for avoidance may, in turn, result in fewer friendships and exacerbate feelings of loneliness.

EPIDEMIOLOGY

Although the exact prevalence depends on the particular sample and assessment strategy, SAD affects 5% to 16% of adolescents and young adults (Essau et al., 1999; Hayward, Killen, Kraemer, & Taylor, 1998; Lewinsohn, Hops, Roberts, Seeley, & Andrews, 1993; Nelson et al., 2000; Wittchen, Stein, & Kessler, 1999). When examined separately by sex, lifetime prevalence is reported as 4.9% for males and 9.0% for females (Wittchen et al., 1999). As adolescents mature into young adults, prevalence increases as well; whereas 4.0% of 14- to 17-year-olds met diagnostic criteria for SAD, 8.7% of 18- to 24-year-olds did so (Wittchen et al., 1999).

TABLE 1.2
Fear and Avoidance of Social Situations by
Adolescents With Social Anxiety Disorder

Situation	% endorsing at least moderate distress	% endorsing avoidance
Oral reports or reading aloud	90.5	65.1
Attending dances, parties, or activity nights	90.5	65.1
Asking the teacher a question or asking for help	87.3	69.8
Starting or joining in on a conversation	87.3	73.0
Musical or athletic performances	87.3	52.4
Speaking to adults	85.7	68.3
Speaking to new or unfamiliar people	85.7	63.5
Inviting a friend to get together	81.0	57.1
Refusing an unreasonable request	77.8	51.0
Taking tests	76.2	22.2
Writing on the chalkboard	76.2	49.2
Gym class	76.2	28.6
Walking in the hallway or standing at a locker	76.2	41.3
Asking someone else to change his/her behavior	76.2	54.0
Answering questions in class	74.6	58.7
Working or playing with a group	74.6	41.3
Using school or public bathrooms	74.6	22.2
Meetings, such as Boy or Girl Scouts	74.6	42.9
Answering or talking on the telephone	74.6	34.9
Having a picture taken	71.4	20.6
Eating in front of others	68.3	25.4
Dating	54.0	31.7

Note. From "Psychopathology of Adolescent Social Phobia," by D. C. Beidel, S. M. Turner, B. J. Young, R. T. Ammerman, R. F. Salle, and L. Crosby, 2007, *Journal of Psychopathology and Behavioral Assessment, 29,* pp. 46–53. Copyright 2007 by SpringerLink. Reprinted with permission.

Examination of the features of SAD among adolescents illustrates the extent and severity of their fears. In one epidemiological sample, fear of testing and examinations, even when well prepared, was the most prevalent social-evaluative fear (18.2%), followed by fears of public speaking (13.2%; Wittchen et al., 1999). In clinical samples (see Table 1.2), a substantial percentage of adolescents with SAD endorse extensive and pervasive patterns of fear and avoidance across a broad range of social situations (Beidel et al., 2007).

COURSE OF ILLNESS AND DETRIMENTAL EFFECTS

The onset of SAD may occur at any age, but an earlier age of onset has significant implications for the course of the illness. As adults, people with SAD who had childhood onset had more severe symptoms than when SAD began in late adolescence (Dalrymple, Herbert, & Gaudiano, 2007; Stemberger, Turner, Beidel, & Calhoun, 1995).

Similar to their younger and older counterparts, adolescents and young adults with SAD experience a myriad of functional impairments, including academic and occupational limitations. Of adolescents and young adults with the generalized subtype and a comorbid condition, 20% were unable to go to school or work because of their SAD (Wittchen et al., 1999). Additionally, between 34% and 43% reported diminished work productivity. Adolescents also report abusing substances in an effort to alleviate their distress (Clark et al., 1995; DeWit, MacDonald, & Offord, 1999).

A relationship between suicidal ideation and behavior and SAD in adolescents has been reported. For example, adolescent girls with SAD were significantly more likely to report suicidal ideation, suicidal plans, and suicidal attempts than adolescent girls without SAD (Nelson et al., 2000), though this relationship was moderated by the presence of comorbid major depressive disorder. Specifically, when symptoms of depression were controlled, only suicidal ideation (but not suicidal plans or suicidal behaviors) remained higher in adolescent girls with SAD. In contrast, among teenage girls with a primary diagnosis of major depression, comorbid SAD was associated with a threefold increase in the risk of suicide attempts and an almost fourfold increase in risk of an attempt when the adolescent reported wanting to die. Although the reason why a comorbid diagnosis would increase suicidal behaviors among adolescent girls with major depressive disorder is unclear, the explanation may hinge on the lack of social support in the form of friendships (see Chapter 8, this volume).

In general, adolescents and young adults do not seek help for SAD. The barriers to treatment are not clear, but less than 44% of one epidemiological sample had ever contacted a mental health professional about their fears (Wittchen et al., 1999). However, having a late adolescent onset was related to substantially lower symptom scores after cognitive behavioral treatment when compared with those with an early childhood onset (Dalrymple et al., 2007). Therefore, the longer the symptoms remain untreated (i.e., greater chronicity), the less likely that the individual will respond positively to treatment.

SOCIAL ANXIETY DISORDER AND SOCIAL SKILLS

There is now substantial evidence that social skills deficits are part of the clinical presentation of SAD at all ages. These deficits are apparent in preadolescent children (Beidel, Turner, & Morris, 1999; Spence et al., 1999) and adolescents with SAD (Beidel et al., 2007). When compared with adolescents with no disorder, adolescents with SAD exhibit skill deficits and excessive anxiety in social interactions and when reading aloud in front of a small group. Independent observers rated adolescents with SAD as significantly more anxious and significantly less effective in their oral presentations when compared with adolescents with no disorder. Likewise, adolescents with SAD displayed significantly more anxiety and significantly less skill during the role play interactions with a same-age peer. In addition to these overall impressions of less skill and more anxiety, adolescents with SAD had significantly longer speech latencies when interacting with a same-age peer. However, adolescents with SAD appear to be more skilled and less anxious in these tasks than preadolescent children with the same disorder (Rao et al., 2007). This suggests that even if adolescents with SAD have deficient social skills as compared with their peers, they are more adept at these brief interactions than preadolescent children with the same disorder.

These data illustrate the importance of assessing social effectiveness within a developmental context. Whereas preadolescent social skills are characterized by brief social interactions ("What's your name? Want to play?"; Obradovic, van Dulmen, Yates, Carlson, & Egeland, 2006), peer engagement during adolescence requires increased sophistication, including the ability to carry on extended, spontaneous conversations (Englund, Levy, Hyson, & Sroufe 2000; Obradovic et al., 2006). Furthermore, adolescent social effectiveness includes the ability to participate in group discussions, articulate ideas, and take the perspective of others (Englund et al., 2000). Therefore, the use of short scripted prompts such as those used in traditional role play assessments may not directly tap the skills necessary for effective adolescent social interaction. Indeed, adolescents without a psychiatric diagnosis, specifically selected for their social abilities, were rated as only moderately effective when they engaged in the structured role play task, suggesting that the task did not allow them to fully display their social abilities. In contrast, an unstructured conversation task appears to be a more valid assessment strategy (Scharfstein, Hall-Brown, & Beidel, 2009).

SHYNESS: A RELATED CONDITION

The concept most closely related to social anxiety is *shyness* (e.g., Beidel & Turner, 1999; Turner, Beidel, & Townsley, 1990), which has been described as discomfort and inhibition in interpersonal situations (Henderson & Zimbardo, 1998) or fear of negative evaluation (Buss, 1985). This conceptual overlap prompted a review of the SAD and shyness literatures (Turner et al., 1990), which indicated much overlap in somatic, cognitive, and behavioral symptoms. However, shyness was different from SAD in prevalence, chronicity, and functional impairment. Whereas the lifetime prevalence of SAD is estimated at about 13% of the general population (Kessler et al., 2004), prevalence estimates for shyness range from 20% to 48% (Carducci & Zimbardo, 1995; Henderson & Zimbardo, 1998; Zimbardo, 1977). Similarly, whereas shyness is often transitory (Beidel & Turner, 1999; Bruch, Giordano, & Pearl, 1986; Zimbardo, 1977), SAD is chronic and unremitting (Keller, 2003) and results in significantly greater functional impairment (Turner et al., 1990).

In one of the first direct examinations of shyness and SAD (Heiser, Turner, & Beidel, 2003), 200 young adults were surveyed regarding the presence of shyness, SAD, and other psychological disorders. Whereas only 3% of self-identified nonshy persons met diagnostic criteria for SAD, 18% of self-described shy persons did so. Even though this difference was statistically significant and there was a positive correlation between severity of shyness and the presence of SAD, a prevalence of 18% means that 82% of shy individuals did not meet diagnostic criteria, suggesting that SAD is not merely severe shyness. Furthermore, the proportion of shy people who met diagnostic criteria for psychiatric diagnoses other than SAD was significantly higher than among the nonshy group, although some psychological disorders existed among the nonshy group as well.

In a follow-up study (Heiser, Turner, Beidel, & Roberson-Nay, 2009), shy young adults with SAD reported more core symptomatology (distress and avoidance of social situations), more functional impairment, and lower scores on a quality-of-life measure than shy young adults without SAD, who, in turn, had more fears and impairment than nonshy young adults. Interestingly, almost one third of the highly shy young adults without SAD reported no social fears, highlighting the heterogeneity of the term *shy*. With respect to social interactions, young adults with SAD were less effective when interacting with a peer than either group without SAD, but there were no group differences on physiological reactivity during the social interactions. Overall, it appears that shyness and SAD share many components, but there are important differences as well.

COMORBID DISORDERS

Adolescents with SAD often have comorbid psychological disorders. As noted previously, SAD with comorbid depression appears to be related to significantly poorer outcomes. However, the data on the number of adolescents and young adults with SAD and comorbid depression are mixed. Whereas most studies suggest that adolescents with SAD are at increased risk of a major depressive disorder (Beesdo et al., 2007; Bittner et al., 2004; Essau et al., 1999; Last, Perrin, Hersen, & Kazdin, 1992; Regier, Rae, Narrow, Kaelber, & Schatzberg, 1998), one large epidemiological sample ($N = 2,242$ high school students) did not find higher rates of major depression among adolescents with SAD (Hayward et al., 1998).

Among clinical samples, the prevalence of secondary Axis I disorders (American Psychiatric Association, 2000) among adolescents and young adults with SAD is greater than 50% (Beidel et al., 2007), and the presence of comorbid disorders among people with SAD increases with age (Fehm, Beesdo, Jacobi, & Fiedler, 2008). Similar to general adult populations, the most common comorbid disorder among adolescents was generalized anxiety disorder (74.1%), followed by specific phobia (11.1%), obsessive–compulsive disorder (2.8%), separation anxiety disorder (2.8%), and selective mutism (2.8%). Mood disorders were diagnosed in 11% of the sample (Beidel et al., 2007). Considerable rates of comorbidity have also been found in a community sample of adolescents with a primary diagnosis of SAD (Herbert et al., 2009). In this sample, 59% of adolescents met diagnostic criteria for at least one comorbid diagnosis, and 26% met criteria for two or more comorbid diagnoses. In another community sample, SAD had nearly a 50% lifetime association with another anxiety disorder among 14- to 24-year-olds (Wittchen et al., 1999). Similar to the clinical samples, generalized anxiety disorder (26%), dysthymia (21%), major depression (8%), and specific phobia (19%) were among the most common comorbid disorders.

Unique patterns of comorbidity exist among subtypes of SAD. In a cross-sectional community-based sample, the generalized subtype was more strongly associated with other anxiety disorders (odds ratio of 14.23) than the nongeneralized (performance-focused) subtype (odds ratio of 5.10; Marmorstein, 2006). In addition, whereas the nongeneralized subtype was associated with comorbid depressive disorders, generalized SAD was only related to major depressive disorder in females. In contrast, other investigators have found that comorbidity is generally more common and consistent over time with the generalized subtype than the nongeneralized subtype (Tillfors, El-Khouri, Stein, & Trost, 2009; Wittchen et al., 1999).

There is now substantial evidence that the onset of SAD precedes the development of many of these comorbid disorders (Wittchen et al., 1999). On the basis of retrospective self-report data, for 85.2% of adolescents and young adults with comorbid substance use disorders, SAD was evident at least 1 year before the onset of substance use. SAD preceded the onset of depressive disorders in 81.6% of cases, and for other anxiety disorders, SAD appeared first in 64.4% of cases (Wittchen et al., 1999). The only exception appears to be comorbid specific phobia, which typically had an earlier age of onset than generalized SAD.

In one prospective sample of adolescents and young adults, SAD at baseline was associated with an increased likelihood (odds ratio of 3.5) of subsequent depression (Stein, Tancer, Gelernter, Vittone, & Uhde 2001), and there appears to be a particular likelihood of the subsequent development of depression with the generalized subtype (Tillfors et al, 2009). Similarly, adolescents and young adults with SAD at baseline were more likely to later develop nicotine dependence (Sonntag, Wittchen, Hofler, Kessler, & Stein, 2000).

On the basis of a twin sample consisting of adolescent girls (Nelson et al., 2000), a primary diagnosis of SAD was significantly associated with comorbid disorders of alcohol dependence and major depressive disorder. When compared with females without a disorder, the presence of these comorbid disorders was at significantly higher prevalence among adolescent girls with SAD. Specifically, among teenage girls with a primary diagnosis of SAD, rates of comorbid alcohol dependence and depression were 17.8% and 30.1%, respectively, whereas the prevalence of these two disorders was 9.3% and 12% among teenage girls without a primary diagnosis of SAD. Consistent with other investigations, the age of onset for social fears was 7.3 years, whereas the first depressive symptoms did not occur until age 13.9 years. Similarly, among the teenage girls with comorbid SAD and alcohol dependence, the onset of social fears was age 10.6 years, whereas the age of first alcohol intoxication was 15.4 years. Because this sample consisted solely of adolescent girls, it is not clear if the same relationships would exist among adolescent boys.

Separation anxiety disorder is defined as a fear of harm befalling, or separation from, a parental or attachment figure. As a comorbid condition, separation anxiety disorder was significantly more common among children than among adolescents with SAD in one clinic sample (14.9% vs. 3.9%; Rao et al., 2007). This outcome is consistent with latent class analysis of scores on separation anxiety disorder and SAD self-report measures for children and adolescents (Ferdinand et al., 2006). Whereas the latent class analysis identified a subgroup of children (ages 8–11) with high scores on separation anxiety and social anxiety measures, no such group was identified for adolescents (ages 12–18). In fact, adolescents in general did not endorse high levels of separation anxiety disorder, again illustrating the impact of developmental factors on the expression of the clinical syndrome of SAD.

CONCLUSIONS

SAD exists across the life span. Its core, "a marked and persistent fear of one or more social or performance situations in which the person is exposed to unfamiliar people or possible scrutiny by others" (American Psychiatric Association, 2000, p. 450), exists in adolescent and young adult populations, consistent with the larger existing literatures for children and general adult populations. Yet it is equally clear that the unique characteristics of the former two age groups lead to different manifestation of the disorder at these different stages of development. One of the clearest examples of the impact of maturation is the area of cognition. The ability to report on one's thoughts requires metacognitive skill (i.e, the ability to think about thinking), a skill not present in young children but emerging in adolescents. This difference in basic cognitive ability provides an explanation for prior research that finds that young children often do not endorse the presence of negative cognitions, considered a hallmark of this disorder in adults. Adolescents and young adults appear to fall between these two groups; a subset of adolescents endorses the presence of negative cognitions. Thus, the presence of negative thinking may reflect general cognitive maturity. Similarly, increases in behavioral avoidance with increasing age may reflect basic physical maturity and emotional development of the adolescent as he or she branches out (or is expected to branch out) from the family unit.

An earlier age of onset is associated with a more complex picture in terms of symptom severity and range of impairment. Furthermore, as age increases, so does the prevalence of comorbid conditions such as anxiety and depression. Also with increasing age, SAD exerts significantly greater impact on emotional, academic, and occupational functioning.

Except for separation anxiety disorder, most conditions that are comorbid with SAD have a later age of onset. Although it is possible that these disorders would have evolved independently, it is more likely that many comorbid conditions, such as depression and substance abuse, represent secondary impairments that occur as a result of SAD. In conjunction with the broad range of situations affected and the functional impairment created, the subsequent onset of comorbid conditions clearly illustrates the severe and impairing nature of this chronic disorder.

REFERENCES

Alfano, C. A., Beidel, D. C., & Turner, S. M. (2006). Cognitive correlates of social phobia among children and adolescents. *Journal of Abnormal Child Psychology, 34*, 189–201. doi:10.1007/s10802-005-9012-9

Alfano, C. A., Beidel, D. C., & Turner, S. M. (2008). Negative self-imagery among adolescents with social phobia: A test of an adult model of the disorder. *Journal of Clinical Child and Adolescent Psychology, 37*, 327–336. doi:10.1080/15374410801955870

American Psychiatric Association. (2000). *Diagnostic and statistical manual of mental disorders* (4th ed., text rev.). Washington, DC: Author.

Anderson, E. R., & Hope, D. A. (2009). The relationship among social phobia, objective and perceived physiological reactivity, and anxiety sensitivity in an adolescent population. *Journal of Anxiety Disorders, 23*, 18–26. doi:10.1016/j.janxdis.2008.03.011

Arnold, P., Banerjee, P., Bhandari, R., Lorch, E., Ivey, J., Rose, M., & Rosenberg, D. R. (2003). Childhood anxiety disorders and developmental issues in anxiety. *Current Psychiatry Reports, 5,* 252–265. doi:10.1007/s11920-003-0054-9

Beesdo, K., Bittner, A., Pine, D. S., Stein, M. B., Hofler, M., Lieb, R., & Wittchen, H. U. (2007). Incidence of social anxiety disorder and the consistent risk for secondary depression in the first three decades of life. *Archives of General Psychiatry, 64,* 903–912. doi:10.1001/archpsyc.64.8.903

Beidel, D. C., Neal, A. M., & Lederer, A. S. (1991). The feasibility and validity of a daily diary for the assessment of anxiety in children. *Behavior Therapy, 22,* 505–517. doi:10.1016/S0005-7894(05)80342-9

Beidel, D. C., & Turner, S. M. (1999). The natural course of shyness and related syndromes. In L. A. Schmidt & J. Schulkin (Eds.), *Extreme fear, shyness, and social phobia: Origins, biological mechanisms, and clinical outcomes. Series in affective science* (pp. 203–223). New York, NY: Oxford University Press.

Beidel, D. C., & Turner, S. M. (2007). *Shy children, phobic adults: Nature and treatment of social anxiety disorders* (2nd ed.). Washington, DC: American Psychological Association. doi:10.1037/11533-000

Beidel, D. C., Turner, S. M., & Dancu, C. (1985). Physiological, cognitive and behavioral aspects of social anxiety. *Behaviour Research and Therapy, 23,* 109–117. doi:10.1016/0005-7967(85)90019-1

Beidel, D. C., Turner, S. M., & Morris, T. L. (1999). Psychopathology of childhood social phobia. *Journal of the American Academy of Child and Adolescent Psychiatry, 38,* 643–650. doi:10.1097/00004583-199906000-00010

Beidel, D. C., Turner, S. M., Young, B. J., Ammerman, R. T., Sallee, R. F., & Crosby, L. (2007). Psychopathology of adolescent social phobia. *Journal of Psychopathology and Behavioral Assessment, 29,* 46–53. doi:10.1007/s10862-006-9021-1

Bittner, A., Goodwin, R. D., Wittchen, H. U., Beesdo, K., Hofler, M., & Lieb, R. (2004). What characteristics of primary anxiety disorders predict subsequent major depressive disorder? *Journal of Clinical Psychiatry, 65,* 618–626. doi:10.4088/JCP.v65n0505

Bruch, M. A., Giordano, S., & Pearl, L. (1986). Differences between fearful and self-conscious shy subtypes in background and current adjustment. *Journal of Research in Personality, 20,* 172–186. doi:10.1016/0092-6566(86)90116-9

Buss, A. H. (1985). Two kinds of shyness. In R. Schwarzer (Ed.), *Anxiety and cognitions* (pp. 65–75). Hillsdale, NJ: Erlbaum.

Carducci, B. J., & Zimbardo, P. G., (1995, November/December). Are you shy? *Psychology Today.* Retrieved from http://www.psychologytoday.com/articles/200910/are-you-shy

Clark, D. B., Bukstein, O., Smith, M., Kaczynski, N., Mezzich, J. A., & Donovan, J. (1995). Identifying anxiety disorders in adolescents hospitalized for alcohol abuse or dependence. *Psychiatric Services, 46,* 618–620.

Clark, D. M., & Wells, A. (1995). A cognitive model of social phobia. In R. G. Heimberg, M. R. Liebowitz, D. A. Hope, & F. R. Schneier (Eds.), *Social phobia: diagnosis, assessment and treatment* (pp. 69–93). New York, NY: Guilford Press.

Dalrymple, K. L., Herbert, J. D., & Gaudiano, B. A. (2007). Onset of illness and developmental factors in social anxiety disorder: Preliminary findings from a retrospective interview. *Journal of Psychopathology and Behavioral Assessment, 29*, 101–110. doi:10.1007/s10862-006-9033-x

DeWit, D. J., MacDonald, K., & Offord, D. (1999). Childhood stress and symptoms of drug dependence in adolescence and early adulthood: Social phobia as a mediator. *American Journal of Orthopsychiatry, 69*, 61–72. doi:10.1037/h0080382

DiBartolo, P. M., Albano, A. M., Barlow, D. H., & Heimberg, R. G. (1998). Cross-informant agreement in the assessment of social phobia in youth. *Journal of Abnormal Child Psychology, 26*, 213–220. doi:10.1023/A:1022624318795

Englund, M. M., Levy, A. K., Hyson, D. M., & Sroufe, L. A. (2000). Adolescent social competence: Effectiveness in a group setting. *Child Development, 71*, 1049–1060. doi:10.1111/1467-8624.00208

Essau, C. A., Conradt, J., & Petermann, F. (1999). Frequency and comorbidity of social phobia fears in adolescents. *Behaviour Research and Therapy, 37*, 831–843. doi:10.1016/S0005-7967(98)00179-X

Fehm, L., Beesdo, K., Jacobi, F., & Fiedler, A. (2008). Social anxiety disorder above and below the diagnostic threshold: Prevalence, comorbidity and impairment in the general population. *Social Psychiatry and Psychiatric Epidemiology, 43*, 257–265. doi:10.1007/s00127-007-0299-4

Ferdinand, R. F., Bongers, I. L., van der Ende, J., van Gastel, W., Tick, N., Utens, E., & Verhulst, F. C. (2006). Distinctions between separation anxiety and social anxiety in children and adolescents. *Behaviour Research and Therapy, 44*, 1523–1535. doi:10.1016/j.brat.2005.11.006

Gorman, J. M., & Gorman, L. (1987). Drug treatment of social phobia. *Journal of Affective Disorders, 13*, 183–192. doi:10.1016/0165-0327(87)90022-X

Hartup, W. W. (1989). Social relationships and their developmental significance. *American Psychologist, 44*, 120–126. doi:10.1037/0003-066X.44.2.120

Hartup, W. W., & Stevens, N. (1999). Friendships and adaptation across the life span. *Current Directions in Psychological Science, 8*, 76–79. doi:10.1111/1467-8721.00018

Hayward, C., Killen, J. D., Kraemer, H. C., & Taylor, C. B. (1998). Linking self-reported behavioral inhibition to adolescent social phobia. *Journal of the American Academy of Child and Adolescent Psychiatry, 37*, 1308–1316.

Heiser, N. A., Turner, S. M., & Beidel, D. C. (2003). Shyness: Relationship to social phobia and other psychiatric disorders. *Behaviour Research and Therapy, 41*, 209–221. doi:10.1016/S0005-7967(02)00003-7

Heiser, N. A., Turner, S. M., Beidel, D. C., & Roberson-Nay, R. (2009). Differentiating social phobia from shyness. *Journal of Anxiety Disorders, 23*, 469–476. doi:10.1016/j.janxdis.2008.10.002

Henderson, L., & Zimbardo, P. (1998). Shyness. In *Encyclopedia of mental health* (Vol. 3, pp. 497–509). San Diego, CA: Academic Press.

Herbert, J. D., Gaudiano, B. A., Rheingold, A. A., Moitra, E., Myers, V. H., Dalrymple, K. L., & Brandsma, L. L. (2009). Cognitive behavior therapy for generalized social anxiety disorder in adolescents: A randomized controlled trial. *Journal of Anxiety Disorders, 23*, 167–177. doi:10.1016/j.janxdis.2008.06.004

Hodson, K. J., McManus, F. V., Clark, D. M., & Doll, H. (2008). Can Clark and Wells' (1995) cognitive model of social phobia be applied to young people? *Behavioural and Cognitive Psychotherapy, 36*, 449–461. doi:10.1017/S1352465808004487

Kashdan, T. B., & Herbert, J. D. (2001). Social anxiety disorder in childhood and adolescence: Current status and future directions. *Clinical Child and Family Psychology Review, 4*, 37–61. doi:10.1023/A:1009576610507

Keller, M. B. (2003). The lifelong course of social anxiety disorder: A clinical perspective. *Acta Psychiatrica Scandinavica, 108*(Suppl. 417), 85–94. doi:10.1034/j.1600-0447.108.s417.6.x

Kessler, R. C., Berglund, P., Chiu, W., Demler, O., Heeringa, S., Hiripi, E., . . . Zheng, H. (2004). The US National Comorbidity Survey Replication (NCS-R): Design and field procedures. *International Journal of Methods in Psychiatric Research, 13*(2), 69–92. doi:10.1002/mpr.167

Lang, P. (1968). Fear reduction and fear behavior: Problems in treating a construct. In J. M. Schlien (Ed.), *Research in psychotherapy* (Vol. 3, pp. 90–102). Washington, DC: American Psychological Association.

Last, C. G., Perrin, S., Hersen, M., & Kazdin, A. E. (1992). *DSM–III–R* anxiety disorders in children: Sociodemographic and clinical characteristics. *Journal of the American Academy of Child and Adolescent Psychiatry, 31*, 1070–1076. doi:10.1097/00004583-199211000-00012

Lewinsohn, P., Hops, H., Roberts, R., Seeley, J., & Andrews, J. A. (1993). Adolescent psychopathology: I. Prevalence and incidence of depression and other *DSM–III–R* disorders in high school students. *Journal of Abnormal Psychology, 102*, 133–144. doi:10.1037/0021-843X.102.1.133

Liebowitz, M. R., Gorman, J. M., Fyer, A. J., & Klein, D. F. (1985). Social phobia: Review of a neglected anxiety disorder. *Archives of General Psychiatry, 42*, 729–736.

Marmorstein, N. R. (2006). Generalized versus performance-focused social phobia: Patterns of comorbidity among youth. *Journal of Anxiety Disorders, 20*, 778–793. doi:10.1016/j.janxdis.2005.08.004

Nelson, E. C., Grant, J. D., Bucholz, K. K., Flowinski, A., Madden, P. A. F., Reich, W., & Heath, A. C. (2000). Social phobia in a population-based female adolescent twin sample: Co-morbidity and associated suicide-related symptoms. *Psychological Medicine, 30*, 797–804. doi:10.1017/S0033291799002275

Obradovic, J., van Dulman, M. H., Yates, T. M., Carlson, E. A., & Egeland, B. (2006). Developmental assessment of competence from early childhood to middle adolescence. *Journal of Adolescence, 29*, 857–889.

Rao, P. A., Beidel, D. C., Turner, S. M., Ammerman, R. T., Crosby, L. E., & Sallee, F. R. (2007). Social anxiety disorder in childhood and adolescence: Descriptive psychopathology. *Behaviour Research and Therapy, 45*, 1181–1191. doi:10.1016/j.brat.2006.07.015

Regier, D., Rae, D., Narrow, W., Kaelber, C., & Schatzberg, A. (1998). Prevalence of anxiety disorders and their comorbidity with mood and addictive disorders. *British Journal of Psychiatry, 173*, 24–28.

Scharfstein, L., Hall-Brown, T., & Beidel, D. C. (2009). The use of an unstructured conversation task to assess social skills in adolescents with social phobia. Unpublished manuscript, Department of Psychology, University of Central Florida.

Silverman, W. K., & Albano, A. M. (1996). *Anxiety Disorders Interview Schedule for Children for DSM–IV: Child and Parent Versions*. San Antonio, TX: Psychological Corporation.

Sonntag, H., Wittchen, H. U., Hofler, M., Kessler, R. C., & Stein, M. B. (2000). Are social fears and *DSM–IV* social anxiety disorder associated with smoking and nicotine dependence in adolescents and young adults? *European Psychiatry, 15*, 67–74. doi:10.1016/S0924-9338(00)00209-1

Spence, S. H., Donovan, C., & Brechman-Toussaint, M. (1999). Social skills, social outcomes, and cognitive features of childhood social phobia. *Journal of Abnormal Psychology, 108*, 211–221. doi:10.1037/0021-843X.108.2.211

Stein, M. B., Tancer, M. E., Gelernter, C. S., Vittone, B. G., & Uhde, T. W. (2001). Major depression in patients with social phobia. *Archives of General Psychiatry, 58*, 251–256. doi:10.1001/archpsyc.58.3.251

Stemberger, R. T., Turner, S. M., Beidel, D. C., & Calhoun, K. S. (1995). Social phobia: An analysis of possible developmental factors. *Journal of Abnormal Psychology, 104*, 526–531. doi:10.1037/0021-843X.104.3.526

Tillfors, M., El-Khouri, B., Stein, M. B., & Trost, K. (2009). Relationships between social anxiety, depressive symptoms, and antisocial behaviors: Evidence from a prospective study of adolescent boys. *Journal of Anxiety Disorders, 23*, 718–724. doi:10.1016/j.janxdis.2009.02.011

Turner, S. M., Beidel, D. C., Dancu, C. V., & Keys, D. J. (1986). Psychopathology of social phobia and comparison to avoidant personality disorder. *Journal of Abnormal Psychology, 95*, 389–394. doi:10.1037/0021-843X.95.4.389

Turner, S. M., Beidel, D. C., & Townsley, R. M. (1990). Social phobia: Relationship to shyness. *Behaviour Research and Therapy, 28*, 497–505. doi:10.1016/0005-7967(90)90136-7

Wittchen, H. U., Stein, M. B., & Kessler, R. C. (1999). Social fears and social phobia in a community sample of adolescents and young adults: Prevalence, risk factors, and co-morbidity. *Psychological Medicine, 29*, 309–323. doi:10.1017/S0033291798008174

Zimbardo, P. G. (1977). *Shyness: What it is, what to do about it*. Reading, MA: Addison-Wesley.

2

THE ETIOLOGY OF SOCIAL ANXIETY DISORDER IN ADOLESCENTS AND YOUNG ADULTS

CHARMAINE K. HIGA-McMILLAN AND CHAD EBESUTANI

As interest in the existence of social anxiety disorder (SAD) has increased, so has the interest in the onset and maintenance of this diagnosis. In this chapter, we review the etiology of SAD using a developmental psychopathology framework. Building on models in the literature, we propose a developmental and maintenance model of the etiology of SAD in adolescence and young adulthood. In addition to reviewing predisposing (e.g., neurobiological vulnerabilities, parenting style) and precipitating (e.g., conditioning experiences) factors, we also propose a transformational model of the etiology and maintenance of SAD.

DEVELOPMENTAL PSYCHOPATHOLOGY

The etiology of SAD in adolescence and young adulthood may be best understood through a developmental psychopathology framework. Conceptually, pathology is assumed to be the result of multiple causal influences (multideterminism) that interact dynamically with each factor, potentially changing and being changed by other factors over time (Cicchetti, 2006; Lewis, 2000; Vasey & Dadds, 2001). Three general factors that are thought to influence psychopathology are predisposing, precipitating, and maintaining factors. Although it is most probable that an individual with SAD has some combination of all three factors, it is also possible for an individual to acquire SAD without a predisposing factor or without a precipitating factor, and what serves to predispose and/or precipitate the onset of SAD may later contribute to its maintenance (Vasey & Dadds, 2001). Furthermore, a core principle of developmental psychopathology is the presence of multiple developmental pathways. For example, an adolescent or young adult may acquire SAD primarily because of an inhibited, shy temperament, whereas another adolescent or young adult may acquire it as a result of a negative conditioning experience.

THEORIES OF THE ORIGINS OF SOCIAL ANXIETY DISORDER

A number of etiological models have been proposed for SAD. It is beyond the scope of this chapter to review all of them. Instead, we briefly summarize a few models in the context of our own developmental and maintenance model of SAD in adolescence and young adulthood. Consistent among most models of SAD, our model emphasizes multiple entry points, multideterminism, equifinality, and nonlinear associations (e.g., Morris, 2001; Beidel & Turner, 2007). There are multiple types of predisposing factors, such as neurobiological vulnerabilities, inhibited temperament, poor attachment, and negative parenting styles. These vulnerabilities interact to set the stage for the development of SAD (see Figure 2.1). Individuals with one or more of these vulnerabilities could go on to develop SAD with or without exposure to a precipitating factor (i.e., negative life event or conditioning experience). Further, an individual may not have a predisposing factor but may encounter a precipitating factor leading to the development of SAD. This path is likely characterized by less severe psychopathology and may be more consistent with nongeneralized SAD, whereas the path characterized by a predisposition may be more consistent with generalized SAD (Beidel & Turner, 2007; Hofmann & Barlow, 2002).

Regardless of the initial pathway, all individuals who develop SAD experience symptoms in the presence of social situations that are perceived as threatening. As suggested by multiple researchers, the experience of a socially threatening situation brings on or heightens anxious apprehension and self-focused attention. Barlow (2002) described anxious apprehension as a repetitive cycle in which a signal of threat leads to attentional narrowing with an increasing self-focus that heightens the experience of negative affect. Clark and Wells (1995) argued that this excessive self-focus interferes with processing of social situations and others' behavior and that interoceptive information is then used to construct a negative mental representation of the self (i.e.,

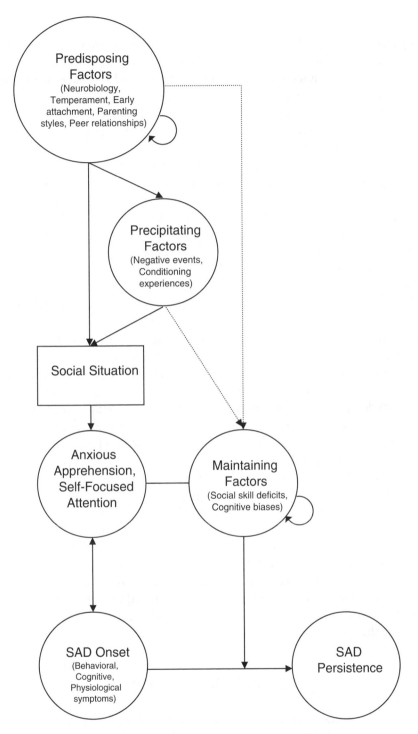

Figure 2.1. Developmental model of the etiology of social anxiety disorder in adolescents. SAD = social anxiety disorder.

negative self-imagery). Furthermore, Rapee and Heimberg (1997) suggested that the socially anxious individual considers what others would expect in terms of a performance standard and then compares his or her own mental image with the expected standard. The discrepancy between the two determines the perceived probability of negative evaluation from other people. This cycle of negative cognitive events is suggested to lead to the development and persistence of SAD.

It is currently unclear, however, how these cognitive models of adult SAD apply to adolescents because few studies have examined their applicability for youth. In a community sample of children and adolescents, Higa and Daleiden (2008) found that youth with elevated social anxiety reported heightened self-focus. However, Alfano, Beidel, and Turner (2008) found that manipulating negative self-imagery among nonanxious adolescents did not increase self- or observer-reported social anxiety. In addition, in a study of physiological arousal, Anderson and Hope (2009) found that despite no differences in objective physiological arousal, adolescents with SAD perceived elevated arousal during two anxiety-provoking situations compared with nonanxious youth. The authors suggested that a heightened self-focus among socially anxious youth made them more aware of small increases in physiological arousal. Finally, Parr and Cartwright-Hatton (2009) found that socially anxious adolescents who received video feedback, a cognitive intervention designed to correct negative self images, developed more positive appraisals of their performance following a speech task and demonstrated a reduction in state anxiety. Thus, a few studies provide preliminary support for the downward extension of adult cognitive models of SAD to younger populations, but more research is clearly indicated.

In the following sections, we first discuss factors that predispose an individual to SAD; then we discuss factors believed to precipitate its onset. Because predisposing and precipitating factors can also act as maintaining factors, they are discussed only once; however, the reader should keep in mind how these factors can reinforce and prolong symptoms of SAD. Social skill deficits and cognitive biases are discussed as maintaining factors. Whether these vulnerabilities are predisposing or maintaining factors will become clearer as researchers more firmly establish whether these vulnerabilities precede disorder onset.

PREDISPOSING FACTORS

Predisposing factors place individuals at risk of the development of SAD. Multiple vulnerabilities can interact to set the stage for the development of SAD. Each is discussed in this section.

Genetic Vulnerabilities

Over the past few decades, research has established that there is a familial or genetic vulnerability to the development of anxiety disorders in general
and social anxiety specifically. The majority of research examining the
genetic contributions to SAD has used family or twin study methods. Family
studies have consistently found significantly higher rates of SAD in the rela-
tives of socially phobic probands compared with nonclinical controls (e.g.,
Fyer, Mannuzza, Chapman, Martin, & Klein, 1995; Hughes, Furr, Sood,
Barmish, & Kendall, 2009; Reich & Yates, 1988). Further, it appears that the
generalized subtype of SAD may indicate increased risk of familial transmission of SAD compared with the nongeneralized subtype (e.g., Mannuzza et al.,
1995; Stein et al., 1998).

Family studies can identify whether offspring are at increased risk of the
development of SAD, but they do not tease apart the relative contribution
of genes and shared environment. In other words, families contribute both
genetic material as well as shared environment that could foster the development of SAD. Twin studies, on the other hand, have the benefit of identifying the unique contribution of genes over shared environmental factors. By
comparing the concordance rates between monozygotic (MZ; identical) twins
who share the same genetic material and dizygotic (DZ; fraternal) twins who
share no more genetic material than siblings (roughly 50%), studies showing
larger concordance rates among MZ than DZ twins indicate a unique genetic
contribution above and beyond shared environment alone.

Twin studies have consistently found evidence for the heritability of
general traits such as behavioral inhibition, shyness, and fear of negative evaluation, which are thought to lead to the development of SAD (e.g., Daniels
& Plomin, 1985; Eley et al., 2003; Stein, Goldin, Sareen, Zorrilla, & Brown,
2002; Warren, Schmitz, & Emde, 1999). Further, a meta-analysis of twin
studies reported a heritability estimate of .65 for social anxiety (Beatty, Heisel,
Hall, Levine, & La France, 2002). However, research has not consistently
supported the specific heritability of SAD. For example, Kendler, Neale,
Kessler, Heath, and Eaves (1992) found a higher concordance rate for SAD
among MZ (24%) than DZ (15%) female twins with an overall heritability
index of 30%. Another study found similar concordance rates for SAD among
MZ and DZ twins, suggesting that there is not a specific genetic contribution
(Skre, Onstad, Torgersen, Lygren, & Kringlen, 1993). More recently, Eley,
Rijsdijk, Perrin, O'Connor, and Bolton (2008) examined a large sample of
6-year-old twin pairs for lifetime presence of social anxiety symptom syndrome
(i.e., SAD diagnosis without impairment criteria). Although they found a
higher concordance rate for MZ (27%) than DZ (14%) twins, the heritability index was nonsignificant at 14% with a majority of the variance being

accounted for by nonshared environment (79%, $p < .05$). Given that SAD onset is typically in adolescence and Eley and colleagues' study examined 6-year-old children, these findings should be interpreted with caution.

Neurobiology

Although relatively less understood, research conducted to date points to several possible neurobiological vulnerabilities underlying SAD. First, as initially suggested by Liebowitz (1987), SAD may be related to dopaminergic dysregulation. Support for this notion comes from research by Tiihonen and colleagues (1997), who examined the density of dopamine reuptake sites via single photon emission computed tomography. They reported that striatal dopamine reuptake site densities were lower among SAD patients than a comparison group matched on age and gender. Tiihonen et al. (1997) also pointed out that SAD patients respond to nonselective monoamine oxidase blockers, implicating the dysregulation of the dopaminergic system in SAD. Schneier and colleagues (2000) also found that patients with generalized SAD show low dopaminergic activity. These researchers, however, also found dysregulated dopaminergic functioning among other populations (e.g., substance abusing), suggesting a more general vulnerability related to psychological distress and highlighting the need for further research.

Research also points to aberrant serotonergic functioning in SAD. In addition to the observation that patients with SAD respond well to drugs inhibiting serotonin reuptake (SSRIs; Bouwer & Stein, 1998; Katzelnick et al., 1995), Tancer and colleagues (1994–1995) found that patients with SAD displayed greater cortisol responses to fenfluramine than a comparison group without anxiety—reflecting differential levels of stimulation of central serotonin $5\text{-}HT_{2C}$ receptors. More recently, Arbelle et al. (2003) and Battaglia et al. (2005) found associations between the serotonin transporter promoter polymorphism genotype and shyness in second-grade children. A recent positron emission tomography study (Lanzenberger et al., 2007) also identified reduced binding of a specific serotonin receptor ($5\text{-}HT_{1A}$) related to SAD.

Temperament

Temperament, defined as biologically based contributions to consistent, basic dispositions that motivate the expression of activity, reactivity, emotionality, and sociability (Rothbart & Mauro, 1990), has been studied in relation to the development of psychopathology. In particular, an inhibited temperament or behavioral inhibition (BI) is often associated with the development of anxiety disorders. *Behavioral inhibition* is defined as withdrawal, wariness, avoidance, shyness, social uneasiness, and fear of unfamiliar situations, people, objects, and events (Coll, Kagan, & Reznick, 1984; Kagan, 1989). Kagan reported that approximately 15% of Caucasian children appear biologically predisposed to be irritable as infants; shy and fearful as toddlers; and cautious, quiet, and shy in middle childhood. Studies have shown that BI marks an increased risk for anxiety disorders in general (e.g., Rosenbaum, Biederman, Hirshfeld, Bolduc, & Chaloff, 1991), and for SAD specifically (e.g., Hayward, Killen, Kraemer, & Taylor, 1998; Schwartz, Snidman, & Kagan, 1999). For instance, Biederman et al. (2001) found that SAD was more common among children with BI than children without BI, and Hayward and colleagues reported that adolescents with childhood BI were at 4 to 5 times greater risk of developing SAD than those who did not exhibit BI. More recently, Hirshfeld-Becker and colleagues (2007) conducted a 5-year follow-up study and found that BI specifically predicted the onset of SAD and was not associated with any other anxiety disorders. These findings substantiated the previous findings that BI was significantly associated with SAD in children ages 2 to 6 years (Biederman et al., 2001). A separate research group also identified BI as specifically predicting lifetime SAD (Chronis-Tuscano et al., 2009).

Some researchers have suggested that there may be two subcomponents of BI: a physical threat component and a social threat component. The physical threat component appears to be less specific, is associated with anxiety disorders other than SAD (Van Ameringen, Mancini, & Oakman 1998), and may be less stable (Asendorpf, 1991; Gest, 1997; Neal, Edelmann, & Glachan, 2002). The social threat component of BI, on the other hand, appears to be more specifically related to fear of social interactions and performance situations and appears to be stable through adulthood (Mick & Telch, 1998; Neal et al., 2002; Van Ameringen et al., 1998). Further, there is some evidence that the social threat component of childhood BI is linked to later depression. This is consistent with findings that in addition to high negative affect, which is consistent across the anxiety disorders and depression, SAD and depression both evidence low positive affect (Brown, Chorpita, & Barlow, 1998; Chorpita, Plummer, & Moffitt, 2000).

Early Attachment

Consistent with attachment theorists' notion that insecure attachment is related to the development of anxiety (Bowlby, 1973; Sroufe & Waters, 1977), studies have since demonstrated that insecure patterns of attachment are related to the development of psychological disorders in general (e.g., Erickson, Sroufe, & Egeland, 1985; Kobak, Sudler, & Gamble, 1991) as well as anxiety specifically (e.g., Barnett, Schaafsma, Guzman, & Parker, 1991; Crowell, O'Connor, Wollmers, Sprafkin, & Rao, 1991). For instance, insecurely attached children are more likely to exhibit symptoms of anxiety than securely attached children (Muris, Mayer, & Meesters, 2000). In a 20-year longitudinal study, individuals who had an anxious–resistant attachment with their caregiver as infants were twice as likely to develop an anxiety disorder later in life compared with other infant–caregiver attachment styles, even when controlling for maternal anxiety and temperament (Warren, Huston, Egeland, & Sroufe, 1997).

Fewer studies have examined the role of early attachment in the development of SAD specifically. Among the studies conducted to date, most indicate that early attachment is related specifically to the development of social anxiety. For instance, Bohlin, Hagekull, and Rydell (2000) conducted a 15-month longitudinal study with children ages 8 to 9 years and found that securely attached children reported significantly less social anxiety, were rated as more socially active, and were more popular among peers at school than children exhibiting anxious–avoidant and anxious–ambivalent attachment styles. Eng, Heimberg, Hart, Schneier, and Liebowitz (2001) examined attachment styles among adults with SAD and found that adults with SAD clustered into two main groups with respect to attachment style—anxious and secure attachment. The anxiously attached adults reported more severe social anxiety, greater avoidance, worse impairment, and lower life satisfaction than the securely attached adults. Overall, however, findings suggest that attachment style is but one factor contributing to SAD, given that a large portion of SAD adults were characterized as securely attached. Other studies have failed to find a significant association between SAD and insecure attachment (Booth, Rose-Krasnor, & Rubin, 1991; Roelofs, Meesters, ter Huurne, Bamelis, & Muris, 2006). Further research is thus needed to clarify whether early attachment is related to SAD specifically or anxiety in general.

Parenting Styles

Research has established that an overcontrolling and rejecting parenting style can also predispose an adolescent or young adult to SAD. Retrospective research has found that socially anxious adults perceived their parents to be overprotective, controlling, insensitive, rejecting, and emotionally distant (Bögels, van Oosten, Muris, & Smulders, 2001; Bruch & Heimberg, 1994; Burgess, Rubin, Cheah, & Nelson, 2001; Parker, 1979; Rapee & Melville, 1997; Schmidt, Polak, & Spooner, 2001; Wood, McLeod, Sigman, Hwang, & Chu, 2003). Studies based on parent reports of their own parenting styles demonstrate that parents of anxious youth view themselves as overprotective and more rejecting than parents of nonanxious youth (e.g., Lieb et al., 2000). Further, research on parent beliefs and observational studies support these retrospective and parental-report-based findings (e.g., Siqueland, Kendall, & Steinberg, 1996). Rubin and Mills (1990), for instance, found that mothers of withdrawn preschoolers tended to report stronger beliefs about parenting in a high-powered and coercive manner and Hudson and Rapee's (2001) observational study demonstrated that mothers of anxious youth were significantly more intrusive during a cognitive task than mothers of nonanxious youth. Additionally, a study of siblings found that parents of anxious youth exhibited more overcontrolling behaviors with their anxious children than with their nonanxious children (Hudson, & Rapee, 2005).

Although the majority of studies on parenting styles have focused largely on mothers, more recent studies have begun to examine the parenting style of fathers of socially anxious youth, yielding mixed results. Some researchers have found that fathers of socially anxious youth also exhibit a high degree of controlling behavior (e.g., Greco & Morris, 2002), whereas other researchers have found that fathers of socially anxious youth do not evidence overinvolvement or controlling behaviors (e.g., Hudson & Rapee, 2002).

In addition to general rearing styles, parents can influence the development of social anxiety through avoidance of social contact and withdrawal from social interaction. Retrospective studies have established that parents of socially anxious individuals tend to overemphasize the opinions of others, underemphasize family sociability, and socially isolate their offspring when they are children (Bruch & Heimberg, 1994; Rapee & Melville, 1997; Stravynski, Elie, & Franche, 1989). Woodruff-Borden, Morrow, Bourland, and Cambron (2002) also found that anxious parents were more withdrawn and disengaged during difficult tasks with their children than nonanxious parents, increasing the likelihood of stress and forcing children to learn to cope with challenges on their own. In a study of children with anxiety disorders and their parents, children were more likely to report responding to a social threat with avoidance after discussing the situation with their parents than before (Barrett, Rapee, Dadds, & Ryan, 1996). In addition, two separate studies using Dutch schoolchildren found that children who reported their parents "warned them against all possible dangers" reported experiencing significantly more anxiety (Gruner, Muris, & Merckelbach, 1999; Muris, Meesters, Merckelbach, & Hulsenbeck, 2000).

PRECIPITATING FACTORS

Whereas predisposing factors set the stage for the development of SAD, precipitating factors generally immediately precede symptom onset and are often referred to as *causal risk factors*. Individuals with one or more of the predisposing factors described previously could go on to develop SAD with or without exposure to a precipitating factor, or individuals may not have any predisposing factors but may encounter a precipitating event that leads to the development of SAD. Various precipitating factors are discussed in the sections that follow.

Negative Life Events

Research on the precipitating factors of SAD has pointed to two main potential contributors. The first implicates early childhood stressors, such as child sexual abuse, child illness, failing a grade, separation from parents, moving multiple times, family conflict, divorce, and parental psychopathology (Bandelow et al., 2004; Kessler, Davis, & Kendler, 1997; Lieb et al., 2000; Magee, 1999). A majority of the research on negative life events and SAD has used retrospective reports and has not examined the proximity of negative events and disorder onset, thus calling into question the precipitous nature of negative life events and SAD onset. However, using a discrete-time event history method, Magee (1999) examined the proximity of life events and SAD onset and found that sexual assault by a family member precipitated the onset of SAD in girls, whereas verbal aggression between parents and verbal aggression by an adult precipitated SAD onset in boys and girls. Additional research is needed examining other negative life events as possible precipitating factors.

Conditioning Experiences

A more compelling set of precipitating factors for SAD may be direct and indirect exposure to conditioning experiences. Direct conditioning experiences related to the development of SAD typically involve exposure to socially related events, such as being called on in class, speaking in public, making a mistake in a social situation, or being at a party. Direct exposure to socially traumatic events is believed to mark the onset or dramatic increase in symptoms, including increased avoidance, internal distress and physiological hyperarousal in response to and in anticipation of such situations. The development of SAD through direct exposure to socially traumatic events is consistent with fear acquisition models, such as those describing the acquisition of specific phobias (e.g., Barlow, 2002; Mineka & Zinbarg, 2006; Mowrer, 1939). That is, a previously neutral socially related event becomes a conditioned stimulus for a set of conditioned responses (e.g., physiological hyperarousal) as a result of the event being paired with perceptions and/or the experience of social defeat, danger, or humiliation. Many individuals with SAD can recall a past traumatic event associated with the onset of their disorder (Beidel & Turner, 2007). Öst and Hugdahl (1981) found that 58% of their SAD sample reported that their SAD-related fears were the result of direct, traumatic social experiences. In another study, 56% of individuals with specific SAD and 40% of individuals with generalized SAD recalled a traumatic event that precipitated the onset and/or increase in their symptoms (Stemberger, Turner, Beidel, & Calhoun, 1995). Beidel, Turner, and Morris (1999) reported that children with SAD reported more negative social events than children without SAD. On the other hand, Kendler, Myers, and Prescott (2002) found that although 23% of adults from a population-based twin registry reported having experienced a socially traumatic event that brought about their social fears, 65% could not recall a conditioning event that marked the onset of their fears.

Although less empirically studied, indirect conditioning—the acquisition of fear through observing another's fearful behavior in response to a perceived threat or through verbal communication or information transfer—is also believed to contribute to the development of SAD (Rachman, 1977). Indeed, Öst and Hugdahl (1981) found that 17% of individuals with SAD recalled vicarious learning experiences and 10% recalled information transfer experiences related to onset of social fears. Vicarious learning of social fears dates back to Cook and Mineka's series of experiments on observational conditioning of snake fear in rhesus monkeys (e.g., Cook & Mineka, 1990; Cook, Mineka, Wolkenstein, & Laitsch, 1985). In humans, parents may "teach" their children to be fearful of social situations through modeling of social fears (e.g., Moore, Whaley, & Sigman, 2004; Turner, Beidel, Roberson-Nay, & Tervo, 2003). For example, Rapee and colleagues (Dubi, Rapee, Emerton, & Schniering, 2008; Gerull & Rapee, 2002) found that toddlers showed greater fear expressions and avoidance of fear-relevant and fear-irrelevant stimuli following negative reactions of their mothers. Additionally, in a study of infants and their nonanxious mothers, infants were more likely to be fearful and avoidant of a stranger after watching their mothers behave in a socially anxious manner with the same stranger (de Rosnay, Cooper, Tsigaras, & Murray, 2006). Taken together, both direct and indirect conditioning experiences, combined with the presence of other precipitating and predisposing factors, likely set the stage for the development of SAD, particularly in the adolescent and young adulthood years, which are laden with an abundance of social demands and expectations.

MAINTAINING FACTORS

As mentioned previously, most of the predisposing or precipitating factors described earlier also serve to maintain SAD after disorder onset. They are not discussed again, but the reader should consider how they could serve to maintain and intensify SAD over time. Social skill deficits and cognitive biases are discussed in the sections that follow as maintaining factors given that research to date has yet to examine the prospective nature of the factors in the development of SAD, particularly in adolescence.

Social Skill Deficits

Some researchers have found that children with SAD exhibit significantly poorer social skills than do normal controls and anxious children without SAD (Alfano, Beidel, & Turner, 2006; Beidel et al., 1999; Inderbitzen-Nolan, Anderson, & Johnson, 2007; Spence, Donovan, & Brechman-Toussaint, 1999). Research has also established that children with SAD display less prosocial behavior and more social withdrawal (Erath, Flanagan, & Bierman, 2007), exhibit reduced nonverbal communication (e.g., reduced facial activity; Melfsen, Osterlow, & Florin, 2000), and demonstrate impaired perception of social cues (e.g., interpretation of facial expressions) relative to nonanxious controls (Melfsen & Florin, 2002; Simonian, Beidel, Turner, Berkes, & Long, 2001). On the other hand, some researchers have found the opposite—that socially anxious children do not exhibit poorer social interaction skills than nonanxious controls (Cartwright-Hatton, Tschernitz, & Gomersall, 2005; Erath et al., 2007). One possible reason for these conflicting findings may be that studies not finding a relationship between skill deficits and social anxiety examined social skills using analogue tasks with adults, which may not adequately approximate social interactions with peers (Erath et al., 2007). In other cases, differences may be related to the type of sample examined (i.e., clinical vs. community samples).

Although it is not clear what the causal direction between social skill deficits and social anxiety may be, it is possible that individuals start with poor social skills (predisposing factor) and encounter a social situation in which their deficits create a socially awkward situation, which then creates anxious apprehension leading to SAD. On the other hand, it is also possible that individuals with performance inhibition caused by anxiety (e.g., behaviorally inhibited) avoid social situations and thus do not have the opportunity to develop social skills (Arkowitz, 1981). Regardless of the pathway, it does appear that skill deficits play some role in the maintenance of SAD.

Cognitive Biases

SAD is also maintained through cognitive biases, or errors in thinking in which individuals preferentially attend to, interpret, and recall information that is schema consistent (e.g., Beck, Emery, & Greenberg, 2005; Williams, Watts, MacLeod, & Mathews, 1988). In social anxiety, cognitive biases such as attending to social threat cues over nonthreat cues, interpreting ambiguous social situations in a threatening manner, and recalling negative social events over neutral social events represent schema-consistent biases. The literature to date has found consistent support for biases in interpretation in socially anxious youth and selective attention in adults. However, research has not consistently found support for memory biases in social anxiety for youth or adults.

Interpretation studies have established that socially anxious youth have more negative interpretations for ambiguous social situations, anticipate negative social outcomes, have lower expectations for their performance in social situations, display lower thresholds for social threat perception, perceive and interpret social threat in ambiguous scenarios, evaluate their own performance in social situations in a critical manner, and overestimate the cost and probability of negative social events (Cartwright-Hatton et al., 2005; Higa & Daleiden, 2008; Miers, Blöte, Bögels, & Westenberg, 2008; Muris, Merckelbach, & Damsma, 2000; Rheingold, Herbert, & Franklin, 2003; Spence et al., 1999). Additionally, Alfano and colleagues (2006) found that some adolescents with SAD, but no children, reported engaging in negative self-talk during a social interaction task.

Research to date has yet to examine selective attention biases in socially anxious adolescents. Research on selective attention and social anxiety in adults, however, is quite extensive. We only include a brief summary of findings; the interested reader is encouraged to read more comprehensive reviews of this literature elsewhere (e.g., Bögels & Mansell, 2004). In a modified Stroop task, studies have shown that adults with SAD are slower in naming socially threatening words than neutral words (Hope, Rapee, Heimberg, & Dombeck, 1990; Mattia, Heimberg, & Hope, 1993). In a probe detection task in which individuals respond after seeing a dot that follows a pair of words (one neutral and one socially threatening), socially anxious adults evidenced shorter response latencies to socially threatening words (Asmundson & Stein, 1994). Although selective attention to social threat has not yet been examined in adolescents with social anxiety, selective attention toward threatening information has been demonstrated in youth with anxiety disorders (Vasey, Daleiden, Williams, & Brown, 1995) and with test anxiety (Vasey, El-Hag, & Daleiden, 1996).

SUMMARY

There are a number of risk factors for SAD, and using a developmental psychopathology framework may be one way to better understand how various causal influences interact to set the stage for development. Predisposing (genetics, neurobiology, temperament, attachment, and parenting), precipitating (negative life and conditioning experiences), and maintaining (skill deficits and cognitive biases) factors are thought to influence SAD development. Although it is most probable that an individual with SAD has some combination of all three factors, it is also possible for an individual to acquire SAD without a predisposing factor or without a precipitating factor, and what serves to predispose and/or precipitate the onset of SAD may later contribute to its maintenance.

Adolescence and young adulthood is a period characterized by significant physical growth, neurobiological and hormonal changes, social–emotional development, and cognitive maturation. There are increasing social demands, pressures from peers, romantic interests, and greater independence from parents and other adults. Adolescence and young adulthood is the "perfect storm" for the development of SAD. Cognitively, adolescents and young adults engage in metacognition (i.e., thinking about their own thoughts) and can also consider the thoughts of others. As a result, combined with the increasing importance of peers as adolescents develop independence from the family, they begin to place greater importance on the opinions and perceptions of their peers. It is during this time that the imaginary audience phenomenon emerges (Elkind, 1967), including enhanced public self-awareness or the perception that other people are as concerned with adolescents' behaviors and appearance as adolescents themselves. Further, research has established that public self-consciousness is related to adolescent social anxiety (Higa, Phillips, Chorpita, & Daleiden, 2008), suggesting that although some heightened public self-consciousness is a normal developmental experience, adolescents with additional risk factors may be at increased risk for the development of SAD.

REFERENCES

Alfano, C. A., Beidel, D. C., & Turner, S. M. (2006). Cognitive correlates of social phobia among children and adolescents. *Journal of Abnormal Child Psychology*, *34*, 182–194. doi:10.1007/s10802-005-9012-9

Alfano, C. A., Beidel, D. C., & Turner, S. M. (2008). Negative self-imagery among adolescents with social phobia: A test of an adult model of the disorder. *Journal of Clinical Child and Adolescent Psychology*, *37*, 327–336. doi:10.1080/15374410801955870

Anderson, E. R., & Hope, D. A. (2009). The relationship among social phobia, objective and perceived physiological reactivity, and anxiety sensitivity in an adolescent population. *Journal of Anxiety Disorders*, *23*, 18–26. doi:10.1016/j.janxdis.2008.03.011

Arbelle, S., Benjamin, J., Golin, M. Kremer, I., Belmaker, R. H., & Ebstein, R. P. (2003). Relation of shyness in grade school children to the genotype for the long form of the serotonin transporter promoter region polymorphism. *The American Journal of Psychiatry, 160,* 671–676.

Arkowitz, H. (1981). Assessment of social skills. In M. Hersen & A. S. Bellack (Eds.), *Behavioral assessment* (pp. 296–327). New York, NY: Pergamon Press.

Asendorpf, J. B. (1991). Development of inhibited children's coping with unfamiliarity. *Child Development, 62,* 1460–1474. doi:10.2307/1130819

Asmundson, G., & Stein, M. (1994). Selective processing of social threat in patients with generalized social phobia: Evaluation using a dot-probe paradigm. *Journal of Anxiety Disorders, 8,* 107–117. doi:10.1016/0887-6185(94)90009-4

Bandelow, B., Torrente, C. A., Wedekind, D., Broocks, A., Hajak, G., & Rüther, E. (2004). Early traumatic life events, parental rearing styles, family history of mental disorders, and birth risk factors in patients with social disorder. *European Archives of Psychiatry and Clinical Neuroscience, 254,* 397–405. doi:10.1007/s00406-004-0521-2

Barlow, D. H. (2002). *Anxiety and its disorders: The nature and treatment of anxiety and panic* (2nd ed.). New York, NY: Guilford Press.

Barnett, B., Schaafsma, M. F., Guzman, A. M., & Parker, G. B. (1991). Maternal anxiety: A 5-year review of an intervention study. *Journal of Child Psychology and Psychiatry, and Allied Disciplines, 32,* 423–438. doi:10.1111/j.1469-7610.1991.tb00321.x

Barrett, P. M., Rapee, R., Dadds, M., & Ryan, S. (1996). Family enhancement of cognitive style in anxious and aggressive children. *Journal of Abnormal Child Psychology, 24,* 187–203. doi:10.1007/BF01441484

Battaglia, M., Ogliari, A., Zanoni, A., Citterio, A., Pozzoli, U., Giorda, R., . . . Marino, C. (2005). Influence of the serotonin transporter promoter gene and shyness on children's cerebral responses to facial expressions. *Archives of General Psychiatry, 62,* 85–94. doi:10.1001/archpsyc.62.1.85

Beatty, M., Heisel, A., Hall, A., Levine, T., & La France, B. (2002). What can we learn from the study of twins about genetic and environmental influences on interpersonal affiliation, aggressiveness, and social anxiety?: A meta-analytic study. *Communication Monographs, 69,* 1–18. doi:10.1080/03637750216534

Beck, A. T., Emery, G., & Greenberg, R. L. (2005). *Anxiety disorders and phobias: A cognitive perspective.* New York, NY: Basic Books.

Beidel, D. C., & Turner, S. M. (2007). *Shy children, phobic adults: The nature and treatment of social anxiety disorder* (2nd ed.). Washington, DC: American Psychological Association. doi:10.1037/11533-000

Beidel, D. C., Turner, S. M., & Morris, T. L. (1999). Psychopathology of childhood social phobia. *Journal of the American Academy of Child and Adolescent Psychiatry, 38,* 643–650. doi:10.1097/00004583-199906000-00010

Biederman, J., Hirshfeld-Becker, D. R., Rosenbaum, J. F., Hérot, C., Friedman, D., Snidman, N., . . . Faraone, S. V. (2001). Further evidence of association between behavioral inhibition and social anxiety in children. *The American Journal of Psychiatry, 158,* 1673–1679. doi:10.1176/appi.ajp.158.10.1673

Bögels, S. M., & Mansell, W. (2004). Attention processes in the maintenance and treatment of social phobia: Hypervigilance, avoidance and self-focused attention. *Clinical Psychology Review, 24*, 827–856. doi:10.1016/j.cpr.2004.06.005

Bögels, S. M., van Oosten, A., Muris, P., & Smulders, D. (2001). Familial correlates of social anxiety in children and adolescents. *Behaviour Research and Therapy, 39*, 273–287. doi:10.1016/S0005-7967(00)00005-X

Bohlin, G., Hagekull, B., & Rydell, A. (2000). Attachment and social functioning: A longitudinal study from infancy to middle childhood. *Social Development, 9*, 24–39. doi:10.1111/1467-9507.00109

Booth, C. L., Rose-Krasnor, L., & Rubin, K. H. (1991). Relating preschoolers' social competence and their mothers' parenting behaviors to early attachment security and high-risk status. *Journal of Social and Personal Relationships, 8*, 363–382. doi:10.1177/0265407591083004

Bouwer, C., & Stein, D. J. (1998). Use of the selective serotonin reuptake inhibitor citalopram in the treatment of generalized social phobia. *Journal of Affective Disorders, 49*, 79–82. doi:10.1016/S0165-0327(97)00182-1

Bowlby, J. (1973). *Attachment and loss: Vol. 2. Separation: Anxiety and anger*. New York, NY: Basic Books.

Brown, T. A., Chorpita, B., & Barlow, D. (1998). Structural relationships among dimensions of the *DSM–IV* anxiety and mood disorders and dimensions of negative affect, positive affect, and autonomic arousal. *Journal of Abnormal Psychology, 107*, 179–192. doi:10.1037/0021-843X.107.2.179

Bruch, M., & Heimberg, R. (1994). Differences in perceptions of parental and personal characteristics between generalized and nongeneralized social phobics. *Journal of Anxiety Disorders, 8*, 155–168. doi:10.1016/0887-6185(94)90013-2

Burgess, K. B., Rubin, K. H., Chea, C. S. L., & Nelson, L. J. (2001). Behavioral inhibition, social withdrawal, and parenting. In W. R. Crozier & L. E. Alden (Eds.), *International handbook of social anxiety: Concepts, research and interventions* (pp. 137–158). New York, NY: Wiley.

Cartwright-Hatton, S., Tschernitz, N., & Gomersall, H. (2005). Social anxiety in children: Social skills deficit, or cognitive distortion? *Behaviour Research and Therapy, 43*, 131–141. doi:10.1016/j.brat.2003.12.003

Chorpita, B. F., Plummer, M., & Moffitt, C. (2000). Relations of tripartite dimensions of emotion to childhood anxiety and mood disorders. *Journal of Abnormal Child Psychology, 28*, 299–310. doi:10.1023/A:1005152505888

Chronis-Tuscano, A., Degnan, K., Pine, D., Perez-Edgar, K., Henderson, H., Diaz, Y., . . . Fox, N. A. (2009). Stable early maternal report of behavioral inhibition predicts lifetime social anxiety disorder in adolescence. *Journal of the American Academy of Child and Adolescent Psychiatry, 48*, 928–935. doi:10.1097/CHI.0b013e3181ae09df

Cicchetti, D. (2006). Development and psychopathology. In D. Cicchetti & D. J. Cohen (Eds.), *Developmental psychopathology: Vol. 1. Theory and methods* (2nd ed., pp. 1–23). New York, NY: Wiley.

Clark, D. M., & Wells, A. (1995). A cognitive model of social phobia. In R. G. Heimberg, M. R. Liebowitz, D. A. Hope, & F. R. Schneier (Eds.), *Social phobia: diagnosis, assessment, and treatment* (pp. 69–93). New York, NY: Guilford Press.

Coll, C. G., Kagan, J., & Reznick, S. (1984). Behavioral inhibition in young children. *Child Development, 55,* 1005–1019. doi:10.2307/1130152

Cook, M., & Mineka, S. (1990). Selective associations in the observational conditioning of fear in rhesus monkeys. *Journal of Experimental Psychology: Animal Behavior Processes, 16,* 372–389. doi:10.1037/0097-7403.16.4.372

Cook, M., Mineka, S., Wolkenstein, B., & Laitsch, K. (1985). Observational conditioning of snake fear in unrelated rhesus monkeys. *Journal of Abnormal Psychology, 94,* 591–610. doi:10.1037/0021-843X.94.4.591

Crowell, J. A., O'Conner, E., Wollmers, G., Sprafkin, J., & Rao, U. (1991). Mothers' conceptualizations of parent–child relationships: Relation to mother–child interaction and child behavior problems. *Development and Psychopathology, 3,* 431–444. doi:10.1017/S0954579400007616

Daniels, D., & Plomin, R. (1985). Origins of individual differences in infant shyness. *Developmental Psychology, 21,* 118–121. doi:10.1037/0012-1649.21.1.118

de Rosnay, M., Cooper, P., Tsigaras, N., & Murray, L. (2006). Transmission of social anxiety from mother to infant: An experimental study using a social referencing paradigm. *Behaviour Research and Therapy, 44,* 1165–1175. doi:10.1016/j.brat.2005.09.003

Dubi, K., Rapee, R. M., Emerton, J. L., & Schniering, C. A. (2008). Maternal modeling and the acquisition of fear and avoidance in toddlers: Influence of stimulus preparedness and child temperament. *Journal of Abnormal Child Psychology, 36,* 499–512. doi:10.1007/s10802-007-9195-3

Eley, T. C., Bolton, D., O'Connor, T. G., Perrin, S., Smith, P., & Plomin, R. (2003). A twin study of anxiety-related behaviours in pre-school children. *Journal of Child Psychology and Psychiatry, and Allied Disciplines, 44,* 945–960. doi:10.1111/1469-7610.00179

Eley, T. C., Rijdijk, F. V., Perrin, S., O'Connor, T. G., & Bolton, D. (2008). A multivariate genetic analysis of specific phobia, separation anxiety, and social phobia in early childhood. *Journal of Abnormal Child Psychology, 36,* 839–848. doi:10.1007/s10802-008-9216-x

Elkind, D. (1967). Egocentrism in adolescence. *Child Development, 38,* 1025–1034. doi:10.2307/1127100

Eng, W., Heimberg, R., Hart, T. A., Schneier, F. R., & Liebowitz, M. R. (2001). Attachment in individuals with social anxiety disorder: The relationship among adult attachment styles, social anxiety, and depression. *Emotion, 1,* 365–380. doi:10.1037/1528-3542.1.4.365

Erath, S. A., Flanagan, K., & Bierman, K. (2007). Social anxiety and peer relations in early adolescence: Behavioral and cognitive factors. *Journal of Abnormal Child Psychology, 35,* 405–416. doi:10.1007/s10802-007-9099-2

Erickson, M. F., Sroufe, A., & Egeland, B. (1985). The relationship between quality of attachment and behavior problems in preschool in a high-risk sample. *Monographs of the Society for Research in Child Development, 50*(1–2), 147–166. doi:10.2307/3333831

Fyer, A. J., Mannuzza, S., Chapman, T. F., Martin, L. Y., & Klein, D. F. (1995). Specificity in familial aggregation of phobic disorders. *Archives of General Psychiatry, 52*, 564–573.

Gerull, F. C., & Rapee, R. M. (2002). Mother knows best: The effects of maternal modelling on the acquisition of fear and avoidance behaviour in toddlers. *Behaviour Research and Therapy, 40*, 279–287. doi:10.1016/S0005-7967(01)00013-4

Gest, S. D. (1997). Behavioral inhibition: Stability and associations with adaptation from childhood to early adulthood. *Journal of Personality and Social Psychology, 72*, 467–475. doi:10.1037/0022-3514.72.2.467

Greco, L., & Morris, T. (2002). Paternal child-rearing style and child social anxiety: Investigation of child perceptions and actual father behavior. *Journal of Psychopathology and Behavioral Assessment, 24*, 259–267. doi:10.1023/A:1020779000183

Grüner, K., Muris, P., & Merckelbach, H. (1999). The relationship between anxious rearing behaviors and anxiety disorders symptomatology in normal children. *Journal of Behavior Therapy and Experimental Psychiatry, 30*, 27–35. doi:10.1016/S0005-7916(99)00004-X

Hayward, C., Killen, J., Kraemer, H., & Taylor, B. (1998). Linking self-reported childhood behavioral inhibition to adolescent social phobia. *Journal of the American Academy of Child and Adolescent Psychiatry, 37*, 1308–1316. doi:10.1097/00004583-199812000-00015

Higa, C. K., & Daleiden, E. L. (2008). Social anxiety and cognitive biases in non-referred children: The interaction of self-focused attention and threat interpretation biases. *Journal of Anxiety Disorders, 22*, 441–452. doi:10.1016/j.janxdis.2007.05.005

Higa, C. K., Phillips, L. K., Chorpita, B. F., & Daleiden, E. L. (2008). The structure of self-consciousness in children and young adolescents and relations to social anxiety. *Journal of Psychopathology and Behavioral Assessment, 30*, 261–271. doi:10.1007/s10862-008-9079-z

Hirshfeld-Becker, D. R., Biederman, J., Henin, A., Faraone, S., Davis, S., Harrington, K., & Rosenbaum, J. (2007). Behavioral inhibition in preschool children at risk is a specific predictor of middle childhood social anxiety: A five-year follow-up. *Journal of Developmental and Behavioral Pediatrics, 28*, 225–233. doi:10.1097/01.DBP.0000268559.34463.d0

Hofmann, S. G., & Barlow, D. H. (2002). Social phobia (social anxiety disorder). In D. H. Barlow (Ed.), *Anxiety and its disorders: The nature and treatment of anxiety and panic* (2nd ed., pp. 454–476). New York, NY: Guilford Press.

Hope, D., Rapee, R., Heimberg, R., & Dombeck, M. (1990). Representations of the self in social phobia: Vulnerability to social threat. *Cognitive Therapy and Research, 14*, 177–189. doi:10.1007/BF01176208

Hudson, J. L., & Rapee, R. (2001). Parent–child interactions and anxiety disorders: An observational study. *Behaviour Research and Therapy, 39,* 1411–1427. doi:10.1016/S0005-7967(00)00107-8

Hudson, J. L., & Rapee, R. (2002). Parent–child interactions in clinically anxious children and their siblings. *Journal of Clinical Child and Adolescent Psychology, 31,* 548–555.

Hudson, J. L., & Rapee, R. (2005). Parental perceptions of overprotection: Specific to anxious children or shared between siblings? *Behaviour Change, 22,* 185–194. doi:10.1375/bech.2005.22.3.185

Hughes, A. A., Furr, J. M., Sood, E. D., Barmish, A. J., & Kendall, P. C. (2009). Anxiety, mood, and substance use disorders in parents of children with anxiety disorders. *Child Psychiatry and Human Development, 40,* 405–419. doi:10.1007/s10578-009-0133-1

Inderbitzen-Nolan, H. M., Anderson, E., & Johnson, H. (2007). Subjective versus objective behavioral ratings following two analogue tasks: A comparison of socially phobic and non-anxious adolescents. *Journal of Anxiety Disorders, 21,* 76–90. doi:10.1016/j.janxdis.2006.03.013

Kagan, J. (1989). Temperamental contributions to social behavior. *American Psychologist, 44,* 668–674. doi:10.1037/0003-066X.44.4.668

Katzelnick, D. J., Kobak, K. A., Greist, J. H., Jefferson, J. W., Mantle, J. M., & Serlin, R. C. (1995). Sertraline for social phobia: A double blind, placebo-controlled crossover study. *The American Journal of Psychiatry, 152,* 1368–1371.

Kendler, K. S., Myers, J., & Prescott, C. A. (2002). The etiology of phobias: An evaluation of the stress-diathesis model. *Archives of General Psychiatry, 59,* 242–248. doi:10.1001/archpsyc.59.3.242

Kendler, K. S., Neale, M. C., Kessler, R. C., Heath, A. C., & Eaves, L. J. (1992). The genetic epidemiology of phobias in women: The interrelationship of agoraphobia, social phobia, situational phobia, and simple phobia. *Archives of General Psychiatry, 49,* 273–281.

Kessler, R. C., Davis, C. G., & Kendler, K. S. (1997). Childhood adversity and adult psychiatric disorder in the US National Comorbidity Survey. *Psychological Medicine 27,* 1101–1119.

Kobak, R., Sudler, N., & Gamble, W. (1991). Attachment and depressive symptoms during adolescence: A developmental pathways analysis. *Development and Psychopathology, 3,* 461–474. doi:10.1017/S095457940000763X

Lanzenberger, R. R., Mitterhauser, M., Spindelegger, C., Wadsak, W., Klein, N., Mien, L., . . . Tauscher, J. (2007). Reduced serotonin-1A receptor binding in social anxiety disorder. *Biological Psychiatry, 61,* 1081–1089. doi:10.1016/j.biopsych.2006.05.022

Lewis, M. (2000). Toward a development of psychopathology: Models, definitions, and prediction. In A. J. Sameroff, M. Lewis, & S. M. Miller (Eds.), *Handbook of developmental psychopathology* (2nd ed., pp. 3–22). Dordrecht, Netherlands: Kluwer Academic.

Lieb, R., Wittchen, H., Hofler, M., Fuetsch, M., Stein, M., & Merikangas, K. (2000). Parental psychopathology, parenting styles, and the risk of social phobia in offspring: A prospective-longitudinal community study. *Archives of General Psychiatry, 57,* 859–866. doi:10.1001/archpsyc.57.9.859

Liebowitz, M. R. (1987). Social phobia. *Modern problems of pharmacopsychiatry, 22,* 141–173.

Magee, W. J. (1999). Effects of negative life experiences on phobia onset. *Social Psychiatry and Psychiatric Epidemiology, 34,* 343–351. doi:10.1007/s001270050154

Mannuzza, S., Schneier, F. R., Chapman, T. F., Liebowitz, M. R., Klein, D. F., & Fyer, A. J. (1995). Generalized social phobia: reliability and validity. *Archives of General Psychiatry, 52,* 230–237.

Mattia, J. I., Heimberg, R., & Hope, D. (1993). The revised Stroop color-naming task in social phobics. *Behaviour Research and Therapy, 31,* 305–313. doi:10.1016/0005-7967(93)90029-T

Melfsen, S., & Florin, I. (2002). Do socially anxious children show deficits in classifying facial expressions of emotions? *Journal of Nonverbal Behavior, 26,* 109–126. doi:10.1023/A:1015665521371

Melfsen, S., Osterlow, J., & Florin, I. (2000). Deliberate emotional expressions of socially anxious children and their mothers. *Journal of Anxiety Disorders, 14,* 249–261. doi:10.1016/S0887-6185(99)00037-7

Mick, M. A., & Telch, M. (1998). Social anxiety and history of behavioral inhibition in young adults. *Journal of Anxiety Disorders, 12,* 1–20. doi:10.1016/S0887-6185(97)00046-7

Miers, A. C., Blöte, A. W., Bögels, S. M., & Westenberg, P. M. (2008). Interpretation bias and social anxiety in adolescents. *Journal of Anxiety Disorders, 22,* 1462–1471. doi:10.1016/j.janxdis.2008.02.010

Mineka, S., & Zinbarg, R. (2006). A contemporary learning theory perspective on the etiology of anxiety disorders: It's not what you thought it was. *American Psychologist, 61,* 10–26. doi:10.1037/0003-066X.61.1.10

Moore, P. S., Whaley, S., & Sigman, M. (2004). Interactions between mothers and children: Impacts of maternal and child anxiety. *Journal of Abnormal Psychology, 113,* 471–476. doi:10.1037/0021-843X.113.3.471

Morris, T. L. (2001). Social phobia. In M. W. Vasey & M. R. Dadds (Eds.), *The developmental psychopathology of anxiety* (pp. 435–458). New York, NY: Oxford University Press.

Mowrer, O. H. (1939). A stimulus–response analysis of anxiety and its role as a reinforcing agent. *Psychological Review, 46,* 553–565. doi:10.1037/h0054288

Muris, P., Mayer, B., & Meesters, C. (2000). Self-reported attachment style, anxiety, and depression in children. *Social Behavior and Personality, 28,* 157–162. doi:10.2224/sbp.2000.28.2.157

Muris, P., Meesters, C., Merckelbach, H., & Hulsenbeck, P. (2000). Worry in children is related to perceived parental rearing and attachment. *Behaviour Research and Therapy, 38,* 487–497. doi:10.1016/S0005-7967(99)00072-8

Muris, P., Merckelbach, H., & Damsma, E. (2000). Threat perception bias in non-referred, socially anxious children. *Journal of Clinical Child Psychology, 29,* 348–359. doi:10.1207/S15374424JCCP2903_6

Neal, J. A., Edelmann, R. J., & Glachan, M. (2002). Behavioural inhibition and symptoms of anxiety and depression: Is there a specific relationship with social phobia? *British Journal of Clinical Psychology, 41,* 361–374. doi:10.1348/014466502760387489

Öst, L. G., & Hugdahl, K. (1981). Acquisition of phobias and anxiety response patterns in clinical patients. *Behaviour Research and Therapy, 19,* 439–447. doi:10.1016/0005-7967(81)90134-0

Parker, G. (1979). Reported parental characteristics of agoraphobics and social phobics. *The British Journal of Psychiatry, 135,* 555–560. doi:10.1192/bjp.135.6.555

Parr, C. J., & Cartwright-Hatton, S. (2009). Social anxiety in adolescents: The effect of video feedback on anxiety and the self-evaluation of performance. *Clinical Psychology & Psychotherapy, 16,* 46–54. doi:10.1002/cpp.599

Rachman, S. (1977). The conditioning theory of fear-acquisition: A critical examination. *Behaviour Research and Therapy, 15,* 375–387. doi:10.1016/0005-7967(77)90041-9

Rapee, R. M., & Heimberg, R. (1997). A cognitive-behavioral model of anxiety in social phobia. *Behaviour Research and Therapy, 35,* 741–756. doi:10.1016/S0005-7967(97)00022-3

Rapee, R. M., & Melville, L. F. (1997). Retrospective recall of family factors in social phobia and panic disorder. *Depression and Anxiety, 5,* 7–11. doi:10.1002/(SICI)1520-6394(1997)5:1<7::AID-DA2>3.0.CO;2-E

Reich, J., & Yates, W. (1988). Family history of psychiatric disorders in social phobia. *Comprehensive Psychiatry, 29,* 72–75. doi:10.1016/0010-440X(88)90039-9

Rheingold, A. A., Herbert, J. D., & Franklin, M. E. (2003). Cognitive bias in adolescents with social anxiety disorder. *Cognitive Therapy and Research, 27,* 639–655. doi:10.1023/A:1026399627766

Roelofs, J., Meesters, C., ter Huurne, M., Bamelis, L., & Muris, P. (2006). On the links between attachment style, parental rearing behaviors, and internalizing and externalizing problems in non-clinical children. *Journal of Child and Family Studies, 15,* 319–332. doi:10.1007/s10826-006-9025-1

Rosenbaum, J. F., Biederman, J., Hirshfeld, D., Bolduc, E., & Chaloff, J. (1991). Further evidence of an association between behavioral inhibition and anxiety disorders: Results from a family study of children from a non-clinical sample. *Journal of Psychiatric Research, 25,* 49–65. doi:10.1016/0022-3956(91)90015-3

Rothbart, M. K., & Mauro, J. A. (1990). Temperament, behavioral inhibition, and shyness in childhood. In H. Leitenberg (Ed.), *Handbook of social and evaluation anxiety* (pp. 139–160). New York, NY: Plenum Press.

Rubin, K. H., & Mills, R. S. L. (1990). Maternal beliefs about adaptive and maladaptive social behaviors in normal, aggressive, and withdrawn preschoolers. *Journal of Abnormal Child Psychology, 18,* 419–435. doi:10.1007/BF00917644

Schmidt, L. A., Polak, C. P., & Spooner, A. L. (2001). Biological and environmental contributions to childhood shyness: A diathesis-stress model. In R. Crozier & L. E. Alden (Eds.), *International handbook of social anxiety: Concepts, research and interventions relating to the self and shyness* (pp. 29–51). London, England: Wiley.

Schneier, F. R., Liebowitz, M. R., Abi-Dargham, A., Zea-Ponce, Y., Lin, S., & Laruelle, M. (2000). Low dopamine D2 receptor binding potential in social phobia. *The American Journal of Psychiatry, 157,* 457–459. doi:10.1176/appi.ajp.157.3.457

Schwartz, C. E., Snidman, N., & Kagan, J. (1999). Adolescent social anxiety as an outcome of inhibited temperament in childhood. *Journal of the American Academy of Child and Adolescent Psychiatry, 38,* 1008–1015. doi:10.1097/00004583-199908000-00017

Simonian, S. J., Beidel, D. C., Turner, S. M., Berkes, J. L., & Long, J. H. (2001). Recognition of facial affect by children and adolescents diagnosed with social phobia. *Child Psychiatry and Human Development, 32,* 137–145. doi:10.1023/A:1012298707253

Siqueland, L., Kendall, P., & Steinberg, L. (1996). Anxiety in children: Perceived family environments and observed family interactions. *Journal of Clinical Child Psychology, 25,* 225–237. doi:10.1207/s15374424jccp2502_12

Skre, I., Onstad, S., Torgersen, S., Lygren, S., & Kringlen, E. (1993). A twin study of *DSM–III–R* anxiety disorders. *Acta Psychiatrica Scandinavica, 88,* 85–92. doi:10.1111/j.1600-0447.1993.tb03419.x

Spence, S. H., Donovan, C., & Brechman-Toussaint, M. (1999). Social skills, social outcomes, and cognitive features of childhood social phobia. *Journal of Abnormal Psychology, 108,* 211–221. doi:10.1037/0021-843X.108.2.211

Sroufe, L. A., & Waters, E. (1977). Attachment as an organizational construct. *Child Development, 48,* 1184–1199. doi:10.2307/1128475

Stein, M. B., Chartier, M. J., Hazen, A. L., Kozak, M. V., Tancer, M. E., Lander, S., . . . Walker, J. R. (1998). A direct-interview family study of generalized social phobia. *The American Journal of Psychiatry, 155,* 90–97.

Stein, M. B., Goldin, P. R., Sareen, J., Zorrilla, L. T., & Brown, G. G. (2002). Increased amygdala activation to angry and contemptuous faces in generalized social phobia. *Archives of General Psychiatry, 59,* 1027–1034. doi:10.1001/archpsyc.59.11.1027

Stemberger, R. T., Turner, S. M., Beidel, D. C., & Calhoun, K. S. (1995). Social phobia: An analysis of possible developmental factors. *Journal of Abnormal Psychology, 104,* 526–531. doi:10.1037/0021-843X.104.3.526

Stravynski, A., Elie, R., & Franche, R. (1989). Perception of early parenting by patients diagnosed avoidant personality disorder: A test of the overprotection hypothesis. *Acta Psychiatrica Scandinavica, 80,* 415–420. doi:10.1111/j.1600-0447.1989.tb02999.x

Tancer, M. E., Mailman, R. B., Stein, M. B., Mason, G. A., Carson, S. W., & Golden, R. N. (1994–1995). Neuroendocrine responsivity to monoaminergic system probes in generalized social phobia. *Anxiety, 1*, 216–223.

Tiihonen, J., Kuikka, J., Bergström, K., Lepola, U., Koponen, H., & Leinonen, E. (1997). Dopamine reuptake site densities in patients with social phobia. *The American Journal of Psychiatry, 154*, 239–242.

Turner, S. M., Beidel, D., Roberson-Nay, R., & Tervo, K. (2003). Parenting behaviors in parents with anxiety disorders. *Behaviour Research and Therapy, 41*, 541–554. doi:10.1016/S0005-7967(02)00028-1

Van Ameringen, M., Mancini, C., & Oakman, J. M. (1998). The relationship of behavioral inhibition and shyness to anxiety disorder. *Journal of Nervous and Mental Disease, 186*, 425–431. doi:10.1097/00005053-199807000-00007

Vasey, M. W., & Dadds, M. (2001). An introduction to the developmental psychopathology of anxiety. In M. Vasey & M. Dadds (Eds.), *The developmental psychopathology of anxiety* (pp. 3–26). New York, NY: Oxford University Press.

Vasey, M. W., Daleiden, E., Williams, L., & Brown, L. (1995). Biased attention in childhood anxiety disorders: A preliminary study. *Journal of Abnormal Child Psychology, 23*, 267–279. doi:10.1007/BF01447092

Vasey, M. W., El-Hag, N., & Daleiden, E. (1996). Anxiety and the processing of emotionally threatening stimuli: Distinctive patterns of selective attention among high- and low-test-anxious children. *Child Development, 67*, 1173–1185. doi:10.2307/1131886

Warren, S. L., Huston, L., Egeland, B., & Sroufe, L. (1997). Child and adolescent anxiety disorders and early attachment. *Journal of the American Academy of Child and Adolescent Psychiatry, 36*, 637–644. doi:10.1097/00004583-199705000-00014

Warren, S. L., Schmitz, S., & Emde, R. N. (1999). Behavioral genetic analyses of self-reported anxiety at 7 years of age. *Journal of the American Academy of Child and Adolescent Psychiatry, 38*, 1403–1408. doi:10.1097/00004583-199911000-00015

Williams, M., Watts, F., MacLeod, C., & Mathews, A. (1988). *Cognitive psychology and emotional disorders. The Wiley series in clinical psychology.* Oxford, England: Wiley.

Wood, J. J., McLeod, B. D., Sigman, M., Hwang, W., & Chu, B. C. (2003). Parenting and childhood anxiety: Theory, empirical findings, and future directions. *Journal of Child Psychology and Psychiatry, and Allied Disciplines, 44*, 134–151. doi:10.1111/1469-7610.00106

Woodruff-Borden, J., Morrow, C., Bourland, S., & Cambron, S. (2002). The behavior of anxious parents: Examining mechanisms of transmission of anxiety from parent to child. *Journal of Clinical Child and Adolescent Psychiatry, 31*, 364–374.

3

NEURODEVELOPMENTAL ASPECTS OF SOCIAL ANXIETY

ROXANN ROBERSON-NAY AND RUTH C. BROWN

Adolescence is clearly a critical period for the maturation of the neuro-biological systems that underlie both emotion and behavior. Adolescence marks a period of great vulnerability for developing disordered levels of social anxiety. Particularly during adolescence, the brain undergoes rapid structural and functional changes affecting social cognition (Paus, 2005). As a result, youth are more able to reflect on their own thoughts (Elkind & Bowen, 1979), and their perspective-taking skills increase (Selman, 1980). Specifically, during this time adolescents become more aware of how others perceive or might perceive them. The emergence of these biological and cognitive changes may explain why adolescence and young adulthood appear to be such critical periods for the emergence of social phobia.

In this chapter, we review the neurodevelopmental aspects of social anxiety disorder (SAD). Although several themes emerge, the most unfortunate theme is that there is relatively little longitudinal research on the development of emotional circuits, particularly as it relates to adolescent SAD. Rather, much of the research base represents cross-sectional snapshots of neural functioning. To supplement the available data, we review cognitive processes related to anxiety (i.e., attention) as well as relevant animal research

53

examining neurobiological systems. We also rely on the adult literature to aid understanding of the neurodevelopmental aspects of adolescent SAD.

TYPICAL BRAIN DEVELOPMENT FROM CHILDHOOD THROUGH ADULTHOOD

Understanding normal brain development is critical to understanding the psychopathology of SAD because there is likely a dynamic interplay between brain maturation and vulnerability to anxiety. Consistent, stable processing of information by the brain greatly depends on the structural quality and maturity of white matter (WM) pathways (Paus, 2005). *White matter* is the tissue through which neural messages pass between different areas of gray matter (GM; e.g., basal ganglia, amygdala) within the nervous system. WM consists mostly of myelinated axons. Research indicates a steady increase in the overall volume of WM throughout childhood, adolescence, and young adulthood (age range 4–21 years; Giedd et al., 1999; Pfefferbaum et al., 1994; Reiss, Abrams, Singer, & Ross, 1996). Moreover, total cerebral volume generally peaks at 10.5 years in female subjects and 14.5 years in male subjects. Around the age of 6 years, the brain is at about 95% of its maxima. Cerebellum volume peaks approximately 2 years after cerebral volume. Giedd et al. (2009) observed that lateral ventricular volume (located within the cerebrum) exhibits the most inter-individual differences and increases throughout childhood and adolescence.

Unlike the linear relationship observed between age and WM volume, an inverted U-shape distribution is observed for GM (Giedd et al., 1999, 2009). Increases in GM volume of the frontal and parietal lobes has been observed, with peaks at about 10 and 12 years of age in girls and boys, respectively (Giedd et al., 1999). Following these peaks, decreases in GM volumes in these two lobes were detected, although GM volumes in the temporal and occipital lobes did not show the same level of diminished volume. These identified decreases have been described as a loss of GM density over the dorsal and parietal lobes between childhood (7–11 years) and adolescence (12–16 years). The apparent loss of GM density appears to accelerate further in the frontal cortex only from adolescence to adulthood (23–30 years; Sowell, 2001). Decrease in GM appears to start around onset of puberty in the sensorimotor areas and spreads ventrally over the frontal cortex and caudally over the parietal and temporal cortices (Gogtay et al., 2004). Data indicate that the dorsolateral prefrontal cortex and the posterior part of the superior temporal gyrus are the last to lose GM (Gogtay, et al., 2004). Interestingly, the loss of GM density is negatively correlated with local brain growth, leading some to question whether there is really a loss of GM or whether the loss is a function of increases in intracortical WM (Paus, 2005).

Structural neuroimaging studies indicate that by early adolescence the brains of males and females exhibit significant morphological differences, with adolescent females having larger subcortical structures, including hippocampal, pallidum, and caudate volumes but significantly smaller amygdala volume compared with males (Caviness, Kennedy, Bates, & Makris, 1996). By contrast, males show significantly greater growth of the left amygdala relative to females during adolescence (Giedd et al., 1996). Moreover, by the time females reach adulthood, they have a significantly larger percentage of GM within the dorsolateral prefrontal cortex compared with males (Schlaepfer, Harris, Tien, & Peng, 1995). This structural dimorphism is likely manifest in sex differences in emotion and behavior response (Killgore, 2000). More specifically, differences in rates of anxiety disorders in males and females may relate, to some extent, to brain-related sex differences. Thus, a comprehensive model of frontal and subcortical development of affective processing must account for the sex differences observed in emotional behavior and brain structure (Killgore, 2000).

ANXIETY, FEAR, THE AMYGDALA, AND THE VENTRAL LATERAL PREFRONTAL CORTEX

Much of what is known about the brain and anxiety is based on magnetic resonance imaging (MRI) and functional MRI (fMRI), which is a type of specialized MRI scan that measures the hemodynamic response related to neural activity in the brain. Changes in blood flow and blood oxygenation in the brain (collectively known as *hemodynamics*) are closely linked to neural activity (Roy & Sherrington, 1980). When nerve cells are active they increase their consumption of oxygen (Raichle & Mintun, 2006). The local response to this oxygen utilization is to increase blood flow to regions of increased neural activity. The blood oxygen level–dependent response generally serves as the dependent variable in fMRI studies.

Although the definitions of anxiety and fear have been debated, it is generally agreed that fear represents a present here-and-now emotion that is closely tied to the innately driven fight or flight response, whereas anxiety is a more diffuse emotion representing a future-oriented anxious apprehension (Barlow, 2004). Although researchers are beginning to better understand the neural pathways and connections that are associated with fear and anxiety, this literature is in its infancy, and the fact is, the experience of these emotions is not fully understood from a neurodevelopmental perspective. What is known is that there appear to be two key neural structures associated with fear and anxiety, including one subcortical structure, the amygdala, which interacts with the prefrontal cortex to mediate processing of emotional information.

These two structures (i.e., amygdala and prefrontal cortex) play critical roles in the *fear circuit*, which is not completely determined and depends, in part, on the process being examined (e.g., emotional memory, avoidance, attentional processes). Other neural structures that have been implicated in the fear circuit include the hippocampus, striatum, and bed nucleus of the stria terminalis (D. S. Pine, personal communication, October 2009). We focus here on the amygdala and ventral lateral prefrontal cortex (vlPFC) because these two structures have reliably emerged as key components of the fear circuit, regardless of process.

The amygdala is a bilateral collection of nuclei found deep in the anterior portions of the temporal lobes in the brains of primates. It is commonly described as a small, almond-shaped structure that receives projections from many parts of the brain, including the frontal cortex, temporal lobe, and olfactory system. The amygdala also sends its afferents to many parts of the brain, such as the frontal, prefrontal, and orbitofrontal cortices; hypothalamus; and hippocampus. Although the subdivisions of the amygdala are debated, there are currently four main subparts that are generally agreed on: the basolateral, lateral, central, and basomedial nuclei. There also is evidence that the subdivisions of the amygdala play differential roles in emotional processing. For example, the basolateral amygdala appears to modulate memory processes (Packard, 2009) and has been implicated in fear extinction (Berlau & McGaugh, 2006; Boccia, Blake, Baratti, & McGaugh, 2009).

The vlPFC lies in the anterior part of the frontal lobe, in front of the motor and premotor areas. This brain region has been implicated in planning complex cognitive behaviors, expression of personality, decision making, and regulating appropriate social behavior. The functional relationship between the amygdala and vlPFC relates to the processing of threat information. That is, the vlPFC is thought to facilitate delayed higher order processes related to emotion regulation (Hariri, Mattay, Tessitore, Fera, & Weinberger, 2003; Nomura, Izaki, Takita, Tanaka, & Hori, 2004), whereas the amygdala supports immediate threat processing (Davis & Whalen, 2001; Phillips, Drevets, Rauch, & Lane, 2003). Perturbation of amygdala–vlPFC interactions are thought to significantly influence anxiety (Hariri et al., 2003; LeDoux, 1996).

Animal studies also implicate a neural circuit connecting the amygdala and vlPFC in the processing of social threat information (Adolphs, 2003; Gross & Hen, 2004). Moreover, research using animals indicates that this circuitry is influenced by the many experiences that occur during development that come to shape processing of environmental threat information (Gross & Hen, 2004). The two primary animal models used to study neural correlates of anxiety are the rat and the monkey.

The rat brain is not completely developed at birth. In fact, processes of brain development continue for the first 3 weeks of a rat's life (Bayer, Altman,

Russo, & Zhang, 1993). This provides researchers with the ability to enact specific changes in the rat brain for the purpose of observing the cascading effects. Because the adolescent period is well defined in the male rat, extending from postnatal day 21 until postnatal day 60, it serves as a useful animal model of the study of human psychiatric conditions. Because rodents and humans share several behavioral similarities during adolescence, including increased novelty seeking, risk taking, and social interactions (Bayer et al., 1993; Beerpoot, Lipska, & Weinberger, 1996), rats provide a heuristic model of the developing brain.

Adolescence is an important period during which social competencies required for adult life are learned. It has been suggested that early stress experiences can affect brain maturity at different developmental periods. These brain-related changes during adolescence may be associated with the development of later life psychological conditions, including SAD. A recent study examined the long-term effects of repeated social stress during adolescence on adult social approach–avoidance behavior (Vidal et al., 2007). This was accomplished by using the resident–intruder paradigm, which involves the introduction of an unfamiliar rat into an existing cage of rats. Adolescent male Wistar rats were exposed at postnatal days 45 and 48 to an intruder rat followed by three experiences including psychosocial threat with the same resident. Subsequently, 3 weeks following the last psychosocial threat experience, the rats were tested in a social approach–avoidance test (comparable to the human behavioral avoidance test). Rats that were exposed previously to social stress spent less time in the interaction zone with an unfamiliar adult male rat. These behavioral findings suggest that animals exposed to social stress during adolescence exhibit higher levels of social anxiety as adult rats.

The monoamines (neurotransmitters) also have been implicated in mood and anxiety disorders. During adolescence, monoaminergic systems in the brain continue to develop (Jinks & McGregor, 1997). A study in rats sought to determine whether stressful social experiences during adolescence interfere with the development of the monoaminergic brain systems, which then might contribute to risk of various psychiatric conditions. The social defeat paradigm is regarded as an animal analogue to study "bullying, victimization and social subjugation" (Paxinos & Watson, 1986). Rodent studies have demonstrated that exposure to acute and chronic social-defeat encounters produces both short- and long-term alterations in a range of hormonal, physiologic, neurobiologic, and behavioral indices (Radhakishun, Wolterink, & Van Ree, 1988; Roth & Katz, 1979). Using this paradigm, researchers found that social defeat produced a series of effects, including reductions in anxious responding as well as perturbed monoaminergic function in adulthood (Watt, Burke, Renner, & Forster, 2009). These data suggest that social stress experienced during the adolescent years may contribute to increased vulnerability to psychopathology in adulthood.

Studies of nonhuman primates suggest that the developmental period during which amygdala damage occurs is critical and can strongly influence threat perception (Amaral, 2003; Sabatini et al., 2007). Some of the most interesting experiments conducted with nonhuman primates are the studies that have bilaterally lesioned the amygdala to examine associated behavioral consequences. It has been observed that these primates retain the capacity for typical social behavior (Bauman, Lavenex, Mason, Capitanio, & Amaral, 2004b). The developmental period when the lesions are performed (birth vs. mature adult) also does not affect this outcome. This finding suggests that the amygdala is not essential to the neural circuit that mediates social cognition (Bauman, Lavenex, Mason, Capitanio, & Amaral, 2004a). Although the bilateral amygdala lesions do not impact social behavior, these animals did exhibit abnormal fear responses to environmental stimuli (i.e., snakes), suggesting that the amygdala plays a key role in assessing and appraising for potential dangers. The amygdala then goes on to play a strategic role in preparing the organism to respond appropriately to detected threats. This particular function has clear adaptive significance for the defense and survival of the organism, and perturbations in this function likely play a role in many psychiatric syndromes such as the anxiety disorders and SAD (Amaral, 2004).

ATTENTION TO THREAT

Most work concerning the interaction of anxiety and cognitive processes focuses on the link between this emotion and attention to threat stimuli. The threat cue most centrally related to social anxiety is the communication of emotions through facial expressions. Numerous studies using nonhuman primates (e.g., Hinde, 1974), infants (e.g., Izard, 1977), and individuals across various cultures (e.g., Ekman, 1973) indicate that people are biologically predisposed to exhibit and recognize facial gestures associated with a range of emotional states. Coevolving with human facial behaviors was an adaptive ability to interpret and respond appropriately to the facial responses of other organisms of the same species. Thus, humans are thought to be evolutionary prepared to act not only as senders of emotional information but also as receivers of information by recognizing and adaptively responding to various displays in face-to-face social exchanges (Buck, 1994; Dimberg, 1988; Dimberg & Öhman, 1983). Given the significant age-related changes that occur in the neural structures associated with social function, the processing of facial stimuli may differentially influence attention orienting in young versus mature persons.

Unfortunately, little research has directly examined developmental differences in the neural architecture associated with attention orienting to emotional processing. However, the PFC and amygdala again appear to be two key structures relevant to threat detection and response (LeDoux, 2000). Researchers also are beginning to better understand attention and its relation to anxiety in adolescents. One tool that has been extensively used to assess age-related changes in attention and its associated neural circuitry is the dot probe task. Typically, two faces (of the same person) appear on the computer screen. One of the faces depicts an emotion (e.g., happy, angry), and the other face is neutral. A probe then appears in the location of either the emotional face or the neutral face. The subject is asked to identify the probe's location by pressing a button. The subject's reaction time serves as a measure of attention. An attention bias toward threat is indicated by slower reaction times on threat-incongruent compared with threat-congruent trials. A threat-incongruent trial occurs if the probe is presented in a different spatial location from the cue.

As mentioned, no study has specifically examined the neural correlates of attention in socially anxious youth. Rather, studies have generally examined attention in adolescents with a cluster of anxiety disorders (most often SAD, generalized anxiety disorder [GAD], and separation anxiety disorder) and/or healthy nonanxious adolescents. Moreover, with the exception of Lindstrom et al. (2009), no study has directly investigated developmental influences on attention and threat processing. Thus, we review here research from the adult and adolescent literatures, with the hopes of drawing some general conclusions regarding the role of attention to threat. A small number of studies have used the dot probe task to examine neural correlates of emotion–attention interactions using fMRI; they are reviewed here as well.

Monk and colleagues (2004) conducted a series of three experiments using dot probe tasks and fMRI with the goal of examining how healthy individuals alter their responses to threat cues over time. Healthy individuals were found to exhibit an increased attention bias away from threat over time, which was associated with increased activation in the occipitotemporal cortex. These data suggest that healthy subjects implicitly learn to avoid threats without activating fear circuitry (i.e., amygdala–prefrontal cortex). By comparison, Monk and colleagues (2006) also conducted one of the first dot probe studies to examine attention to threat in anxious youth. Their sample included 18 adolescents with GAD (M age = 12.3) and 15 nonanxious control adolescents (M age = 13.5; Monk et al., 2006). Adolescents with GAD manifested greater right vlPFC activation for trials containing angry faces. Youth with GAD also showed greater attention bias away from angry faces. Moreover, vlPFC activation differences continued even after controlling for attention bias, and a negative association was observed such that as vlPFC activation increased, severity of anxiety symptoms decreased. This finding suggests that attenuation of vlPFC modulation of the amygdala increases as anxiety levels increase.

In a related study, a dot probe task using masked threat stimuli was completed by 12 healthy adolescents and 17 adolescents with GAD (Monk et al., 2008). Results indicated that adolescents with GAD showed greater right amygdala activation when viewing masked angry faces, and amygdala activation was positively correlated with anxiety disorder severity. A functional connectivity analysis also indicated that the right amygdala and the right vlPFC exhibited strong negative coupling specifically to masked angry faces. Negative coupling tended to be weaker in youth with GAD than in comparison adolescents, however. The observed negative connectivity between the right vlPFC and amygdala implicates PFC modulation of amygdala response to threat. These findings collectively suggest that age may moderate the neural correlates of attention–emotion interactions (Fox, Hane, & Pine, 2007).

Lindstrom and colleagues (2009) recently sought to determine whether age moderated the neural correlates of attention–emotion interactions. This study also examined the relation between attention and reward (defined as neural response to positive emotional stimuli) because age-related changes in behavior during adolescence (e.g., increased risk taking, novelty seeking) may be accompanied by alterations in sensitivity to both rewards and threats (Ernst & Fudge, 2009; Nelson, Leibenluft, McClure, & Pine, 1999). In this study, 37 individuals between the ages of 9 and 40 completed the dot probe task while undergoing an fMRI scan. Although angry face attention bias scores and brain activation to angry faces were not associated with age, a positive correlation between age and attention bias toward happy faces was observed. Age also was negatively correlated with left cuneus and left caudate activation for a happy bias fMRI contrast. Overall, younger children exhibited a tendency to direct their attention away from happy faces (relative to neutral faces), but this pattern was attenuated in the older age groups along with increasing neural hypoactivation. Thus, age was associated with behavioral and neural indices of biased attention allocation to rewarding (i.e., happy faces) but not to threatening (i.e., angry faces) stimuli.

NEUROIMAGING RESEARCH: WHAT THE ADULT LITERATURE HAS TAUGHT RESEARCHERS

Amygdala hyperactivation has been consistently observed among adults with SAD (Birbaumer et al., 1998; Lorberbaum et al., 2004; Phan, Fitzgerald, Nathan, & Tancer, 2006; Stein, Goldin, Sareen, Zorilla, & Brown, 2002; Straube, Kolassa, Glauer, Mentzel, & Miltner, 2004; Tillfors, Furmark, Marteinsdottir, & Fredrikson, 2002; Veit et al., 2002). Amygdala hyperactivation in adult anxiety is generally observed when attention is focused on nonthreatening aspects as opposed to threatening aspects of negative social stimuli (Blair et al., 2008; Straube et al., 2004;). By contrast, anxious adolescents exhibit amygdala dysfunction when attention is focused on threatening aspects of social cues (McClure et al., 2007). This difference may be a function of more extensive dysfunction in a circuit encompassing the vlPFC and amygdala among adolescents with this disorder (Baxter, Parker, Lindner, Izquierdo, & Murray, 2000; Hariri et al., 2003; McClure et al., 2007).

Among individuals with generalized SAD, neuroimaging studies that engage emotion-processing resources through anticipated public-speaking tasks (Furmark et al., 2005; Furmark et al., 2002; Lorberbaum et al., 2004; Tillfors et al., 2002) or viewing negative emotional faces have demonstrated increased activation of regions associated with emotion processing such as the amygdala, PFC, and insula compared with matched control subjects (Amir et al., 2005; Birbaumer et al., 1998; Phan et al., 2005; Stein et al., 2002; Straube et al., 2004; Straube, Mentzel, & Miltner, 2005). These findings of increased activity of emotion-processing regions, especially the amygdala, during the processing of anxiety-provoking stimuli are not specific to SAD, however. Similar findings have been noted for a range of other anxiety disorders, including posttraumatic stress disorder (Armony, Corbo, Clément, & Brunei, 2005; Shin et al., 2005), obsessive–compulsive disorder (Mataix-Cols et al., 2003), and panic disorder (Sakai et al., 2005), suggesting that nearly all anxiety disorders are associated with increased activity of fear circuitry.

Blair et al. (2008) compared neural activation among adults with SAD (without comorbid GAD), GAD, and healthy controls. Persons with SAD showed increased amygdala activation in response to fearful relative to neutral facial expressions (and several other regions) compared with healthy controls. Amygdala hyperactivation also correlated with self-reported anxiety in persons with SAD. Persons with GAD, however, showed significantly less activation to fearful relative to neutral faces compared with the healthy control group. Persons with GAD did exhibit significantly increased neural response to angry expressions relative to healthy individuals in a lateral region of the middle frontal gyrus, and this increased lateral frontal response also was associated with self-report of anxiety. Thus, although most anxiety disorders are associated with increased fear circuit activation, there is a level of specificity of activation that is driven by the nature of the threat stimulus.

FINDINGS FROM THE ADOLESCENT NEUROIMAGING LITERATURE

With rare exception (e.g., Guyer et al., 2008), almost all neuroimaging studies of adolescents have relied on face emotion tasks to explore the neural circuitry associated with anxiety. Moreover, only one study has specifically focused on adolescent SAD (i.e., Guyer et al., 2008). All other studies have generally examined healthy children and adolescents and/or combine youth with various anxiety disorders. During an fMRI scan, participants view 32 different actors, each displaying one of four face emotions (happy, fearful, angry, or neutral). With this design, a total of eight different actors are seen for each of the four emotions. Subjects view each of these 32 actors four times. There are four different rating conditions; for each actor, subjects make ratings on a 5-point Likert scale, once on each of the four rating conditions. Three of these conditions were designed to manipulate attention ("How afraid are you?" "How hostile is the face?" and "How wide is the nose?"), and one involves a passive viewing condition. Thus, each face stimulus is presented a total of four times (4-s duration for each viewing), once during each of four different rating conditions.

The most recent and comprehensive developmental study of nonanxious youths' neural response to emotional faces was conducted by Daniel Pine's research group at the National Institute of Mental Health (Guyer et al., 2008). Drawing on previous research, this study sought to examine developmental alterations in the amygdala's response to fearful faces. A second aim was to examine the degree to which functional connections between the amygdala and other brain regions exhibit meaningful age-related functional connectivity (i.e., patterns of connection between neural structures) during face emotion processing.

A total of 30 healthy adults (21–40 years old) and 31 adolescents (9–17 years old) underwent fMRI while viewing faces depicting various emotions. During passive viewing (i.e., no ratings made while viewing faces), adolescents demonstrated greater amygdala and fusiform gyrus (which is responsible for face and body recognition) activation in response to fearful faces relative to adults. Functional connectivity analysis also indicated stronger connectivity between the amygdala and the hippocampus in adults than in adolescents. Within each age group, variability in age was not associated with amygdala response, and sex-related developmental differences were not observed. The authors maintained that amygdala hyperactivation in response to fearful faces among adolescents may have helped explain increased vulnerability to affective disorders during this developmental period. Moreover, the more robust amygdala-hippocampus connectivity detected in adults relative to adolescents may have suggested maturation in learning or habituation to facial expressions by adulthood.

Pine and colleagues also developed an ecologically valid fMRI paradigm that used anticipation of peer evaluation within a simulated Internet chat room to induce feelings of social threat in adolescents with and without SAD (or heightened social anxiety) to assess changes in amygdala response. More important, the degree to which amygdala–vlPFC connectivity relates to between-groups differences in a real-world social context was considered. This task required adolescent participants to rate their desire to interact with a group of unknown peers. After 2 weeks, they were asked to rate how they thought these same peers would evaluate them for a social interaction. As part of the task, participants were led to believe that the unknown peers would be told how the research participant rated them. Thus, it was predicated that peers rated as undesirable would elicit amygdala hyperactivation and positive amygdala–vlPFC connectivity in socially anxious versus socially nonanxious adolescents. Two main findings emerged from this study. First, socially anxious adolescents exhibited increased amygdala activity compared with healthy adolescents when viewing photographs of peers they rated as less desirable relative to those they rated as more desirable for an expected social interaction. Second, connectivity analyses indicated a significant positive association between amygdala and vlPFC activation in socially anxious versus healthy adolescents in response to this social situation. These findings were observed along with behaviorally based differences. Compared with healthy adolescents, socially anxious adolescents rated unfamiliar peers as being less likely to want to chat with them. This study adds and extends previous findings concerning adolescent social anxiety on the basis of findings of a cognitive bias concerning social evaluation and related observation of fear circuitry activation. As the authors noted, social stimuli generally considered nonthreatening (i.e., smiling peers) provoked strong amygdala activation in adolescents with SAD, particularly when viewing peers whom they had rated as undesirable.

Although results from this study implicated amygdala-vlPFC coactivation in adolescent social anxiety, neuroimaging research suggests that the amygdala-vlPFC circuitry is broadly related to adolescent anxiety in general (McClure et al., 2007; Monk et al., 2006; Monk et al., 2008; Thomas et al., 2001). As stated previously, what appears to be the key difference is the type of threat stimulus that activates this circuit. Voxel-based morphometry is a neuroimaging method that uses a statistical approach (parametric mapping) that permits investigation of differences in brain anatomy. This is achieved by drawing regions of interest (ROIs) in brain images and calculating the volume. Recently, automated methods have been developed and used, negating reliance on hand tracing ROIs. To the best of our knowledge, there is only one study that has examined voxel-based morphometry in a youth-based anxiety sample (Milham et al., 2005). This study compared GM volume throughout the brains of 17 children with anxiety disorders and 34 healthy youth. Of the 17 children with anxiety disorders, nine were diagnosed with SAD, 13 with GAD, and three with separation anxiety disorder. The average age of participants was about 13 years. Surprisingly, findings suggested diminished GM volume in the left amygdala for youth with anxiety disorders relative to comparison participants. A subthreshold right amygdala volume decrease also was observed but did not meet small volume correction criteria for statistical significance. A recurrent theme of this chapter is the consistent finding of amygdala hyperactivation among anxious adolescents and adults, which seems at odds with the results of this study. A recent study in adult major depressive disorder, however, also observed an inverse association between amygdala activation and left amygdala volume (Siegle, Konecky, Thase, & Carter, 2003). This relation is thought to indicate the end product of excitotoxicity (i.e., exaggerated and continuous stimulation by a neurotransmitter). Thus, a comparable excitotoxic process might be causally related to the decreased GM volumes observed in the Milham et al. (2005) study.

Of the original 17 youth with anxiety disorders from the Milham et al. (2005) study, seven participated in a second imaging session after 8 weeks of treatment with either a selective serotonin reuptake inhibitor medication or cognitive behavioral therapy. All seven youth exhibited improvement with treatment as measured by the Improvement scale of the Clinical Global Impressions Scale. On the basis of the same left amygdala ROI mask used in the original study, comparison of pre- and posttreatment GM volume revealed significant increases after 8 weeks of either pharmacological or psychosocial treatment. No significant changes were observed for whole brain GM volume or any of the other ROIs. Although this finding suggests that therapeutic interventions may reverse some neural perturbations associated with anxiety disorders, these data should be considered with caution given their reliance on a small sample size and absence of matched healthy comparisons.

CONCLUSIONS

Overall, it is clear that relatively little research has been conducted on the development of emotional circuits in socially anxious adolescents. This transitional period involves critical changes in physical and cognitive functioning as well as the capacity to process affect. During adolescence there is a general increase in myelinated axonal projections to the prefrontal lobes (Caviness et al., 1996; Pfefferbaum et al., 1994; Reiss et al., 1996) consistent with evidence that the prefrontal lobes are generally among the last cerebral structures to reach full development (Huttenlocher, 1990). Neuroimaging studies show that maturation during adolescence is paralleled by age-related increases in frontal lobe activation (Rubia et al., 2000). Collectively, these findings suggest that adolescent development may involve a transition within the brain whereby "executive control is transferred from the more primitive, immature subcortical systems to frontal lobe cortex, particularly left prefrontal cortex" (Killgore, 2000, p. 528).

A second major theme is that the amygdala and vlPFC are consistently identified as key components of the fear circuit. However, the type of threat stimulus that arouses this circuit appears to vary as a function of the disorder being studied. Although negatively valenced faces and anticipatory social anxiety seem to reliably trigger this pathway in socially anxious adolescents compared with nonsocially-anxious adolescents, specificity of this response remains unclear. There is a need for additional comparisons using adolescents with various anxiety disorders and healthy adolescents on amygdala-vlPFC activation and their coactivation.

There are now numerous tools and methods available that allow researchers to probe and measure brain structure and function during this period. In addition to fMRI, several other techniques, particularly electro- and magnetoencephalography, can help shed light on the dynamics of the brain during development (Paus, 2005). The integration of data from multiple imaging methods would provide a more complete picture of the relations between emotion expression and the brain as it undergoes the maturational process. Multimethod longitudinal assessments within the same individual will allow researchers to better understand both intra- and interindividual variance for behaviors and emotions (Paus, 2005). Finally, no study of adolescent social anxiety has examined the interplay of genes and neural functioning. Although it is likely that genes related to SAD are pleiotropic (i.e., a single gene influences multiple phenotypic traits), mapping the neural networks underlying socioemotional processing and the genes that influence this network will be critical to fully understanding the disorder.

REFERENCES

Adolphs, R. (2003). Is the human amygdala specialized for processing social information? *Annals of the New York Academy of Sciences, 985*, 326–340. doi:10.1111/j.1749-6632.2003.tb07091.x

Amaral, D. G. (2003). The amygdala, social behavior, and danger detection. *Annals of the New York Academy of Sciences, 1000*, 337–347. doi:10.1196/annals.1280.015

Amaral, D. G. (2004). The amygdala and social behavior: What's fear got to do with it? In J. M. Gorman (Ed.), *Fear and anxiety: The benefits of translational research* (pp. 251–263). Arlington, VA: American Psychiatric Publishing.

Amir, N., Klumpp, H., Elias, J., Bedwell, J. S., Yanasak, N., & Miller, L. S. (2005). Increased activation of the anterior cingulate cortex during processing of disgust faces in individuals with social phobia. *Biological Psychiatry, 57*, 975–981. doi:10.1016/j.biopsych.2005.01.044

Armony, J. L., Corbo, V., Clément, M., & Brunei, A. (2005). Amygdala response in patients with acute PTSD to masked and unmasked emotional facial expressions. *The American Journal of Psychiatry, 162,* 1961–1963. doi:10.1176/appi.ajp.162.10.1961

Barlow, D. H. (2004). *Anxiety and its disorders.* NewYork, NY: Guilford Press.

Bauman, M. D., Lavenex, P., Mason, W. A., Capitanio, J. P., & Amaral, D. G. (2004a). The development of mother–infant interaction after neonatal amygdale lesions in rhesus monkeys. *The Journal of Neuroscience, 24,* 711–721.

Bauman, M. D., Lavenex, P., Mason, W., Capitanio, J. P., & Amaral, D. G. (2004b). The development of social behavior following neonatal amygdala lesions in rhesus monkeys. *Journal of Cognitive Neuroscience, 16,* 1388–1411. doi:10.1162/0898929042304741

Baxter, M. G., Parker, A., Lindner, C. C., Izquierdo, A. D., & Murray, E. A. (2000). Control of response selection by reinforcer value requires interaction of amygdala and orbital prefrontal cortex. *The Journal of Neuroscience, 20,* 4311–4319.

Bayer, S. A., Altman, J., Russo, R. J., & Zhang, X. (1993). Timetables of neurogenesis in the human brain based on experimentally determined patterns in the rat. *Neurotoxicology, 14,* 83–144.

Beerpoot, L. J., Lipska, B. K., & Weinberger, D. R. (1996). Neurobiology of treatment-resistant schizophrenia: New insights and new models. *European Neuropsychopharmacology, 6*(Suppl. 2), 27–34. doi:10.1016/0924-977X(96)00008-9

Berlau, D. J., & McGaugh, J. (2006). Enhancement of extinction memory consolidation: The role of the noradrenergic and GABAergic systems within the basolateral amygdala. *Neurobiology of Learning and Memory, 86,* 123–132. doi:10.1016/j.nlm.2005.12.008

Birbaumer, N., Grodd, W., Diedrich, O., Klose, U., Erb, M., Lotze, M., . . . Flor, H. (1998). fMRI reveals amygdala activation to human faces in social phobics. *Neuroreport, 9,* 1223–1226. doi:10.1097/00001756-199804200-00048

Blair, K., Geraci, M., Devido, J., McCaffrey, D., Chen, G., Vythilingam, M., . . . Pine, D. S. (2008). Neural response to self- and other referential praise and criticism in generalized social phobia. *Archives of General Psychiatry, 65,* 1176–1184. doi:10.1001/archpsyc.65.10.1176

Boccia, M. M., Blake, M., Baratti, C., & McGaugh, J. (2009). Involvement of the basolateral amygdala in muscarinic cholinergic modulation of extinction memory consolidation. *Neurobiology of Learning and Memory, 91,* 93–97. doi:10.1016/j.nlm.2008.07.012

Buck, R. (1994). Social and emotional functions in facial expression and communication: The readout hypothesis. *Biological Psychology, 38,* 95–115. doi:10.1016/0301-0511(94)90032-9

Caviness, V., Kennedy, D., Bates, J., & Makris, N. (1996). *The developing human brain: A morphometric profile. Developmental neuroimaging: Mapping the development of brain and behavior* (pp. 3–14). San Diego, CA: Academic Press.

Davis, M., & Whalen, P. (2001). The amygdala: Vigilance and emotion. *Molecular Psychiatry, 6,* 13–34. doi:10.1038/sj.mp.4000812

Dimberg, U. (1988). Facial electromyography and the experience of emotion. *Journal of Psychophysiology, 2*, 277–282.

Dimberg, U., & Öhman, A. (1983). The effects of directional facial cues on electrodermal conditioning to facial stimuli. *Psychophysiology, 20*, 160–167. doi:10.1111/j.1469-8986.1983.tb03282.x

Ekman, P. (1973). Universal facial expressions in emotion. *Studia Psychologica, 15*, 140–147.

Elkind, D., & Bowen, R. (1979). Imaginary audience behavior in children and adolescents. *Developmental Psychology, 15*, 38–44. doi:10.1037/0012-1649.15.1.38

Ernst, M., & Fudge, J. L. (2009). Developmental neurobiological model of motivated behavior: Anatomy, connectivity and ontogeny of the triadic nodes. *Neuroscience and Biobehavioral Reviews, 33*, 367–382. doi:10.1016/j.neubiorev.2008.10.009

Fox, N. A., Hane, A. A., & Pine, D. S. (2007). Plasticity for affective neurocircuitry: How the environment affects gene expression. *Current Directions in Psychological Science, 16*, 1–5. doi:10.1111/j.1467-8721.2007.00464.x

Furmark, T., Appel, L., Michelgård, Å., Wahlstedt, K., Åhs, F., Zancan, S., . . . Fredrikson, M. (2005). Cerebral blood flow changes after treatment of social phobia with the neurokinin-1 antagonist GR205171, citalopram, or placebo. *Biological Psychiatry, 58*, 132–142. doi:10.1016/j.biopsych.2005.03.029

Furmark, T., Tillfors, M., Marteinsdottir, I., Fischer, H., Pissiota, A., Långström, B., & Fredrikson, M. (2002). Common changes in cerebral blood flow in patients with social phobia treated with citalopram or cognitive-behavioral therapy. *Archives of General Psychiatry, 59*, 425–433. doi:10.1001/archpsyc.59.5.425

Giedd, J. N., Blumenthal, J., Jeffries, N., Rajapakse, J., Vaituzis, A., Liu, H., . . . Castellanos, F. X. (1999). Development of the human corpus callosum during childhood and adolescence: A longitudinal MRI study. *Progress in Neuro-Psychopharmacology & Biological Psychiatry, 23*, 571–588. doi:10.1016/S0278-5846(99)00017-2

Giedd, J. N., Lalonde, F. M., Celano, M. J., White, S. L., Wallace, G. L., Lee, N. R., & Lenroot, R. K. (2009). Anatomical brain magnetic resonance imaging of typically developing children and adolescents. *Journal of the American Academy of Child and Adolescent Psychiatry, 48*, 465–470. doi:10.1097/CHI.0b013e31819f2715

Giedd, J. N., Snell, J. W., Lange, N., Rajapakse, J. C., Casey, B. J., Kozuch, P. L., . . . Rapoport, J. L. (1996). A quantitative MRI study of the corpus callosum in children and adolescents. *Developmental Brain Research, 91*, 1274–1280.

Gogtay, N., Giedd, J. N., Lusk, L., Hayashi, K. M., Greenstein, D., Vaituzis, A. C., . . . Thompson, P. M. (2004). Dynamic mapping of human cortical development during childhood through early adulthood. *Proceedings of the National Academy of Sciences of the United States of America, 101*, 8174–8179. doi:10.1073/pnas.0402680101

Gross, C., & Hen, R. (2004). The developmental origins of anxiety. *Nature Reviews Neuroscience, 5,* 545–552. doi:10.1038/nrn1429

Guyer, A. E., Lau, J. Y. F., McClure-Tone, E., Parrish, J., Shiffrin, N. D., Reynolds, R. C., . . . Nelson, E. E. (2008). Amygdala and ventrolateral prefrontal cortex function during anticipated peer evaluation in pediatric social anxiety. *Archives of General Psychiatry, 65,* 1303–1312. doi:10.1001/archpsyc.65.11.1303

Hariri, A. R., Mattay, V. S., Tessitore, A., Fera, F., & Weinberger, D. R. (2003). Neocortical modulation of the amygdala response to fearful stimuli. *Biological Psychiatry, 53,* 494–501. doi:10.1016/S0006-3223(02)01786-9

Hinde, R. (1974). *Biological bases of human social behaviour.* New York, NY: McGraw-Hill.

Huttenlocher, P. R. (1990). Morphometric study of human cerebral cortex development. *Neuropsychologia, 28,* 517–527. doi:10.1016/0028-3932(90)90031-I

Izard, C. E. (1977). *Human emotions.* New York, NY: Plenum Press.

Jinks, A. L., & McGregor, I. (1997). Modulation of anxiety-related behaviours following lesions of the prelimbic or infralimbic cortex in the rat. *Brain Research, 772,* 181–190. doi:10.1016/S0006-8993(97)00810-X

Killgore, W. D. (2000). Sex differences in identifying the facial affect of normal and mirror-reversed faces. *Perceptual and Motor Skills, 91,* 525–530. doi:10.2466/PMS.91.6.525-530

LeDoux, J. E. (1996). *The emotional brain: The mysterious underpinnings of emotional life.* New York, NY: Simon & Schuster.

LeDoux, J. E. (2000). Emotion circuits in the brain. *Annual Review of Neuroscience, 23,* 155–184. doi:10.1146/annurev.neuro.23.1.155

Lindstrom, K. M., Guyer, A. E., Mogg, K., Bradley, B. P., Fox, N. A., Ernst, M., . . . Bar-Haim, Y. (2009). Normative data on development of neural and behavioral mechanisms underlying attention orienting toward social–emotional stimuli: An exploratory study. *Brain Research, 1292,* 61–70. doi:10.1016/j.brainres.2009.07.045

Lorberbaum, J. P., Kose, S., Johnson, M. R., Arana, G. W., Sullivan, L. K., Hamner, M. B., . . . George, M. S. (2004). Neural correlates of speech anticipatory anxiety in generalized social phobia. *Neuroreport, 15,* 2701–2705.

Mataix-Cols, D., Cullen, S., Lange, K., Zelaya, F., Andrew, C., Amaro, E., . . . Phillips. M. L. (2003). Neural correlates of anxiety associated with obsessive-compulsive symptom dimensions in normal volunteers. *Biological Psychiatry, 53,* 482–493. doi:10.1016/S0006-3223(02)01504-4

McClure, E. B., Monk, C. S., Nelson, E. E., Parrish, J. M., Adler, A., Blair, R. J., . . . Pine, D. S. (2007). Abnormal attention modulation of fear circuit function in pediatric generalized anxiety disorder. *Archives of General Psychiatry, 64,* 97–106. doi:10.1001/archpsyc.64.1.97

McClure, E. B., Monk, C., Nelson, E. E., Zarahn, E., Leibenluft, E., Bilder, R., . . . Pine, D. S. (2004). A developmental examination of gender differences in brain engagement during evaluation of threat. *Biological Psychiatry, 55,* 1047–1055. doi:10.1016/j.biopsych.2004.02.013

Milham, M. P., Nugent, A. C., Drevets, W. C., Dickstein, D. P., Leibenluft, E., Ernst, M., . . . Pine, D. S. (2005). Selective reduction in amygdala volume in pediatric anxiety disorders: A voxel-based morphometry investigation. *Biological Psychiatry, 57,* 961–966. doi:10.1016/j.biopsych.2005.01.038

Monk, C. S., Nelson, E. E., McClure, E. B., Mogg, K., Bradley, B. P., Leibenluft, E., . . . Pine, D. S. (2006). Ventrolateral prefrontal cortex activation and attentional bias in response to angry faces in adolescents with generalized anxiety disorder. *The American Journal of Psychiatry, 163,* 1091–1097. doi:10.1176/appi.ajp.163.6.1091

Monk, C. S., Nelson, E. E., Woldehawariat, G., Montgomery, L. A., Zarahn, E., McClure, E. B., & Pine, D. S. (2004). Experience-dependent plasticity for attention to threat: Behavioral and neurophysiological evidence in humans. *Biological Psychiatry, 56,* 607–610. doi:10.1016/j.biopsych.2004.07.012

Monk, C. S., Telzer, E. H., Mogg, K., Bradley, B. P., Mai, X., Louro, H. M., . . . Pine, D. S. (2008). Amygdala and ventrolateral prefrontal cortex activation to masked angry faces in children and adolescents with generalized anxiety disorder. *Archives of General Psychiatry, 65,* 568–576. doi:10.1001/archpsyc.65.5.568

Nelson, E. E., Leibenluft, E., McClure, E., & Pine, D. S. (1999). The social reorientation of adolescence: A neuroscience perspective on the process and its relation to psychopathology. *Psychological Medicine, 35,* 163–174. doi:10.1017/S0033291704003915

Nomura, M., Izaki, Y., Takita, M., Tanaka, J., & Hori, K. (2004). Extracellular level of basolateral amygdalar dopamine responding to reversal of appetitive-conditioned discrimination in young and old rats. *Brain Research, 1018,* 241–246. doi:10.1016/j.brainres.2004.05.077

Packard, M. G. (2009). Anxiety, cognition, and habit: A multiple memory systems perspective. *Brain Research, 1293,* 121–128. doi:10.1016/j.brainres.2009.03.029

Paus, T. (2005). Mapping brain maturation and cognitive development during adolescence. *Trends in Cognitive Sciences, 9,* 60–68. doi:10.1016/j.tics.2004.12.008

Paxinos, G., & Watson, C. (1986). *The rat brain in stereotaxic coordinates.* New York, NY: Academic Press.

Pfefferbaum, A., Mathalon, D. H., Sullivan, E. V., Rawles, J. M., Zipursky, R. B., & Lim, K. O. (1994). A quantitative magnetic resonance imaging study of changes in brain morphology from infancy to late adulthood. *Archives of Neurology, 5,* 1874–1887.

Phan, K. L., Fitzgerald, D. A., Nathan, P. J., Moore, G. J., Uhde, T. W., & Tancer, M. E. (2005). Neural substrates for voluntary suppression of negative affect: A functional magnetic resonance imaging study. *Biological Psychiatry, 57,* 210–219. doi:10.1016/j.biopsych.2004.10.030

Phan, K. L., Fitzgerald, D. A., Nathan, P. J., & Tancer, M. E. (2006). Association between amygdala hyperactivity to harsh faces and severity of social anxiety in

generalized social phobia. *Biological Psychiatry, 59,* 424–429. doi:10.1016/
j.biopsych.2005.08.012

Phillips, M. L., Drevets, W., Rauch, S., & Lane, R. (2003). Neurobiology of emotion
perception I: The neural basis of normal emotion perception. *Biological Psychiatry, 54,* 504–514. doi:10.1016/S0006-3223(03)00168-9

Radhakishun, F. S., Wolterink, G., & Van Ree, J. (1988). The response of apomor-
phine administered into the accumbens in rats with bilateral lesions of the
nucleus accumbens, induced with 6-hydroxydopamine. *Neuropharmacology, 27,*
1111–1116. doi:10.1016/0028-3908(88)90005-6

Raichle, M. E., & Mintun, M. A. (2006). Brain work and brain imaging. *Annual Review
of Neuroscience, 29,* 449–476. doi:10.1146/annurev.neuro.29.051605.112819

Reiss, A., Abrams, M., Singer, H., & Ross, J. (1996). Brain development, gender and
IQ in children: A volumetric imaging study. *Brain: A Journal of Neurology, 119,*
1763–1774.

Roth, K. A., & Katz, R. (1979). Stress, behavioral arousal, and open field activity: A
reexamination of emotionality in the rat. *Neuroscience and Biobehavioral Reviews,
3,* 247–263. doi:10.1016/0149-7634(79)90012-5

Roy, C. S., & Sherrington, C. S. (1980). On the regulation of the blood-supply of the
brain. *The Journal of Physiology, 11,* 85–108.

Rubia, K., Overmeyer, S., Taylor, E., Brammer, M., Williams, S. C. R., Simmons, A.,
. . . Bullmore, E. T. (2000). Functional frontalisation with age: Mapping neurodevelopmental trajectories with fMRI. *Neuroscience and Biobehavioral Reviews,
24,* 13–19. doi:10.1016/S0149-7634(99)00055-X

Sabatini, M. J., Ebert, P., Lewis, D. A., Levitt, P., Cameron, J. L., & Mirnics, K.
(2007). Amygdala gene expression correlates of social behavior in monkeys
experiencing maternal separation. *The Journal of Neuroscience, 27,* 3295–3304.
doi:10.1523/JNEUROSCI.4765-06.2007

Sakai, Y., Kumano, H., Nishikawa, M., Sakano, Y., Kaiya, H., Imabayashi, E.,
. . . Kuboki, T. (2005). Cerebral glucose metabolism associated with a fear
network in panic disorder. *Neuroreport, 16,* 927–931. doi:10.1097/00001756-
200506210-00010

Schlaepfer, T., Harris, G., Tien, A., & Peng, L. (1995). Structural differences in the
cerebral cortex of healthy female and male subjects: A magnetic resonance imaging study. *Psychiatry Research: Neuroimaging, 61,* 129–135. doi:10.1016/0925-
4927(95)02634-A

Selman, R. L. (1980). *The growth of interpersonal understanding: Developmental and
clinical analyses.* New York, NY: Academic Press.

Shin, L. M., Wright, C., Cannistraro, P., Wedig, M., McMullin, K., Martis, B.,
. . . Rauch, S. L. (2005). A functional magnetic resonance imaging study of
amygdala and medial prefrontal cortex responses to overtly presented fearful
faces in posttraumatic stress disorder. *Archives of General Psychiatry, 62,* 273–281.
doi:10.1001/archpsyc.62.3.273

Siegle, G. J., Konecky, R. O., Thase, M. E., & Carter, C. S. (2003). Relationships between amygdala volume and activity during emotional information processing tasks in depressed and never-depressed individuals: An fMRI investigation. *Annals of the New York Academy of Sciences, 985*, 481–484. doi:10.1111/j.1749-6632.2003.tb07105.x

Sowell, E. R. (2001). Mapping continued brain growth and gray matter density reduction in dorsal frontal cortex: Inverse relationships during postadolescent brain maturation. *The Journal of Neuroscience, 21*, 8819–8829.

Stein, M. B., Goldin, P. R., Sareen, J., Zorrilla, L. T., & Brown, G. G. (2002). Increased amygdala activation to angry and contemptuous faces in generalized social phobia. *Archives of General Psychiatry, 59*, 1027–1034. doi:10.1001/archpsyc.59.11.1027

Straube, T., Kolassa, I. T., Glauer, M., Mentzel, H. J., & Miltner, W. H. (2004). Effect of task conditions on brain responses to threatening faces in social phobics: An event-related functional magnetic resonance imaging study. *Biological Psychiatry, 56*, 921–930. doi:10.1016/j.biopsych.2004.09.024

Straube, T., Mentzel, H. J., & Miltner, W. H. R. (2005). Common and distinct brain activation to threat and safety signals in social phobia. *Neuropsychobiology, 52*, 163–168. doi:10.1159/000087987

Thomas, K. M., Drevets, W. C., Dahl, R. E., Ryan, N. D., Birmaher, B., Eccard, C. H., . . . Casey, B. J. (2001). Amygdala response to fearful faces in anxious and depressed children. *Archives of General Psychiatry, 58*, 1057–1063. doi:10.1001/archpsyc.58.11.1057

Tillfors, M., Furmark, T., Marteinsdottir, I., & Fredrikson, M. (2002). Cerebral blood flow during anticipation of public speaking in social phobia: A PET study. *Biological Psychiatry, 52*, 1113–1119. doi:10.1016/S0006-3223(02)01396-3

Veit, R., Flor, H., Erb, M., Hermann, C., Lotze, M., Grodd, W., & Birbaumer, N. (2002). Brain circuits involved in emotional learning in antisocial behavior and social phobia in humans. *Neuroscience Letters, 328*, 233–236. doi:10.1016/S0304-3940(02)00519-0

Vidal, J., de Bie, J., Granneman, R. A., Wallinga, A. E., Koolhaas, J. M., & Buwalda, B. (2007). Social stress during adolescence in Wistar rats induces social anxiety in adulthood without affecting brain monoaminergic content and activity. *Physiology & Behavior, 92*, 824–830. doi:10.1016/j.physbeh.2007.06.004

Watt, M. J., Burke, A. R., Renner, K. J., & Forster, G. L. (2009). Adolescent male rats exposed to social defeat exhibit altered anxiety behavior and limbic monoamines as adults. *Behavioral Neuroscience, 123*, 564–576. doi:10.1037/a0015752

II

INDIVIDUAL DIFFERENCES, CONTEXTS, AND INFLUENCES OF SOCIAL ANXIETY IN YOUNG PEOPLE

II

4

SOCIAL ANXIETY AND DEPRESSION: THE TEENAGE AND EARLY ADULT YEARS

LISA R. STARR, JOANNE DAVILA, ANNETTE LA GRECA, AND RYAN R. LANDOLL

Anxiety disorders in general show pronounced comorbidity with depression (Brady & Kendall, 1992; Essau, 2003; Lewinsohn, Zinbarg, Seeley, Lewinsohn, & Sack, 1997), and social anxiety disorder (SAD) is no exception. In the general population, 34.2% of people with SAD are also depressed compared with only 14.5% of people without SAD (Kessler, Stang, Wittchen, Stein, & Walters, 1999). Looking specifically at adolescent samples, Essau, Conradt, and Petermann (1999) reported comorbidity rates of 29.4% between SAD and depression; Wittchen, Stein, and Kessler (1999) found similar rates that were especially pronounced among those with SAD.

Examining the comorbidity between SAD and depression is important for several reasons. First, comorbidity appears to have negative implications that go beyond those of each individual disorder. For example, youth with comorbid disorders (as with adults with comorbid disorders; Kessler et al., 1999; Rush et al., 2005) report more severe symptoms, including more recurrences of depression, greater likelihood of suicide attempts, and more overall psychosocial impairment (Lewinsohn, Rohde, & Seeley, 1995). Comorbidity may also impair adolescent interpersonal functioning because it is associated with greater familial conflict, greater peer and parental alienation, and a decreased numbers of friends (Lewinsohn, et al., 1995; Starr & Davila, 2008b). There is also some evidence that treatment outcomes are negatively impacted for youth with comorbid depression and anxiety (Ledley et al., 2005; Young, Mufson, & Davies, 2006).

Comorbidity also has very important implications for research. Many investigations of SAD have failed to control for comorbid depression. As a result, it is unclear whether reported outcomes are specific to SAD or if comorbid depressive symptoms confounded results. When research excludes people with comorbid conditions, internal validity is improved but external validity is reduced, making results more difficult to generalize.

In this chapter, we examine SAD and depression during adolescence and the transition to adulthood. First, we review temporal sequencing of comorbid SAD and depression. Second, we discuss distinguishing features and correlates of these disorders during this age period, including associated cognitive factors, neurobiological processes, interpersonal correlates, and personality features. Finally, we explore sex differences underlying SAD and depression in adolescence and discuss possible implications for differences in the presentation of these highly comorbid conditions.

TIMING OF COMORBID SYMPTOMS

The temporal sequencing of SAD and depression may offer some clues regarding the presence of comorbidity. Several studies suggest that anxiety disorders, including SAD, typically precede depressive disorders (Essau, 2003; Orvaschel, Lewinsohn, & Seeley, 1995; Wittchen, Kessler, Pfister, & Lieb, 2000), leading some researchers (Starr & Davila, 2008a; Stein et al., 2001; Wittchen, Beesdo, Bittner, & Goodwin, 2003; Wittchen et al., 2000) to speculate that this temporal ordering may reflect a causal role for anxiety. Few studies, however, have actually tested this hypothesis with regard to SAD. In one of the few available studies, Grant, Beck, Farrow, and Davila (2007) found that social anxiety predicted depressive symptoms 1 year later in a sample of emerging adults and that social-anxiety-related interpersonal styles (e.g., avoidance of expressing emotion) mediated this relationship.

Adolescence is, in many ways, an ideal time to evaluate such models. SAD usually emerges by early adolescence, with 83% of cases developing before age 14 (Giaconia, Reinherz, Silverman, & Pakiz, 1994; Kessler et al., 2005). Risk of depression, in contrast, increases throughout adolescence (especially for girls; Giaconia et al., 1994; Lewinsohn, Clark, Seeley, & Rohde, 1994; Nolen-Hoeksema & Girgus, 1994). Thus, adolescence may be the time when the mechanisms emerge that cause social anxiety to lead into depression.

UNIQUE AND SHARED FEATURES OF
SOCIAL ANXIETY IN DEPRESSION

Although there is a need for further research that examines comorbidity models, current research has elucidated several individual factors related to both SAD and depression in adolescence as well as several factors that uniquely predict SAD and depression. In particular, cognitive, interpersonal, and termperament or personality domains appear to be most promising for differentiating between SAD and depression. These domains are therefore reviewed in the sections that follow.

Cognitive Factors

In recent years, there has been increased attention to the role of cognitive factors in anxiety disorders and, in particular, a focus on how cognitive processes affect emotion regulation (Hannesdottir & Ollendick, 2007; Southam-Gerow & Kendall, 2000; Stirling, Eley, & Clark, 2006). Emotion regulation can include a variety of complex cognitive and emotional behaviors, each of which has unique ties to an equal variety of psychopathology outcomes (see Southam-Gerow & Kendall, 2002). In fact, there is much debate about what constitutes emotion regulation and a need to establish a solid working definition of the term (Cole, Martin, & Dennis, 2004). Thus, to avoid confusion, the focus of this review is on identifying specific cognitive factors that affect emotional regulation that may be most relevant to differentiating between SAD and depression among youth.

Avoidance is a hallmark of all anxiety disorders, including SAD (American Psychiatric Association, 2000). It is important to note that although avoidance is a behavioral act, it also reflects a cognitive appraisal of a situation as dangerous or threatening. Although cognitive avoidance may be somewhat unique to anxiety disorders, other cognitive aspects of emotion regulation may overlap with mood disorders, like depression. One such factor appears to be *rumination* (Kashdan & Roberts, 2007). Rumination, or the focus and rethinking about thoughts related to a negative event, has been most often associated with depressive symptoms (Garnefski & Kraaij, 2006; Hankin, 2008; Joormann, Dkane, & Gotlib, 2006; Nolen-Hoeksema, 2000). In fact, Garnefski and Kraaij (2006) found that rumination was one of the components of emotion regulation most strongly associated with depressive symptoms across five independent samples, ranging in age from early adolescents to elderly people.

At the same time, emerging research suggests an association between rumination and social anxiety (Morgan & Banerjee, 2008; Wong & Moulds, 2009). In particular, postevent processing of a social event may be the area in which social anxiety and depression share cognitive influences. Because social anxiety, but not general anxiety, is associated with postevent processing (Fehm, Schneider, & Hoyer, 2007), rumination (i.e., postevent processing) may distinguish SAD from other anxiety disorders and may be one of the shared factors with depression. Among college-age youth, the strongest associations between social anxiety and negative postevent rumination occurred among individuals with elevated depressive symptoms (Kashdan & Roberts, 2007). However, the majority of these studies were conducted with college-age adults (i.e., Kashdan & Roberts, 2007; Morgan & Banerjee, 2008; Wong & Moulds, 2009), and replication with adolescents is important. In one study using an adolescent sample (Prinstein, Cheah, & Guyer, 2005), the combination of negative peer experiences and critical self-attributions of these experiences (a form of postevent processing) predicted increases in social anxiety and depression over time.

Neurobiology Underlying Cognitive Processes in Social Anxiety and Depression

In addition to examining psychological and behavioral indicators of cognitive processes related to emotion regulation, researchers have begun to examine the neurobiological processes that may underlie these indicators. This research is in its infancy, however. Few studies exist among adolescents and even fewer that directly examine shared and unique risk factors across depression and SAD. However, there are data examining social information processing, threat processing, memory biases, reward processing, decision making, and facial processing. Further, a number of these studies focus on social anxiety or depression within an interpersonal context, such as processing of threatening social information or fearful faces (e.g., Guyer et al., 2008; Monk et al., 2008). Despite the relatively limited research, these data offer tentative clues about unique differences in processing. For example, youth with anxiety disorders consistently show specific types of threat-processing biases (i.e., greater attention to threat and biased appraisal of threat), whereas youth with depression do not (see Pine, 2007, 2009). However, youth with depression tend to show more memory biases (e.g., retention of negative information) as well as reduced neural response to reward, whereas anxious youth do not. Research that continues to examine the neurobiology underlying cognitive processes in SAD and depression may help further elucidate mechanisms of comorbidity as well as factors that distinguish risk among these disorders.

Interpersonal Factors

Interpersonal models and correlates of depression and social anxiety are well documented (Coyne, 1976; Joiner, Alfano, & Metalsky, 1992; La Greca

& Harrison, 2005; La Greca & Mackey, 2007; Prinstein, Borelli, Cheah, Simon, & Aikins, 2005; Siegel, La Greca, & Harrison, 2009; Starr & Davila, 2008b). Among adolescents, family and peers represent key interpersonal domains, and it appears that these interpersonal relationships play a prominent role in understanding both social anxiety and depression.

With respect to family factors, family sociability, parental overprotection, and parents' concern over others' opinions are associated with social anxiety in adolescents (Bögels, van Oosten, Muris, & Smulders, 2001; Caster, Inderbitzen, & Hope, 1999). Evidence also supports an interpersonal model of social anxiety whereby genetic vulnerabilities toward social anxiety are reinforced by the early social environment of the family (for a review, see Alden & Taylor, 2004). Similar family factors have been associated with adolescents' depressive symptoms. For example, both maternal and paternal history of depression are associated with higher levels of depression in offspring, particularly for adolescent girls (Reeb & Conger, 2009). Other research suggests that parental conflict and maternal hostility are associated with depression in adolescence (see Hammen, 2009). These findings are consistent with interpersonal theories of depression (Coyne, 1976; Joiner et al., 1992), which suggest that depressed individuals respond negatively to interpersonal stressors such as stressful family interactions and that in turn individuals' negative behaviors further exacerbate family and interpersonal stressors. Heightened genetic vulnerability to depressive symptoms may make children of depressed mothers and fathers particularly vulnerable to these processes.

The high degree of comorbidity between SAD and depression, evident in youth and in adults, presents methodological challenges for research examining the intergenerational transmission of these disorders because there is a lack of specificity between parental and childhood disorders (Knappe, Beesdo, Fehm, Lieb, & Wittchen, 2009; Loeber, Hipwell, Battista, Sembower, & Stouthamer-Loeber, 2009; Ohannessian et al., 2005). Findings suggest that several forms of parental psychopathology, including SAD, other anxiety disorders, and depressive disorders, are all associated with childhood social anxiety (Knappe et al., 2009). Similarly, parental depression is associated with both adolescent depression and anxiety (Ohannessian et al., 2005).

Only recently have investigators begun to account for the comorbidity between SAD and depression when examining family contributions to childhood disorders. This line of research suggests that family factors play a stronger, more significant role in youths' depression than in their social anxiety. When the comorbidity between SAD and depression is considered, family factors such as decreased trust, conflict, and low levels of family sociability are more strongly associated with adolescent depression than with adolescent SAD (Johnson, Inderbitzen-Nolan, & Schapman, 2005; Starr & Davila, 2008a). Although adolescent depression appears to be more specifically linked to family factors than adolescent social anxiety, the offspring of parents with comorbid anxiety and depressive disorders are at higher risk of psychopathology than those whose parents do not have a comorbid disorder, suggesting the importance of both parental disorders in the transmission of psychopathology (Dozois, Dobson, & Westra, 2004).

With respect to peer relations, peer processes may play an even greater role in the development of SAD in adolescents and young adults compared with family factors. Specifically, feelings of social anxiety may inhibit the positive social interactions necessary for satisfactory social and emotional development (see Davila, La Greca, Starr, & Landoll, 2010; La Greca & Landoll, in press). For adolescents and young adults, acceptance from peers and companionship, intimacy, and emotional support from close friends are extremely important (Buote et al., 2007; La Greca & Prinstein, 1999). Adolescents who are actively rejected by peers (or who have low peer acceptance) report significantly higher levels of social anxiety and depressive symptoms than those who are more accepted (Inderbitzen, Walters, & Bukowski, 1997; La Greca & Lopez, 1998). Additionally, peer rejection of young adults who are socially anxious leads to decreases in their prosocial behavior in future interactions (Mallott, Maner, DeWall, & Schmidt, 2009). There are parallel findings for depression. Depressed youth who experience negative social feedback seek more negative social feedback, placing them at further risk of rejection (Casbon, Burns, Bradbury, & Joiner, 2005).

More recently, *peer victimization* (PV) has been identified as an interpersonal stressor that affects adolescent adjustment (e.g., De Los Reyes & Prinstein, 2004; Hawker & Boulton, 2000; La Greca & Harrison, 2005; La Greca & Mackey, 2007; Prinstein, Boergers, & Vernberg, 2001). Prospective work indicates that PV leads to increases in adolescents' social anxiety over time (Siegel et al., 2009) and to increased rates of SAD (Storch, Masia-Warner, Crisp, & Klein, 2005). PV also has been associated with adolescents' symptoms of depression (e.g., Hawker & Boulton, 2000; La Greca & Harrison, 2005; McLaughlin, Hatzenbuehler, & Hilt, 2009; Prinstein et al., 2005). Emerging evidence has begun to disentangle the specific pathways between PV and SAD versus depression. Studies by Ranta, Kaltiala-Heino, Pelkonen, and Marttunen (2009) strongly suggested that PV is uniquely associated with social anxiety rather than depression. Adolescents (12–17 years old) who met criteria for SAD had substantially higher rates of PV than those without SAD, and PV was highest among adolescents with SAD comorbid with depression; in contrast, PV was not associated with adolescent depression alone.

Because close friendships are critical to adolescents' and young adults' interpersonal functioning, problems in this area represent another interpersonal stressor that may contribute to feelings of social anxiety, which in turn could lead to avoidance or inhibition in close relationships and interfere with the further development of close, supportive ties. For example, socially anxious adolescents have fewer close friends, perceive themselves to be less competent in their friendships, and perceive the qualities of their close friendships to be low (i.e., less supportive, less intimate, and lower in companionship; La Greca & Lopez, 1998). Even after controlling for factors such as PV, adolescents who reported fewer positive and more negative interactions in friendships reported significantly higher levels of social anxiety (La Greca & Harrison, 2005). Only high levels of negative interactions with friends predicted adolescents' depressive symptoms. There is, in fact, a wealth of literature documenting associations between the quality of close friendships and depression in adolescents (Borelli & Prinstein, 2006; Demir & Urberg, 2004; Hussong, 2000; La Greca & Harrison, 2005). Depressed adolescents and adults cause erosion in social support through maladaptive interpersonal behaviors such as seeking negative feedback and excessive reassurance (Burns, Brown, & Plant, 2006; Joiner et al., 1992; Stice, Ragan, & Randall, 2004). Thus, whereas global negative social interactions may more strongly influence social anxiety, it is the quality of close friendships that appears to be more closely tied to depression in young people.

Temperament and Personality Factors

Temperament and personality factors also shed light on the unique and shared features of SAD and depression as well as on the timing and course of their comorbidity. Although the literature is sparse, research has focused particularly on positive and negative emotionality (PE and NE, respectively) and behavioral inhibition (BI). With regard to PE and NE, high NE appears to be more strongly associated with depression than social anxiety, whereas low PE is associated is associated with both (and more so than with other disorders; Watson, Gamez, & Sims, 2005). Given this, researchers have attempted to identify aspects of PE that may be specific to each disorder. Naragon-Gainey, Watson, and Markon (2009) examined four facets of PE—sociability, positive emotionality, ascendance, and fun-seeking—and found that depression was associated specifically with low positive emotionality, whereas social anxiety was associated with low scores on all four facets and most strongly with sociability and ascendance. These findings help to elucidate potential sources or areas of comorbidity.

With regard to BI (for a more detailed description, see Chapter 2, this volume), numerous studies (although not all; see Caspi, Moffitt, Newman, & Silva, 1996) have found increased risk of SAD among children and adolescents with high levels of BI (e.g., Biederman et al., 2001; Gladstone, Parker, Mitchell, Wilhelm, & Malhi, 2005; Hayward, Killen, Kraemer, & Taylor, 1998). A similar finding has emerged for depression as well (e.g., Caspi et al.,

1996; Jaffee, Moffitt, Caspi, Fombonne, & Martin, 2002; Muris, Merckelbach, Schmidt, Gadet, & Bogie, 2001), suggesting that BI is a nonspecific risk factor for both disorders and may account for at least part of their comorbidity. Gladstone and Parker (2006) also found an association between lifetime depression and self-reported BI, but this association was attenuated when controlling for current social anxiety symptoms. Although this study used a retrospective cross-sectional design, the authors suggested that the findings may indicate that social anxiety mediates the association between BI and depression. If longitudinal research were to confirm this speculation, it would help clarify how BI relates to both depression and SAD as well as to the temporal order of their development. Consistent with this notion, one study (Eng, Heimberg, Hart, Schneier, & Liebowitz, 2001) found that social anxiety mediated the association between attachment insecurity (which is associated with BI; e.g., Calkins & Fox, 1992) and depressive symptoms, although, again, this was a self-report, cross-sectional study. Nonetheless, the findings point to an important hypothesis for future research.

SEX DIFFERENCES

SAD afflicts both sexes but is disproportionately found in girls. In a sample of German adolescents (Essau et al., 1999), girls were substantially more likely than boys to meet criteria for SAD and express subsyndromal social fears. In the Oregon Adolescent Depression project, lifetime prevalence of SAD was 2.36% for girls compared with 0.49% for boys. These differences remain fairly constant over time (Hale, Raaijmakers, Muris, van Hoof, & Meeus, 2008), and similar sex disparities are found among adults (Chapman, Mannuzza, & Fyer, 1995) and younger children (Anderson, Williams, McGee, & Silva, 1987).

Depression is also more prevalent among girls during adolescence. In contrast to SAD, girls' depression rates are relatively similar to boys' during childhood but then markedly increase throughout adolescence, reaching an approximately 2:1 female-to-male ratio by age 15 (see Nolen-Hoeksema & Girgus, 1994). This disproportion persists into adulthood (Weissman & Klerman, 1977). Given that both SAD and depression are considerably more common in females, SAD and depression tend to co-occur, and SAD tends to precede depression, a logical question is whether sex differences in depression are secondary to sex differences in preexisting SAD. A few researchers have empirically examined this question (looking at anxiety disorders in general, rather than SAD specifically) and have found that sex differences in anxiety disorders at least partially account for sex differences in depression (Breslau, Schultz, & Peterson, 1995; Parker & Hadzi-Pavlovic, 2001, 2004). Notably, previous research has not supported gender as a moderator of anxiety disorder and depression comorbidity (Breslau et al., 1995; Parker & Hadzi-Pavlovic, 2001). In other words, anxiety confers the same degree of risk of depression across males and females, but because girls and women show higher rates anxiety in the first place, this in turn may translate into higher depression rates among females. However, this question has never been examined (to our knowledge) in adolescent samples.

Although sex differences in anxiety are as pronounced as sex differences in depression, the latter have received substantially more research attention. One avenue for generating hypotheses on the origins of sex differences in SAD is by exploring gender differences in social-anxiety-related behaviors. In addition to biological differences, girls and boys are socialized in dramatically different ways, so it is not surprising that they tend to engage in sharply different interpersonal behaviors (Block, 1983). Furthermore, the social challenges that emerge in adolescence may have different meaning for each sex because boys and girls are scrutinized according to different standards. This may in turn lead to differential implications for SAD and depression.

In their review of the literature, Rose and Rudolph (2006) noted several consistent findings. First, the content and social structure of children's and adolescents' social interactions differ by gender. Boys tend to have larger social networks with well-defined social hierarchies, whereas girls spend more extended time in dyadic interaction and use this time for engaging in prosocial behavior and self-disclosure. In addition, adolescent girls generally value and show more affiliative characteristics within their peer relationships, including greater caring, more support, and more nurturance (Benenson & Benarroch, 1998; Jarvinen & Nicholls, 1996; Rose & Rudolph, 2006). On the one hand, these affilliative qualities may protect girls from the development of antisocial behaviors and other externalizing problems and ultimately promote self-worth (Rose & Rudolph, 2006). However, compared with boys, girls also tend to worry more about peer relationships and experience and generate more interpersonal stress (Kuperminc, Blatt, & Leadbeater, 1997; Rudolph & Hammen, 1999). These tendencies may place girls at added risk of depression and SAD.

CONCLUSION

In this chapter, we examined several important literatures toward elucidating the common overlap between SAD and depression, including the temporal sequencing of these disorders as well as shared underlying factors. Although available data offer clear directions for future research, each of the areas is in need of further development, exploring the cognitive, neurobiological, interpersonal, and personality factors in SAD and depression, with an eye toward determining distinguishing factors that are unique to each disorder as well as toward identifying shared features that may act as common risk factors for the development of comorbid disorders.

REFERENCES

Alden, L. E., & Taylor, C. T. (2004). Interpersonal processes in social phobia. *Clinical Psychology Review, 24*, 857–882. doi:10.1016/j.cpr.2004.07.006

American Psychiatric Association. (2000). *Diagnostic and statistical manual of mental disorders* (4th ed., text rev.). Washington, DC: American Psychiatric Association.

Anderson, J. C., Williams, S., McGee, R., & Silva, P. A. (1987). *DSM–III* disorders in preadolescent children: Prevalence in a large sample from the general population. *Archives of General Psychiatry, 44*, 69–76.

Benenson, J. F., & Benarroch, D. (1998). Gender differences in responses to friends' hypothetical greater success. *The Journal of Early Adolescence, 18*, 192–208. doi:10.1177/0272431698018002004

Biederman, J., Hirshfeld-Becker, D. R., Rosenbaum, J. F., Herot, C., Friedman, D., Snidman, N., . . . Faraone, S. V. (2001). Further evidence of association between behavioural inhibition and social anxiety in children. *The American Journal of Psychiatry, 158*, 1673–1679. doi:10.1176/appi.ajp.158.10.1673

Block, J. H. (1983). Differential premises arising from differential socialization of the sexes: Some conjectures. *Child Development, 54*, 1335–1354. doi:10.2307/1129799

Bögels, S. M., van Oosten, A., Muris, P., & Smulders, D. (2001). Familial correlates of social anxiety in children and adolescents. *Behaviour Research and Therapy, 39*, 273–287. doi:10.1016/S0005-7967(00)00005-X

Borelli, J. L., & Prinstein, M. J. (2006). Reciprocal, longitudinal associations among adolescent's negative feedback-seeking, depressive symptoms, and peer relations. *Journal of Abnormal Child Psychology, 34*, 154–164. doi:10.1007/s10802-005-9010-y

Brady, E. U., & Kendall, P. C. (1992). Comorbidity of anxiety and depression in children and adolescents. *Psychological Bulletin, 111*, 244–255. doi:10.1037/0033-2909.111.2.244

Breslau, N., Schultz, L., & Peterson, E. (1995). Sex differences in depression: A role for preexisting anxiety. *Psychiatry Research, 58*(1), 1–12. doi:10.1016/0165-1781(95)02765-O

Buote, V. M., Pancer, S. M., Pratt, M. W., Adams, G., Birnie-Lefcovitch, S., Polivy, J., & Wintre, M. G. (2007). The importance of friends: Friendship and adjustment among 1st-year university students. *Journal of Adolescent Research, 22*, 665–689. doi:10.1177/0743558407306344

Burns, A. B., Brown, J. S., & Plant, E. A. (2006). On the specific depressotypic nature of excessive reassurance-seeking. *Personality and Individual Differences, 40*, 135–145. doi:10.1016/j.paid.2005.05.019

Calkins, S. D., & Fox, N. A. (1992). The relations among infant temperament, security of attachment, and behavioral inhibition at twenty-four months. *Child Development, 63*, 1456–1472. doi:10.2307/1131568

Casbon, T. S., Burns, A. B., Bradbury, T. N., & Joiner, T. E., Jr. (2005). Receipt of negative feedback is related to increased negative feedback seeking among individuals with depressive symptoms. *Behaviour Research and Therapy, 43*, 485–504. doi:10.1016/j.brat.2004.03.009

Caspi, A., Moffitt, T. E., Newman, D. L., & Silva, P. A. (1996). Behavioral observations at age 3 years predict adult psychiatric disorders. *Archives of General Psychiatry, 53*, 1033–1039.

Caster, J. B., Inderbitzen, H. M., & Hope, D. (1999). Relationship between youth and parent perceptions of family environment and social anxiety. *Journal of Anxiety Disorders, 13*, 237–251. doi:10.1016/S0887-6185(99)00002-X

Chapman, T. F., Mannuzza, S., & Fyer, A. J. (1995). Epidemiology and family studies of social phobia. In R. G. Heimberg, M. R. Liebowitz, D. A. Hope, & F. R. Schneier (Eds.), *Social phobia: Diagnosis, assessment, and treatment* (pp. 21–40). New York, NY: Guilford Press.

Cole, P. M., Martin, S. E., & Dennis, T. A. (2004). Emotion regulation as a scientific construct: Methodological challenges and directions for child development research. *Child Development, 75*, 317–333. doi:10.1111/j.1467-8624.2004.00673.x

Coyne, J. C. (1976). Toward an interactional description of depression. *Psychiatry, 39*, 28–40.

Davila, J., La Greca, A. M., Starr, L. R., & Landoll, R. R. (2010). Anxiety disorders in adolescence. In J. G. Beck (Ed.), *Interpersonal processes in the anxiety disorders: Implications for understanding psychopathology and treatment* (pp. 97–124). Washington, DC: American Psychological Association. doi:10.1037/12084-004

De Los Reyes, A., & Prinstein, M. J. (2004). Applying depression-distortion hypotheses to the assessment of peer victimization in adolescents. *Journal of Clinical Child and Adolescent Psychology, 33*, 325–335. doi:10.1207/s15374424jccp3302_14

Demir, M., & Urberg, K. A. (2004). Friendship and adjustment among adolescents. *Journal of Experimental Child Psychology, 88*, 68–82. doi:10.1016/j.jecp.2004.02.006

Dozois, D. J. A., Dobson, K. S., & Westra, H. A. (2004). The comorbidity of anxiety and depression, and the implications of comorbidity for prevention. In D. J. A. Dozois & K. S. Dobson (Eds.), *The prevention of anxiety and depression* (pp. 261–280). Washington, DC: American Psychological Association. doi:10.1037/10722-011

Eng, W., Heimberg, R. G., Hart, T. A., Schneier, F. R., & Liebowitz, M. R. (2001). Attachment in individuals with social anxiety disorder: The relationship among adult attachment styles, social anxiety, and depression. *Emotion, 1*, 365–380. doi:10.1037/1528-3542.1.4.365

Essau, C. A. (2003). Comorbidity of anxiety disorders in adolescents. *Depression and Anxiety, 18*, 1–6. doi:10.1002/da.10107

Essau, C. A., Conradt, J., & Petermann, F. (1999). Frequency and comorbidity of social phobia and social fears in adolescents. *Behaviour Research and Therapy, 37,* 831–843. doi:10.1016/S0005-7967(98)00179-X

Fehm, L., Schneider, G., & Hoyer, J. (2007). Is post-event processing specific for social anxiety? *Journal of Behavior Therapy and Experimental Psychiatry, 38,* 11–22. doi:10.1016/j.jbtep.2006.02.004

Garnefski, N., & Kraaij, V. (2006). Relationships between cognitive emotion regulation strategies and depressive symptoms: A comparative study of five specific samples. *Personality and Individual Differences, 40,* 1659–1669. doi:10.1016/j.paid.2005.12.009

Giaconia, R. M., Reinherz, H. Z., Silverman, A. B., & Pakiz, B. (1994). Ages of onset of psychiatric disorders in a community population of older adolescents. *Journal of the American Academy of Child and Adolescent Psychiatry, 33,* 706–717. doi:10.1097/00004583-199406000-00012

Gladstone, G. L., & Parker, G. B. (2006). Is behavioral inhibition a risk factor for depression? *Journal of Affective Disorders, 95,* 85–94. doi:10.1016/j.jad.2006.04.015

Gladstone, G. L., Parker, G. B., Mitchell, P. B., Wilhelm, K. A., & Malhi, G. S. (2005). Relationship between self-reported childhood behavioral inhibition and lifetime anxiety disorders in a clinical sample. *Depression and Anxiety, 22,* 103–113. doi:10.1002/da.20082

Grant, D. M., Beck, J. G., Farrow, S. M., & Davila, J. (2007). Do interpersonal features of social anxiety influence the development of depressive symptoms? *Cognition and Emotion, 21,* 646–663. doi:10.1080/02699930600713036

Guyer, A. E., Lau, J. Y. F., McClure-Tone, E. B., Shiffrin, N. D., Chen, G., Leibenluft, E., . . . Nelson, E. E. (2008). Amygdala and ventrolateral prefrontal cortex function during anticipated peer evaluation in pediatric social anxiety. *Archives of General Psychiatry, 65,* 1303–1312. doi:10.1001/archpsyc.65.11.1303

Hale, W. W., III, Raaijmakers, Q., Muris, P., van Hoof, A., & Meeus, W. (2008). Developmental trajectories of adolescent anxiety disorder symptoms: A 5-year prospective community study. *Journal of the American Academy of Child and Adolescent Psychiatry, 47,* 556–564. doi:10.1097/CHI.0b013e3181676583

Hammen, C. (2009). Adolescent depression: Stressful interpersonal contexts for risk for recurrence. *Current Directions in Psychological Science, 18,* 200–204. doi:10.1111/j.1467-8721.2009.01636.x

Hankin, B. L. (2008). Rumination and depression in adolescence: Investigating symptom specificity in a multiwave prospective study. *Journal of Clinical Child and Adolescent Psychology, 37,* 701–713. doi:10.1080/15374410802359627

Hannesdottir, D. K., & Ollendick, T. H. (2007). The role of emotion regulation in the treatment of child anxiety disorders. *Clinical Child and Family Psychology Review, 10,* 275–293. doi:10.1007/s10567-007-0024-6

Hawker, D. S. J., & Boulton, M. J. (2000). Twenty years' research on peer victimization and psychosocial maladjustment: A meta-analytic review of cross-sectional studies. *The Journal of Child Psychology and Psychiatry and Allied Disciplines, 41*, 441–455. doi:10.1111/1469-7610.00629

Hayward, C., Killen, J. D., Kraemer, H. C., & Taylor, C. B. (1998). Linking self-reported childhood behavioral inhibition to adolescent social phobia. *Journal of the American Academy of Child and Adolescent Psychiatry, 37*, 1308–1316. doi:10.1097/00004583-199812000-00015

Hussong, A. M. (2000). Perceived peer context and adolescent adjustment. *Journal of Research on Adolescence, 10*, 391–415.

Inderbitzen, H. M., Walters, K. S., & Bukowski, A. L. (1997). The role of social anxiety in adolescent peer relations: Differences among sociometric status groups and rejected subgroups. *Journal of Clinical Child Psychology, 26*, 338–348. doi:10.1207/s15374424jccp2604_2

Jaffee, S. R., Moffitt, T. E., Caspi, A., Fombonne, E. P. R., & Martin, J. (2002). Differences in early childhood risk factors for juvenile-onset and adult-onset depression. *Archives of General Psychiatry, 59*, 215–222. doi:10.1001/archpsyc.59.3.215

Jarvinen, D. W., & Nicholls, J. G. (1996). Adolescents' social goals, beliefs about the causes of social success, and satisfaction in peer relations. *Developmental Psychology, 32*, 435–441. doi:10.1037/0012-1649.32.3.435

Johnson, H. S., Inderbitzen-Nolan, H. M., & Schapman, A. M. (2005). A comparison between socially anxious and depressive symptomatology in youth: A focus on perceived family environment. *Journal of Anxiety Disorders, 19*, 423–442. doi:10.1016/j.janxdis.2004.04.004

Joiner, T. E., Alfano, M. S., & Metalsky, G. I. (1992). When depression breeds contempt: Reassurance seeking, self-esteem, and rejection of depressed college students by their roommates. *Journal of Abnormal Psychology, 101*, 165–173. doi:10.1037/0021-843X.101.1.165

Joormann, J., Dkane, M., & Gotlib, I. H. (2006). Adaptive and maladaptive components of rumination? Diagnostic specificity and relation to depressive biases. *Behavior Therapy, 37*, 269–280. doi:10.1016/j.beth.2006.01.002

Kashdan, T. B., & Roberts, J. E. (2007). Social anxiety, depressive symptoms, and post-event rumination: Affective consequences and social contextual influences. *Journal of Anxiety Disorders, 21*, 284–301. doi:10.1016/j.janxdis.2006.05.009

Kessler, R. C., Berglund, P., Demler, O., Jin, R., Merkingas, K. R., & Walters, E. E. (2005). Lifetime prevalence and age-of-onset distributions of DSM–IV disorders in the National Comorbidity Survey Replication. *Archives of General Psychiatry, 62*, 593–602. doi:10.1001/archpsyc.62.6.593

Kessler, R. C., Stang, P., Wittchen, H. U., Stein, M., & Walters, E. E. (1999). Lifetime comorbidities between social phobia and mood disorders in the U.S. National Comorbidity Survey. *Psychological Medicine, 29*, 555–567. doi:10.1017/S0033291799008375

Knappe, S., Beesdo, K., Fehm, L., Lieb, R., & Wittchen, H. (2009). Associations of familial risk factors with social fears and social phobia: Evidence for continuum hypothesis in social anxiety disorder? *Journal of Neural Transmission, 116,* 639–648. doi:10.1007/s00702-008-0118-4

Kuperminc, G. P., Blatt, S. J., & Leadbeater, B. J. (1997). Relatedness, self-definition, and early adolescent adjustment. *Cognitive Therapy and Research, 21,* 301–320. doi:10.1023/A:1021826500037

La Greca, A. M., & Harrison, H. W. (2005). Adolescent peer relations, friendships and romantic relationships: Do they predict social anxiety and depression? *Journal of Clinical Child and Adolescent Psychology, 34,* 49–61. doi:10.1207/s15374424jccp3401_5

La Greca, A. M., & Landoll, R. R. (in press). Peer influences. In W. K. Silverman & A. Fields (Eds.), *Anxiety disorders in children and adolescents: Research, assessment and intervention* (2nd ed.). Cambridge, England: Cambridge University Press.

La Greca, A. M., & Lopez, N. (1998). Social anxiety among adolescents: Linkages with peer relations and friendships. *Journal of Abnormal Child Psychology, 26*(2), 83–94. doi:10.1023/A:1022684520514

La Greca, A. M., & Mackey, E. R. (2007). Adolescents' anxiety in dating situations: Do friends and romantic partners contribute? *Journal of Clinical Child and Adolescent Psychology, 36,* 522–533. doi:10.1080/15374410701662097

La Greca, A. M., & Prinstein, M. J. (1999). Peer group. In W. K. Silverman & T. H. Ollendick (Eds.), *Developmental issues in the clinical treatment of children* (pp. 171–198). Needham Heights, MA: Allyn & Bacon.

Ledley, D. R., Huppert, J. D., Foa, E. B., Davidson, J. R. T., Keefe, F. J., & Potts, N. L. S. (2005). Impact of depressive symptoms on the treatment of generalized social anxiety disorder. *Depression and Anxiety, 22,* 161–167. doi:10.1002/da.20121

Lewinsohn, P. M., Clarke, G. N., Seeley, J. R., & Rohde, P. (1994). Major depression in community adolescents: Age at onset, episode duration, and time to recurrence. *Journal of the American Academy of Child and Adolescent Psychiatry, 33,* 809–818. doi:10.1097/00004583-199407000-00006

Lewinsohn, P. M., Rohde, P., & Seeley, J. R. (1995). Adolescent psychopathology: III. The clinical consequences of comorbidity. *Journal of the American Academy of Child and Adolescent Psychiatry, 34,* 510–519. doi:10.1097/00004583-199504000-00018

Lewinsohn, P. M., Zinbarg, R., Seeley, J. R., Lewinsohn, M., & Sack, W. H. (1997). Lifetime comorbidity among anxiety disorders and between anxiety disorders and other mental disorders in adolescents. *Journal of Anxiety Disorders, 11,* 377–394. doi:10.1016/S0887-6185(97)00017-0

Loeber, R., Hipwell, A., Battista, D., Sembower, M., & Stouthamer-Loeber, M. (2009). Intergenerational transmission of multiple problem behaviors: Prospective relationships between mothers and daughters. *Journal of Abnormal Child Psychology, 37,* 1035–1048. doi:10.1007/s10802-009-9337-x

Mallott, M. A., Maner, J. K., DeWall, N., & Schmidt, N. B. (2009). Compensatory deficits following rejection: The role of social anxiety in disrupting affiliative behavior. *Depression and Anxiety, 26,* 438–446. doi:10.1002/da.20555

McLaughlin, K. A., Hatzenbuehler, M. L., & Hilt, L. M. (2009). Emotion dysregulation as a mechanism linking peer victimization to internalizing symptoms in adolescents. *Journal of Consulting and Clinical Psychology, 77,* 894–904. doi:10.1037/a0015760

Monk, C. S., Klein, R. G., Telzer, E. H., Mannuzza, S., Guardino, M., McClure-Tone, E. B., . . . Ernst, M. (2008). Amygdala and nucleus accumbens activation to emotional facial expressions in children and adolescents at risk for major depression. *The American Journal of Psychiatry, 165,* 90–98. doi:10.1176/appi.ajp. 2007.06111917

Morgan, J., & Banerjee, R. (2008). Post-event processing and autobiological memory in social anxiety: The influence of negative feedback and rumination. *Journal of Anxiety Disorders, 22,* 1190–1204. doi:10.1016/j.janxdis.2008.01.001

Muris, P., Merckelbach, H., Schmidt, H., Gadet, B., & Bogie, N. (2001). Anxiety and depression as correlates of self-reported behavioral inhibition in normal adolescents. *Behaviour Research and Therapy, 39,* 1051–1061. doi:10.1016/S0005-7967(00)00081-4

Naragon-Gainey, K., Watson, D., & Markon, K. E. (2009). Differential relations of depression and social anxiety symptoms to the facets of extraversion/positive emotionality. *Journal of Abnormal Psychology, 118,* 299–310. doi:10.1037/a0015637

Nolen-Hoeksema, S. (2000). The role of rumination in depressive disorders and mixed anxiety/depressive symptoms. *Journal of Abnormal Psychology, 109,* 504–511. doi:10.1037/0021-843X.109.3.504

Nolen-Hoeksema, S., & Girgus, J. S. (1994). The emergence of gender differences in depression during adolescence. *Psychological Bulletin, 115,* 424–443. doi:10.1037/0033-2909.115.3.424

Ohannessian, C. M., Hesselbrock, V. M., Kramer, J., Kuperman, S., Bucholz, K. K., Schuckit, M. A., & Nurnberger, J. I. (2005). The relationship between parental psychopathology and adolescent psychopathology: An examination of gender patterns. *Journal of Emotional and Behavioral Disorders, 13,* 67–76. doi:10.1177/10634266050130020101

Orvaschel, H., Lewinsohn, P. M., & Seeley, J. R. (1995). Continuity of psychopathology in a community sample of adolescents. *Journal of the American Academy of Child and Adolescent Psychiatry, 34,* 1525–1535. doi:10.1097/00004583-199511000-00020

Parker, G., & Hadzi-Pavlovic, D. (2001). Is any female preponderance in depression secondary to a primary female preponderance in anxiety disorders? *Acta Psychiatrica Scandinavica, 103,* 252–256. doi:10.1034/j.1600-0447.2001.00375.x

Parker, G., & Hadzi-Pavlovic, D. (2004). Is the female preponderance in major depression secondary to a gender difference in specific anxiety disorders? *Psychological Medicine, 34,* 461–470. doi:10.1017/S0033291703001181

Pine, D. S. (2007). Research review: A neuroscience framework for pediatric anxiety disorders. *Journal of Child Psychology and Psychiatry, and Allied Disciplines, 48,* 631–648. doi:10.1111/j.1469-7610.2007.01751.x

Pine, D. S. (2009). A social neuroscience approach to adolescent depression. In M. de Haan & M. R. Gunnar (Eds.), *Handbook of developmental social neuroscience* (pp. 339–418). New York, NY: Guilford Press.

Prinstein, M. J., Boergers, J., & Vernberg, E. M. (2001). Overt and relational aggression in adolescents: Social-psychological functioning of aggressors and victims. *Journal of Clinical Child Psychology, 30,* 447–489.

Prinstein, M. J., Borelli, J. L., Cheah, C. S. L., Simon, V. A., & Aikins, J. W. (2005). Adolescent girls' interpersonal vulnerability to depressive symptoms: A longitudinal examination of reassurance-seeking and peer relationships. *Journal of Abnormal Psychology, 114,* 676–688. doi:10.1037/0021-843X.114.4.676

Prinstein, M. J., Cheah, C. S. L., & Guyer, A. E. (2005). Peer victimization, cue interpretation, and internalizing symptoms: Preliminary concurrent and longitudinal findings for children and adolescents. *Journal of Clinical Child and Adolescent Psychology, 34,* 11–24. doi:10.1207/s15374424jccp3401_2

Ranta, K., Kaltiala-Heino, R., Pelkonen, M., & Marttunen, M. (2009). Associations between peer victimization, self-reported depression and social phobia among adolescents: The role of comorbidity. *Journal of Adolescence, 32,* 77–93. doi:10.1016/j.adolescence.2007.11.005

Reeb, B. T., & Conger, K. J. (2009). The unique effect of paternal depressive symptoms on adolescent functioning: Associations with gender and father–adolescent relationship closeness. *Journal of Family Psychology, 23,* 758–761. doi:10.1037/a0016354

Rose, A. J., & Rudolph, K. D. (2006). A review of sex differences in peer relationship processes: Potential trade-offs for the emotional and behavioral development of girls and boys. *Psychological Bulletin, 132,* 98–131. doi:10.1037/0033-2909.132.1.98

Rudolph, K. D., & Hammen, C. (1999). Age and gender as determinants of stress exposure, generation, and reactions in youngsters: A transactional perspective. *Child Development, 70,* 660–677. doi:10.1111/1467-8624.00048

Rush, A. J., Zimmerman, M., Wisniewski, S. R., Fava, M., Hollon, S. D., Warden, D., . . . Trivedi, M. H. (2005). Comorbid psychiatric disorders in depressed outpatients: Demographic and clinical features. *Journal of Affective Disorders, 87,* 43–55. doi:10.1016/j.jad.2005.03.005

Siegel, R. S., La Greca, A. M., & Harrison, H. M. (2009). Peer victimization and social anxiety in adolescents: Prospective and reciprocal relationships. *Journal of Youth and Adolescence, 38,* 1096–1109. doi:10.1007/s10964-009-9392-1

Southam-Gerow, M. A., & Kendall, P. C. (2000). A preliminary study of the emotion understanding of youths referred for treatment of anxiety disorders. *Journal of Clinical Child Psychology, 29,* 319–327. doi:10.1207/S15374424JCCP2903_3

Southam-Gerow, M. A., & Kendall, P. C. (2002). Emotion regulation and understanding: Implications for child psychopathology and therapy. *Clinical Psychology Review, 22,* 189–222. doi:10.1016/S0272-7358(01)00087-3

Starr, L. R., & Davila, J. (2008a). Differentiating interpersonal correlates of depressive symptoms and social anxiety in adolescence: Implications for models of comorbidity. *Journal of Clinical Child and Adolescent Psychology, 37*, 337–349. doi:10.1080/15374410801955854

Starr, L. R., & Davila, J. (2008b). Excessive reassurance seeking, depression, and interpersonal rejection: A meta-analytic review. *Journal of Abnormal Psychology, 117*, 762–775. doi:10.1037/a0013866

Stein, M. B., Fuetsch, M., Müller, N., Höfler, M., Lieb, R., & Wittchen, H.-U. (2001). Social anxiety disorder and the risk of depression: A prospective community study of adolescents and young adults. *Archives of General Psychiatry, 58*, 251–256. doi:10.1001/archpsyc.58.3.251

Stice, E., Ragan, J., & Randall, P. (2004). Prospective relations between social support and depression: Differential direction of effects for parent and peer support? *Journal of Abnormal Psychology, 113*, 155–159. doi:10.1037/0021-843X.113.1.155

Stirling, L. J., Eley, T. C., & Clark, D. M. (2006). Preliminary evidence for an association between social anxiety and avoidance of negative faces in school-age children. *Journal of Clinical Child and Adolescent Psychology, 35*, 431–439. doi:10.1207/s15374424jccp3503_9

Storch, E. A., Masia-Warner, C., Crisp, H., & Klein, R. G. (2005). Peer victimization and social anxiety in adolescence: A prospective study. *Aggressive Behavior, 31*, 437–452. doi:10.1002/ab.20093

Watson, D., Gamez, W., & Simms, L. J. (2005). Basic dimensions of temperament and their relation to anxiety and depression: A symptom-based perspective. *Journal of Research in Personality, 39*, 46–66. doi:10.1016/j.jrp.2004.09.006

Weissman, M. M., & Klerman, G. L. (1977). Sex differences and the epidemiology of depression. *Archives of General Psychiatry, 34*, 98–111.

Wittchen, H.-U., Beesdo, K., Bittner, A., & Goodwin, R. D. (2003). Depressive episodes—Evidence for a causal role of primary anxiety disorders? *European Psychiatry, 18*, 384–393. doi:10.1016/j.eurpsy.2003.10.001

Wittchen, H.-U., Kessler, R. C., Pfister, H., & Lieb, M. (2000). Why do people with anxiety disorders become depressed? A prospective-longitudinal community study. *Acta Psychiatrica Scandinavica, 102*, 14–23. doi:10.1111/j.0065-1591.2000.acp29-03.x

Wittchen, H.-U., Stein, M. B., & Kessler, R. C. (1999). Social fears and social phobia in a community sample of adolescents and young adults: Prevalence, risk factors and co-morbidity. *Psychological Medicine, 29*, 309–323. doi:10.1017/S0033291798008174

Wong, Q. J. J., & Moulds, M. L. (2009). Impact of rumination versus distraction on anxiety and maladaptive self-beliefs in socially anxious individuals. *Behaviour Research and Therapy, 47*, 861–867. doi:10.1016/j.brat.2009.06.014

Young, J. F., Mufson, L., & Davies, M. (2006). Impact of comorbid anxiety in an effectiveness study of interpersonal psychotherapy for depressed adolescents. *Journal of the American Academy of Child and Adolescent Psychiatry, 45*, 904–912. doi:10.1097/01.chi.0000222791.23927.5f

5

DATING, ROMANTIC RELATIONSHIPS, AND SOCIAL ANXIETY IN YOUNG PEOPLE

ANNETTE LA GRECA, JOANNE DAVILA, RYAN R. LANDOLL, AND REBECCA SIEGEL

Romantic relationships represent an important but relatively under-studied aspect of adolescent peer relations. This is surprising given that by age 16 most adolescents have had a romantic relationship (Carver, Joyner, & Udry, 2003). These relationships represent a normative aspect of development and may be beneficial to adolescents' emotional functioning. They provide social support, enhance self-esteem, and prepare adolescents for adult relationships and the development of intimacy (Collins, 2003; Connolly & Goldberg, 1999). At the same time, adolescent romantic relationships can be a significant source of psychosocial distress. Romantic relationships explain 25% to 34% of the strong emotions that high school students experience, and about 42% of these strong emotions are negative feelings, such as anxiety, anger, jealousy, and depression (Larson, Clore, & Wood, 1999). Growing evidence suggests that involvement in dating and romantic relationships during adolescence, particularly if frequent or steady, is associated with internalizing and depressive symptoms (e.g., Davila, Steinberg, Kachadourian, Cobb, & Fincham, 2004; see also La Greca, Davila, & Siegel, 2008).

In this chapter, we review research focusing on the complex associations between romantic (heterosexual) relationships and social anxiety during adolescence (for an examination of these issues in lesbian, gay, bisexual, and transgender populations, see Chapter 9, this volume). To set the stage for understanding these relationships, we briefly focus on the broad developmental and qualitative aspects of dating and romantic relationships during the period from mid-adolescence to late adolescence (early adulthood). Next we examine the interplay between romantic relationships and social anxiety more specifically and address other issues such as the impact of violence or victimization in dating relationships. We conclude with a discussion of limitations of existing research on romantic relationships, social anxiety, and social anxiety disorder (SAD) and suggest directions for future research.

DEVELOPMENTAL AND QUALITATIVE ASPECTS OF EARLY ROMANTIC RELATIONSHIPS

In adolescence, puberty typically brings greater awareness of romantic attraction and sexual desire, which prompt interest and engagement in romantic and sexual activity (e.g., Bellis, Downing, & Ashton, 2006). Most adolescents in the United States report having had a romantic relationship by mid-adolescence (Carver et al., 2003), and these numbers continue to increase through early adulthood. Further, approximately 13% of girls and 15% of boys have engaged in sexual intercourse before age 15; by ages 15 to 17 years, approximately 30% of girls and 31% of boys have done so; and by ages 18 to 19 years, the rates of sexual intercourse reach 69% of young women and 64% of young men (Abma, Martinez, Mosher, & Dawson, 2004). Not surprisingly, for most adolescents, dating activities and romantic relationships provide the context for engaging in sexual activities (Kuttler & La Greca, 2004).

Among heterosexual adolescents, romantic development progresses across relatively predictable stages (e.g., Brown, 1999; Connolly & Goldberg, 1999; Furman & Wehner, 1994). In early adolescence, teens primarily engage in mixed-gender group interactions, or group dating, that is characterized by affiliation and companionship rather than intimacy (Shulman & Scharf, 2000). As adolescents mature, they are more likely to engage in dyadic dating that involves higher levels of intimacy and closeness, deeper mutual feelings, and more extensive sexual activity (Connolly & Goldberg, 1999; Shulman & Scharf, 2000). By late adolescence, romantic relationships also include caretaking and caregiving and begin to resemble what one typically thinks of as adult dyadic relationships (Furman & Wehner, 1994). Thus, romantic and sexual activities serve important functions with regard to identity development (see Collins, 2003; Furman & Shaffer, 2003).

Adolescent relationships also provide social learning experiences that can set the stage for interpersonal functioning in adulthood. For example, less romantic competence among early adolescent girls more strongly predicts being unmarried and greater engagement in potentially risky sexual activity (Davila et al., 2009). Conversely, higher quality romantic relationships in mid-adolescence are associated with positive relationships and commitment in early adulthood (Seiffge-Krenke & Lang, 2002). Positive romantic experiences and relationships also may help young people develop adaptive interpersonal skills (Seiffge-Krenke & Lang, 2002), foster self-esteem (Connolly & Konarski, 1994), reduce anxiety (Glickman & La Greca, 2004; La Greca & Harrison, 2005), and allow for healthy sexual development (Welsh, Haugen, Widman, Darling, & Grello, 2005).

GENDER AND ETHNIC CONSIDERATIONS

Not all adolescents follow the same progression of romantic and sexual development, and some may have very different experiences than others. For example, adolescent girls are more likely than boys to be romantically involved (Glickman & La Greca, 2004; La Greca & Harrison, 2005; La Greca & Mackey, 2007). Gender differences in the qualities of adolescents' romantic relationships have been observed, with girls reporting more positive (La Greca & Mackey, 2007) and fewer negative interactions in their romantic relationships (La Greca & Harrison, 2005) than adolescent boys. Data from the National Longitudinal Study of Adolescent Health (Carver et al., 2003; O'Sullivan, Cheng, Harris, & Brooks-Gunn, 2007) suggest that the occurrence and progression of adolescents' romantic relationships are substantially similar across different U.S. ethnic groups (White, Black, Asian, Hispanic or Latino, and mixed ethnicity). One exception is that Asian adolescents are less likely to report having a romantic relationship than adolescents from other major ethnic groups (O'Sullivan et al., 2007). Asian and Hispanic or Latino adolescents who are involved in romantic relationships also are less likely to report engaging in sexual behaviors (e.g., touching partner under clothing, sexual intercourse) than White or Black adolescents (O'Sullivan et al., 2007).

OTHER IMPORTANT CONTEXTS

Adolescent romantic activities occur in the context of salient situational factors such as the peer context (e.g., Brown, 1999; Connolly & Goldberg, 1999; Kuttler & La Greca, 2004; Shulman & Scharf, 2000). For instance, adolescent girls who date frequently have more close friends and more opposite-sex friends than those who date rarely or not at all (Kuttler & La Greca,

2004). Thus, heterosocial friendships set the stage and provide opportunities for romantic relationships (Feiring, 1999). In addition, girls who are involved in serious and steady romantic relationships have more close friends with romantic partners than those who are dating casually or not at all (Kuttler & La Greca, 2004).

Recent technological advances that allow for immediate, rapid, and readily available communication represent another important context that affects adolescents' romantic relations. Online communication tools, such as instant messaging, chat rooms, online social sites, e-mail, and text messaging, have the potential to reinforce existing relationships with romantic partners (Subrahmanyam & Greenfield, 2008), enabling them to stay in touch. Indeed, greater instant messaging use was associated with greater romantic relationship quality in adolescence (Blais, Craig, Pepler, & Connolly, 2008). However, as we discuss later, such technological advances can also complicate romantic relationships.

ROMANTIC RELATIONSHIPS AND SOCIAL (AND DATING) ANXIETY

As noted earlier, romantic relationships have protective aspects (e.g., social support, esteem enhancement) for optimal mental health. At the same time, however, they can be stressful, especially for adolescents who place considerable importance on romantic relationships yet are just learning how to navigate them (Downey, Bonica, & Rincon, 1999). As such, romantic relationships (and even their absence) may contribute to feelings of social anxiety; social anxiety may also influence the presence and quality of romantic relationships.

As it does in adults, social anxiety in youth has the potential to interfere with intimate relationships. Inhibition, avoidance, and negative appraisals of socially anxious adolescents may present considerable challenges for forming romantic relationships. Consistent with this view, data indicate that heterosexual socially anxious adolescents are less likely to be involved in a romantic relationship (La Greca & Harrison, 2005), perhaps because they avoid or are uncomfortable in heterosocial situations that might lead to opportunities for dating or romantic relationships (Glickman & La Greca, 2004). Similarly, epidemiological studies have found adults with SAD to be more likely to have been never married, separated, or divorced than their nonanxious counterparts (Lampe, Slade, Issakidis, & Andrews, 2003; Wittchen, Fuetsch, Sonntag, Müller, & Liebowiz, 2000). In fact, even among children followed longitudinally, shy and socially inhibited boys were more likely to marry later in life than comparison youth (Caspi, Elder, & Bem, 1988). Thus, because they avoid dating and other social activities, socially anxious youth miss out on the psychological benefits that romantic relationships can convey.

Once dating or romantic relationships are established, the qualities of such relationships appear to be less adequate or skillful among socially anxious individuals. Although research is scant, socially anxious adults and adults with SAD display less emotional expression, fewer positive behaviors, less self-disclosure, and decreased intimacy in their romantic relationships (Sparrevohn & Rapee, 2009; Wenzel, Graff-Dolezal, Macho, & Brendle, 2005). Kashdan and colleagues (2007) found that for individuals low in social anxiety, the ability to express negative emotions in an open and uninhibited way fostered a good quality romantic relationship; for individuals high in social anxiety, the expression of negative emotions in the context of a romantic relationship was associated with deteriorating relationship quality. Socially anxious young adults also demonstrate more negative and fewer positive interactions with their romantic partner during an observed communication task (Wenzel et al., 2005). Thus, it appears that negative emotional expression is a common factor in the romantic relationships of socially anxious individuals.

For the most part, this research does not clarify the directionality of the relationship. It is possible that social anxiety leads to inhibited social behavior that limits the intimacy and quality of a romantic relationship. However, it is also plausible that negative interactions in romantic relationships contribute to or exacerbate adolescents' and young adults' feelings of distress and, specifically, social anxiety (e.g., La Greca & Mackey, 2007). This view is consistent with other data that adolescents and young adults demonstrate increased sensitivity to rejection from romantic partners (Downey et al., 1999) and greater interpersonal dependence (Darcy, Davila, & Beck, 2005; Grant, Beck, & Farrow, 2007). Thus, negative interactions with a romantic partner, which are fairly common, might directly contribute to feelings of social anxiety. Moreover, once engaged in a romantic relationship, socially anxious individuals may have increased difficulties with social appraisal and evaluation, which in turn increase symptoms of social anxiety.

A complementary literature has examined the association between romantic relationships and dating anxiety. The term *dating anxiety* refers to worry, distress, and inhibition in heterosocial situations involving dating partners or potential dating partners (see Chorney & Morris, 2008; Glickman & La Greca, 2004). Social anxiety and dating anxiety are strongly related but distinct constructs (Glickman & La Greca, 2004). Similar to social anxiety, dating anxiety is conceptualized as consisting of fear of negative evaluation (in dating situations or with other-sex individuals) and social inhibition and distress (either with a dating partner, a potential dating partner, or during heterosocial group situations; Glickman & La Greca, 2004).

Research findings on the romantic relationships of adolescents who exhibit dating anxiety parallel those obtained for socially anxious individuals. Adolescents who report more dating anxiety are significantly less likely to be currently dating (Glickman & La Greca, 2004) and are more likely to report that they have never dated (La Greca & Mackey, 2007). Such adolescents also have fewer close friends of the opposite sex (La Greca & Mackey, 2007), which, as noted earlier, is an important avenue for the development of romantic relationships.

Dating anxiety is also associated with potential problems in romantic relationships, even when controlling for other indicators of social competence (e.g., number of close friends, qualities of close friendships). Among adolescents who were currently dating (and thus less likely to be socially or dating anxious), fewer positive and more negative qualities in the romantic relationship predicted higher levels of dating anxiety (La Greca & Mackey, 2007).

These findings suggest that heterosexual adolescents who are anxious about dating might avoid heterosocial situations, thus making it difficult to develop a romantic relationship. It is possible, however, that once romantically involved, fears and worries about dating may become less salient. Some evidence supports this view. In a rare prospective study, Nieder and Seiffge-Krenke (2001) tracked the romantic relationships of adolescents from ages 14 to 17 years. Across the 3 years, stress in romantic situations decreased, and romantic relationship quality increased. As these authors suggested, increased exposure to dating relationships during adolescence may decrease anxiety in dating situations over time (Nieder & Seiffge-Krenke, 2001) and positively impact a sense of social competence. Although not studied directly, it seems reasonable to expect that greater experience with romantic relationships would be most likely to reduce dating and/or social anxiety if the relationships are generally positive. In contrast, high levels of negative interactions with a romantic partner (e.g., criticism, pressure, conflict) might well exacerbate feelings of social anxiety and serve to increase social fears.

ADVANCES IN TECHNOLOGY AND THEIR IMPACT ON ROMANTIC RELATIONS

As noted earlier, advances in communication technology have had a major impact on youths' and adults' romantic interactions and relationships. Although often a benefit to close relationships, cell phones, social networking sites, and the Internet all have the potential to complicate and even undermine romantic relationships. Adolescents and young adults report that cell phones and the Internet have been used by their romantic partners to stalk, harass, and "spy on" them (Magid, 2009).

Using online communication tools may attenuate social anxiety in adolescence (Subrahmanyam & Greenfield, 2008). Pierce (2009) found that greater discomfort talking with others face-to-face was associated with more interaction online and via text messaging. However, greater comfort talking with others was associated with a greater likelihood of making friends online. Therefore, in adolescence, social anxiety may be associated with more online communication but not necessarily with the development of close relationships. In contrast, socially isolated adolescents were less likely than other adolescents to use online communication (Bryant, Sanders-Jackson, & Smallwood, 2006). Clearly, more research examining how online communication tools affect the onset, course, and outcome of adolescent romantic (and sexual) activities, particularly among socially anxious adolescents, is needed.

Issues of Dating Violence or Victimization

Dating and romantic relationships are important for social and emotional development, but there is a dark side characterized by their potential for dating violence or victimization and the resultant negative emotional repercussions. In fact, dating violence is considered to be a significant social and public health concern (Lewis & Fremouw, 2001; Wolitzky-Taylor et al., 2008). Statistics on the prevalence of dating violence are startling. Perhaps up to one third of high-school-age adolescents reported some form of physical abuse in a dating or romantic relationship (Callahan, Tolman, & Saunders, 2003; Malik, Sorenson, & Aneshensel, 1997). About 10% of adolescents reported being hurt by a romantic partner in the previous 12 months (Eaton et al., 2008). Among 681 African American and Caucasian adolescents, 37% reported physical dating violence, and 62% reported emotional abuse in dating relationships (Holt & Espelage, 2005). A phone survey of a nationally representative sample of adolescents found that 2.7% of adolescent girls and 0.6% of adolescent boys report being the victims of serious dating violence, defined as physical assault and/or drug- or alcohol-facilitated rape perpetrated by a girlfriend or boyfriend or dating partner (Wolitzky-Taylor et al., 2008).

Adolescent girls and young women appear to be at higher risk of dating violence victimization (Molidor & Tolman, 1998; Vézina & Hebert, 2007) and of more severe and higher rates of sexual victimization than are adolescent boys and young men (e.g. Bergman, 1992; Foshee, 1996; Molidor & Tolman, 1998; Vézina & Hebert, 2007). Adolescent girls and young women are also likely to sustain more injuries than adolescent boys or young men (Foshee, 1996; Molidor & Tolman, 1998). It is not surprising, then, that victims of dating violence (especially girls and young women) also report significant fear and anxiety (e.g., Follingstad, Wright, Lloyd, & Sebastian, 1991; Holt & Espelage, 2005; Kaura & Lohman, 2007). Dating violence or victimization among adolescents also is related to lower psychological well-being and symptoms of posttraumatic stress (e.g., Callahan et al., 2003; Wolitzky-Taylor et al., 2008) and to higher levels of anxiety and depression (Holt & Espelge, 2005; Wolitzky-Taylor et al., 2008), even when controlling for demographic characteristics and other traumatic stressors. Emotional forms of dating victimization are also significantly associated with adolescents' levels of anxiety and depression (Holt & Espelage, 2005).

Among girls in romantic relationships, negative experiences, such as relational victimization (i.e., deliberate exclusion) perpetrated by their partner, may increase symptoms of anxiety and depression (Ellis, Crooks, & Wolfe, 2009). Aversive peer experiences have been strongly associated with the development and maintenance of social anxiety in adolescents and young adults (e.g., La Greca & Harrison, 2005; Siegel, La Greca, & Harrison, 2009; for a review, see La Greca & Landoll, in press). Aversive dating experiences also would likely contribute to greater social and dating anxiety for adolescents and young adults. This will be an important avenue for further inquiry.

Social Anxiety and Risky Sexual Behaviors

As noted earlier, dating and romantic relationships set the stage for sexual relationships. Interestingly, social anxiety may serve as both a risk and protective factor for risky sexual behaviors that, in turn, are associated with sexually transmitted diseases. For example, because socially anxious adolescents are less likely to date or be involved in a romantic relationship, they also have fewer sexual partners and a lower likelihood of engaging in risky sexual behaviors (La Greca, Landoll, Lai, & Siegel, 2008; Leary & Dobbins, 1983). However, once one is involved in a romantic relationship, social anxiety may contribute to risky sexual behaviors, such as reduced or inconsistent birth control or condom use, that are associated with increased risk for HIV infection and sexually transmitted diseases. High levels of social anxiety are associated with lack of assertion in personal relationships (Grant et al., 2007), which can make it difficult to request condom use with a romantic partner (La Greca, Landoll, et al., 2008). Lack of assertion can also result in the avoidance of requesting information or guidance from professionals, parents, and peers about safe sex practices (Nangle & Hansen, 1998). In fact, among adolescents, social anxiety predicts less contraceptive use among adolescents who are romantically involved and sexually active (La Greca, Landoll, et al., 2008; Landoll, La Greca, Lai, & Siegel, 2008).

SUMMARY AND CONCLUSIONS

As we illustrated in this chapter, emerging evidence suggests that social anxiety can be a predictor, correlate, and consequence of romantic activity, particularly negative romantic experiences. In addition, the association between social anxiety and romantic experiences develops within a number of developmentally relevant contexts, including peer relationships and social networking technology. There may be some experiences (e.g., dating violence) and some populations (e.g., sexual minority youth) in which the inherent stressors involved may make social anxiety a particularly likely occurrence.

These provocative findings, however, must be considered preliminary, given that this is a newly emerging area of research. Moreover, there are few prospective studies, thereby limiting researchers' ability to examine the temporal associations between social anxiety and romantic relationships among youth. Existing studies mainly examine social anxiety along a dimension, using nonclinical samples. As such, it is not clear how the findings generalize to youth with SAD. Further, most existing studies have used self-report methodologies, leaving gaps in the understanding of associations between social anxiety and romantic relations relate to specific behaviors. Thus, we hope this chapter encourages researchers to conduct studies that build on the findings reviewed here using methods that can advance knowledge of developmentally and socially relevant factors.

REFERENCES

Abma, J. C., Martinez, G. M., Mosher, W. D., & Dawson, B.S. (2004). *Teenagers in the United States: Sexual activity, contraceptive use, and childbearing, 2002.* National Center for Health Statistics. *Vital Health Statistics*, Series 23(Suppl. 24).

Bellis, M. A., Downing, J., & Ashton, J. R. (2006). Adults at 12? Trends in puberty and their public health consequences. *Journal of Epidemiology and Community Health, 60,* 910–911. doi:10.1136/jech.2006.049379

Bergman, L. (1992). Dating violence among high school students. *Social Work, 37,* 21–27.

Blais, J. J., Craig, W. M., Pepler, D., & Connolly, J. (2008). Adolescents online: The importance of Internet activity choices to salient relationships. *Journal of Youth and Adolescence, 37,* 522–536. doi:10.1007/s10964-007-9262-7

Brown, B. B. (1999). "You're going out with who?": Peer group influences on adolescent romantic relationships. In W. Furman, B. B. Brown, & C. Feiring (Eds.), *The development of romantic relationships in adolescence* (pp. 291–329). Cambridge, England: Cambridge University Press.

Bryant, J. A., Sanders-Jackson, A., & Smallwood, A. M. K. (2006). IMing, text messaging, and adolescent social networks. *Journal of Computer-Mediated Communication, 11,* 577–592. doi:10.1111/j.1083-6101.2006.00028.x

Callahan, M. R., Tolman, R. M., & Saunders, D. G. (2003). Adolescent dating violence victimization and psychological well-being. *Journal of Adolescent Research, 18,* 664–681. doi:10.1177/0743558403254784

Carver, K., Joyner, K., & Udry, J. R. (2003). National estimates of adolescent romantic relationships. In P. Florsheim (Ed.), *Adolescent romantic relationships and sexual behavior: Theory, research, and practical implications* (pp. 23–56). New York, NY: Cambridge University Press.

Caspi, A., Elder, G. H., & Bem, D. J. (1988). Moving away from the world: Life-course patterns of shy children. *Developmental Psychology, 24,* 824–831. doi:10.1037/0012-1649.24.6.824

Chorney, D. B., & Morris, T. L. (2008). The changing face of dating anxiety: Issues in assessment with special populations. *Clinical Psychology: Science and Practice, 15,* 224–238. doi:10.1111/j.1468-2850.2008.00132.x

Collins, W. A. (2003). More than myth: the developmental significance of romantic relationships during adolescence. *Journal of Research on Adolescence, 13,* 1–24. doi:10.1111/1532-7795.1301001

Connolly, J. A., & Goldberg, A. (1999). Romantic relationships in adolescence: The role of friends and peers in their emergence and development. In W. Furman, B. B. Brown, & C. Feiring (Eds.), *The development of romantic relationships in adolescence* (pp. 266–290). New York, NY: Cambridge University Press.

Connolly, J. A., & Konarski, R. (1994). Peer self-concept in adolescence: analysis of factor structure and of associations with peer experience. *Journal of Research on Adolescence, 4,* 385–403. doi:10.1207/s15327795jra0403_3

Darcy, K., Davila, J., & Beck, J. G. (2005). Is social anxiety associated with both interpersonal avoidance and dependence? *Cognitive Therapy and Research, 29,* 171–186. doi:10.1007/s10608-005-3163-4

Davila, J., Steinberg, S. J., Kachadourian, L., Cobb, R., & Fincham, F. (2004). Romantic involvement and depressive symptoms in early and late adolescence: The role of a preoccupied relational style. *Personal Relationships, 11,* 161–178. doi:10.1111/j.1475-6811.2004.00076.x

Davila, J., Steinberg, S. J., Ramsay, M., Stroud, C. B., Starr, L., & Yoneda, A. (2009). Assessing romantic competence in adolescence: The romantic competence interview. *Journal of Adolescence, 32,* 55–75. doi:10.1016/j.adolescence.2007.12.001

Downey, G., Bonica, C., & Rincon, C. (1999). Rejection sensitivity and adolescent romantic relationships. In W. Furman, B. B. Brown, & C. Feiring (Eds.), *The development of romantic relationships in adolescence* (pp. 148–174). New York, NY: Cambridge University Press.

Eaton, D.K., Kann, L. Kinchen, S., Shanklin, S., Ross, J. Hawkins, J., . . . Wechsler, H. (2008). Youth risk behavior surveillance—United States, 2007. *Morbidity and Mortality Weekly Report: Surveillance Summaries, 57*(4), 1–131.

Ellis, W. E., Crooks, C. V., & Wolfe, D. A. (2009). Relational aggression in peer and dating relationships: Links to psychological and behavioral adjustment. *Social Development, 18*, 253–269. doi:10.1111/j.1467-9507.2008.00468.x

Feiring, C. (1999). Other-sex friendship networks and the development of romantic relationships in adolescence. *Journal of Youth and Adolescence, 28*, 495–512. doi:10.1023/A:1021621108890

Follingstad, D. R., Wright, S., Lloyd, S., & Sebastian, J. A. (1991). Sex differences in motivations and effects in dating violence. *Family Relations, 40*, 51–57. doi:10.2307/585658

Foshee, V. (1996). Gender differences in adolescent dating abuse prevalence, types and injuries. *Health Education Research, 11*, 275–286. doi:10.1093/her/11.3.275-a

Furman, W., & Shaffer, L. (2003). The role of romantic relationships in adolescent development. In P. Florsheim (Ed.), *Adolescent romantic relations and sexual behavior: Theory, research, and practical implications* (pp. 3–22). Mahwah, NJ: Erlbaum.

Furman, W., & Wehner, E. A. (1994). Romantic views: Toward a theory of adolescent romantic relationships. In R. Montemayor, G. R. Adams, & T. P. Gullotta (Eds.), *Personal relationships during adolescence* (pp. 168–195). Thousand Oaks, CA: Sage.

Glickman, A. R., & La Greca, A. M. (2004). The Dating Anxiety Scale for Adolescents: Scale development and associations with adolescent functioning. *Journal of Clinical Child and Adolescent Psychology, 33*, 566–578. doi:10.1207/s15374424jccp3303_14

Grant, D. M., Beck, J. G., Farrow, S. M., & Davila, J. (2007). Do interpersonal features of social anxiety influence the development of depressive symptoms? *Cognition and Emotion, 21*, 646–663. doi:10.1080/02699930600713036

Holt, M. K., & Espelage, D. L. (2005). Social support as a moderator between dating violence victimization and depression/anxiety among African American and Caucasian adolescents. *School Psychology Review, 34*, 309–328.

Kashdan, T. B., Volkmann, J. R., Breen, W. E., & Han, S. (2007). Social anxiety and romantic relationships: The costs and benefits of negative emotion expression are context-dependent. *Journal of Anxiety Disorders, 21*, 475–492. doi:10.1016/j.janxdis.2006.08.007

Kaura, S. A., & Lohman, B. J. (2007). Dating violence victimization, relationship satisfaction, mental health problems, and acceptability of violence: A comparison of men and women. *Journal of Family Violence, 22*, 367–381. doi:10.1007/s10896-007-9092-0

Kuttler, A. F., & La Greca, A. M. (2004). Linkages among adolescent girls' romantic relationships, best friendships, and peer networks. *Journal of Adolescence, 27*, 395–414. doi:10.1016/j.adolescence.2004.05.002

La Greca, A. M., Davila, J., & Siegel, R. (2008). Friendships, romantic relationships, and depression. In N. Allen & L. Sheeber (Eds.), *Adolescent emotional development and the emergence of depressive disorders* (pp. 318–336). New York, NY: Cambridge University Press. doi:10.1017/CBO9780511551963.017

La Greca, A. M., & Harrison, H. W. (2005). Adolescent peer relations, Friendships and romantic relationships: Do they predict social anxiety and depression? *Journal of Clinical Child and Adolescent Psychology, 34,* 49–61. doi:10.1207/s15374424jccp3401_5

La Greca, A. M., & Landoll, R. R. (in press). Peer influences in the development and maintenance of anxiety disorders. In W. K. Silverman & A. Field (Eds.), *Anxiety disorders in children and adolescents: Research, assessment, and intervention* (2nd ed.). London, England: Cambridge University Press.

La Greca, A. M., Landoll, R. R., Lai, B. S., & Siegel, R. S. (2008, August). *Potential peer influences on risky sexual behaviors among adolescents: Peer crowds, romantic relationships, and feelings of social anxiety.* Paper presented at the meeting of the International Congress of Behavioral Medicine, Tokyo, Japan.

La Greca, A. M., & Mackey, E. R. (2007). Adolescents' anxiety in dating situations: Do friends and romantic partners contribute? *Journal of Clinical Child and Adolescent Psychology, 36,* 522–533. doi:10.1080/15374410701662097

Lampe, L., Slade, T., Issakidis, C., & Andrews, G. (2003). Social phobia in the Australian National Survey of Mental Health and Well-Being (NSMHWB). *Psychological Medicine, 33,* 637–646. doi:10.1017/S0033291703007621

Landoll, R., La Greca, A. M., Lai, B. S., & Siegel, R. S. (2008, April). *Social anxiety and sexual risk behavior: Risk and protective factors for an ethnically diverse sample of socially anxious adolescents.* Paper presented at the 2008 National Conference in Child Health Psychology, Miami, FL.

Larson, R. W., Clore, G. L., & Wood, G. A. (1999). The emotions of romantic relationships: Do they wreck havoc on adolescents? In W. Furman, B. B. Brown, & C. Feiring (Eds.), *The development of romantic relationships in adolescence* (pp. 19–49). New York, NY: Cambridge University Press.

Leary, M. R., & Dobbins, S. R. (1983). Social anxiety, sexual behavior, and contraceptive use. *Journal of Personality and Social Psychology, 45,* 1347–1354. doi:10.1037/0022-3514.45.6.1347

Lewis, S. F., & Fremouw, W. (2001). Dating violence: A critical review of the literature. *Clinical Psychology Review, 21,* 105–127. doi:10.1016/S0272-7358(99)00042-2

Magid, L. (2009). *Youth cell phones for "dating abuse."* Retrieved from http://www.safekids.com/2009/12/08/youth-use-cell-phones-for-dating-abuse/

Malik, S., Sorenson, S. B., & Aneshensel, C. S. (1997). Community and dating violence among adolescents: Perpetration and victimization. *The Journal of Adolescent Health, 21,* 291–302. doi:10.1016/S1054-139X(97)00143-2

Molidor, C., & Tolman, R. M. (1998). Gender and contextual factors in adolescent dating violence. *Violence Against Women, 4,* 180–194. doi:10.1177/1077801298004002004

Nangle, D. W., & Hansen, D. J. (1998). Adolescent heterosocial competence revisited: Implications of an extended conceptualization for the prevention of high-risk sexual interactions. *Education & Treatment of Children, 21,* 431–446.

Nieder, T., & Seiffge-Krenke, I. (2001). Coping with stress in different phases of romantic development. *Journal of Adolescence, 24,* 297–311. doi:10.1006/jado.2001.0407

O'Sullivan, L. F., Cheng, M. M., Harris, K. M., & Brooks-Gunn, J. (2007). I wanna hold your hand: The progression of social, romantic and sexual events in adolescent relationships. *Perspectives on Sexual and Reproductive Health, 39,* 100–107. doi:10.1363/3910007

Pierce, T. (2009). Social anxiety and technology: Face-to-face communication versus technological communication among teens. *Computers in Human Behavior, 25,* 1367–1372. doi:10.1016/j.chb.2009.06.003

Seiffge-Krenke, I., & Lang, J. (2002, April). *Forming and maintaining romantic relations from early adolescence to young adulthood: Evidence of a developmental sequence.* Paper presented at the meeting of the Society for Research on Adolescence, New Orleans, LA.

Shulman, S., & Scharf, M. (2000). Adolescent romantic behaviors and perceptions: Age- and gender-related differences, and links with family and peer relationships. *Journal of Research on Adolescence, 10,* 99–118. doi:10.1207/SJRA1001_5

Siegel, R. S., La Greca, A. M., & Harrison, H. M. (2009). Peer victimization and social anxiety in adolescents: Prospective and reciprocal relationships. *Journal of Youth and Adolescence, 38,* 1096–1109. doi:10.1007/s10964-009-9392-1

Sparrevohn, R. M., & Rapee, R. M. (2009). Self-disclosure, emotional expression and intimacy within romantic relationships of people with social phobia. *Behaviour Research and Therapy, 47,* 1074–1078. doi:10.1016/j.brat.2009.07.016

Subrahmanyam, K., & Greenfield, P. (2008). Online communication and adolescent relationships [Special issue]. *The Future of Children, 18,* 119–146.

Vézina, J., & Hebert, M. (2007). Risk factors for victimization in romantic relationships of young women: A review of empirical studies and implications for prevention. *Trauma, Violence, & Abuse, 8,* 33–66. doi:10.1177/1524838006297029

Welsh, D. P., Haugen, P. T., Widman, L., Darling, N., & Grello, C. M. (2005). Kissing is good: A developmental investigation of sexuality in adolescent romantic couples. *Sexuality Research & Social Policy, 2,* 32–41. doi:10.1525/srsp.2005.2.4.32

Wenzel, A., Graff-Dolezal, J., Macho, M., & Brendle, J. R. (2005). Communication and social skills in socially anxious and nonanxious individuals in the context of romantic relationships. *Behaviour Research and Therapy, 43,* 505–519. doi:10.1016/j.brat.2004.03.010

Wittchen, H.-U., Fuetsch, M., Sonntag, H., Müller, N., & Liebowiz, M. (2000). Disability and quality of life in pure and comorbid social phobia: Findings from a controlled study. *European Psychiatry, 15,* 46–58. doi:10.1016/S0924-9338(00)00211-X

Wolitzky-Taylor, K. B., Ruggiero, K. J., Danielson, C. K., Resnick, H. S., Hanson, R. F., Smith, D. W., . . . Kilpatrick, D. G. (2008). Prevalence and correlates of dating violence in a national sample of adolescents. *Journal of the American Academy of Child and Adolescent Psychiatry, 47,* 755–762. doi:10.1097/CHI.0b013e318172ef5f

6

ALCOHOL AND DRUG USE IN SOCIALLY ANXIOUS YOUNG ADULTS

RACHEL D. THOMPSON, ABIGAIL A. GOLDSMITH, AND GIAO Q. TRAN

OVERVIEW

Adults with social anxiety disorder (SAD) commonly use alcohol and drugs to cope with social discomfort. Among the internalizing disorders, SAD serves as a unique risk factor for the subsequent onset of alcohol or drug dependence. Although coping motives, alcohol- and drug-related expectancies, and negative consequences associated with these behaviors are well studied in adults, investigation is particularly relevant during the adolescent and college years when heavy drinking and drug use more often occur. Evolving social norms, peer pressure, conformity, and greater independence contribute to the increased risks associated with this developmental period. In this chapter, we review current theoretical models accounting for the relationship between SAD and alcohol and drug in adults and examine their applicability to adolescents on the basis of this limited but emerging body of research.

Etiological models for comorbid SAD and substance use disorders (SUDs) generally propose three types of causal mechanisms: (a) SAD causes or increases the risk of SUDs; (b) SUDs cause or increase the risk of SAD; and/or (c) a third variable causes or increases the risks of both disorders. The first model, often known as *self-medication*, proposes that pharmacological or psychological effects of alcohol and other drugs function as negative rein-forcers by reducing the aversive effects of anxiety symptoms (Khantzian, 1997). Anxiety researchers tend to support the self-medication view, whereas SUD researchers often promote the second view that posits anxiety as a largely physiological consequence of chronic substance use and social withdrawal. However, given the strong influence of environmental factors and experi-ences on the development of adolescents and young adults, other factors (e.g., peer substance use) may also increase risk of both SAD and SUDs.

PREVALENCE AND TRENDS

SAD has long been associated with alcohol use and comorbid alcohol use disorder (AUD; e.g., Amies, Gelder, & Shaw, 1983; Van Ameringen, Mancini, Styan, & Donison, 1991). In the National Comorbidity Survey, researchers (Kessler et al., 1996, 1997) noted that individuals with SAD are about twice as likely to meet diagnostic criteria for alcohol dependence than those without SAD. More recent data from the National Epidemiologic Sur-vey on Alcohol and Related Conditions confirmed these odds and estimated the 12-month prevalence of AUD among individuals with SAD to be about 13% (Grant et al., 2004). Patterns have emerged with regard to the specificity of this relationship, with a number of reports suggesting that SAD is associ-ated with greater risk of alcohol dependence than alcohol abuse (Buckner, Schmidt, et al., 2008; Buckner, Timpano, Zvolensky, Sachs-Ericsson, & Schmidt, 2008; Grant et al., 2004; Kessler et al., 1997) and that this risk may be stronger among socially anxious women than men (Buckner & Turner, 2009; Merikangas et al., 1998).

Some evidence suggests that individuals with subclinical social anxiety (i.e., an unreasonable fear of social situations that does not meet avoidance or impairment criteria) may be at greater risk of heavy drinking and AUD than those at the extremes of the social anxiety continuum (Crum & Pratt, 2001). Specifically, Merikangas, Avenevoli, Acharyya, Zhang, and Angst (2002) found that young adults with subclinical social anxiety were 3 times more likely to develop AUD than those with no diagnosis and had almost twice the odds of developing AUD than those with SAD. One possible expla-nation may be that because socially avoidant behavior tends to increase with SAD severity, more pervasive patterns of avoidance associated with SAD may protect against AUD by limiting involvement in social scenarios where alcohol is accessible.

One of the most consistent findings within the comorbidity literature is that SAD tends to predate the development of AUD (Carrigan & Randall, 2003). Cross-sectional research among clinical and community samples supports this claim, though these findings are based largely on retrospective reports of the disorders' onset (Buckner, Timpano, et al., 2008; Kessler et al., 1997; Nelson et al., 2000; Van Ameringen et al., 1991). Prospective studies among adolescent and young adult cohorts yield the most convincing evidence because they establish timing of onset across multiple assessment points and allow for the examination of longitudinal relationships. The Zurich Cohort Study of Young Adults, a 15-year longitudinal investigation, found that the age of social anxiety symptom onset was typically during adolescence (14–16 years old) and prior to AUD development (Merikangas et al., 2002). As an extension of these findings, a 14-year longitudinal study among high school students found that SAD at study entry was associated with more than a fourfold increase in the likelihood of alcohol dependence at study follow-up (Buckner, Schmidt, et al., 2008). Moreover, SAD remained a unique predictor of AUD after controlling for other psychiatric variables in a 3-year prospective investigation conducted among young adults (Buckner & Turner, 2009). On the basis of this body of work, the existing literature favors etiological models supporting SAD as a causal or contributing factor in the development of AUD.

SELF-MEDICATION HYPOTHESIS

The self-medication model of alcohol use was derived from early tension-reduction theories, which postulated that some individuals consume alcohol to reduce anxious internal states. In an early review article, Conger (1956) outlined how this stimulus–response association can be learned over time through negative reinforcement; the consumption of alcohol in response to an anxious stimulus results in anxiety dampening effects. In the application of this concept to SAD, individuals with social anxiety may consume alcohol to reduce anxious arousal in social situations. The symptom relief gained may then lead to continued and excessive alcohol use.

Multiple studies show that socially anxious individuals often report self-medicating with alcohol. Among inpatient alcoholics, individuals with comorbid SAD reported the highest rate of self-medication relative to people with other anxiety disorders (Chambless, Cherney, Caputo, & Rheinstein, 1987). In a more recent report, socially anxious individuals were significantly more likely to report avoiding social situations where no alcohol was present, using alcohol to feel more comfortable and experiencing greater symptom relief from alcohol than control subjects (Thomas, Randall, & Carrigan, 2003). Yet, only a few published studies have experimentally examined the anxiolytic effects of alcohol on social anxiety symptomatology (Carrigan & Randall, 2003). In support of the self-medication hypothesis, Abrams, Kushner, Medina, and Voight (2001, 2002) showed that individuals with SAD (on the basis of *Diagnostic and Statistical Manual of Mental Disorders* criteria [4th ed.; *DSM–IV*; American Psychiatric Association, 1994]) consumed more alcohol in response to a speech challenge than after a control task and that the pharmacological properties of alcohol additively contributed to self-reports of reduced performance anxiety. In contrast, two experimental speech challenges conducted among individuals with SAD (on the basis of *Diagnostic and Statistical Manual of Mental Disorders* criteria [3rd ed.; *DSM–III*; American Psychiatric Association, 1980]) found no evidence of alcohol producing a change in participants' subjective experience of anxiety or physiological stress responses (Himle et al., 1999; Naftolowitz, Vaughn, Ranc, & Tancer, 1994). One possible reason for these seemingly contradictory findings is the difference in diagnostic criteria specified in the *DSM–III* and *DSM–IV* for SAD. Specifically, the *DSM–III* required avoidance of social situations that provoke anxiety; however, this criterion was subsequently dropped in the *DSM–IV*. This is particularly relevant to the present discussion because individuals who do not avoid social situations may be particularly vulnerable to problematic alcohol use because they may use alcohol to cope with these situations. High levels of avoidance may serve a protective function because they effectively limit access to social situations where alcohol may be present, in turn limiting exposure to and engagement in alcohol-related behaviors.

In sum, the literature shows partial support for the self-medication model's ability to account for the relationship between SAD and AUD. It is clear that individuals with social anxiety report drinking to cope with their distress; however, there is little evidence to suggest that drinking alcohol actually reduces social anxiety (Carrigan & Randall, 2003). Given that null findings were reported when examining the self-medicating effects of alcohol among individuals diagnosed with *DSM–III* compared with *DSM–IV* SAD, extent of social avoidance may be a critical factor in understanding vulnerability to self-medicating behavior.

SOCIAL ANXIETY AS A PROTECTIVE MECHANISM

In contrast to the self-medication model, a number of cross-sectional investigations have challenged the notion that socially anxious individuals drink to reduce their symptoms. Results of these studies suggest that social anxiety may serve a protective function against alcohol use, particularly in college populations (Eggleston, Woolaway-Bickel, & Schmidt, 2004; Ham, Bonin, & Hope, 2007; Ham & Hope, 2005). For example, social anxiety was negatively related to quantity and frequency of alcohol consumption among a sample of undergraduate college students (Eggleston et al., 2004). Similarly, social anxiety may be either negatively related or unrelated to alcohol use, problematic drinking, and drinking consequences (Ham et al., 2007; Ham & Hope, 2005; Stewart, Morris, Mellings, & Komar, 2006; Tran, Haaga, & Chambless, 1997). Again, socially avoidant behaviors may explain these findings because limited engagement in social activities may in turn result in reduced exposure to alcohol. This protective relationship may extend to even younger adolescents, with greater levels of substance use predicting decreased levels of social anxiety among high school students (Myers, Aarons, Tomlinson, & Stein, 2003).

SOCIAL-COGNITIVE MODELS

Mixed findings regarding the direct links between social anxiety and alcohol use have led to an examination of individual differences that may predispose certain individuals to consume alcohol in response to social anxiety. Cognitive models have been increasingly used to explain conflicting results and provide support for the role of alcohol expectancies, drink refusal self-efficacy, and drinking motives as potential intervening variables (Burke & Stephens, 1999; Morris, Stewart, & Ham, 2005). These models stem from social learning theory, which proposes that cognitive expectations are established and reinforced through interactions with others and the environment, in turn guiding individuals' decision making and behavior.

Alcohol Expectancies and Drink Refusal Self-Efficacy

One individual difference that has emerged in the literature is the cognitive concept of *alcohol expectancies*, defined as beliefs about the anticipated positive and negative consequences of alcohol on cognition, mood, and behavior. In a cross-sectional study using community volunteers (Tran & Haaga, 2002), individuals with comorbid SAD and AUD had significantly stronger expectancies that alcohol would facilitate interaction in stressful social situations (when alcohol was accessible) than those with SAD but without AUD. Building on these findings, Ham, Carrigan, Moak, and Randall (2005) showed that socially anxious individuals not only reported significantly higher expectancies that alcohol would facilitate social interaction and assertion than did their nonsocially anxious counterparts but also that increases in alcohol expectancies specific to social situations actually predicted greater alcohol consumption and alcohol dependence levels. In fact, the longitudinal relationship between social facilitation expectancies and drinking behaviors among adolescents across middle and high school showed a reciprocal positive feedback relationship. Specifically, greater initial alcohol expectancies were linked to increased drinking behaviors, and increased drinking was subsequently related to greater expectations regarding the alcohol's effects (Smith, Goldman, Greenbaum, & Christiansen, 1995).

In addition to alcohol expectancies regarding social facilitation, Abrams and Kushner (2004) experimentally demonstrated the role of tension reduction expectancies, showing that among males with SAD, those with stronger beliefs about the tension-reducing effects of alcohol experienced less fear of negative evaluation and emotional distress after drinking a beverage they believed contained alcohol. Positive expectancies for both social assertion and tension reduction predicted alcohol consumption over the past month among a clinical sample with SAD (Ham, Hope, White, & Rivers, 2002). Similarly, Carrigan and colleagues (2008) simultaneously examined the predictive utility of both assertion and tension reduction expectancies and found that both types of alcohol expectancies uniquely discriminated between individuals with high and low levels of drinking in terms of their ability to cope with discomfort in social situations.

One's belief about one's ability to successfully refuse an alcoholic drink, known as drink refusal self-efficacy, is another type of expectancy that has received increasing attention and is postulated to be a robust predictor of drinking behavior (Greenfield et al., 2000; Oei & Burrow, 2000; Yeh, Chiang, & Huang, 2006). Burke and Stephens (1999) developed a cognitive model incorporating alcohol expectancies and drink refusal self-efficacy that outlines the relationship between social anxiety and alcohol use among college students. Their social-cognitive theory of heavy drinking proposes that alcohol expectancies and drink refusal self-efficacy moderate the relationship between social anxiety and drinking behavior. Individuals with high expectations about the positive effects of alcohol and low confidence regarding their ability to refuse alcohol are more likely to drink in situations that provoke social anxiety. In support of this model, Tran, Athenelli, Smith, Corcoran, and Rofey (2004) showed that among hazardous college drinkers, those with high social anxiety reported significantly stronger alcohol expectancies of social anxiety reduction and lower drink refusal self-efficacy than hazardous drinkers with low social anxiety. More recently, Gilles, Turk, and Fresco (2006) reported findings that directly supported all the hypothesized interactional effects of social anxiety, alcohol expectancy, and drink refusal self-efficacy in predicting amount and frequency of alcohol consumption in a collegiate sample. However, support for this model has not been shown consistently (Eggleston et al., 2004; Ham & Hope, 2005).

Drinking Motives

Individuals' reasons for drinking alcohol, commonly referred to as *drinking motives*, are another type of individual difference that has been linked to problematic alcohol use (Cooper, Frone, Russell, & Mudar, 1995). Drinking motives are distinct from alcohol expectancies in that they appear to reflect the perceived motivations driving individuals' engagement in alcohol use. On the other hand, alcohol expectancies reflect anticipated outcomes of drinking behavior, consequences that may or may not be preferred (Ham et al., 2007). According to Cooper and colleagues' (1995) motivational model of alcohol use, motives for drinking are the most proximal antecedent to alcohol use through which the effects of expectancies and affective experience are mediated. The relevancy of this model to social anxiety and alcohol use has received increasing attention in recent years, as use of alcohol as an emotional regulation strategy has been linked to the development of disordered drinking patterns (e.g., Carpenter & Hasin, 1998, 1999; Khantzian, 1997; Kushner, Sher, & Beitman, 1990). The majority of research in this area has examined college populations but could be extended to younger adolescents.

Because individuals with social anxiety may drink primarily to alleviate distress (e.g., Kuntsche, Knibbe, Gmel, & Engels, 2005), the role of negative-reinforcement motives may be most salient (Lewis et al., 2008). These motives include coping (i.e., drinking to reduce or regulate negative affect) and conformity (i.e., drinking to avoid social reproach or in response to social pressure). Both reasons appear to be highly relevant to individuals with SAD, given the anxious affect and fear of negative evaluation (or embarrassment) associated with the condition (Ham et al., 2007). In support of this hypothesis, coping and conformity motives were related to greater alcohol use and related problems for those with high and moderate levels of social anxiety symptomatology (Ham et al., 2007). In two cross-sectional investigations among college students, social anxiety and fear of negative evaluation were positively related to negative consequences of drinking, and these relationships were found to be mediated by coping and conformity motives (Lewis et al., 2008; Stewart et al., 2006).

PEER EFFECTS ON THE RELATIONSHIP BETWEEN ALCOHOL USE AND SOCIAL ANXIETY

Peer influences and perceptions of friends' drinking behaviors are consistently identified as strong predictors of college drinking (Bruch, Rivet, Heimberg, & Levin, 1997; Campo et al. 2003; Tran et al., 1997). Many colleges have high drinking norms, with hazardous drinking ranging from 44% to 70% of the students (Wechsler, Davenport, Dowdall, Moeykens, & Castillo, 1994). Social anxiety, characterized in part by a preoccupation with negative evaluation, is associated with an increased susceptibility to peer influences on drinking among college students. Results from one study revealed that although both socially anxious and healthy control students perceived similar drinking norms (i.e., overestimated how much alcohol their peers drank), socially anxious students were more likely to drink heavily in response to perceived high drinking norms (Neighbors et al., 2007). These findings suggest that young adults with high levels of social anxiety or SAD may be more susceptible to peer influences regarding alcohol consumption.

CANNABIS USE DISORDER: PREVALENCE AND TRENDS

The relationship between SAD and cannabis use disorder (CUD) has received comparatively less attention than SAD and AUD. The majority of studies have been cross-sectional in nature (e.g., Buckner, Mallott, Schmidt, & Taylor, 2006; Buckner & Schmidt, 2008), with only two longitudinal investigations examining temporal sequencing (Buckner, Schmidt, et al., 2008; Merikangas et al., 2002). However, a number of interesting trends have materialized that appear to parallel findings from the SAD and AUD literature.

Epidemiological data (Agosti, Nunes, & Levin, 2002) from the National Comorbidity Survey show that the lifetime prevalence of cannabis dependence among individuals with SAD is 29%, which is considerably higher than the rate in the general population (4%). It has been estimated that individuals with SAD are nearly 5 times more likely to meet the *DSM–IV* diagnostic criteria for cannabis dependence (Buckner, Schmidt, et al., 2008). This prospective relationship remained even after controlling for a number of potentially confounding variables, including sex, conduct disorder, depression, and other anxiety disorders, suggesting that social anxiety is a relatively robust and unique predictor of subsequent cannabis dependence. Similar to findings from the alcohol literature, subclinical levels of social anxiety have been associated with an increased risk of subsequent CUD development relative to those with SAD (Merikangas et al., 2002). Moreover, it has been suggested that SAD typically precedes the development of CUD and is generally more strongly related to cannabis dependence than abuse (Buckner, Schmidt, et al., 2008; Merikangas et al., 2002).

THEORETICAL CONSIDERATIONS

Despite support establishing a longitudinal link between SAD and subsequent CUD, there are few data examining the mechanisms that link social anxiety with problematic cannabis use. Among undergraduate students, perceived substance use norms moderated the relationship between SAD and CUD; increased perception of peer substance use contributed to increased

CUD symptomatology (Buckner, Mallott, et al., 2006). Similarly, individuals' perceived coping abilities (i.e., the extent to which one believes one can effectively cope with a stressor) also moderated the relationship between SAD and CUD (Buckner, Schmidt, Bobadilla, & Taylor, 2006). In contrast to the interaction uncovered with perceived substance use norms, perceived coping was negatively related to CUD symptoms, indicating that a perceived inability to effectively cope is linked to increased CUD symptomatology.

The relevancy of expectancies and motives for cannabis use has also been examined in an effort to better understand the social-cognitive variables that may serve as vulnerabilities to cannabis use in response to symptoms of social anxiety. Consistent with the alcohol literature, emerging evidence suggests that social anxiety may be more robustly related to cannabis use problems than to actual cannabis use frequency (Buckner, Bonn-Miller, Zvolensky, & Schmidt, 2007; Buckner & Schmidt, 2008). The innovative work of Buckner and her colleagues (2007) has also implicated the potential role of cannabis use motives in accounting for this relationship. Among undergraduate (lifetime) cannabis users, social anxiety was a significant predictor of the strength of engagement in coping and conformity motives for cannabis use, extending the relevancy of negative-reinforcement motives to comorbid SAD and CUD. Moreover, coping motives for cannabis use were found to mediate the association between social anxiety and cannabis use problems (Buckner et al., 2007), highlighting that the link between social anxiety and cannabis use appears to be indirect and that specific motives for use may be a more proximal determinant of cannabis use behavior. In support of the role of cannabis expectancies, preliminary research has demonstrated that social anxiety is significantly related to cannabis outcome expectancies, including impairment, tension reduction, and enhancement expectancies (Buckner & Schmidt, 2008). Interestingly, cannabis expectancies for cognitive and behavioral impairment moderated the social anxiety and cannabis use relationship such that increased expectancies for impairment actually predicted increased use. Moreover, overall negative expectancies (i.e., beliefs that cannabis use will result in impairment and more globally negative outcomes) partially mediated the relationship between social anxiety and cannabis use problems (Buckner & Schmidt, 2008). Taken together, it appears that cannabis use expectancies for impairment and other negative outcomes are related to increased use of cannabis, suggesting that individuals continue to use cannabis to cope with social anxiety despite expected negative consequences. Unlike a social-cognitive model of alcohol use and SAD, however, a specific model for understanding the associations between cannabis use and SAD has not been formally proposed. Future research examining the unique relationships between SAD, cannabis expectancies, motives, and CUD may be particularly helpful.

The research examining the relationship between social anxiety and nicotine use has been limited. The studies that have been conducted appear to suggest a unidirectional relationship, and a number of interesting trends are beginning to emerge. However, the results are quite preliminary and need to be more fully explored among adolescent samples.

NICOTINE USE: PREVALENCE AND TRENDS

Individuals with SAD are 2 to 3 times more likely to meet criteria for nicotine dependence (Grant et al., 2004). Epidemiological data from the National Epidemiologic Survey on Alcohol and Related Conditions show that the 12-month prevalence of nicotine dependence among individuals with SAD is 27%, doubling the rate of nicotine dependence in the general population (13%; Grant et al., 2004). Similarly, in a study of adults, the rate for nicotine dependence among individuals with SAD was twice that of a matched control group (Wittchen, Fuetsch, Sonntag, Müller, & Liebowitz, 2000).

In a 4-year longitudinal study including adolescents and young adults, nonsmokers and non-nicotine-dependent smokers with social anxiety had a greater risk of developing later nicotine dependence than those without social anxiety (Sonntag, Wittchen, Höfler, Kessler, & Stein, 2000). The reverse has not been shown to be true. That is, the prospective relationship between smoking and subsequent SAD is nonsignificant when examined among an adolescent and young adult sample (Johnson, et al., 2000). Consistent with trends observed in the alcohol and cannabis literatures, a high level of social anxiety is associated with an elevated risk of subsequent nicotine dependence compared with those with SAD (Merikangas et al., 2002). Taken together, these studies suggest that individuals with subthreshold SAD symptoms may be a group particularly vulnerable to smoking, supporting the theory that preexisting social anxiety may increase the risk of later nicotine dependence. However, the literature remains somewhat mixed. For example, Baker-Morissette, Gulliver, Wiegel, and Barlow (2004) reported that the prevalence rate of nicotine dependence decreased considerably among socially anxious individuals without comorbid alcohol or other substance use disorders (14%).

SOCIAL ANXIETY DISORDER AS CAUSAL FACTOR

Models examining the relationship between nicotine and SAD have focused on the predictive role of SAD in the development of smoking behavior. Although several epidemiological and longitudinal studies have indirectly supported the self-medication hypothesis (e.g., Grant et al., 2004;

Sonntag et al., 2000), to our knowledge no studies have examined the hypothesis that smoking actually reduces socially anxious individuals' experience of social anxiety.

One theory in the adolescent literature is *impression management*, defined as an individual's attempt to convey a desired self-image, in turn facilitating the formation of social relationships (Leventhal, Keeshan, Baker, & Wetter, 1991). Only two published studies have tested this hypothesis in adolescents and young adults. O'Callaghan and Doyle's (2001) study of cigarette smoking among high school students found that both nonsmokers and frequent smokers were more socially anxious than occasional smokers. These groups also had lower levels of self-esteem and perceived success in impression management relative to their counterparts. In contrast, a study with a young adult sample (Sharp & Getz, 1996) supported the role of impression management with regard to alcohol use but not nicotine use. Given the mixed and preliminary nature of these findings, much more research is needed to better understand these specific mechanisms.

CONCLUSIONS AND FUTURE DIRECTIONS

Clearly, much work remains in order to develop empirically based theoretical models for the complex relationships between SAD and various SUDs, though several important themes are apparent. Cross-sectional and longitudinal studies show striking similarities in social anxiety's relationships to alcohol and cannabis use, despite a much smaller body of evidence for the latter. First, SAD increases the risk of alcohol or cannabis dependence, and SAD onset typically precedes the onsets of both substance use disorders. Second, subclinical levels of social anxiety appear to be associated with higher risk of developing AUD or CUD than SAD. This counterintuitive finding makes conceptual sense considering the fact that individuals with SAD are often highly avoidant of social situations and, consequently, may have less access to and need for alcohol as a form of self-medication. Third, empirical research emphasizes the moderating and mediating roles of alcohol expectancies, drink refusal self-efficacy, and coping motives help to explain these etiological relationships. Fourth, emerging data suggest that social anxiety has a more consistent and stronger positive association with substance-use-related problems rather than use itself.

Overall, proposed etiological models are still in their early development. The most commonly tested causal model is based on a self-medication hypothesis for which there is some support across adolescent and adult populations. In light of well-established findings pointing to the social environment as critical for adolescent and young adult substance use, developing models of comorbidity that consider potential moderating and mediating factors (Buckner, Mallott, et al., 2006; Buckner, Schmidt, et al., 2006; Neighbors et al., 2007) will likely enrich the theoretical conceptualization of the relationships between social anxiety and substance use as well as their negative consequences.

REFERENCES

Abrams, K., & Kushner, M. G. (2004). The moderating effects of tension-reduction alcohol outcome expectancies on placebo responding in individuals with social phobia. *Addictive Behaviors, 29,* 1221–1224. doi:10.1016/j.addbeh.2004.03.020

Abrams, K., Kushner, M. G., Medina, K. L., & Voight, A. (2001). The pharmacologic and expectancy effects of alcohol on social anxiety in individuals with social phobia. *Drug and Alcohol Dependence, 64,* 219–231. doi:10.1016/S0376-8716(01)00125-9

Abrams, K., Kushner, M. G., Medina, K. L., & Voight, A. (2002). Self-administration of alcohol before and after a public speaking challenge by individuals with social phobia. *Psychology of Addictive Behaviors, 16,* 121–128. doi:10.1037/0893-164X.16.2.121

Agosti, V., Nunes, E., & Levin, F. (2002). Rates of psychiatric comorbidity among U.S. residents with lifetime cannabis dependence. *The American Journal of Drug and Alcohol Abuse, 28,* 643–652. doi:10.1081/ADA-120015873

American Psychiatric Association. (1980). *Diagnostic and statistical manual of mental disorders* (3rd ed.). Washington, DC: Author.

American Psychiatric Association. (1994). *Diagnostic and statistical manual of mental disorders* (4th ed.). Washington, DC: Author.

Amies, P. L., Gelder, M. G., & Shaw, P. M. (1983). Social phobia: A comparative clinical study. *The British Journal of Psychiatry, 142,* 174–179. doi:10.1192/bjp.142.2.174

Baker-Morissette, S. L., Gulliver, S. B., Wiegel, M., & Barlow, D. H. (2004). Prevalence of smoking in anxiety disorders uncomplicated by comorbid alcohol or substance abuse. *Journal of Psychopathology and Behavioral Assessment, 26,* 107–112. doi:10.1023/B:JOBA.0000013658.50297.ff

Bruch, M. A., Rivet, K. M., Heimberg, R. G., & Levin, M. A. (1997). Shyness, alcohol expectancies, and drinking behaviors: Replication and extension of suppressor effect. *Personality and Individual Differences, 22,* 193–200. doi:10.1016/S0191-8869(96)00190-0

Buckner, J. D., Bonn-Miller, M. O., Zvolensky, M. J., & Schmidt, N. B. (2007). Marijuana use motives and social anxiety among marijuana-using young adults. *Addictive Behaviors, 32,* 2238–2252. doi:10.1016/j.addbeh.2007.04.004

Buckner, J. D., Mallott, M. A., Schmidt, N. B., & Taylor, J. (2006). Peer influence and gender differences in problematic cannabis use among individuals with social anxiety. *Journal of Anxiety Disorders, 20,* 1087–1102. doi:10.1016/j.janxdis.2006.03.002

Buckner, J. D., & Schmidt, N. B. (2008). Marijuana effect expectancies: Relations to social anxiety and marijuana use problems. *Addictive Behaviors, 33,* 1477–1483. doi:10.1016/j.addbeh.2008.06.017

Buckner, J. D., Schmidt, N. B., Bobadilla, L., & Taylor, J. (2006). Social anxiety and problematic cannabis use: Evaluating the moderating role of stress reactivity and perceived coping. *Behaviour Research and Therapy, 44,* 1007–1015. doi:10.1016/j.brat.2005.08.002

Buckner, J. D., Schmidt, N. B., Lang, A. R., Small, J. W., Schlauch, R. C., & Lewinsohn, P. M. (2008). Specificity of social anxiety disorder as a risk factor for alcohol and cannabis dependence. *Journal of Psychiatric Research, 42,* 230–239. doi:10.1016/j.jpsychires.2007.01.002

Buckner, J. D., Timpano, K. R., Zvolensky, M. J., Sachs-Ericsson, N., & Schmidt, N. B. (2008). Implications of comorbid alcohol dependence among individuals with social anxiety disorder. *Depression and Anxiety, 25,* 1028–1037. doi:10.1002/da.20442

Buckner, J. D., & Turner, R. J. (2009). Social anxiety disorder as a risk factor for alcohol use disorders: A prospective examination of parental and peer influences. *Drug and Alcohol Dependence, 100,* 128–137. doi:10.1016/j.drugalcdep.2008.09.018

Burke, R. S., & Stephens, R. S. (1999). Social anxiety and drinking in college students: A social cognitive theory analysis. *Clinical Psychology Review, 19,* 513–530. doi:10.1016/S0272-7358(98)00058-0

Campo, S., Brossard, D., Frazer, M. S., Marchell, T., Lewis, D., & Talbot, J. (2003). Are social norms campaigns really magic bullets? Assessing effects of students' misperceptions on drinking behaviors. *Health Communication, 15,* 481–497. doi:10.1207/S15327027HC1504_06

Carpenter, K. M., & Hasin, D. S. (1998). Reasons for drinking alcohol: Relationships with *DSM–IV* alcohol diagnoses and alcohol consumption in a community sample. *Psychology of Addictive Behaviors, 12,* 168–184. doi:10.1037/0893-164X.12.3.168

Carpenter, K. M., & Hasin, D. S. (1999). Drinking to cope with negative affect and *DSM–IV* alcohol use disorders: A test of three alternative explanations. *Journal of Studies on Alcohol, 60,* 694–704.

Carrigan, M. H., Ham, L. S., Thomas, S. E., & Randall, C. L. (2008). Alcohol outcome expectancies and drinking to cope with social situations. *Addictive Behaviors, 33,* 1162–1166. doi:10.1016/j.addbeh.2008.04.020

Carrigan, M. H., & Randall, C. L. (2003). Self-medication in social phobia: A review of the alcohol literature. *Addictive Behaviors, 28,* 269–284. doi:10.1016/S0306-4603(01)00235-0

Chambless, D. L., Cherney, J., Caputo, G. C., & Rheinstein, B. J. G. (1987). Anxiety disorders and alcoholism: A study with inpatient alcoholics. *Journal of Anxiety Disorders, 1,* 29–40. doi:10.1016/0887-6185(87)90020-X

Conger, J. J. (1956). Reinforcement theory and the dynamics of alcoholism. *Journal of Studies on Alcohol, 17,* 296–305.

Cooper, M. L., Frone, M. R., Russell, M., & Mudar, P. (1995). Drinking to regulate positive and negative emotions: A motivational model of alcohol use. *Journal of Personality and Social Psychology, 69,* 990–1005. doi:10.1037/0022-3514. 69.5.990

Crum, R. M., & Pratt, L. A. (2001). Risk of heavy drinking and alcohol use disorders in social phobia: A prospective analysis. *The American Journal of Psychiatry, 158,* 1693–1700. doi:10.1176/appi.ajp.158.10.1693

Eggleston, A. M., Woolaway-Bickel, K., & Schmidt, N. B. (2004). Social anxiety and alcohol use: Evaluation of the moderating and mediating effects of alcohol expectancies. *Journal of Anxiety Disorders, 18,* 33–49. doi:10.1016/j.janxdis. 2003.07.005

Gilles, D. M., Turk, C. L., & Fresco, D. M. (2006). Social anxiety, alcohol expectancies, and self-efficacy as predictors of heavy drinking in college students. *Addictive Behaviors, 31,* 388–398. doi:10.1016/j.addbeh.2005.05.020

Grant, B. F., Stinson, F., S., Dawson, D. A., Chou, S. P., Dufour, M. C., Compton, W., . . . Kaplan, K. (2004). Prevalence and co-occurrence of substance use disorders and independent mood and anxiety disorders. *Archives of General Psychiatry, 61,* 807–816. doi:10.1001/archpsyc.61.8.807

Greenfield, S. F., Hufford, M. R., Vagge, L. M., Muenz, L. R., Costello, M. E., & Weiss, R. D. (2000). The relationship of self-efficacy expectancies to relapse among alcohol dependent men and women: A prospective study. *Journal of Studies on Alcohol, 61,* 345–351.

Ham, L. S., Bonin, M., & Hope, D. A. (2007). The role of drinking motives in social anxiety and alcohol use. *Journal of Anxiety Disorders, 21,* 991–1003. doi:10.1016/ j.janxdis.2006.10.014

Ham, L. S., Carrigan, M. H., Moak, D. H., & Randall, C. L. (2005). Social anxiety and specificity of positive alcohol expectancies: Preliminary findings. *Journal of Psychopathology and Behavioral Assessment, 27,* 115–121. doi:10.1007/s10862-005-5385-x

Ham, L. S., & Hope, D. A. (2005). Incorporating social anxiety into a model of college student problematic drinking. *Addictive Behaviors, 30,* 127–150. doi:10.1016/ j.addbeh.2004.04.018

Ham, L. S., Hope, D. A., White, C. S., & Rivers, P. C. (2002). Alcohol expectancies and drinking behavior in adults with social anxiety disorder and dysthymia. *Cognitive Therapy and Research, 26,* 275–288. doi:10.1023/A:1014582005745

Himle, J. A., Abelson, J. L., Haghightgou, H., Hill, E. M., Nesse, R. M., & Curtis, G. C. (1999). Effect of alcohol on social phobic anxiety. *The American Journal of Psychiatry, 156,* 1237–1243.

Johnson, J. G., Cohen, P., Pine, D. S., Klein, D. F., Kasen, S., & Brook, J. S. (2000). Association between cigarette smoking and anxiety disorders during adolescence and early adulthood. *JAMA, 284,* 2348–2351. doi:10.1001/jama.284.18.2348

Kessler, R. C., Crum, R. M., Warner, L. A., Nelson, C. B., Schulenberg, C. B., & Anthony, J. C. (1997). Lifetime co-occurrence of *DSM–III–R* alcohol abuse and dependence with other psychiatric disorders in the National Comorbidity Survey. *Archives of General Psychiatry, 54,* 313–321.

Kessler, R. C., Nelson, C. B., McGonagle, K. A., Edlund, M. J., Frank, R. G., & Leaf, P. J. (1996). The epidemiology of co-occurring addictive and mental disorders: Implications for prevention and service utilization. *American Journal of Orthopsychiatry, 66,* 17–31. doi:10.1037/h0080151

Khantzian, E. J. (1997). The self-medication hypothesis of substance use disorders: A reconsideration and recent applications. *Harvard Review of Psychiatry, 4,* 231–244. doi:10.3109/10673229709030550

Kuntsche, E., Knibbe, R., Gmel, G., & Engels, R. (2005). Why do young people drink? A review of drinking motives. *Clinical Psychology Review, 25,* 841–861. doi:10.1016/j.cpr.2005.06.002

Kushner, M. G., Sher, K. J., & Beitman, B. D. (1990). The relation between alcohol problems and the anxiety disorders. *The American Journal of Psychiatry, 147,* 685–695.

Leventhal, H., Keeshan, P., Baker, T., & Wetter, D. (1991). Smoking prevention: Towards a process approach. *British Journal of Addiction, 86,* 583–587.

Lewis, M. A., Hove, M. C., Whiteside, U., Lee, C. M., Kirkeby, B. S., Oster-Aaland, L., . . . Larimer, M. E. (2008). Fitting in and feeling fine: Conformity and coping motives as mediators of the relationship between social anxiety and problematic drinking. *Psychology of Addictive Behaviors, 22,* 58–67. doi:10.1037/0893-164X.22.1.58

Merikangas, K. R., Avenevoli, S., Acharyya, S., Zhang, H., & Angst, J. (2002). The spectrum of social phobia in the Zurich Cohort Study of Young Adults. *Biological Psychiatry, 51,* 81–91. doi:10.1016/S0006-3223(01)01309-9

Merikangas, K. R., Stevens, D. E., Fenton, B., Stolar, M., O'Malley, S., Woods, S. W., & Risch, N. (1998). Co-morbidity and familial aggregation of alcoholism and anxiety disorders. *Psychological Medicine, 28,* 773–788. doi:10.1017/S0033291798006941

Morris, E. P., Stewart, S. H., & Ham, L. S. (2005). The relationship between social anxiety disorder and alcohol use disorders: A critical review. *Clinical Psychology Review, 25,* 734–760. doi:10.1016/j.cpr.2005.05.004

Myers, M. G., Aarons, G. A., Tomlinson, K., & Stein, M. B. (2003). Social anxiety, negative affectivity, and substance use among high school students. *Psychology of Addictive Behaviors, 17,* 277–283. doi:10.1037/0893-164X.17.4.277

Naftolowitz, D. F., Vaughn, B. V., Ranc, J., & Tancer, M. E. (1994). Response to alcohol in social phobia. *Anxiety, 1,* 96–99.

Neighbors, C., Fossos, N., Woods, B. A., Fabiano, P., Sledge, M., & Frost, D. (2007). Social anxiety as moderator of the relationship between perceived norms and drinking. *Journal of Studies on Alcohol, 68,* 91–96.

Nelson, E. C., Grant, J. D., Bucholz, K. K., Glowinski, A., Madden, P. A. F., Reich, W., & Heath, A. C. (2000). Social phobia in a population-based female adolescent twin sample: Co-morbidity and associated suicide-related symptoms. *Psychological Medicine*, *30*, 797–804. doi:10.1017/S0033291799002275

O'Callaghan, F., & Doyle, J. (2001). What is the role of impression management in adolescent cigarette smoking? *Journal of Substance Abuse*, *13*, 459–470. doi:10.1016/S0899-3289(01)00089-X

Oei, T. P. S., & Burrow, T. (2000). Alcohol expectancy and drinking refusal self-efficacy: A test of specificity theory. *Addictive Behaviors*, *25*, 499–507. doi:10.1016/S0306-4603(99)00044-1

Sharp, M. J., & Getz, J. G. (1996). Substance use as impression management. *Personality and Social Psychology Bulletin*, *22*, 60–67.

Smith, G. T., Goldman, M. S., Greenbaum, P. E., & Christiansen, B. A. (1995). Expectancy for social facilitation from drinking: The divergent paths of high-expectancy and low-expectancy adolescents. *Journal of Abnormal Psychology*, *104*, 32–40. doi:10.1037/0021-843X.104.1.32

Sonntag H., Wittchen H.-U., Höfler, M., Kessler, R., C., & Stein, M., B. (2000). Are social fears and *DSM–IV* social anxiety disorder associated with smoking and nicotine dependence in adolescents and young adults? *European Psychiatry*, *15*, 67–74. doi:10.1016/S0924-9338(00)00209-1

Stewart, S. H., Morris, E., Mellings, T., & Komar, J. (2006). Relations of social anxiety variables to drinking motives, drinking quantity and frequency, and alcohol-related problems in undergraduates. *Journal of Mental Health*, *15*, 671–682. doi:10.1080/09638230600998904

Thomas, S. E., Randall, C. L., & Carrigan, M. H. (2003). Drinking to cope in socially anxious individuals: A controlled study. *Alcoholism, Clinical and Experimental Research*, *27*, 1937–1943. doi:10.1097/01.ALC.0000100942.30743.8C

Tran, G. Q., Anthenelli, R. M., Smith, J. P., Corcoran, K. J., & Rofey, D. L. (2004). Alcohol use, cognitive correlates of drinking, and change readiness in hazardous drinkers with high level versus low social anxiety. *Journal of Studies on Alcohol*, *65*, 715–724.

Tran, G. Q., & Haaga, D. A. F. (2002). Coping responses and alcohol outcome expectancies in alcohol abusing and nonabusing social phobics. *Cognitive Therapy and Research*, *26*, 1–17. doi:10.1023/A:1013803803192

Tran, G. Q., Haaga, D. A. F., & Chambless, D. L. (1997). Expecting that alcohol use will reduce social anxiety moderates the relation between social anxiety and alcohol consumption. *Cognitive Therapy and Research*, *21*, 535–553. doi:10.1023/A:1021857402164

Van Ameringen, M., Mancini, C., Styan, G., & Donison, D. (1991). Relationship of social phobia with other psychiatric illness. *Journal of Affective Disorders*, *21*, 93–99. doi:10.1016/0165-0327(91)90055-W

Wechsler, H., Davenport, A., Dowdall, G., Moeykens, B., & Castillo, S. (1994). Health and behavioral consequences of binge drinking in college: A national survey of students at 140 campuses. *JAMA, 272*, 1672–1677. doi:10.1001/jama. 272.21.1672

Wittchen, H.-U., Fuetsch, M., Sonntag, H., Müller, N., & Liebowitz, M. (2000). Disability and quality of life in pure and comorbid social phobia—Findings from a controlled study. *European Psychiatry, 15*, 46–58. doi:10.1016/S0924-9338(00)00211-X

Yeh, M., Chiang, I, & Huang, S. (2006). Gender differences in predictors of drinking behavior in adolescents. *Addictive Behaviors, 31*, 1929–1938.

7

SOCIAL AND PERFORMANCE ANXIETY AND OPPOSITIONAL AND SCHOOL REFUSAL BEHAVIOR IN ADOLESCENTS

CHRISTOPHER A. KEARNEY, MARISA GAUGER,
RACHEL SCHAFER, AND TIMOTHY DAY

A particularly underrecognized area of clinical psychology involves youth with social and performance anxiety as well as oppositional and school refusal behavior. *Social* and *performance anxiety* refer to adverse physiological arousal or distress in social or performance situations involving possible negative evaluation from others, worry or fear of psychological harm, and/or desire to avoid or escape these situations (La Greca & Stone, 1993; Schlenker & Leary, 1982). *Oppositional behavior* refers to defiance, noncompliance, tantrums, argumentativeness, and/or vindictiveness. Oppositional behavior sometimes overlaps with *conduct disorder*, or "a repetitive and persistent pattern of behavior in which the basic rights of others or major age-appropriate societal norms or rules are violated." One symptom of conduct disorder is "often truant from school, beginning before age 13 years" (American Psychiatric Association, 2000, pp. 98, 99).

School refusal behavior refers to youth-motivated refusal to attend school and/or difficulties remaining in classes for an entire day (Kearney & Silverman, 1996). School refusal behavior may come in the form of extended or periodic school absences, skipped classes, chronic tardiness, morning misbehaviors in an attempt to refuse school, and substantial distress while attending school that precipitates pleas for future nonattendance. Problematic school absenteeism involves school-age youths who (a) have missed at least 25% of total school time for at least 2 weeks, (b) experience severe difficulty attending classes for at least 2 weeks with significant interference in a youth's or family's daily routine, and/or (c) are absent for at least 10 days of school during any 15-week period while school is in session, with a daily absence defined as 25% or more of school time missed (Kearney, 2008b). In this chapter, we examine the clinical syndrome, assessment, and treatment of social anxiety and oppositional behaviors, including school refusal.

SOCIAL AND PERFORMANCE ANXIETY AND OPPOSITIONAL AND SCHOOL REFUSAL BEHAVIOR

Several researchers over past decades have alluded to the association between social and performance anxiety and oppositional and school refusal behavior. Broadwin (1932) stated that some cases of school absenteeism "represent an act of defiance, an attempt to obtain love, or escapes from real situations to which it is difficult to adjust" (p. 254). Partridge (1939) claimed that one form of truancy included youths who displayed timidity, guilt, anxiety, tantrums, and aggression. Kennedy (1965) proposed that one form of school phobia included youths with poor parental relations and adjustment. Later studies involved statistical techniques to group youths with school refusal behavior, but heterogeneity of internalizing and externalizing behavior problems was common, and many youths could not be adequately classified (Atkinson, Quarrington, Cyr, & Atkinson, 1989; Berg et al., 1985; Kolvin, Berney, & Bhate, 1984). Other researchers examined youths with school refusal behavior diagnostically or phenomenologically and found overlap with social and performance anxiety and oppositionality (Berg et al., 1993; Bernstein & Garfinkel, 1986; Granell de Aldaz, Feldman, Vivas, & Gelfand, 1987).

More contemporary studies of comorbidity have involved structured diagnostic interviews and other dependent measures with strong psychometric properties. An association between social and performance anxiety and oppositional and school refusal behavior continues to receive support. Mcshane, Walter, and Rey (2001) evaluated 192 adolescents with school refusal behavior and found that many had social phobia (8%), oppositional defiant disorder (24%), conduct disorder (3%), and disruptive behavior disorder not otherwise specified (5%). Egger, Costello, and Angold (2003) compared nine 13-year-old youths with pure anxious school refusal ($n = 130$), pure truancy ($n = 482$), or a mixture of symptoms ($n = 35$) from these categories along several variables, some of which are presented in Table 7.1. Considerable linkages were evident for social and performance anxiety and peer relationship variables such as shy-

TABLE 7.1
Comparison of Youths With Anxious School Refusal,
Truancy, and Mixed Symptoms

Variable	Anxious school refusal (%)	Truancy (%)	Mixed symptoms (%)
Diagnosis			
Social phobia	3.2	0.2	0.0
Oppositional defiant disorder	5.6	9.7	17.9
Conduct disorder	5.0	14.8	43.4
Symptom			
Performance anxiety	6.7	0.8	1.4
Social anxiety	8.5	1.8	14.2
Peer relationship variable			
Shy with peers	28.2	10.3	6.7
Bullied/teased	28.9	8.5	31.2
Difficulty making friends because of withdrawal	18.9	5.6	17.8
Difficulty making friends because of aggression	17.5	3.9	34.1
Conflictual peer relationships	27.0	16.2	22.1

Note. Adapted from "School Refusal and Psychiatric Disorders: A Community Study," by H. L. Egger, E. J. Costello, and A. Angold, 2003, *Journal of the American Academy of Child & Adolescent Psychiatry, 42,* pp. 797–807. Copyright 2003 by the American Academy of Child & Adolescent Psychiatry. Adapted with permission.

ness across all three conditions, including the truancy group that is often associated with greater oppositional behavior.

Kearney and colleagues (Kearney, 2007; 2008c; Kearney & Albano, 2007; Kearney & Silverman, 1996) outlined a functional model of school refusal behavior based on the primary reasons a youth misses school. Primary functions include avoidance of school-related stimuli that provoke negative affectivity, escape from aversive school-based social and/or evaluative situations, pursuit of attention from significant others, and pursuit of tangible rewards outside of school. Kearney and Albano (2004) examined 143 youths with school refusal behavior and found some overlap of oppositional defiant and conduct disorder in youths who wished to escape aversive school-based social and/or evaluative situations. Other researchers have also examined broader groups of youths with school absenteeism and found that peer victimization, social fear and isolation, inhibition, association with deviant peers, and poor relationships with peers and teachers are key contributing factors (Attwood & Croll, 2006; Buitelaar, van Andel, Duyx, & van Strien, 1994; Henry & Huizinga, 2007; Kearney, 2008b; Weiss & Burke, 1967).

Outcome studies also indicate that chronic absenteeism relates to problems in social and marital functioning for teens and young adults (Berg &

Jackson, 1985; Flakierska-Praquin, Lindstrom, & Gillberg, 1997; Hibbett & Fogelman, 1990; McCune & Hynes, 2005). Mcshane, Walter, and Rey (2004) found that social phobia was associated with poorer functional outcome over 3 years among adolescents treated for school refusal behavior. Peer competence also predicts whether a child remains in school (Jimerson, Egeland, Sroufe, & Carlson, 2000). Adults with social phobia also report that they were more often truant and more likely to be expelled from school than controls (Davidson, Hughes, George, & Blazer, 1993). Adults with subthreshold social phobia were also more likely than controls to report work attendance problems, poor school grades, and have less income and education (Davidson, Hughes, George, & Blazer, 1994).

Other researchers have found similar links by examining different samples of youth. Beidel, Turner, and Morris (1999) found that 10% of youths with social phobia refused to attend school. In addition, youths with social phobia commonly avoided social situations that are present at school, including reading or writing before a class, musical or athletic performances, conversations, dances, asking a teacher for help, eating in the cafeteria, and walking in hallways. Harada, Yamazaki, and Saitoh (2002) found school refusal to be common among youths with attention-deficit/hyperactivity disorder (17%), oppositional defiant disorder (80%), or combined diagnoses (42%). Social isolation was also common to each group (39%, 30%, 19%, respectively). Others have noted a link between social skills deficits, social withdrawal, externalizing behavior problems, and school maladjustment (Rubin, Burgess, Kennedy, & Stewart, 2003; Tarolla, Wagner, Rabinowitz, & Tubman, 2002).

Many youths with these comorbid characteristics display inappropriate or maladaptive interpersonal styles, inaccurate perceptions of social cues, inaccurate estimations of threat by others, difficulty making or keeping friends, and impaired social problem-solving skills (Albano & Detweiler, 2001; Kearney, 2005). In addition, externalizing behavior problems in youths with school refusal behavior are sometimes an expression of covert symptoms such as social anxiety (Kearney, 2001).

ASSESSING SOCIAL AND PERFORMANCE ANXIETY WITH OPPOSITIONAL AND SCHOOL REFUSAL BEHAVIOR

The assessment of youths with both anxiety and oppositional behaviors must involve multiple methods and multiple sources of information about several key variables. Common methods for this population include structured diagnostic interviews, youth self-reports and parent and teacher questionnaires, observations, and reviews of records. Important sources of information include the youth and his or her parents, school officials, and other professionals who may be involved with a case, such as a probation or truant officer, pediatrician, or psychiatrist. Key variables to be targeted during an assessment include school attendance, grades, course schedule, required make-up work, legal status, avoided social and performance situations, and oppositional behavior to maintain absenteeism, among others (Kearney & Albano, 2007). A summary of common methods to assess this population follows.

Structured Diagnostic Interview

Structured diagnostic interviews are important for youths with social and performance anxiety and oppositional and school refusal behavior because of the heterogeneity of the symptoms involved. Most youths in this population display a combination of internalizing and externalizing disorders, so a diagnostic interview allows a clinician to prioritize treatment targets. For some youths, social and performance anxiety is the primary issue, and oppositional behavior will subside once anxiety is reduced. For other youths, oppositionality is the primary issue and may be aggravated by social and performance anxiety. Many youths, for example, have been out of school for a lengthy period of time and are understandably anxious about returning to interact with and face questions from peers, teachers, and others.

Several diagnostic interviews are available for youths, but a common one for the population discussed in this chapter is the Anxiety Disorders Interview Schedule for *DSM–IV*: Child and Parent Versions (ADIS for *DSM–IV*: C/P; Silverman & Albano, 1996). The ADIS for *DSM–IV*: C/P has excellent psychometric properties and contains sections for school refusal behavior as well as various anxiety, mood, and disruptive behavior disorders, among others (Silverman, Saavedra, & Pina, 2001; Wood, Piacentini, Bergman, McCracken, & Barrios, 2002). The ADIS for *DSM–IV*: C/P is widely used in empirical studies of anxious youth and as an outcome measure. The ADIS for *DSM–IV*: C/P allows clinicians to identify and prioritize relevant diagnoses for a given case but also contributes to the development of a hierarchy of items of most concern for youths and their parents.

Youth Self-Report and Parent and Teacher Questionnaires

Several youth self-report and parent and teacher questionnaires are relevant for the population discussed in this chapter. Some of these measures are covered in other chapters (see Chapters 10 and 12, this volume), and the reader is referred to those sections for more information. The measures discussed next have excellent psychometric properties. Common youth self-report measures regarding social and performance anxiety include the Social Anxiety Scale for Adolescents (La Greca & Lopez, 1998) and Social Phobia and Anxiety Inventory for Children (Beidel, Turner, & Morris, 1995). Key concepts covered by these scales include fear of negative evaluation, social situation fears, assertiveness, general conversation, physical and cognitive symptoms, avoidance, and public performance (Beidel, Turner, & Fink, 1996; La Greca, 1998). Other youth self-report measures have subscales devoted to social and performance anxiety. These measures include the Multidimensional Anxiety Scale for Children (including humiliation and performance fears; March, 1997), Screen for Child Anxiety-Related Disorders (Birmaher et al., 1999), and Spence Children's Anxiety Scale (Spence, Barrett, & Turner, 2003). A popular youth self-report measure of internalizing and externalizing behavior problems that includes aspects of social anxiety and oppositionality is the Youth Self-Report (Achenbach & Rescorla, 2001).

Parent and teacher questionnaires typically cover internalizing and externalizing behavior problems and often shed light on the considerable symptom heterogeneity evident in the population discussed in this chapter. Relevant measures include the Child Behavior Checklist and Teacher's Report Form (Achenbach & Rescorla, 2001), Conners Parent Rating Scale and Conners Teacher Rating Scale (Conners, 2008), and Behavior Assessment System for Children—2 (Reynolds & Kamphaus, 2004). The Behavior Assessment System for Children—2, for example, covers a range of behaviors applicable to school-refusing youths, including adaptability, anxiety, conduct problems, depression, learning problems, social skills, somatization, study skills, and withdrawal.

Another set of measures more specific to youths with difficulties attending school includes the School Refusal Assessment Scale—Revised (child and parent versions; SRAS–R–C/SRAS–R–P; Kearney, 2002, 2006). The SRAS–R is a 24-item measure of the relative influence of the primary functions or maintaining variables of school refusal behavior: school-related stimuli that provoke negative affectivity, escape from aversive school-based social and/or evaluative situations, pursuit of attention from significant others, and pursuit of tangible rewards outside of school (six items per function). Youths and parents complete their relevant version of the SRAS–R and the clinician calculates item means for each function. The function with the highest item mean score across administrations of the SRAS–R is considered the primary maintaining variable of school refusal behavior.

Observations

Structured diagnostic interviews and youth self-report and parent and teacher questionnaires provide a good overview of social and performance anxiety with oppositional and school refusal behavior. Observations, however, help provide more specific information about a youth's daily behaviors. Many youths of this population, for example, demonstrate fluid changes in attendance, anxiety, and noncompliance that are not adequately captured by questionnaires (Kearney & Bates, 2005). In addition, parent and school official responses to a youth's school refusal behavior are important influences that should be assessed. Observations, especially in the morning before school and during high-risk times throughout the day when a youth may leave the school campus, are quite useful for determining treatment targets.

Observations can be formal or informal in nature. Formal observations involve specified procedures to record verbal and physical resistance to school preparation and attendance, ratings of negative affectivity before and during school, actual time spent in school, and noncompliance at school (Kearney & Tillotson, 1998). Youths and parents may also engage in self-monitoring practices or logbooks to provide daily ratings of negative affectivity and noncompliance (Kearney & Silverman, 1999). Informal observations can also be conducted by a clinician, parent, or school official to support or refute a hypothesis about the primary function of school refusal behavior.

Review of Records

Clinicians who assess cases of school refusal behavior involving social and performance anxiety and oppositionality should also review relevant academic, formal testing, and attendance records available at most schools (Kearney, 2008a). Academic records include information about grades and class schedules, and formal testing results may reveal cognitive, learning, or other behavioral problems that need to be addressed in treatment. Clinicians should also maintain regular contact with school guidance counselors and psychologists to coordinate further testing as necessary. Attendance records are important for understanding the developmental trajectory of a youth's absenteeism.

TREATING SOCIAL AND PERFORMANCE ANXIETY WITH OPPOSITIONAL AND SCHOOL REFUSAL BEHAVIOR

Treating youths with social and performance anxiety and oppositional and school refusal behavior requires a delicate but intense process with various goals. The most urgent goal is usually to stabilize school attendance or establish full-time attendance but within the context of reducing social and performance anxiety and oppositionality. Some cases involve less severity and a relatively straightforward clinical approach, but other cases involve more complexity because of increased severity and greater number of contributing contextual variables (for a complete listing, see Kearney, 2008b). The following sections outline treatment strategies for less severe and more severe cases of social and performance anxiety with oppositional and school refusal behavior.

Clinical Strategies for Less Severe Cases

Less severe cases of social and performance anxiety with oppositional and school refusal behavior often involve emerging symptomatology and absenteeism, fewer contextual variables, and more circumscribed avoidance. Clinicians and researchers often use several cognitive behavioral family systems techniques to address such cases (Bernstein et al., 2000; Heyne et al., 2002; Kearney & Silverman, 1999; King et al., 1998; Last, Hansen, & Franco, 1998). These clinical techniques are summarized in Exhibit 7.1 and concentrate primarily on anxiety management, parent training, and family-based intervention to reduce distress and ease reentry to full-time school attendance. Anxiety management techniques include psychoeducation regarding key aspects of anxiety, somatic control exercises to reduce physical symptoms of anxiety, cognitive restructuring to modify inaccurate thoughts regarding school-based social and evaluative situations, and hierarchies with exposure-based practice to gradually reintegrate a child to school and perform effectively

EXHIBIT 7.1
Cognitive Behavioral Techniques for School Refusal Behavior
With Social and Performance Anxiety and Oppositionality

Cognitive restructuring: Youth-based approach to identify and modify maladaptive thoughts about peers and other stimuli at school, especially in social and evaluative situations, to boost adaptive and realistic thinking.

Contingency contracting: Family-based approach emphasizing written contracts between parents and a youth to increase incentives for school attendance, disincentives for school nonattendance, and daily supervision of the youth.

Contingency management: Parent-based approach to develop regular morning and daily routines, alter commands toward brevity and clarity, ignore school refusal behaviors such as tantrums, and provide consequences for attendance and nonattendance; school-based personnel may also be included in this process.

Coping skills training: Youth-based approach to increase problem-solving ability and assertiveness at school; may be combined with social and peer refusal skills training.

Exposure-based practice: Gradual or stepwise reintegration of a youth into school, such as one class or hour at a time; often conducted with anxiety management techniques such as hierarchy development, cognitive restructuring and somatic control exercises.

Hierarchy development: Construction of a list of school-related social and other situations that range from least to most anxiety provoking to provide structure for exposure-based practice.

Peer refusal skills training: Youth-based approach to teach a youth methods to refuse offers to miss school or avoid high-risk situations that provoke absenteeism.

Psychoeducation: Educating youth and parents about the primary components of a youth's absentee behaviors and providing a rationale for treatment; often conducted with rapport-building.

Somatic control exercises: Youth-based relaxation training and breathing retraining to reduce physical symptoms of anxiety associated with school attendance.

in social and performance situations. Youths may also be taught coping and social skills to increase problem-solving ability and assertiveness as well as peer refusal skills to decline offers to miss school (Kearney & Albano, 2007). Parent training techniques typically focus on contingency management practices to reestablish parental control over daily routines and consequences for behavior, especially attendance and nonattendance. Parent training techniques also can be modified for school-based professionals, such as teachers (King et al., 1998).

Pina, Zerr, Gonzales, and Ortiz (2009) conducted a meta-analysis of cognitive behavioral interventions for school refusal behavior that largely involved the techniques listed in Exhibit 7.1. Across the included studies, school attendance improved from 30% at pretest to 75% at posttest (range at posttest: 47%–100%). Cognitive behavioral therapy was found to be effective for some domains (e.g., anxiety) more so than others (e.g., depression). A downside to cognitive behavioral therapy approaches, however, is that they may not be applicable to a wider range of youths who refuse school, especially those who display more severe social and performance anxiety and oppositional and school refusal behavior as well as contributing contextual factors. A broader approach to address these more severe cases is presented next.

Broader Strategies for More Severe Cases

Several researchers have called for a broader approach to address youths with various levels of social and performance anxiety and oppositional and school refusal behavior (Kearney, 2003, 2008a; Lyon & Cotler, 2007; Reid, 2003). This approach often involves expansive and multidisciplinary strategies to address ongoing episodes of school refusal behavior that include a wide array of reasons for nonattendance, more severe social and performance anxiety, and greater disruption in a family's or youth's daily functioning. Anxiety management and some contingency management techniques (e.g., structured morning routine) described previously are likely necessary, but a family-based approach is often critical as well. Such an approach may include contingency contracting to boost incentives for attendance and disincentives for nonattendance (Vaal, 1973). Part-time attendance schedules may be used first and include some favorite classes or times of the day or attendance in a supervised school area that does not necessarily involve a classroom (e.g., nurse's office, library; Kearney & Bensaheb, 2006).

A broader approach to treatment for more severe cases must also involve extensive collaboration with school-based personnel such as guidance counselors, school psychologists, school-based social workers, principals, teachers, and attendance officers. Such collaboration should focus on developing a clear and gradual strategy for reintegrating a youth to school, resolving academic deficiencies that have resulted from nonattendance, reducing obstacles to attendance, identifying and addressing high-risk times for premature departure from school, and bolstering parent–school official contact. Clinicians with more complex school refusal behavior cases may meet with parents and school officials together to develop a consensual plan for remediating attendance and related problems (Kearney & Hugelshofer, 2000).

Once a part-time school attendance schedule is stabilized, intervention must then turn to related issues. Related issues often involve extensive family conflict, oppositional behavior, alienation from or intimidation by peers at school, association with deviant peers, adjustment difficulties, and legal problems (King & Bernstein, 2001). Family conflict will often abate once school attendance resumes and some semblance of a daily routine is restored. Family conflict in these cases can be addressed as well by incorporating communication skills training in the problem-solving and contracting process. A key goal is to enhance a family's ability to define problems, collaboratively develop solutions, refrain from maladaptive behaviors such as lecturing, and prioritize, implement, and evaluate effective solutions. School attendance, school preparation behaviors, and clear rules and expectations for behavior are common targets of this process for the population discussed in this chapter.

Peers are an important influence on adolescents with school refusal behavior as well and social and performance anxiety and must therefore be addressed in treatment (Egger et al., 2003; Mcshane et al., 2001). This may involve greater participation of the adolescent in school-based extracurricular activities, integration of positive peers in morning classes and lunch to build social support, and greater exposure to peers of similar ethnicity if desired. Friends may be incorporated as well into exposure-based practices needed to reduce social and performance anxiety in school-based situations.

Clinicians also need to address the matter of deviant peers who issue offers to miss school or who intimidate. *Peer refusal skills training* refers to the acquisition of methods to refuse offers to miss school or avoid high-risk situations that provoke absenteeism (Kearney & Albano, 2007). Youths should also be taught methods necessary to address teasing, bullying, or other forms of peer victimization (Salmivalli, Kaukiainen, & Voeten, 2005). Such methods may include reducing social isolation, informing adults of a threatening situation, and providing effective rejoinders to verbal jabs from others. Contracts may be manipulated as well to increase association with positive peers.

The oppositional behavior demonstrated by many of these adolescents, especially those who miss parts of a school day, means that increased parent and school official supervision is necessary. Some youths will agree to provisions of a contract but remain unable to attend school and thus receive appropriate rewards. Parents and school officials may need to escort a youth to school and from class to class and monitor high-risk times for premature departure from school. These methods must be used with great discretion, however, given the importance of peer perceptions during adolescence as well as social anxiety that may lead to greater school avoidance. Attendance journals are recommended as well and require a youth to secure signatures from teachers in each class to demonstrate evidence of attendance (Kearney & Bates, 2005). If a youth is found to be out of school during regular school hours, then attempts should be made to locate him or her and return him or her to school.

Intervention with more complicated cases may also require mobilizing a family's social support network; easing logistical problems such as transportation and language barriers; expanding the treatment plan to address other common comorbid conditions, such as depression or suicidality; pursuing a slower pace of school reintegration; and mediating between parents and school officials. Clinicians may find it necessary to work with school officials to develop individualized education or 504 plans that allow for part-time attendance, curriculum revision, modifications in class schedule and academic work, escorts to school and class, attendance journals, increased supervision, and regular feedback to parents regarding attendance and academic performance (Terjesen, Jacofsky, Froh, & DiGiuseppe, 2004). Clinicians should note that restoring full-time attendance is not always possible in extended cases of school refusal behavior with substantial oppositionality and social and performance anxiety. The final goal is sometimes a modified educational program that allows for more gradual accumulation of academic credit and that may involve summer classes, alternative educational programs, and partial classroom attendance.

Others contend that clinicians could become involved in *exosystem* interventions that focus on social structures and policies that create a general impact on absenteeism (Lyon & Cotler, 2009). Clinicians could donate services to local truancy court and truancy diversion programs; consult with juvenile justice and other agencies regarding extant legal procedures to reduce absenteeism; participate in research-based trials of systemic interventions that include school attendance as a key variable; develop multidisciplinary teams within their locale to boost availability and consistency of health-based services; and investigate interventions that focus on crisis resolution, mobilization of family resources, and links to community resources.

The prognosis in more severe cases of school refusal is fair to good if relapse prevention strategies also are established and practiced. Such strategies include continued close supervision of attendance, fast resolution of obstacles to attendance, ongoing practice of therapeutic strategies that helped improve attendance, and continued collaboration between parents and school officials. In addition, youths will benefit greatly from increased social and academic competence and association with prosocial peers. Other important relapse prevention ideas include maintaining regular morning routines, easing adjustment problems following a long break from school, and providing booster sessions as needed to enhance social and academic skills (Kearney, 2008a).

SUMMARY AND CONCLUSIONS

Adolescents with oppositional behavior, social anxiety, and school refusal behavior represent an important clinical population that deserves more research attention. Specific models have been designed to conceptualize each of these behavior problems in isolation, but less work has been done on youths with all three characteristics. Clinicians may wish to engage in a thorough behavioral assessment of these adolescents, especially in cases involving extensive absenteeism, and focus most urgently on returning a youth to school as quickly as possible. In many cases, resolving an absentee problem greatly facilitates the treatment of related issues such as noncompliance and social anxiety. Youths with oppositional behavior, social anxiety, and school refusal behavior also require extensive follow-up to prevent remission toward avoidance or absenteeism.

REFERENCES

Achenbach, T. M., & Rescorla, L. A. (2001). *Manual for the ASEBA school-age forms and profiles*. Burlington, VT: University of Vermont Research Center for Children, Youth, & Families.

Albano, A. M., & Detweiler, M. F. (2001). The developmental and clinical impact of social anxiety and social phobia in children and adolescents. In S. G. Hofmann & P. M. DiBartolo (Eds.), *From social anxiety to social phobia: Multiple perspectives* (pp. 162–178). Needham Heights, MA: Allyn & Bacon.

American Psychiatric Association. (2000). *Diagnostic and statistical manual of mental disorders* (4th ed., text rev.). Washington, DC: Author.

Atkinson, L., Quarrington, B., Cyr, J. J., & Atkinson, F. V. (1989). Differential classification of school refusal. *The British Journal of Psychiatry, 155*, 191–195. doi:10.1192/bjp.155.2.191

Attwood, G., & Croll, P. (2006). Truancy in secondary school pupils: Prevalence, trajectories and pupil perspectives. *Research Papers in Education, 21*, 467–484. doi:10.1080/02671520600942446

Beidel, D. C., Turner, S. M., & Fink, C. M. (1996). Assessment of childhood social phobia: Construct, convergent, and discriminative validity of the Social Phobia and Anxiety Inventory for Children (SPAI-C). *Psychological Assessment, 8*, 235–240. doi:10.1037/1040-3590.8.3.235

Beidel, D. C., Turner, S. M., & Morris, T. L. (1995). A new inventory to assess childhood social anxiety and phobia: The Social Phobia and Anxiety Inventory for Children. *Psychological Assessment, 7*, 73–79. doi:10.1037/1040-3590.7.1.73

Beidel, D. C., Turner, S. M., & Morris, T. L. (1999). Psychopathology of childhood social phobia. *Journal of the American Academy of Child and Adolescent Psychiatry, 38*, 643–650. doi:10.1097/00004583-199906000-00010

Berg, I., Butler, A., Franklin, J., Hayes, H., Lucas, C., & Sims, R. (1993). DSM–III–R disorders, social factors and management of school attendance problems in the normal population. *Journal of Child Psychology and Psychiatry, and Allied Disciplines, 34*, 1187–1203. doi:10.1111/j.1469-7610.1993.tb01782.x

Berg, I., Casswell, G., Goodwin, A., Hullin, R., McGuire, R., & Tagg, G. (1985). Classification of severe attendance problems. *Psychological Medicine, 15*, 157–165. doi:10.1017/S0033291700021024

Berg, I., & Jackson, A. (1985). Teenage school refusers grow up: A follow-up study of 168 subjects, ten years on average after inpatient treatment. *The British Journal of Psychiatry, 147*, 366–370. doi:10.1192/bjp.147.4.366

Bernstein, G. A., Borchardt, C. M., Perwein, A. R., Crosby, R. D., Kushner, M. G., Thuras, P. D., & Last, C. G. (2000). Imipramine plus cognitive-behavioral therapy in the treatment of school refusal. *Journal of the American Academy of Child and Adolescent Psychiatry, 39*, 276–283. doi:10.1097/00004583-200003000-00008

Bernstein, G. A., & Garfinkel, B. D. (1986). School phobia: The overlap of affective and anxiety disorders. *Journal of the American Academy of Child Psychiatry, 25*, 235–241. doi:10.1016/S0002-7138(09)60231-4

Birmaher, B., Brent, D. A., Chiappetta, L., Bridge, J., Monga, S., & Baugher, M. (1999). Psychometric properties of the Screen for Child Anxiety Related Emotional Disorders (SCARED): A replication study. *Journal of the American Academy of Child and Adolescent Psychiatry, 38*, 1230–1236. doi:10.1097/00004583-199910000-00011

Broadwin, I. T. (1932). A contribution to the study of truancy. *American Journal of Orthopsychiatry, 2*, 253–259. doi:10.1111/j.1939-0025.1932.tb05183.x

Buitelaar, J. K., van Andel, H., Duyx, J. H. M., & van Strien, D. C. (1994). Depressive and anxiety disorders in adolescence: A follow-up study of adolescents with school refusal. *Acta Paedopsychiatrica, 56*, 249–253.

Conners, C. K. (2008). *Conners third edition* (Conners 3). Retrieved from http://www.pearsonassessments.com/HAIWEB/Cultures/en-us/Productdetail.htm?Pid=Conners_3

Davidson, J. R. T., Hughes, D. L., George, L. K., & Blazer, D. G. (1993). The epidemiology of social phobia: Findings from the Duke Epidemiological Catchment Area Study. *Psychological Medicine, 23*, 709–718. doi:10.1017/S0033291700025484

Davidson, J. R. T., Hughes, D. L., George, L. K., & Blazer, D. G. (1994). The boundary of social phobia: Exploring the threshold. *Archives of General Psychiatry, 51*, 975–983.

Egger, H. L., Costello, E. J., & Angold, A. (2003). School refusal and psychiatric disorders: A community study. *Journal of the American Academy of Child and Adolescent Psychiatry, 42,* 797–807. doi:10.1097/01.CHI.0000046865.56865.79

Flakierska-Praquin, N., Lindstrom, M., & Gillberg, C. (1997). School phobia with separation anxiety disorder: A comparative 20- to 29-year follow-up study of 35 school refusers. *Comprehensive Psychiatry, 38,* 17–22. doi:10.1016/S0010-440X(97)90048-1

Granell de Aldaz, E., Feldman, L., Vivas, E., & Gelfand, D. M. (1987). Characteristics of Venezuelan school refusers: Toward the development of a high-risk profile. *Journal of Nervous and Mental Disease, 175,* 402–407. doi:10.1097/00005053-198707000-00003

Harada, Y., Yamazaki, T., & Saitoh, K. (2002). Psychosocial problems in attention-deficit hyperactivity disorder with oppositional defiant disorder. *Psychiatry and Clinical Neurosciences, 56,* 365–369. doi:10.1046/j.1440-1819.2002.01024.x

Henry, K. L., & Huizinga, D.H. (2007). Truancy's effect on the onset of drug use among urban adolescents placed at risk. *Journal of Adolescent Health, 40,* 358.e9-358.e17.

Heyne, D., King, N. J., Tonge, B. J., Rollings, S., Young, D., Pritchard, M., & Ollendick, T. H. (2002). Evaluation of child therapy and caregiver training in the treatment of school refusal. *Journal of the American Academy of Child and Adolescent Psychiatry, 41,* 687–695. doi:10.1097/00004583-200206000-00008

Hibbett, A., & Fogelman, K. (1990). Future lives of truants: Family formation and health-related behaviour. *The British Journal of Educational Psychology, 60,* 171–179.

Jimerson, S., Egeland, B., Sroufe, L. A., & Carlson, B. (2000). A prospective longitudinal study of high school dropouts examining multiple predictors across development. *Journal of School Psychology, 38,* 525–549. doi:10.1016/S0022-4405(00)00051-0

Kearney, C. A. (2001). *School refusal behavior in youth: A functional approach to assessment and treatment.* Washington, DC: American Psychological Association. doi:10.1037/10426-000

Kearney, C. A. (2002). Identifying the function of school refusal behavior: A revision of the School Refusal Assessment Scale. *Journal of Psychopathology and Behavioral Assessment, 24,* 235–245. doi:10.1023/A:1020774932043

Kearney, C. A. (2003). Bridging the gap among professionals who address youth with school absenteeism: Overview and suggestions for consensus. *Professional Psychology, Research and Practice, 34,* 57–65. doi:10.1037/0735-7028.34.1.57

Kearney, C. A. (2005). *Social anxiety and social phobia in youth: Characteristics, assessment, and psychological treatment.* New York, NY: Springer.

Kearney, C. A. (2006). Confirmatory factor analysis of the School Refusal Assessment Scale—Revised: Child and parent versions. *Journal of Psychopathology and Behavioral Assessment, 28,* 139–144. doi:10.1007/s10862-005-9005-6

Kearney, C. A. (2007). Forms and functions of school refusal behavior in youth: An empirical analysis of absenteeism severity. *Journal of Child Psychology and Psychiatry, and Allied Disciplines, 48*, 53–61. doi:10.1111/j.1469-7610.2006.01634.x

Kearney, C. A. (2008a). *Helping school refusing children and their parents: A guide for school-based professionals*. New York, NY: Oxford University Press.

Kearney, C. A. (2008b). An interdisciplinary model of school absenteeism in youth to inform professional practice and public policy. *Educational Psychology Review, 20*, 257–282. doi:10.1007/s10648-008-9078-3

Kearney, C. A. (2008c). School absenteeism and school refusal behavior in youth: A contemporary review. *Clinical Psychology Review, 28*, 451–471. doi:10.1016/j.cpr.2007.07.012

Kearney, C. A., & Albano, A. M. (2004). The functional profiles of school refusal behavior: Diagnostic aspects. *Behavior Modification, 28*, 147–161. doi:10.1177/0145445503259263

Kearney, C. A., & Albano, A. M. (2007). *When children refuse school: A cognitive-behavioral therapy approach—Therapist guide*. New York, NY: Oxford University Press.

Kearney, C. A., & Bates, M. (2005). Addressing school refusal behavior: Suggestions for frontline professionals. *Children & Schools, 27*, 207–216.

Kearney, C. A., & Bensaheb, A. (2006). School absenteeism and school refusal behavior: A review and suggestions for school-based health professionals. *The Journal of School Health, 76*, 3–7. doi:10.1111/j.1746-1561.2006.00060.x

Kearney, C. A., & Hugelshofer, D. S. (2000). Systemic and clinical strategies for preventing school refusal behavior in youth. *Journal of Cognitive Psychotherapy, 14*, 51–65.

Kearney, C. A., & Silverman, W. K. (1996). The evolution and reconciliation of taxonomic strategies for school refusal behavior. *Clinical Psychology: Science and Practice, 3*, 339–354. doi:10.1111/j.1468-2850.1996.tb00087.x

Kearney, C. A., & Silverman, W. K. (1999). Functionally-based prescriptive and non-prescriptive treatment for children and adolescents with school refusal behavior. *Behavior Therapy, 30*, 673–695. doi:10.1016/S0005-7894(99)80032-X

Kearney, C. A., & Tillotson, C. A. (1998). School attendance. In T. S. Watson & F. M. Gresham (Eds.), *Handbook of child behavior therapy* (pp. 143–161). New York, NY: Plenum Press.

Kennedy, W. A. (1965). School phobia: Rapid treatment of 50 cases. *Journal of Abnormal Psychology, 70*, 285–289. doi:10.1037/h0022440

King, N. J., & Bernstein, G. A. (2001). School refusal in children and adolescents: A review of the past 10 years. *Journal of the American Academy of Child and Adolescent Psychiatry, 40*, 197–205. doi:10.1097/00004583-200102000-00014

King, N. J., Tonge, B. J., Heyne, D., Pritchard, M., Rollings, S., Young, D., . . . Ollendick, T. H. (1998). Cognitive-behavioral treatment of school-refusing children: A controlled evaluation. *Journal of the American Academy of Child and Adolescent Psychiatry, 37*, 395–403. doi:10.1097/00004583-199804000-00017

Kolvin, I., Berney, T. P., & Bhate, S. R. (1984). Classification and diagnosis of depression in school phobia. *The British Journal of Psychiatry, 145*, 347–357. doi:10.1192/bjp.145.4.347

La Greca, A. M. (1998). *Social anxiety scales for children and adolescents: Manual and instructions for the SASC, SASC–R, SAS–A (adolescents), and parent versions of the scales.* Miami, FL: Author.

La Greca, A. M., & Lopez, N. (1998). Social anxiety among adolescents: Linkages with peer relations and friendships. *Journal of Abnormal Child Psychology, 26*, 83–94. doi:10.1023/A:1022684520514

La Greca, A. M., & Stone, W. L. (1993). Social Anxiety Scale for Children— Revised: Factor structure and concurrent validity. *Journal of Clinical Child Psychology, 22*, 17–27. doi:10.1207/s15374424jccp2201_2

Last, C. G., Hansen, C., & Franco, N. (1998). Cognitive-behavioral treatment of school phobia. *Journal of the American Academy of Child and Adolescent Psychiatry, 37*, 404–411. doi:10.1097/00004583-199804000-00018

Lyon, A. R., & Cotler, S. (2007). Toward reduced bias and increased utility in the assessment of school refusal behavior: The case for divergent samples and evaluation of context. *Psychology in the Schools, 44*, 551–565. doi:10.1002/pits.20247

Lyon, A. R., & Cotler, S. (2009). Multi-systemic intervention for school refusal behavior: Integrating approaches across disciplines. *Advances in School Mental Health Promotion, 2*, 20–34.

March, J. (1997). *Multidimensional Anxiety Scale for Children.* North Tonawanda, NY: Multi-Health Systems.

McCune, N., & Hynes, J. (2005). Ten year follow-up of children with school refusal. *International Journal of Psychiatry in Medicine, 22*, 56–58.

Mcshane, G., Walter, G., & Rey, J. M. (2001). Characteristics of adolescents with school refusal. *The Australian and New Zealand Journal of Psychiatry, 35*, 822–826. doi:10.1046/j.1440-1614.2001.00955.x

Mcshane, G., Walter, G., & Rey, J. M. (2004). Functional outcome of adolescents with 'school refusal.' *Clinical Child Psychology and Psychiatry, 9*, 53–60. doi:10.1177/1359104504039172

Partridge, J. M. (1939). Truancy. *The Journal of Mental Science, 85*, 45–81.

Pina, A. A., Zerr, A. A., Gonzales, N. A., & Ortiz, C. D. (2009). Psychosocial interventions for school refusal behavior in children and adolescents. *Child Development Perspectives, 3*, 11–20. doi:10.1111/j.1750-8606.2008.00070.x

Reid, K. (2003). A strategic approach for tackling school absenteeism and truancy: The PSCC scheme. *Educational Studies, 29*, 351–371. doi:10.1080/0305569032000159660

Reynolds, C. R., & Kamphaus, R. W. (2004). *Behavior Assessment System for Children—2*. Circle Pines, MN: American Guidance Service.

Rubin, K. H., Burgess, K. B., Kennedy, A. E., & Stewart, S. L. (2003). Social withdrawal in childhood. In E. J. Mash & R. A. Barkley (Eds.), *Child psychopathology* (2nd ed., pp. 372–406). New York, NY: Guilford Press.

Salmivalli, C., Kaukiainen, A., & Voeten, M. (2005). Anti-bullying intervention: Implementation and outcome. *The British Journal of Educational Psychology, 75*, 465–487. doi:10.1348/000709905X26011

Schlenker, B. R., & Leary, M. R. (1982). Social anxiety and self-presentation: A conceptualization and model. *Psychological Bulletin, 92*, 641–669. doi:10.1037/0033-2909.92.3.641

Silverman, W. K., & Albano, A. M. (1996). *The Anxiety Disorders Interview Schedule for Children for DSM–IV: Child and Parent Versions*. San Antonio, TX: Psychological Corporation.

Silverman, W. K., Saavedra, L. M., & Pina, A. A. (2001). Test–retest reliability of anxiety symptoms and diagnoses with the Anxiety Disorders Interview Schedule for DSM–IV: Child and Parent Versions. *Journal of the American Academy of Child and Adolescent Psychiatry, 40*, 937–944. doi:10.1097/00004583-200108000-00016

Spence, S. H., Barrett, P. M., & Turner, C. M. (2003). Psychometric properties of the Spence Children's Anxiety Scale with young adolescents. *Journal of Anxiety Disorders, 17*, 605–625. doi:10.1016/S0887-6185(02)00236-0

Tarolla, S. M., Wagner, E. F., Rabinowitz, J., & Tubman, J. G. (2002). Understanding and treating juvenile offenders: A review of current knowledge and future directions. *Aggression and Violent Behavior, 7*, 125–144. doi:10.1016/S1359-1789(00)00041-0

Terjesen, M. D., Jacofsky, M., Froh, J., & DiGiuseppe, R. (2004). Integrating positive psychology into schools: Implications for practice. *Psychology in the Schools, 41*, 163–172. doi:10.1002/pits.10148

Vaal, J. J. (1973). Applying contingency contracting to a school phobic: A case study. *Journal of Behavior Therapy and Experimental Psychiatry, 4*, 371–373. doi:10.1016/0005-7916(73)90012-8

Weiss, M., & Burke, A. G. (1967). A five to ten-year follow-up of hospitalized school phobic children and adolescents. *American Journal of Orthopsychiatry, 37*, 294–295.

Wood, J. J., Piacentini, J. C., Bergman, L., McCracken, J., & Barrios, V. (2002). Concurrent validity of the anxiety disorders section of the Anxiety Disorders Interview Schedule for DSM–IV: Child and Parent Versions. *Journal of Clinical Child and Adolescent Psychology, 31*, 335–342.

8

PEER RELATIONS AND VICTIMIZATION IN ADOLESCENTS WITH SOCIAL ANXIETY DISORDER

BRIDGET K. BIGGS, MARILYN L. SAMPILO,
AND MEGAN M. McFADDEN

In this chapter, we provide an overview of the interpersonal function-ing of adolescents and young adults with social anxiety disorder (SAD). We begin with a description of the social worlds of socially anxious adolescents, including the number and quality of friendships, social standing within the larger peer group, and experiences with peer victimization. Next, we describe a conceptual model for the relationship between SAD and peer relational dif-ficulties. We then look more closely at social skills and thought processes asso-ciated with social anxiety that could affect social interactions and lead to the development of SAD. Understanding these processes is important for identi-fying targets for intervention. Throughout the chapter, we highlight charac-teristics of individuals or their environments that may increase the severity of symptoms and dysfunction (i.e., risk factors) and factors that may lead to more positive outcomes (i.e., protective factors). Because, in many cases, research among young people with SAD is not available, we review findings for social anxiety and peer relationships more broadly.

THE SOCIAL WORLD OF ADOLESCENTS
WITH SOCIAL ANXIETY DISORDER

The peer networks of adolescents and young adults consist of complex webs of close relationships (e.g., friendships, romantic relationships), which are embedded in groups of friends (i.e., cliques), formal (e.g., clubs) and informal (e.g., Saturday pickup basketball) groups, and reputational crowds (e.g., "athletes," "brains," "populars"). Although some studies have described the social functioning of youth with SAD, much of what researchers know currently about the connection between social anxiety and peer relations comes from research investigating peer relations among community samples. Nonetheless, this body of work provides a picture of the quality of relationships and social challenges youth with high levels of social anxiety experience.

Friendships

Friendships in adolescence are generally described as close relationships built on shared interests and mutual appreciation and liking. They differ from younger children's friendships in that they are among the most significant sources of emotional support as adolescents grow in independence from parents and gravitate toward their peers (Buhrmester & Furman, 1987). Adolescents look to close friendships for intimacy and acceptance (Berndt, 2004). Friendships provide opportunities for reciprocal feedback regarding social behavior, are linked to positive outcomes in adjustment (Hartup, 1996), and can protect against negative treatment from other peers (e.g., Hodges, Boivin, Vitaro, & Bukowski, 1999).

Adolescents who report high social anxiety tend to have a smaller network of friends from which to draw support (La Greca & Lopez, 1998). Further, these few friends may not provide the same level of benefit typically expected in good quality friendships because social anxiety symptoms are correlated with lower friendship quality, including less time spent together, fewer intimate exchanges, higher conflict, and poor conflict resolution (La Greca & Lopez, 1998; Vernberg, Abwender, Ewell, & Beery, 1992). These effects differ slightly for boys and girls such that girls report greater social anxiety, which is more strongly related to friendship quantity and quality among girls (La Greca & Lopez, 1998).

Part of the problem might be that shy, anxious youth form friendships with others who have similar social difficulties. For example, Rubin, Wojslawowicz, Rose-Kasnor, Booth-LaForce, and Burgess (2006) examined the friendships of shy or withdrawn children and found that they and their identified best friends were similarly withdrawn, rejected, and victimized in their peer groups. These authors posited that these children may experience more limited benefits of friendships and their friendships may have less protective power against negative events such as peer victimization. This idea is consistent with the writings of Berndt (2002), who suggested that the repertoire of behaviors developed within friendships will generalize to youths' interactions with others outside the immediate friendship circle. Youth in poor-quality friendships may develop patterns of social behavior that elicit negative reactions not only from friends but also from others.

Relations With Peer Groups

Youth high in social anxiety are also likely to experience difficulties with the larger peer group. Social anxiety is associated with lower peer acceptance (Erath, Flanagan, & Bierman, 2007; Inderbitzen, Walters, & Bukowski, 1997) and lower support from classmates (La Greca & Lopez, 1998). Neglected and rejected adolescents appear particularly vulnerable to social anxiety (Inderbitzen et al., 1997). Research suggests that socially anxious adolescents are likely to cope with social discomfort by withdrawing, which in turn limits the frequency of positive contact and leads to lower peer acceptance (Erath et al., 2007).

Adolescents tend to categorize their peer group into reputational crowds (e.g., brains, athletes, populars), and the groups to which adolescents are assigned are meaningfully related to internalizing problems both concurrently and longitudinally (Prinstein & La Greca, 2002). Specifically, level of social anxiety decreased over time for all peer crowd groups, with the exception of the brains (Prinstein & La Greca, 2002), suggesting that the brains appeared to be most vulnerable to persistent social anxiety. Prinstein and La Greca (2002) suggested that adolescent peer crowds influence individuals' self-concepts and subsequent well-being, including feelings of social anxiety. Although more research is needed to understand the influence of peer crowd affiliation on development and maintenance of SAD, these findings speak to the importance of understanding peer crowd affiliation.

Peer Victimization

Socially anxious adolescents are also at increased risk of peer victimization. The relationship between social anxiety and peer victimization appears to be bidirectional with each predicting the other in various studies. From these studies (Erath et al., 2007; Slee, 1994; Storch, Brassard, & Masia-Warner, 2003), victimization appears to be associated with fear of negative evaluation, a component of social anxiety, which can then lead to subsequent withdrawal or avoidance of both general and novel situations among adolescents and/or continued victimization. Furthermore, negative performance expectations and social disengagement appear to contribute to peer problems, perhaps because withdrawal from the peer group reduces opportunities for positive social engagement (Erath et al., 2007).

HOW DO DIFFICULTIES IN PEER RELATIONS DEVELOP? A VICIOUS CYCLE

By nature of their disorder, individuals with SAD find social situations, particularly new or unfamiliar ones, distressing. Theory and research (Erath et al., 2007; Rubin & Burgess, 2001) suggest that socially anxious youth may not know how to make friends or interact effectively with peers. Even if they have a sense of what to do, they may doubt their ability or fear negative responses from others. Rather than risk humiliation, they may find themselves on the fringes of a school dance or birthday party (or absent altogether). Many feel quite lonely and unsure how to improve their social situation. This plight does not emerge overnight; rather, it develops gradually over a series of connected events stemming from individual characteristics, behavior, and social experiences. Figure 8.1 provides a model for understanding the vicious cycle in which young people with SAD appear to be caught. It is important to keep in mind the unique experience of the individual and that not all adolescents with SAD follow the exact same path.

Early Risk of Social Anxiety and Peer Relations

It is our contention that by the time an individual develops SAD, early risk factors and manifestations of social anxiety may have had a mark on social

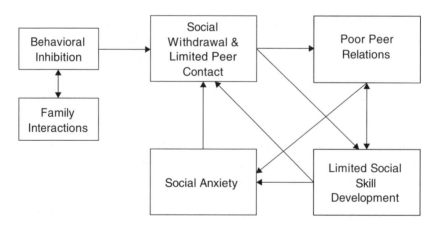

Figure 8.1. Conceptual model of the vicious cycle leading to the emergence of social anxiety and poor peer relations.

functioning and/or social problems may have influenced the development of the disorder. Thus, it is important to understand adolescents' current symptoms and social functioning as well as the development of those symptoms in relation to the individual's unique social history. Although every individual is different, the literature on the developmental psychopathology of SAD highlights several factors that could lead to both social anxiety and problematic peer relations, including temperamental characteristics, parenting practices, and negative peer interactions. Here, we focus our discussion on the role these factors could play in the social functioning of adolescents with or at risk of SAD.

An inhibited temperament has been implicated as a risk factor for internalizing problems generally and for SAD in particular (Kagan, 2008). A consistent pattern of caution and reserve can affect growing children's entry into the peer world, their level of comfort and behavior with peers, and the way in which peers respond to them. Inhibited temperament has been conceptually and empirically linked to socially withdrawn behavior in childhood (Rubin, Stewart, & Coplan, 1995). Shy temperament, as rated by parents, is one of the strongest predictors of low sociability with peers in preschool when multiple domains of temperament and parenting are considered (Russell, Hart, Robinson, & Olsen, 2003). In adolescence, individuals with SAD report a childhood history of greater inhibition than individuals with and without other anxiety disorders and are more likely to have problematic peer relations (Cunha, Soares, & Pinto-Gouveia, 2008).

Although there appears to be a strong biological basis, not all young children who are temperamentally inhibited shy away from peers, and few actually develop SAD (Kagan, 2008). Research has identified several moderating factors of the stability of behavioral inhibition, many of which involve parents. Theory and research on the development of social competence suggest that parents influence their children's social development by (a) providing an early model of social relationships and how they function, (b) teaching and advising how to interact with others, and (c) acting as social managers and supervisors of their children's peer activities (Parke et al., 2002). Interestingly, inhibition in toddlerhood has been associated with reticent social behavior in preschool only among children whose mothers were intrusive or hypercritical (Rubin, Burgess, & Hastings, 2002). Conceivably, if parents are overprotective and intrusive in their children's social lives, they could restrict their children's social contacts and opportunities to engage freely and confidently with other children. Although relatively little research has investigated the role of parents in the social lives of youth with SAD, intrusive and rejecting parenting styles are associated with risk for peer victimization (Finnegan, Hodges, & Perry, 1998).

On a positive note, parents of temperamentally inhibited children could arguably foster social competence and positive peer experiences by fostering a positive relationship with their child, modeling and teaching effective social skills, and facilitating positive social contacts. Research on parent facilitation of adolescents' friendships following relocation to a new community indicates that adolescents whose parents actively encouraged their adolescents' social engagement had higher quality friendships in their 1st year in the new community (Vernberg, Beery, Ewell, & Abwender, 1993). This effect was observed across groups of adolescents with various behavioral profiles, including those with elevated social anxiety and internalizing symptoms (Vernberg, Greenhoot, & Biggs, 2006).

Social Reticence and Withdrawal Affect Socialization

Shy, withdrawn children tend to remain on the outskirts of peer interactions, looking on without engaging with peers in both familiar and unfamiliar unstructured social settings (Rubin & Coplan, 2004). A tendency to keep to oneself combined with less positive peer interactions is believed to raise the risk of increasingly greater social isolation, which further limits opportunities for socialization and social skills development (Rubin et al., 1995).

Unfortunately, socially withdrawn behavior is fairly stable across childhood (Rubin, Hymel, & Mills, 1989) and early adolescence (Schneider, Younger, Smith, & Freeman, 1998), becomes less acceptable to peers from middle childhood through early adolescence (Younger & Piccinin, 1989), and is associated with a number of negative peer group experiences, including rejection and victimization (Erath et al., 2007; Rubin et al., 2006). Although some evidence suggests that shy and withdrawn youth are just as likely as their peers to have a best friend, research suggests their friends are similarly withdrawn and victimized and the quality of these friendships is not as strong (Rubin et al., 2006).

With limited peer socialization comes fewer opportunities to learn the skills to foster friendships and gain acceptance within the larger peer group. A growing body of research suggests that youth who are socially withdrawn or who have SAD are less socially skilled (e.g., Beidel, Turner, & Morris, 1999; Erath et al., 2007). It appears that social skills deficits and social anxiety are additively predictive of social withdrawal, which might lead to peer rejection and an ongoing cycle of social anxiety and social difficulties. The body of research on social anxiety and social skills is described in greater detail in the Keys to the Cycle sections.

On the other hand, positive experiences with peers could break this cycle. For example, high-quality friendships protect children with internalizing behaviors from peer victimization and the development of internalizing problems when an individual is victimized by peers (Hodges et al., 1999). In addition, peers can facilitate the development of social skills among youth with increased levels of social anxiety. Less understood is whether naturally occurring friendships and peer groups could alter the developmental course leading to and following the development of SAD. For example, caring, socially skilled friends; a supportive school class; or an encouraging sports team might facilitate greater social connection for youth with or at risk of SAD.

Poor Quality Peer Relations Increase Social Withdrawal and Anxiety

Socially withdrawn youth are at increased risk of social isolation. Exclusion from peers, friendlessness, and friendship instability (Oh et al., 2008) are associated with continued or increased social withdrawal in elementary school and adolescence. Further, social withdrawal becomes more strongly associated with internalizing psychopathology as children approach adolescence, and rejection from peers confers added risk of internalizing problems (Ladd, 2006). Apart from social withdrawal, studies support the idea that poor peer relations could contribute to the development of SAD specifically, and it appears that multiple aspects of adolescents' social worlds are important. In one study, positive peer nominations (the number of classmates who nominate an individual as a friend), peer victimization, and perceived friendship quality were uniquely associated with symptoms of social anxiety in early adolescence (Flanagan, Erath, & Bierman, 2008). Prospective work indicates that increases in social anxiety over time are associated with peer victimization (Storch, Masia-Warner, Crisp, & Klein, 2005), peer rejection experiences, and friendship quality (Vernberg et al., 1992).

Other Developmental Considerations

Adolescence is a period of transition that includes multiple points of change, including the onset of puberty (often identified as the onset of adolescence) and, at least in most industrialized nations, multiple school transitions. One could argue that these points in time are pivotal moments in the lives of youth with or at risk of SAD. Although few studies have investigated these topics directly as they relate to SAD, the current knowledge base points to potential risk factors and possible opportunities to shift the cycle of peer relations.

Puberty has been implicated in the emergence of gender differences in emotional distress during adolescence (Ge, Conger, & Elder, 2001). According to research, the further along girls are in their pubertal development, the greater their vulnerability to symptoms of social anxiety; in contrast, puberty does not appear to be related to social anxiety symptoms for boys (Deardorff et al., 2007). Girls who mature earlier than their peers show increased vulnerability to psychological distress in the face of prepuberty stressors. They are also more likely to associate with mixed-sex and deviant peer groups and tend to feel more socially isolated than their peers who started puberty "on time" or later (Ge et al., 1996). The authors interpreted these findings as evidence for the *early timing hypothesis*, which predicts that early pubertal onset places girls at risk of emotional and behavioral problems because their mature physical appearance elicits responses and expectations from their environment that they are not yet prepared to manage (Ge et al., 1996). Further, the quality of peer relations may matter because problematic peer relations have been associated with social anxiety symptoms among early maturing adolescents (Blumenthal, Leen-Feldner, Trainor, Babson, & Bunaciu, 2009). Clinically, these findings suggest that attention to pubertal timing and quality of peer relations are both important, particularly among girls.

During school transitions, having friends and fitting in are primary social goals for many adolescents. The importance placed on peers in school transitions appears warranted because shifts in social networks are common, at least in U.S. samples. In the transition to middle school, Aikins, Bierman, and Parker (2005) found that 63% of their sample reported a new best friend after starting middle school. Hardy, Bukowski, and Sippola (2002) similarly found that boys and girls formed new friendships with previously unfamiliar peers at increasing rates as they ended old friendships during the 1st year of junior high. School transitions are associated with a temporary increase in loneliness for the average adolescent (Pellegrini & Bartini, 2000), although having a consistent friend may protect adolescents from feelings of isolation during this time (Berndt, Hawkins, & Jiao, 1999). Further, adolescents who maintain friendships from elementary to middle school are more likely to enjoy positive social and academic adjustment in the new school environment (Aikins et al., 2005).

What might these findings mean for the lives of adolescents and young adults with SAD? Like many of their peers, adolescents with SAD might look forward to the opportunity to reinvent their social lives, especially if they have been dissatisfied with the social scene at their previous school. On the other hand, large school and class sizes, the potential ending of current friendships, and demands to make new friends may be daunting. Because active efforts are often needed to maintain and make new friendships (Oswald & Clark, 2003), adolescents who cope with these challenges by retreating or waiting passively for others to initiate interaction could be left behind. Given the importance of friendship as a buffer against loneliness and facilitator of overall adjustment to the new school, it makes sense that clinicians working with adolescents approaching school transitions focus on skills and actions to maintain and/or initiate friendships. For example, engagement in organized activities might help individuals with poor pretransition social adjustment form friendships and ward off loneliness in the new school, as has been found among individuals in the first year of college (Bohnert, Aikins, & Edidin, 2007).

KEYS TO THE CYCLE: SOCIAL SKILLS

As the model depicted in Figure 8.1 illustrates, socially anxious adolescents have a tendency to cope with anxious feelings that arise in social situations by avoiding or withdrawing. Avoidance strategies include pretending not to hear someone talking to them, pretending to be sick, staying away from distressing places, or avoiding involvement in extracurricular activities (Beidel et al., 1999). Children with SAD have demonstrated a lower frequency of initiated interactions and a shorter duration of interactions with peers (Spence, Donovan, & Brechman-Toussaint, 1999), habits that might contribute to increased patterns of social withdrawal observed in adolescence (Erath et al., 2007). Social avoidance is believed to limit positive peer interactions and make the acquisition of social skills more difficult.

There is mixed evidence as to whether social skills deficits are closely associated with SAD in childhood and adolescence, and little research has looked specifically at adolescents (Inderbitzen-Nolan, Anderson, & Johnson, 2007). A few recent observational studies found that adolescents with SAD were globally less effective than nonanxious peers in speech and role-play tasks according to self- and observer ratings (Inderbitzen-Nolan et al., 2007; Beidel et al., 2007). In their study of peer ratings of the degree to which youth appeared likable on the basis of videotaped interactions, Verduin and Kendall (2008) found that youth with SAD were less liked than youth with other anxiety disorders, regardless of the degree to which they appeared anxious. These results imply that youth with SAD behave in a manner that hinders their social competence over and above that of general anxiety.

Although research has provided initial evidence that socially anxious adolescents lack effective social skills, very little research has examined specific skills that are deficient, an important next step for improving intervention. One possibility may be longer speech latencies, which have been noted in socially anxious youth compared with nonanxious youth (Beidel et al., 1999). Other skills that may be lacking in socially anxious youth may be discerned by examining intervention research. For example, Social Effectiveness Therapy for Children has been effective in treating SAD and teaches greetings and introductions, starting and maintaining conversations, listening and remembering skills, skills for joining groups, positive and negative assertion, and telephone skills (Beidel et al., 2007; see also Chapter 13, this volume). Clinical experience and reports have corroborated the presence of social skills deficits in adults with social anxiety, in that skills such as listening, maintaining conversations, initiating conversations, and perceiving social cues appear to be limited in this population (Beidel & Turner, 2007).

Given the complexity of adolescents' and young adults' social worlds, we posit that a different set of social skills may be needed in different contexts, although much more research is needed to reach any firm conclusions. In a larger group of peers, skills such as cooperation, assertion, and self-control may be instrumental in gaining acceptance and liking. Greco and Morris (2005) found evidence to support their idea that deficits in social skills are one of the reasons socially anxious youth tend to be less accepted by peers, in that social skills fully mediated the association between social anxiety and peer acceptance. For this study they assessed social skills with teachers' responses to the Social Skills Rating System, a measure that includes items assessing cooperation, assertion, and self-control. Although these authors did not look at specific skills individually, similar findings regarding cooperation have been observed among adolescents of average versus rejected status (Parkhurst & Asher, 1992) and male adolescents' popular versus rejected status (Elliott & Gresham, 1989).

Other research highlights the importance of a specific social skill, assertion. In an observational study of adolescents interacting with a group of peers, adolescents who effectively guided and influenced other members of the group and expressed ideas freely and confidently tended to receive a higher number of peer nominations than adolescents who were less assertive (Englund, Levy, Hyson & Sroufe, 2000). Although rarely analyzed as a lone construct, social initiation is another skill that has been included in many studies (e.g., Buhrmester, Furman, Wittenberg, & Reis, 1988; La Greca & Santogrossi, 1980). Social initiation among the general peer group arguably becomes more important in adolescence and young adulthood as individuals have more freedom to choose their friends and activities.

In contrast to group acceptance, a different set of skills might be needed to form close friendships in adolescence and young adulthood. Adolescence brings growing emphasis on reciprocal sharing of personal experiences, or intimacy, in friendships (Hartup, 1993). Fostering close and meaningful friendships likely requires a particular skill set including self-disclosure, provision of emotional support to friends, management of conflicts, negative assertion, and initiation of friendships (Buhrmester, 1990). Compared with nonanxious adolescents, anxious adolescents seem to emphasize intimacy less in their friendships (Schneider & Tessier, 2007). In addition, observations of preadolescents in interactions with close friends revealed that socially anxious youth tended to talk less and demonstrated more neutral and less positive affect when interacting with best friends (Schneider, 2009), a trend that may continue into adolescence and beyond, hindering the development of close friendships.

KEYS TO THE CYCLE: SOCIAL INFORMATION PROCESSING

Social information processing models help explain the cognitive processes that bidirectionally relate to the social behavior of adults with SAD (Clark & McManus, 2002) and many be somewhat applicable to youth. Crick and Dodge (1994) provided a reformulation of a social information processing model that can be used to illustrate the ways that social information processing influences and maintains SAD. There are four steps (encoding situational cues, interpreting those cues, searching for possible responses, and selecting a response) thought to influence each other in a series of feedback loops rather than in a step-by-step fashion (Crick & Dodge, 1994).

Encoding situational cues involves detecting external and internal stimuli (Clark & McManus, 2002). Anxious individuals, in general, have a bias toward noticing threat cues over positive (Bradley, Mogg, White, Groom, & de Bono, 1999) or neutral (Bradley, Mogg, Millar, & White, 1995) cues, whereas the opposite holds for nonanxious individuals. Further, anxious individuals tend to identify threat cues more quickly, with less information, and more frequently than nonanxious individuals (Muris, Merckelbach, & Damsma, 2000) but focus for shorter periods on threat cues than neutral cues (Clark, 1999), indicating ultimate avoidance of threatening stimuli. In addition, individuals with SAD have been found to engage in greater self-focus (Hope, Heimberg, & Klein, 1990). In social situations, they focus on and monitor their own actions, appearance, and emotions, making them more likely to miss a view of the overall situation (Coles, Turk, Heimberg, & Fresco, 2001) and hindering their ability to recall information (Hope et al., 1990).

Individuals with SAD also demonstrate biases in interpretation of the cues within and around them. Ambiguous situations tend to be interpreted more often in a negative light (Bögels & Zigterman, 2000), and mildly negative social situations are interpreted as catastrophic (Rheingold, Herbert, & Franklin, 2003). Moreover, individuals with SAD show a trend toward attributing negative social situations to internal, personal causes (Coles et al., 2001), but when conversations are going well, they are more likely attribute their success to external causes (George & Stopa, 2008). However, Burgess, Wojslawowicz, Rubin, Rose-Krasnor, and Booth-LaForce (2006) found that shy or withdrawn children blamed themselves less if the situation involved a close friend, suggesting that the cognitive processes of socially anxious youth may differ from adults.

The interpretation of cues revolves around a person's schemas, causal attributions, and perceptions of others' intentions (Crick & Dodge, 1994), and several studies point to self- and social schemas that could influence socially anxious adolescents' social functioning. For example, the relatively immature understanding of friendship observed among socially withdrawn and anxious adolescents (i.e., emphasis on receiving help more than intimacy) is indicative of slightly different schemas used to interpret friends' actions. Arguably, differences in friendship expectations could lead to disagreements and disappointments, perhaps explaining previous links between social anxiety and negative friendship quality (e.g., La Greca & Lopez, 1998). In addition, individuals with SAD see themselves as socially unskilled in threatening situations (Pinto-Gouveia, Castilho, Galhardo, & Cunha, 2006) and underestimate their performance in social situations (Cartwright-Hatton, Hodges, & Porter, 2003), which could make them less likely to engage socially.

Individuals' search for possible responses is influenced by their goals, threat interpretation, and emotion states. When faced with potentially conflictual social situations in hypothetical vignettes, socially withdrawn children rated relationship-oriented and avoidance goals highly (Erdley & Asher, 1996). They may also gravitate toward avoidant responses over prosocial responses as a result of a tendency to interpret situations as threatening. Emotions related to memories of past responses are thought to play a role in the generation of responses as well (Lemerise & Arsenio, 2000). If adolescents with SAD remember a similar event as being particularly catastrophic or unpleasant, their response options might be limited to avoidant strategies to avert a recurrence.

After examining their response options, socially anxious individuals select a response based on expected outcomes and their sense of efficacy in skillfully implementing the response (Crick & Dodge, 1994). Research shows that adolescents with SAD expect to perform poorly in social situations (Erath et al., 2007), and they view negative social events as costly (Rheingold et al., 2003). Adults with SAD often think that they will be unable to cope with the perceived threat of the social situation (Hofmann, 2007). Past experiences may support this perception, given that early adolescents with SAD tend to choose maladaptive coping strategies such as social withdrawal that put them at greater risk of victimization and low peer acceptance (Erath et al., 2007).

SUMMARY AND CONCLUSIONS

Research and clinical experience in the area of social anxiety and peer relations indicate that socially anxious young people typically face a number of social challenges believed to be a consequence of and contributor to SAD. These challenges include limited access to the benefits of friendship, low acceptance from the peer group, and peer victimization. By the time individuals seek treatment, their social difficulties may be long-standing, and they likely have developed ways of thinking about and responding to social situations that exacerbate their social difficulties and discomfort. A persistent theme in this literature is the role of avoidant coping and social withdrawal in the emergence and maintenance of SAD, problematic peer relations, and their association. Social withdrawal is believed to limit positive socialization experiences and connections with peers and to interfere with the development of skills and confidence for engaging in one's social world. Social anxiety and withdrawal also appear to elicit negative responses from peers, which add fuel to the cycle.

It follows that treatment aimed at reversing this process would help young people increase their social engagement and develop the skills to do so more successfully. Potentially fruitful directions for future research and treatment development include further delineation of social skills needed for the various social contexts in which adolescents and young adults live. Exploration of the potential protective function of positive friendships and supportive peer groups could also further inform treatment. Clearly, good friends can protect youth from negative social experiences, and engagement in structured activities can facilitate friendships and social adjustment. With further research and clinical creativity, additional ideas for helping youth with SAD break the cycle and develop positive, rewarding relationships will emerge.

REFERENCES

Aikins, J. W., Bierman, K. L., & Parker, J. G. (2005). Navigating the transition to junior high school: The influence of pre-transition friendship and self-system characteristics. *Social Development, 14*, 42–60. doi:10.1111/j.1467-9507.2005.00290.x

Beidel, D. C., & Turner, S. M. (2006). Clinical presentation of social anxiety disorder in adults. In D. C. Beidel & S. M. Turner (Eds.), *Shy children, phobic adults: Nature and treatment of social anxiety disorder* (2nd ed., pp. 11–46). Washington, DC: American Psychological Association.

Beidel, D. C., Turner, S. M., & Morris, T. L. (1999). Psychopathology of childhood social phobia. *Journal of the American Academy of Child and Adolescent Psychiatry, 38*, 643–650. doi:10.1097/00004583-199906000-00010

Beidel, D. C., Turner, S. M., Young, B. J., Ammerman, R. T., Sallee, F. R., & Crosby, L. (2007). Psychopathology of adolescent social phobia. *Journal of Psychopathology and Behavioral Assessment, 29*, 46–53. doi:10.1007/s10862-006-9021-1

Berndt, T. J. (2002). Friendship quality and social development. *Current Directions in Psychological Science, 11*, 7–10. doi:10.1111/1467-8721.00157

Berndt, T. J. (2004). Children's friendships: Shifts over a half-century in perspectives on their development and their effects. *Merrill-Palmer Quarterly, 50*, 206–223. doi:10.1353/mpq.2004.0014

Berndt, T. J., Hawkins, J. A., & Jiao, Z. (1999). Influences of friends and friendships on adjustment to junior high school. *Merrill-Palmer Quarterly, 45*, 13–41.

Blumenthal, H., Leen-Feldner, E. W., Trainor, C. D., Babson, K. A., & Bunaciu, L. (2009). Interactive roles of pubertal timing and peer relations in predicting social anxiety symptoms among youth. *The Journal of Adolescent Health, 44,* 401–403. doi:10.1016/j.jadohealth.2008.08.023

Bögels, S. M., & Zigterman, D. (2000). Dysfunctional cognitions in children with social phobia, separation anxiety disorder, and generalized anxiety disorder. *Journal of Abnormal Child Psychology, 28,* 205–211. doi:10.1023/A:1005179032470

Bohnert, A. M., Aikins, J. W., & Edidin, J. (2007). The role of organized activities in facilitating social adaptation across the transition to college. *Journal of Adolescent Research, 22,* 189–208. doi:10.1177/0743558406297940

Bradley, B. P., Mogg, K., Millar, N., & White, J. (1995). Selective processing of negative information: Effects of clinical anxiety, concurrent depression, and awareness. *Journal of Abnormal Psychology, 104,* 532–536. doi:10.1037/0021-843X.104.3.532

Bradley, B. P., Mogg, K., White, J., Groom, C., & de Bono, J. (1999). Attentional bias for emotional faces in generalized anxiety disorder. *The British Journal of Clinical Psychology, 38,* 267–278. doi:10.1348/014466599162845

Buhrmester, D. (1990). Intimacy of friendship, interpersonal competence, and adjustment during preadolescence and adolescence. *Child Development, 61,* 1101–1111. doi:10.2307/1130878

Buhrmester, D., & Furman, W. (1987). The development of companionship and intimacy. *Child Development, 58,* 1101–1113. doi:10.2307/1130550

Buhrmester, D., Furman, W., Wittenberg, M. T., & Reis, H. T. (1988). Five domains of interpersonal competence in peer relationships. *Journal of Personality and Social Psychology, 55,* 991–1008. doi:10.1037/0022-3514.55.6.991

Burgess, K. B., Wojslawowicz, J. C., Rubin, K. H., Rose-Krasnor, L., & Booth-LaForce, C. (2006). Social information processing and coping strategies of shy/withdrawn and aggressive children: Does friendship matter? *Child Development, 77,* 371–383. doi:10.1111/j.1467-8624.2006.00876.x

Cartwright-Hatton, S., Hodges, L., & Porter, J. (2003). Social anxiety in childhood: The relationship with self and observer rated social skills. *Journal of Child Psychology and Psychiatry, and Allied Disciplines, 44,* 737–742. doi:10.1111/1469-7610.00159

Clark, D. M. (1999). Anxiety disorders: Why they persist and how to treat them. *Behaviour Research and Therapy, 37,* S5–S27.

Clark, D. M., & McManus, F. (2002). Information processing in social phobia. *Biological Psychiatry, 51,* 92–100. doi:10.1016/S0006-3223(01)01296-3

Coles, M. E., Turk, C. L., Heimberg, R. G., & Fresco, D. M. (2001). Effects of varying levels of anxiety within social situations: Relationship to memory perspective and attributions in social phobia. *Behaviour Research and Therapy, 39,* 651–665. doi:10.1016/S0005-7967(00)00035-8

Crick, N. R., & Dodge, K. A. (1994). A review and reformulation of social information-processing mechanisms in children's social adjustment. *Psychological Bulletin, 115,* 74–101. doi:10.1037/0033-2909.115.1.74

Cunha, M., Soares, I., & Pinto-Gouveia, J. (2008). The role of individual temperament, family and peers in social anxiety disorder: A controlled study. *International Journal of Clinical and Health Psychology, 8*, 631–655.

Deardorff, J., Hayward, C., Wilson, K. A., Bryson, S., Hammer, L. D., & Agras, S. (2007). Puberty and gender interact to predict social anxiety symptoms in early adolescence. *The Journal of Adolescent Health, 41*, 102–104. doi:10.1016/j.jadohealth.2007.02.013

Elliott, S. N., & Gresham, F. M. (1989). Teacher and self-ratings of popular and rejected adolescent boys' behavior. *Journal of Psychoeducational Assessment, 7*, 323–334. doi:10.1177/073428298900700405

Englund, M. M., Levy, A. K., Hyson, D. M., & Sroufe, L. A. (2000). Adolescent social competence: Effectiveness in a group setting. *Child Development, 71*, 1049–1060. doi:10.1111/1467-8624.00208

Erath, S. A., Flanagan, K. S., & Bierman, K. L. (2007). Social anxiety and peer relations in early adolescence: Behavioral and cognitive factors. *Journal of Abnormal Child Psychology, 35*, 405–416. doi:10.1007/s10802-007-9099-2

Erdley, C. A., & Asher, S. R. (1996). Children's social goals and self-efficacy perceptions as influences on their responses to ambiguous provocation. *Child Development, 67*, 1329–1344. doi:10.2307/1131703

Finnegan, R. A., Hodges, E. V. E., & Perry, D. G. (1998). Victimization by peers: Associations with children's reports of mother–child interaction. *Journal of Personality and Social Psychology, 75*, 1076–1086. doi:10.1037/0022-3514.75.4.1076

Flanagan, K. S., Erath, S. A., & Bierman, K. L. (2008). Unique associations between peer relations and social anxiety in early adolescence. *Journal of Clinical Child and Adolescent Psychology, 37*, 759–769. doi:10.1080/15374410802359700

Ge, X., Conger, R. D., & Elder, G. H. (2001). Pubertal transition, stressful life events, and the emergence of gender differences in adolescent depressive symptoms. *Developmental Psychology, 37*, 404–417. doi:10.1037/0012-1649.37.3.404

George, L., & Stopa, L. (2008). Private and public self-awareness in social anxiety. *Journal of Behavior Therapy and Experimental Psychiatry, 39*, 57–72. doi:10.1016/j.jbtep.2006.09.004

Greco, L. A., & Morris, T. L. (2005). Factors influencing the link between social anxiety and peer acceptance: Contribution of social skills and close friendships during middle childhood. *Behavior Therapy, 36*, 197–205. doi:10.1016/S0005-7894(05)80068-1

Hardy, C. L., Bukowski, W. M., & Sippola, L. K. (2002). Stability and change in peer relationships during the transition to middle-level school. *The Journal of Early Adolescence, 22*, 117–142. doi:10.1177/0272431602022002001

Hartup, W. W. (1993). Adolescents and their friends. In B. Laursen (Ed.), *Close friendships in adolescence* (pp. 3–22). San Francisco, CA: Jossey-Bass.

Hartup, W. W. (1996). The company they keep: Friendships and their developmental significance. *Child Development, 67*, 1–13. doi:10.2307/1131681

Hodges, E. V. E., Boivin, M., Vitaro, F., & Bukowski, W. M. (1999). The power of friendship: Protection against an escalating cycle of peer victimization. *Developmental Psychology, 35,* 94–101. doi:10.1037/0012-1649.35.1.94

Hofmann, S. G. (2007). Cognitive factors that maintain social anxiety disorder: A comprehensive model and its treatment implications. *Cognitive Behaviour Therapy, 36,* 193–209. doi:10.1080/16506070701421313

Hope, D. A., Heimberg, R. G., & Klein, J. F. (1990). Social anxiety and the recall of interpersonal information. *Journal of Cognitive Psychotherapy, 4,* 185–195.

Inderbitzen, H. M., Walters, K. S., & Bukowski, A. L. (1997). The role of social anxiety in adolescents peer relations: Differences among sociometric status groups and rejected subgroups. *Journal of Clinical Child Psychology, 26,* 338–348. doi:10.1207/s15374424jccp2604_2

Inderbitzen-Nolan, H. M., Anderson, E. R., & Johnson, H. S. (2007). Subjective versus objective behavioral ratings following two analogue tasks: A comparison of socially phobic and non-anxious adolescents. *Journal of Anxiety Disorders, 21,* 76–90. doi:10.1016/j.janxdis.2006.03.013

Kagan, J. (2008). Behavioral inhibition as a risk factor for psychopathology. In T. P. Beauchaine & S. P. Hinshaw (Eds.), *Child and adolescent psychopathology* (pp. 157–179). Hoboken, NJ: Wiley.

Ladd, G. W. (2006). Peer rejection, aggressive or withdrawn behavior, and psychological maladjustment from ages 5 to 12: An examination of four predictive models. *Child Development, 77,* 822–846. doi:10.1111/j.1467-8624.2006.00905.x

La Greca, A. M., & Lopez, N. (1998). Social anxiety among adolescents: Linkages with peer relations and friendships. *Journal of Abnormal Child Psychology, 26,* 83–94.

La Greca, A. M., & Santogrossi, D. A. (1980). Social skills training with elementary school students: A behavioral group approach. *Journal of Consulting and Clinical Psychology, 48,* 220–227. doi:10.1037/0022-006X.48.2.220

Lemerise, E. A., & Arsenio, W. F. (2000). An integrated model of emotion processes and cognition in social information processing. *Child Development, 71,* 107–118. doi:10.1111/1467-8624.00124

Muris, P., Merckelbach, H., & Damsma, E. (2000). Threat perception bias in non-referred, socially anxious children. *Journal of Clinical Child Psychology, 29,* 348–359. doi:10.1207/S15374424JCCP2903_6

Oh, W., Rubin, K. H., Bowker, J. C., Booth-LaForce, C., Rose-Krasnor, L. A., & Laursen, B. (2008). Trajectories of social withdrawal from middle childhood to early adolescence. *Journal of Abnormal Child Psychology, 36,* 553–566. doi:10.1007/s10802-007-9199-z

Oswald, D. L., & Clark, E. M. (2003). Best friends forever? High school best friendships and the transition to college. *Personal Relationships, 10,* 187–196. doi:10.1111/1475-6811.00045

Parke, R. D., Simpkins, S. D., McDowell, D. J., Kim, M., Killian, C., Dennis, J., . . . Rah, Y. (2002). Relative contributions of families and peers to children's social development. In P. K. Smith & C. H. Hart (Eds.), *Blackwell handbook of childhood social development* (pp. 156–177). Malden, MA: Blackwell.

Parkhurst, J. T., & Asher, S. R. (1992). Peer rejection in middle school: Subgroup differences in behavior, loneliness, and interpersonal concerns. *Developmental Psychology, 28,* 231–241. doi:10.1037/0012-1649.28.2.231

Pellegrini, A. D., & Bartini, M. (2000). A longitudinal study of bullying, victimization, and peer affiliation during the transition from primary school to middle school. *American Educational Research Journal, 37,* 699–725.

Pinto-Gouveia, J., Castilho, P., Galhardo, A., & Cunha, M. (2006). Early maladaptive schemas and social phobia. *Cognitive Therapy and Research, 30,* 571–584. doi:10.1007/s10608-006-9027-8

Prinstein, M. J., & La Greca, A. M. (2002). Peer crowd affiliation and internalizing distress in childhood and adolescence: A longitudinal follow-back study. *Journal of Research on Adolescence, 12,* 325–351. doi:10.1111/1532-7795.00036

Rheingold, A., Herbert, J., & Franklin, M. (2003). Cognitive bias in adolescents with social anxiety disorder. *Cognitive Therapy and Research, 27,* 639–655. doi:10.1023/A:1026399627766

Rubin, K. H., & Burgess, K. B. (2001). Social withdrawal and anxiety. In M. W. Vasey & M. R. Dadds (Eds.), *The developmental psychopathology of anxiety* (pp. 407–434). New York, NY: Oxford University Press.

Rubin, K. H., Burgess, K. B., & Hastings, P. D. (2002). Stability and social-behavioral consequences of toddlers' inhibited temperament and parenting behaviors. *Child Development, 73,* 483–495. doi:10.1111/1467-8624.00419

Rubin, K. H., & Coplan, R. J. (2004). Paying attention to and not neglecting social withdrawal and social isolation. *Merrill-Palmer Quarterly, 50,* 506–534.

Rubin, K. H., Hymel, S., & Mills, R. S. (1989). Sociability and social withdrawal in childhood: Stability and outcomes. *Journal of Personality, 57,* 237–255. doi:10.1111/j.1467-6494.1989.tb00482.x

Rubin, K. H., Stewart, S. L., & Coplan, R. J. (1995). Social withdrawal in childhood: Conceptual and empirical perspectives. In T. Ollendick & R. Prinz (Eds.), *Advances in clinical child psychology* (Vol. 17, pp. 157–196). New York, NY: Plenum Press.

Rubin, K. H., Wojslawowicz, J. C., Rose-Krasnor, L., Booth-LaForce, C., & Burgess, K. B. (2006). The best friendships of shy/withdrawn children: Prevalence, stability, and relationship quality. *Journal of Abnormal Child Psychology, 34,* 139–153.

Russell, A., Hart, C. H., Robinson, C. C., & Olsen, S. F. (2003). Children's sociable and aggressive behavior with peers: A comparison of the US and Australia, and contributions of temperament and parenting styles. *International Journal of Behavioral Development, 27,* 74–86. doi:10.1080/01650250244000038

Schneider, B. H. (2009). An observational study of the interactions of socially withdrawn/anxious early adolescents and their friends. *Journal of Child Psychology and Psychiatry, and Allied Disciplines, 50,* 799–806. doi:10.1111/j.1469-7610.2008.02056.x

Schneider, B. H., & Tessier, N. G. (2007). Close friendship as understood by socially withdrawn, anxious early adolescents. *Child Psychiatry and Human Development, 38,* 339–351. doi:10.1007/s10578-007-0071-8

Schneider, B. H., Younger, A. J., Smith, T., & Freeman, P. (1998). A longitudinal exploration of the cross-contextual stability of social withdrawal in early adolescence. *The Journal of Early Adolescence, 18,* 374–396. doi:10.1177/0272431698018004003

Slee, P. T. (1994). Situational and interpersonal correlates of anxiety associated with peer victimization. *Child Psychiatry and Human Development, 25,* 97–107. doi:10.1007/BF02253289

Spence, S. H., Donovan, C., & Brechman-Toussaint, M. (1999). Social skills, social outcomes, and cognitive features of childhood social phobia. *Journal of Abnormal Psychology, 108,* 211–221. doi:10.1037/0021-843X.108.2.211

Storch, E. A., Brassard, M. R., & Masia-Warner, C. L. (2003). The relationship of peer victimization to social anxiety and loneliness in adolescence. *Child Study Journal, 33,* 1–18.

Storch, E. A., Masia-Warner, C., Crisp, H., & Klein, R. G. (2005). Peer victimization and social anxiety in adolescence: A prospective study. *Aggressive Behavior, 31,* 437–452. doi:10.1002/ab.20093

Verduin, T. L., & Kendall, P. C. (2008). Peer perceptions and liking of children with anxiety disorders. *Journal of Abnormal Child Psychology, 36,* 459–469. doi:10.1007/s10802-007-9192-6

Vernberg, E. M., Abwender, D. A., Ewell, K. K., & Beery, S. H. (1992). Social anxiety and peer relationships in early adolescence: A prospective analysis. *Journal of Clinical Child Psychology, 21,* 189–196. doi:10.1207/s15374424jccp2102_11

Vernberg, E. M., Beery, S. H., Ewell, K. K., & Abwender, D. A. (1993). Parents' use of friendship facilitation strategies and the formation of friendships in early adolescence: A prospective study. *Journal of Family Psychology, 7,* 356–369. doi:10.1037/0893-3200.7.3.356

Vernberg, E. M., Greenhoot, A. F., & Biggs, B. K. (2006). Intercommunity relocation and adolescent friendships: Who struggles and why? *Journal of Consulting and Clinical Psychology, 74,* 511–523. doi:10.1037/0022-006X.74.3.511

Younger, A. J., & Piccinin, A. M. (1989). Children's recall of aggressive and withdrawal behaviors: Recognition memory and likeability judgments. *Child Development, 60,* 580–590. doi:10.2307/1130724

9

SOCIAL ANXIETY AMONG LESBIAN, GAY, BISEXUAL, AND TRANSGENDER ADOLESCENTS AND YOUNG ADULTS

KAREN E. ROBERTS, DANIELLE SCHWARTZ, AND TREVOR A. HART

Lesbian, gay, bisexual, and transgender (LGBT) adolescents and adults are notably underrepresented in the social anxiety literature. The lack of research on LGBT populations is striking in the face of evidence that social anxiety is higher among LGBT youth and adults than among heterosexuals (Bostwick, Boyd, Hughes, & McCabe, 2010; Pachankis & Goldfried, 2006; Safren & Pantalone, 2006; Sandfort, de Graaf, Bijl, & Schnabel, 2001). Among a large sample of American adults, the lifetime prevalence of social anxiety disorder (SAD) was 12.4% in gay men versus 5.8% in heterosexual men and 18.2% in bisexual women versus 7.9% in heterosexual women (Bostwick et al., 2010). In a sample of Dutch adults (Sandfort et al., 2001), gay men (14.6%) were more than twice as likely as heterosexual men (5.5%) to have SAD. LGBT individuals are also more likely than heterosexuals to meet criteria for any anxiety disorder (King et al., 2008; Meyer, 2003), including generalized anxiety disorder (Fergusson, Horwood, & Beautrais, 1999), which often includes worry about social situations.

The vast majority of studies on social anxiety and SAD fail to report statistics on sexual orientation or gender identities. Further, many studies that include LGBT samples have grouped these individuals together, despite research indicating that symptoms of social anxiety vary within this broad population. For example, data from the National Epidemiologic Survey on Alcohol and Related Conditions found that lesbians had a 9.6% lifetime prevalence of SAD versus 12.4% for gay men, 14.2% for bisexual men, and 18.2% for bisexual women (Bostwick et al., 2010). Researchers have therefore suggested the need for more research on social anxiety and SAD in nonheterosexual populations (Eckleberry-Hunt & Dohrenwend, 2005; Hope & Heimberg, 1990; Leary & Kowalski, 1995; Pachankis, Goldfried, & Ramrattan, 2008). Moreover, the need to study how social anxiety affects behavior in both heterosexual and LGBT populations since the onset of the human immunodeficiency virus (HIV)/acquired immune deficiency syndrome (AIDS) epidemic has been underscored (Brown, Macintyre & Trujillo, 2003; Courtenay-Quirk, Wolitski, Parsons, & Gómez, 2006; Devine, Plant, & Harrison, 1999; Hope & Heimberg, 1990).

What variables might contribute to greater social anxiety in this population? In addition to identified etiological factors common to all individuals, other potential factors include gender role nonconformity, sexual orientation victimization (SOV), developmental issues, and abusive and negative familial experiences (Bailey & Zucker, 1995; Corliss, Cochran, & Mays, 2002; Garofalo, Wolf, Kessel, Palfrey, & DuRant, 1998; Poteat, Espelage, & Koenig, 2009). LGBT youth also experience greater psychological and social problems related to being LGBT, including alcohol and drug use, engagement in sexual risk behaviors, decreased social support, and suicidality (Eisenberg & Resnick, 2006; Hart & Heimberg, 2005; Marshal et al., 2008; Safren & Pantalone, 2006), and these problems also may be related to higher social anxiety. Whereas broad etiological factors are discussed in Chapter 2, in this chapter we outline potential causes and effects specific to LGBT youth. Because research on SAD is highly limited in this population, the primary focus of this chapter is on social anxiety symptoms more broadly.

POTENTIAL CAUSAL FACTORS OF SOCIAL ANXIETY SPECIFIC TO LESBIAN, GAY, BISEXUAL, AND TRANSGENDER YOUTH

There are many potential causal factors of social anxiety among LGBT youth. In the following sections, we review factors that have been investigated in the current literature.

Victimization Because of Gender Role Nonconformity

Lesbians and gay men report higher rates of gender nonconformity during childhood than heterosexual individuals (Bailey & Zucker, 1995), and these youth are often labeled as *sissies* or *tomboys*. Awareness of one's own nontraditional gender presentation may be partially responsible for the perceptions of a majority of sexual minority youth that strangers are likely to identify them as LGBT. In fact, males perceiving themselves as more feminine and females perceiving themselves as more masculine than their peers feel they are significantly more identifiable as LGBT than other LGBT peers (D'Augelli & Hershberger, 1993). Youth who report being gender atypical during childhood report more victimization experiences, mental health problems, and traumatic stress (D'Augelli, Grossman, & Starks, 2006). In turn, this early gender nonconformity has been linked to later anxiety, particularly in gay men (Lippa, 2008; Weinrich, Atkinson, McCutchan, & Grant, 1995). As would be expected, transgender individuals also report many instances of gender nonconformity in childhood (e.g., cross-dressing) and negative familial reactions such as name-calling and parental attempts to suppress gender atypical behaviors (Gagné, Tewksbury, & McGaughey, 1997).

Lesbians may recall higher levels of childhood gender nonconformity than gay men (Lippa, 2008). However, in terms of parental responses to gender atypical behaviors, gay and bisexual males perceived their parents' reactions more negatively than lesbian and bisexual females (D'Augelli et al., 2006). Consistent with these perceptions, mothers and fathers appear more accepting of gender atypical behaviors in young girls than in young boys (Kane, 2006).

Stigmatizing Attitudes

Negative attitudes toward LGBT individuals are widespread. For example, 50% of boys and 26% of girls (ages 11–16) in the United Kingdom indicated that homosexuality is "always wrong" or "usually wrong" (Sharpe, 2002). Two surveys of more than 16,000 U.S. middle school and high school students found that 10% to 30% of students agreed with the statement "I could never stay friends with someone who told me he or she was gay or lesbian," and 20% to 44% agreed with the statement "I would rather attend a school where there are no gay or lesbian students" (Poteat et al., 2009). There is evidence that homophobia decreases with age and education (Marsiglio, 1993; Poteat et al., 2009), yet stigmatizing attitudes are found at postsecondary institutions as well (Lambert, Ventura, Hall, & Cluse-Tolar, 2006; Pettijohn & Walzer, 2008). Moreover, many studies indicate gender differences in self-reported attitudes, with males consistently reporting more negative views of LGBT youth than females (D'Augelli & Rose, 1990; Fisher & Banik, 2007; Herek & Glunt, 1993; Hinrichs & Rosenberg, 2002; Louderback & Whitley, 1997; Nagoshi et al, 2008; Roper & Halloran, 2007; Sharpe, 2002). Further, perceived stigmatization (e.g., losing a close friend because of homosexuality or bisexuality) at baseline predicted symptoms of anxiety at 6-month follow-up among a sample of 140 gay, lesbian, and bisexual youth ages 14 to 21 years (Rosario, Schrimshaw, Hunter, & Gwadz, 2002). Although no longitudinal studies have examined if and how stigmatization leads specifically to social anxiety or SAD, the importance of peers during the period of adolescence suggests a powerful relationship.

HIV/AIDS Stigma

With the advent of the HIV/AIDS epidemic, stigmatization of persons with HIV/AIDS and persons at risk of contracting HIV has become a widespread phenomenon that has disproportionately affected the LGBT community (Herek & Capitanio, 1999; Swendeman, Rotherham-Borus, Comulada, Weiss, & Ramos, 2006). The general public often associates HIV/AIDS with a nonheterosexual orientation, and many are misinformed about the transmission of HIV, believing they can contract HIV from casual contact (e.g., kissing, sharing a glass; Herek, Capitanio, & Widaman, 2002). In fact, gay and bisexual youth who are HIV positive are twice as likely to experience HIV/AIDS stigma (e.g., avoidance of physical contact, verbal abuse, loss of a friend because of one's HIV positive status) as heterosexual youth who are HIV positive (Swendeman et al., 2006).

Internalized Homophobia

Theory and research suggest that society's homophobic attitudes can become internalized in LGBT individuals. Many of these youth experience negative feelings about homosexuality (Kubicek et al., 2007; Rosario, Schrimshaw, & Hunter, 2008). Internalized homophobia predicted anxiety symptoms among a sample of lesbian, gay, and bisexual adults, including patients from a psychiatric outpatient sexual identity clinic (Igartua, Gill, & Montoro, 2003). Symptoms of anxiety have also been shown to mediate the relationship between internalized homophobia and substance abuse in gay and bisexual males ages 14 to 21 years (Rosario, Scrimshaw, & Hunter, 2006).

Some evidence suggests that attitudes toward lesbians are less negative than attitudes toward gay males (Schellenberg, Hirt, & Sears, 1999), possibly because sexual behavior between two females is often considered more acceptable (Louderback & Whitley, 1997). It is also possible, however, that lesbians encounter different or more subtle forms of stigmatizing attitudes. However, this possibility awaits research inquiry.

Sexual Orientation Victimization

Negative attitudes are regularly verbalized, particularly in school environments (Poteat & Espelage, 2007; Russell, Franz, & Driscoll, 2001). Almost

60% of LGB youth ages 14 to 21 years reported experiencing verbal abuse at their high schools. Further, they reported other SOV: having objects thrown at them; being punched, kicked, or beaten; being threatened with a weapon; and being sexually assaulted. Gay and bisexual men report more instances of SOV than gay and bisexual women (D'Augelli, Pilkington, & Hershberger, 2002). LGB youth are also more likely to have missed school because of fear (25% vs. 5%) and to have been threatened with a weapon at school within the past 30 days (33% vs. 7%; Garofalo et al., 1998).

SOV is also common at colleges and universities (Evans, 2001; Evans & D'Augelli, 1996; Love, 1997; Waldo, Hesson-McInnis, & D'Augelli, 1998). Over one third of undergraduate students indicated that they had experienced SOV in the past year, including derogatory remarks, verbal harassment, threats of physical violence, and physical assaults. Further, the majority of students acknowledged that they hide their sexual orientation or gender identity to avoid intimidation. These SOV experiences occurred in multiple venues, including public areas on campus, on-campus residences, and in the classroom. The perpetrators were predominantly other students. SOV among sexual minority youth has been related to increased distress, and verbal abuse has been related to symptoms of posttraumatic stress (D'Augelli et al., 2002).

Transgender youth appear to be at higher risk of victimization than LGB youth. A higher proportion of transgender individuals (41%) compared with lesbian (33%), gay (31%), and bisexual (28%) individuals reported being harassed on college or university campuses. In terms of perceived discrimination, students, staff, faculty, and administrators indicated that transgender individuals (71%) are the most likely victims of harassment, followed by gay men (61%), lesbians (53%), and then bisexuals (38%; Rankin, 2003).

Feeling "Different" From Others

LGBT development is fraught with challenges related to society's negative evaluation (Rotherham-Borus & Langabeer, 2001). Aside from the awareness that one's own sexual orientation or gender identity may be viewed with disdain, this conflict may begin early in life, at approximately 10 years for boys and 11 years for girls (D'Augelli, 2002). Moreover, LGB youth report "feeling different from others" at an even earlier mean age (D'Augelli et al., 2006), and disclosure often does not occur until years after awareness of same-sex attraction (D'Augelli, 2002). A long-standing feeling of being different in ways deemed unacceptable by society may explain empirical findings of higher social anxiety among LGBT youth (Bostwick et al., 2010; Pachankis & Goldfried, 2006; Safren & Pantalone, 2006). Further, social anxiety may be implicated in a research finding of a delay between the mean age of first feeling different and mean age of first disclosure of sexual orientation (D'Augelli, 2002; D'Augelli et al., 2006; D'Augelli & Hershberger, 1993).

Abusive and Negative Family Experiences

One area in which LGBT youth may experience social anxiety and distress is in the family environment (Hart & Heimberg, 2001). Undoubtedly, these youth experience a fear of rejection when contemplating disclosure to others, especially parents. When disclosing to parents, other anxieties include fear of disappointing or hurting parents, fear of verbal or physical abuse, and fear of relationship deterioration. Many parents do initially respond negatively to disclosure (Savin-Williams, 1994), and extreme reactions include eviction from the family home, a possible explanation for the increased number of LGB individuals who are homeless (Goldfried & Goldfried, 2001; Hunter, 2008). Recent estimates of parental responses suggest that 30% to 40% of parents respond negatively to their children's disclosure but also that LGB youth tend to overestimate the likelihood of negative parental reactions. Further, youth who reported more positive reactions by parents revealed that they worried less about rejection (D'Augelli, Grossman, & Starks, 2008). In general, LGB youth are more likely to disclose their sexual orientation to their mothers than their fathers potentially because mothers respond more positively than fathers to such disclosure (D'Augelli, 2002; D'Augelli, Hershberger, & Pilkington, 1998).

Given the possibility of parental rejection, a minority of LGB youth do not disclose their sexual orientation to parents (D'Augelli, 2002; D'Augelli, Grossman, & Starks, 2005). Youth who had not disclosed their sexual orientation to parents reported more fear of rejection by parents and siblings and higher internalized homophobia (D'Augelli et al., 2008).

Childhood Abuse

There is a higher prevalence of childhood sexual and physical abuse among LGB youth than among heterosexual youth, including major physical maltreatment, such as being beaten up, choked, or burned (Corliss et al., 2002; Saewyc et al., 2006). The prevalence of reported childhood sexual abuse among LGBT adults is high (> 40% in Kenagy, 2005; Tomeo, Templer, Anderson, & Kotler, 2001). Verbal abuse is also common (Grossman & D'Augelli, 2007; Pilkington & D'Augelli, 1995), and family members, particularly parents, are often the perpetrators (Rivers & D'Augelli, 2001). For example, 33.6% of lesbian and bisexual women and 26.9% of gay and bisexual men reported major physical maltreatment by their parents during childhood compared with 10.3% of heterosexual women and 12.5% of heterosexual men (Corliss et al., 2002). More than 25% of a sample of transgender youth reported being slapped, beaten, or hit by parents in relation to gender atypical expression (Grossman & D'Augelli, 2007), and the greater the self-reported gender atypicality, the more likely were reports of childhood abuse or victimization (Waldo et al., 1998). Although specific data for LGBT youth are not available, population data suggest that youth who experience childhood or adolescent abuse are more likely to have decreased psychosocial functioning, including social problems and SAD during adolescence and young adulthood (He, Pan, & Meng, 2008; Silverman, Reinherz, & Giaconia, 1996).

POTENTIAL EFFECTS OF SOCIAL ANXIETY ON LESBIAN, GAY, BISEXUAL, AND TRANSGENDER YOUTH

There are many potential effects of social anxiety on LGBT youth. In the following sections, we review factors that have been investigated in the current literature.

Alcohol and Drug Use

The relationship between SAD and substance use among LGBT youth is particularly important to consider given its high comorbidity in the general population (e.g., Buckner et al., 2008; Schneier et al., 2010). Although this relationship has not been investigated empirically in LGBT youth, it has been suggested that LGBT individuals may engage in alcohol and substance use to reduce inhibitions, increase assertiveness, and engage in behaviors with which they may otherwise be uncomfortable (Faltz, 1992).

Alcohol and substance use is more prevalent among LGBT youth than in heterosexual youth (Marshal et al., 2008; Noell & Ochs, 2001; Rosario, Hunter, & Gwadz, 1997; Rotheram-Borus, Hunter, & Rosario, 1994). In a recent meta-analysis, the odds of substance use among LGB youth were 190% higher than for heterosexual youth (Marshal et al., 2008). Another study comparing LGB youth to national data found that the prevalence of substance abuse was 6.4 times higher among lesbian and bisexual females compared with heterosexual females and 4.4 times higher among gay and bisexual males compared with heterosexual males (Rosario et al., 1997).

LGBT youth may be inclined toward substance use as a result of marginalization, feelings of depression and loneliness, and stress related to interpersonal and intrapersonal stigmatization (Jordan, 2000). Factors such as victimization, perceived discrimination, homophobia, and shame may contribute to greater alcohol and substance use among these youth (Cochran, 2001; Herbert, Hunt, & Dell, 1994; Hughes & Eliason, 2002; Mays & Cochran, 2001; McDermott, Roen, & Scourfield, 2008; Rosario et al., 1997).

LGB youth who had experienced high levels of victimization reported significantly more substance use compared with heterosexual youth and LGB youth who were not victimized (Bontempo & D'Augelli, 2002).

Sexual Risk Behaviors

There is very little research examining the relationship between social anxiety and sexual risk behaviors among LGBT youth. To date, only one study has examined this association in gay and bisexual male youth (Hart & Heimberg, 2005). This study examined the relationship between two dimensions of social anxiety—(a) observation anxiety, which is anxiety about being observed or scrutinized by others, and (b) social interaction anxiety, which is anxiety about interacting in dyads or groups—and unprotected anal intercourse in a sample of 100 gay and bisexual male youth (ages 16–21). Social anxiety predicted an increased probability of having engaged in unprotected insertive anal intercourse in the past 6 months and was associated with unprotected intercourse above and beyond the effects of communication about condom use. The authors posited that gay or bisexual youth who are high in social anxiety may be excessively focused on their performance and therefore neglect health-related issues such as condom use. Further, these individuals may avoid putting on condoms because of embarrassment about being watched.

Social Support

As discussed earlier, the negative reactions LGBT youth face when they disclose their sexual orientation may have profound effects on their well-being (e.g., Hershberger, Pilkington, & D'Augelli, 1997; Pilkington & D'Augelli, 1995). Sexual minority youth report fewer social supports and lower satisfaction with social support compared with heterosexual youth (Safren & Heimberg, 1999; Safren & Pantalone, 2006). In one study, a high percentage of lesbian and bisexual women reported relationship concerns and lack of adequate social networks (Rogers, Emanuel, & Bradford, 2002). A study of LGB and heterosexual youth (ages 16–21) found that, controlling for the effects of sexual orientation, social anxiety was associated with less satisfaction with social support among LGB youth (Safren & Pantalone, 2006). The increased stressors that these youth experience during adolescence may predispose them to social anxiety or SAD, which may subsequently impair their ability to develop strong social support networks.

Another study examined the mediating role of social support in the relationship between social anxiety and ego identity in LGB individuals (ages 18–74; Potioczniak, Aldea, & DeBlaere, 2007). Ego identity was defined across two dimensions: (a) exploration, which refers to an individual's efforts to discover the self; and (b) commitment, which refers to an individual's adherence to particular beliefs and values about the self. Social anxiety was negatively associated with social support, whereas social support was positively associated with ego identity. As well, social support mediated the relationship between social anxiety and ego identity, and social anxiety and self-concealment. Social anxiety may therefore negatively impact LGBT individuals' social support and lead to self-concealment and lack of self-acceptance.

Potoczniak and colleagues (2007) found differences in the impact of perceived social support among LGBT youth. Perceived social support had a stronger impact on ego identity for females than males, and self-concealment had a stronger impact on ego identity for males than females. These findings are consistent with past studies revealing that females are more interpersonally oriented (Meeus, Iedema, Helsen, & Vollebergh, 1999) and that social stigma about same-sex behavior may be greater for sexual minority men than women (Herek, 2000).

Depression and Suicidality

Compared with heterosexual youth, LGBT youth are at an increased risk of depression and suicidality (Almeida, Johnson, Corliss, Molnar, & Azrael, 2009; Eisenberg & Resnick, 2006; Garofalo et al., 1998; Hershberger & D'Augelli, 1995; Remafedi, 2002; Remafedi, French, Story, Resnick, & Blum, 1998; Safren & Heimberg, 1999). Eisenberg and Resnick (2006) found that 53.4% of lesbian and bisexual females and 29% of gay and bisexual males reported past suicide attempts compared with 24.8% of heterosexual females and 12.6% of heterosexual males. In another study, over one third of LGB youth reported a past suicide attempt (D'Augelli, 2002). Disclosure of sexual orientation, loss of friends as a result of disclosure, and victimization were predictors of past suicide attempts among LGB youth (Hershberger et al., 1997). In a review of this literature, Remafedi (1999) noted that gender noncomformity, violence, lack of support, school dropout, and family problems were all associated with suicide attempts among sexual minority youth. Although social anxiety per se has not been examined as a risk factor for suicide in LGBT youth, it may be an important variable to explore.

An Integrative Model of Social Anxiety Among Lesbian, Gay, Bisexual, and Transgender Youth

Figure 9.1 presents an integrative model of the possible causes and effects of social anxiety among LGBT youth. The reviewed literature highlights a range of early life experiences that may directly or indirectly contribute to the development of social anxiety or SAD, with subsequent effects

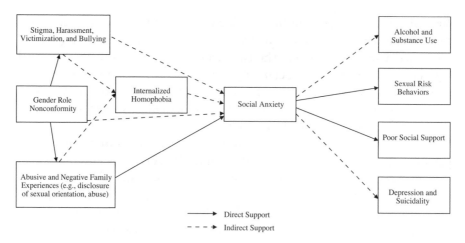

Figure 9.1. An integrative model of social anxiety among lesbian, gay, bisexual, and transgender youth.

on long-term behavioral, psychological, and social functioning. In this figure, relationships that have been directly supported in past research are indicated with a solid line. Possible relationships that have been suggested by researchers but not yet directly examined through empirical data are indicated with a broken line. Thus, in addition to providing a guide for clinicians conducting psychological therapies, major gaps in current understanding of social anxiety and SAD among sexual minority youth also are highlighted.

Limitations and Future Directions

Despite the growing body of research examining social anxiety among LGBT youth, there are still many gaps in the literature. Although previous research assessing adult heterosexual samples provides guidance as to specific relationships between SAD and impaired psychosocial functioning (Rapaport, Clary, Fayyad, & Endicott, 2005; Safren, Heimberg, Brown, & Holle, 1996), the extent of generalizability to LGBT youth is unknown. In fact, previous research suggests that LGBT youth may follow different developmental pathways than their heterosexual counterparts with respect to psychopathology (Rotheram-Borus, Rosario, Van Rossem, Reid, & Gillis, 1995). Future research is therefore needed to understand how social anxiety may develop and worsen in LGBT youth and how it affects the lives of people in this vulnerable population.

In this chapter, we highlight that LGBT youth are often grouped together in research studies despite their different life experiences. Depending on their specific gender and sexual orientation, these youth may encounter unique psychosocial stressors predisposing them to social anxiety and/or

SAD. For example, transgender youth face many of the same adverse life experiences as LGB adolescents but may also face personal distress regarding discomfort with their sex, gender, and body as well as confusion regarding their sexual orientation (Bockting, Benner, & Coleman, 2009; Ryan & Futterman, 1998). These important differences highlight the need for more research that examines LGBT youth as separate entities, taking into account their unique developmental experiences.

Another concern is the paucity of research examining SAD among LGBT youth. Almost all of the relevant research focuses on social anxiety in nonclinical samples without exploring clinically significant levels of social anxiety. Therefore, it is unclear whether the findings from nonclinical samples generalize to individuals with SAD. Future research should examine predictors and consequences of SAD among LGBT youth and investigate whether differences exist between clinical and nonclinical populations.

Finally, future research should use longitudinal designs. To capture the developmental processes underlying these relationships, more research is needed to determine how these variables interact over time and whether causal relationships exist. Longitudinal studies beginning in preadolescence would allow researchers to investigate how early childhood experiences and family and peer relationships interact with sexual development to predict social anxiety and other mental and physical health outcomes.

Social and Clinical Implications

There are many social and clinical implications that follow from the reviewed research. In the following sections, we consider some of the most important implications.

Changes Needed in Societal Attitudes and Protections for Lesbian, Gay, Bisexual, and Transgender Youth

In this chapter, we highlight the need for clinical interventions aimed at reducing social anxiety among LGBT youth. In their developmental years, LGBT adolescents commonly face adverse experiences such as bullying and victimization, social isolation, and loss of friends and family (e.g., Garofalo et al., 1998; Hershberger et al., 1997), which may predispose them to the development of SAD and a host of other problems. To reduce these negative outcomes, preventative efforts are necessary. Given the amount of time adolescents spend in school, a large portion of social, emotional, and sexual development occurs within this environment. Unfortunately, a high proportion of LGBT adolescents report feeling unsafe at school and may miss school to ensure their safety (Eisenberg & Resnick, 2006; Garofalo et al., 1998). School safety is therefore critical in protecting these youth from negative outcomes (Garofalo et al.,

1998), and efforts to decrease social stigma toward LGBT youth within the school environment are essential. Students, faculty, administration, and families need to be educated on the critical importance of support in the lives of LGBT youth and on the devastating effects of bullying and harassment, which may potentially include increased social withdrawal and SAD.

Psychological Treatments Needed

Psychological treatments are recommended to reduce the incidence of SAD and its negative consequences among LGBT youth. Cognitive behavior therapy, in particular, has been shown to reduce symptoms of SAD in both adolescent and adult populations (Abramowitz, Moore, Braddok, & Harrington, 2009; Blackmore & Heimberg, 2009; Clark et al., 2006; Davidson et al., 2004; Eng, Coles, Heimberg, & Safren, 2005; Feske & Chambless, 1995; Gould, Otto, Pollack, Yap, 1997; Herbert et al., 2009; Taylor, 1996; Hambrick, Weeks, Harb, & Heimberg, 2003). Although treatment of social anxiety with cognitive behavior therapy has not been extensively studied among LGBT youth, there is preliminary evidence of its effectiveness among LGB adult clients (see Martell, Safren, & Prince, 2004; Safren & Rogers, 2001). These interventions may have significant clinical implications for LGBT youth not only in treating social anxiety but also in preventing related adverse outcomes including alcohol and substance use, sexual risk behaviors, poor social support, and suicidality. Several articles present case studies that may be useful for clinicians treating social anxiety among LGBT youth (e.g., Hart & Heimberg, 2001; Safren, Hollander, Hart, & Heimberg, 2001). However, additional research is needed to demonstrate the generalizability of findings from primary heterosexual samples of adolescents and young adults to LGBT youth.

Finally, it is important to note that many of the concerns among LGBT youth regarding negative social evaluation may be rooted in actual experiences of bullying, harassment, and social isolation. Therefore, interventions developed for LGBT adolescents should not focus exclusively on reducing irrational thoughts but also on methods of coping with real-life stressors. As well, because social support is a critical protective factor against negative psychological outcomes, clinicians must make efforts to assist LGBT youth in seeking out and attaining supportive social networks that may buffer them against further harm.

CONCLUSION

Although it is certainly possible that LGBT adolescents and young adults may acquire SAD in the same manner as heterosexuals, these individuals face a myriad of unique risk factors that may contribute to persistent social anxiety and avoidance. LGBT youth are a high-risk population, vulnerable to a range of life stressors and negative mental and physical health outcomes. In this chapter, we highlighted that social anxiety and SAD may be both a cause and consequence of adverse social, emotional, and physical experiences beginning during childhood. To improve the quality of life of LGBT youth, more research is needed to understand the unique experiences of this population and to guide future interventions that will reduce social anxiety and improve long-term health outcomes in this vulnerable population.

REFERENCES

Abramowitz, J. S., Moore, E. L., Braddock, A. E., & Harrington, D. L. (2009). Self-help cognitive-behavioral therapy with minimal therapist contact for social phobia: A controlled trial. *Journal of Behavior Therapy and Experimental Psychiatry, 40*, 98–105. doi:10.1016/j.jbtep.2008.04.004

Almeida, J., Johnson, R. M., Corliss, H. L., Molnar, B. E., & Azrael, D. (2009). Emotional distress among LGBT youth: The influence of perceived discrimination based on sexual orientation. *Journal of Youth and Adolescence, 38*, 1001–1014. doi:10.1007/s10964-009-9397-9

Bailey, J. M., & Zucker, K. J. (1995). Childhood sex-typed behavior and sexual orientation: A conceptual analysis and quantitative review. *Developmental Psychology, 31*, 43–55. doi:10.1037/0012-1649.31.1.43

Blackmore, M. A., & Heimberg, R. G. (2009). Cognitive behavior therapy for social anxiety disorder. In G. Simos (Ed.), *Cognitive behaviour therapy: A guide for the practising clinician* (Vol. 2, pp. 48–63). London, England: Routledge.

Bockting, W., Benner, A., & Coleman, E. (2009). Gay and bisexual identity development among female-to-male transsexuals in North America: Emergence of a transgender sexuality. *Archives of Sexual Behavior, 38*, 688–701. doi:10.1007/s10508-009-9489-3

Bontempo, D. E., & D'Augelli, A. R. (2002). Effects of at-school victimization and sexual orientation on lesbian, gay, or bisexual youths' health risk behavior. *The Journal of Adolescent Health, 30*, 364–374. doi:10.1016/S1054-139X(01)00415-3

Bostwick, W. B., Boyd, C. J., Hughes, T. L., & McCabe, S. E. (2010). Dimensions of sexual orientation and the prevalence of mood and anxiety disorders in the United States. *American Journal of Public Health, 100*, 468–475.

Brown, L., Macintyre, K., & Trujillo, L. (2003). Interventions to reduce HIV/AIDS stigma: What have we learned? *AIDS Education and Prevention, 15*, 49–69. doi:10.1521/aeap.15.1.49.23844

Buckner, J. D., Schmidt, N. B., Lang, A. R., Small, J. W., Schlauch, R. C., & Lewinsohn, P. M. (2008). Specificity of social anxiety disorder as a risk factor for alcohol and cannabis dependence. *Journal of Psychiatric Research, 42*, 230–239. doi:10.1016/j.jpsychires.2007.01.002

Clark, D. M., Ehlers, A., Hackmann, A., McManus, F., Fennell, M., Grey, N., . . . Wild, J. (2006). Cognitive therapy versus exposure and applied relaxation in social phobia: A randomized controlled trial. *Journal of Consulting and Clinical Psychology, 74,* 568–578.

Cochran, S. D. (2001). Emerging issues in research on lesbians' and gay men's mental health: Does sexual orientation really matter? *American Psychologist, 56,* 931–947. doi:10.1037/0003-066X.56.11.931

Corliss, H. L., Cochran, S. D., & Mays, V. M. (2002). Reports of parental maltreatment during childhood in a United States population-based survey of homosexual, bisexual, and heterosexual adults. *Child Abuse & Neglect, 26,* 1165–1178. doi:10.1016/S0145-2134(02)00385-X

Courtenay-Quirk, C., Wolitski, R. J., Parsons, J. T., & Gómez, C. A. (2006). Is HIV/AIDS stigma dividing the gay community? Perceptions of HIV-positive men who have sex with men. *AIDS Education and Prevention, 18,* 56–67. doi:10.1521/aeap.2006.18.1.56

D'Augelli, A. R. (2002). Mental health problems among lesbian, gay, and bisexual youths ages 14–21. *Clinical Child Psychology and Psychiatry, 7,* 433–456.

D'Augelli, A. R., Grossman, A. H., & Starks, M. T. (2005). Parents' awareness of lesbian, gay, and bisexual youths' sexual orientation. *Journal of Marriage and the Family, 67,* 474–482. doi:10.1111/j.0022-2445.2005.00129.x

D'Augelli, A. R., Grossman, A. H., & Starks, M. T. (2006). Childhood gender atypicality, victimization, and PTSD among lesbian, gay, and bisexual youth. *Journal of Interpersonal Violence, 21,* 1462–1482. doi:10.1177/0886260506293482

D'Augelli, A. R., Grossman, A. H., & Starks, M. T. (2008). Families of gay, lesbian, and bisexual youth: What do parents and siblings know and how do they react? *Journal of GLBT Family Studies, 4,* 95–115.

D'Augelli, A. R., & Hershberger, S. L. (1993). Lesbian, gay and bisexual youth in community settings: Personal challenges and mental health problems. *American Journal of Community Psychology, 21,* 421–448. doi:10.1007/BF00942151

D'Augelli, A. R., Hershberger, S., & Pilkington, N. W. (1998). Lesbian, gay, and bisexual youths and their families: Disclosure of sexual orientation and its consequences. *American Journal of Orthopsychiatry, 68,* 361–371. doi:10.1037/h0080345

D'Augelli, A. R., Pilkington, N. W., & Hershberger, S. L. (2002). Incidence and mental health impact of sexual orientation victimization of lesbian, gay, and bisexual youths in high school. *School Psychology Quarterly, 17,* 148–167. doi:10.1521/scpq.17.2.148.20854

D'Augelli, A. R., & Rose, M. L. (1990). Homophobia in a university community: Attitudes and experiences of heterosexual freshmen. *Journal of College Student Development, 31,* 484–491.

Davidson, J. R. T., Foa, E. B., Huppert, J. D., Keefe, F. J., Franklin, M. E., Compton, J. S., . . . Gadde, K. M. (2004). Fluoxetine, comprehensive cognitive behavioral therapy, and placebo in generalized social phobia. *Archives of General Psychiatry, 61,* 1005–1013. doi:10.1001/archpsyc.61.10.1005

Devine, P. G., Plant, E. A., & Harrison, K. (1999). The problem of "us" versus "them" and AIDS stigma. *American Behavioral Scientist, 42,* 1212–1228. doi:10.1177/00027649921954732

Eckleberry-Hunt, J. G., & Dohrenwend, A. (2005). Sociocultural interpretations of social phobia in a non-heterosexual female. *Journal of Homosexuality, 49,* 103–117. doi:10.1300/J082v49n02_06

Eisenberg, M. E., & Resnick, M. D. (2006). Suicidality among gay, lesbian and bisexual youth: The role of protective factors. *The Journal of Adolescent Health, 39,* 662–668. doi:10.1016/j.jadohealth.2006.04.024

Eng, W., Coles, M. E., Heimberg, R. G., & Safren, S. A. (2005). Domains of life satisfaction in social anxiety disorder: Relation to symptoms and response to cognitive-behavioral therapy. *Journal of Anxiety Disorders, 19,* 143–156. doi:10.1016/j.janxdis.2004.01.007

Evans, N. J. (2001). The experiences of lesbian, gay, and bisexual youths in university communities. In A. R. D'Augelli & C. J. Patterson (Eds.), *Lesbian, gay, and bisexual identities and youth: Psychological perspectives* (pp. 181–198). New York, NY: Oxford University.

Evans, N. J., & D'Augelli, A. R. (1996). Lesbians, gay men, and bisexual people in college. In R. C. Savin-Williams & K. M. Cohen (Eds.), *The lives of lesbians, gays, and bisexuals: Children to adults* (pp. 201–226). Fort Worth, TX: Harcourt Brace College.

Faltz, B. G. (1992). Coping with AIDS and substance abuse. In P. A. Ahmend & N. Ahmed (Eds.), *Living and dying with AIDS* (pp. 137–150). New York, NY: Plenum Press.

Fergusson, D. M., Horwood, L. J., & Beautrais, A. L. (1999). Is sexual orientation related to mental health problems and suicidality in young people? *Archives of General Psychiatry, 56,* 876–880. doi:10.1001/archpsyc.56.10.876

Feske, U., & Chambless, D. L. (1995). Cognitive behavioral versus exposure only treatment for social phobia: A meta-analysis. *Behavior Therapy, 26,* 695–720. doi:10.1016/S0005-7894(05)80040-1

Fisher, L. E., & Banik, S. (2007). College major, gender and heterosexism reconsidered under more controlled conditions. *Journal of LGBT Health Research, 3,* 49–53. doi:10.1300/J463v03n01_06

Gagné, P., Tewksbury, R., & McGaughey, D. (1997). Coming out and crossing over: Identity formation and proclamation in a transgender community. *Gender & Society, 11,* 478–508. doi:10.1177/089124397011004006

Garofalo, R. R., Wolf, C., Kessel, S., Palfrey, J., & DuRant, R. H. (1998). The association between health risk behaviors and sexual orientation among a school-based sample of adolescents. *Pediatrics, 101,* 895–902. doi:10.1542/peds.101.5.895

Goldfried, M. R., & Goldfried, A. P. (2001). The importance of parental support in the lives of gay, lesbian, and bisexual individuals. *Journal of Clinical Psychology, 57,* 681–693. doi:10.1002/jclp.1037

Gould, R. A., Otto, M. W., Pollack, M. H., & Yap, L. (1997). Cognitive behavioral and pharmacological treatment of generalized anxiety disorder: A preliminary meta-analysis. *Behavior Therapy, 28,* 285–305. doi:10.1016/S0005-7894(97)80048-2

Grossman, A. H., & D'Augelli, A. R. (2007). Transgender youth and life-threatening behaviors. *Suicide & Life-Threatening Behavior, 37,* 527–537. doi:10.1521/suli.2007.37.5.527

Hambrick, J. P., Weeks, J. W., Harb, G. C., & Heimberg, R. G. (2003). Cognitive-behavioral therapy for social anxiety disorder: Supporting evidence and future directions. *CNS Spectrums, 8,* 373–381.

Hart, T. A., & Heimberg, R. G. (2001). Presenting problems among treatment-seeking gay, lesbian, and bisexual youth. *Journal of Clinical Psychology, 57,* 615–627. doi:10.1002/jclp.1032

Hart, T. A., & Heimberg, R. G. (2005). Social anxiety as a risk factor for unprotected intercourse among gay and bisexual male youth. *AIDS and Behavior, 9,* 505–512. doi:10.1007/s10461-005-9021-2

He, Q.-M., Pan, R.-D., & Meng, X.-Z. (2008). Relationship of social anxiety disorder and child abuse and trauma. *Chinese Journal of Clinical Psychology, 16,* 40–42.

Herbert, J. D., Gaudiano, B. A., Rheingold, A. A., Moitra, E., Myers, V. H., Dalrymple, K. L., & Brandsma, L. L. (2009). Cognitive behavior therapy for generalized social anxiety disorder in adolescents: A randomized controlled trial. *Journal of Anxiety Disorders, 23,* 167–177. doi:10.1016/j.janxdis.2008.06.004

Herbert, J. T., Hunt, B., & Dell, G. (1994). Counseling gay men and lesbians with alcohol problems. *The Journal of Rehabilitation, 60,* 52–58.

Herek, G. M. (2000). Sexual prejudice and gender: Do heterosexuals' attitudes toward lesbians and gay men differ? *Journal of Social Issues, 56,* 251–266. doi:10.1111/0022-4537.00164

Herek, G. M., & Capitanio, J. P. (1999). AIDS stigma and sexual prejudice. *American Behavioral Scientist, 42,* 1130–1147.

Herek, G. M., Capitanio, J. P., & Widaman, K. F. (2002). HIV-related stigma and knowledge in the United States: Prevalence and trends, 1991–1999. *American Journal of Public Health, 92,* 371–377.

Herek, G. M., & Glunt, E. K. (1993). Interpersonal contact and heterosexuals' attitudes toward gay men: Results from a national survey. *Journal of Sex Research, 30,* 239–244. doi:10.1080/00224499309551707

Hershberger, S. L., & D'Augelli, A. R. (1995). The impact of victimization on the mental health and suicidality of lesbian, gay, and bisexual youths. *Developmental Psychology, 31,* 65–74.

Hershberger, S. L., Pilkington, N. W., & D'Augelli, A. R. (1997). Predictors of suicide attempts among gay, lesbian, and bisexual youth. *Journal of Adolescent Research, 12,* 477–497. doi:10.1177/0743554897124004

Hinrichs, D. W., & Rosenberg, P. J. (2002). Attitudes toward gay, lesbian, and bisexual persons among heterosexual liberal arts college students. *Journal of Homosexuality, 43,* 61–84. doi:10.1300/J082v43n01_04

Hope, D. A., & Heimberg, R. G. (1990). Dating anxiety. In H. Leitenberg (Ed.), *Handbook of social and evaluation anxiety* (pp. 217–246). New York, NY: Plenum Press.

Hughes, T. L., & Eliason, M. (2002). Substance use and abuse in lesbian, gay, bisexual, and transgender population. *The Journal of Primary Prevention, 22*, 263–298. doi:10.1023/A:1013669705086

Hunter, E. (2008). What's good for the gays is good for the gander: Making homeless youth housing safer for lesbian, gay, bisexual, and transgender youth. *Family Court Review, 46*, 543–557. doi:10.1111/j.1744-1617.2008.00220.x

Igartua, K. J., Gill, K., & Montoro, R. (2003). Internalized homophobia: A factor in depression, anxiety, and suicide in the gay and lesbian population. *Canadian Journal of Community Mental Health, 22*, 15–30.

Jordan, K. M. (2000). Substance abuse among gay, lesbian, bisexual, transgender, and questioning adolescents. *School Psychology Review, 29*, 201–206.

Kane, E. W. (2006). "No way my boys are going to be like that!": Parents' responses to children's gender nonconformity. *Gender & Society, 20*, 149–176.

Kenagy, G. P. (2005). Transgender health: Findings from two needs assessment studies in Philadelphia. *Health & Social Work, 30*, 19–26.

King, M., Semlyen, J., Tai, S. S., Killaspy, H., Osborn, D., Popelyuk, D., & Nazareth, I. (2008, August 18). A systematic review of mental disorder, suicide, and deliberate self harm in lesbian, gay, and bisexual people. *BMC Psychiatry, 8*, Article 70. Retrieved from http://www.biomedcentral.com/1471-244X/8/70

Kubicek, K., McDavitt, B., Carpineto, J., Weiss, G., Iverson, E. F., & Kipke, M. D. (2007). Making informed decisions: How attitudes and perceptions affect the use of crystal, cocaine, and ecstasy among young men who have sex with men. *Journal of Drug Issues, 37*, 643–674.

Lambert, E. G., Ventura, L. A., Hall, D. E., & Cluse-Tolar, T. (2006). College students' views on gay and lesbian issues: Does education make a difference. *Journal of Homosexuality, 50*, 1–30. doi:10.1300/J082v50n04_01

Leary, M. R., & Kowalski, R. M. (1995). *Social anxiety*. New York, NY: Guilford Press.

Lippa, R. A. (2008). The relation between childhood gender nonconformity and adult masculinity–femininity and anxiety in heterosexual and homosexual men and women. *Sex Roles, 59*, 684–693. doi:10.1007/s11199-008-9476-5

Louderback, L. A., & Whitley, B. E., Jr. (1997). Perceived erotic value of homosexuality and sex-role attitudes as mediators of sex differences in heterosexual college students' attitudes toward lesbians and gay men. *Journal of Sex Research, 34*, 175–182. doi:10.1080/00224499709551882

Love, P. (1997). Contradiction and paradox: Attempting to change the culture of sexual orientation at a small Catholic college. *Review of Higher Education, 20*, 381–398.

Marshal, M. P., Friedman, M. S., Stall, R., King, K. M., Miles, J., Gold, M. A., . . . Morse, J. Q. (2008). Sexual orientation and adolescent substance use: A meta-analysis

and methodological review. *Addiction, 103,* 546–556. doi:10.1111/j.1360-0443.
2008.02149.x

Marsiglio, W. (1993). Attitudes toward homosexual activity and gays as friends: A
national survey of heterosexual 15- to 19-year-old males. *Journal of Sex Research,
30,* 12–17. doi:10.1080/00224499309551673

Martell, C. R., Safren, S. A., & Prince, S. E. (2004). *Cognitive-behavioral therapies with
lesbian, gay, and bisexual clients.* New York, NY: Guilford Press.

Mays, V. M., & Cochran, S. D. (2001). Mental health correlates of perceived discrimination among lesbian, gay, and bisexual adults in the United States.
American Journal of Public Health, 91, 1869–1876.

McDermott, E., Roen, K., & Scourfield, J. (2008). Avoiding shame: Young LGBT
people, homophobia and self-destructive behaviours. *Culture, Health & Sexuality,
10,* 815–829. doi:10.1080/13691050802380974

Meeus, W., Iedema, J., Helsen, M., & Volleberg, W. (1999). Patterns of adolescent
identity development: Review of literature and longitudinal analysis. *Developmental Review, 19,* 419–461. doi:10.1006/drev.1999.0483

Meyer, I. H. (2003). Prejudice, social stress, and mental health in lesbian, gay, and
bisexual populations: Conceptual issues and research evidence. *Psychological
Bulletin, 129,* 674–697. doi:10.1037/0033-2909.129.5.674

Nagoshi, J. L., Adams, K., Terrell, H. K., Hill, E. D., Brzuzy, S., & Nagoshi, C. T.
(2008). Gender differences in correlates of homophobia and transphobia. *Sex
Roles, 59,* 521–531. doi:10.1007/s11199-008-9458-7

Noell, J. W., & Ochs, L. M. (2001). Relationship of sexual orientation to substance use,
suicidal ideation, suicide attempts, and other factors in a population of homeless
adolescents. *The Journal of Adolescent Health, 29,* 31–36. doi:10.1016/S1054-139X
(01)00205-1

Pachankis, J. E., & Goldfried, M. R. (2006). Social anxiety in young gay men. *Journal of
Anxiety Disorders, 20,* 996–1015. doi:10.1016/j.janxdis.2006.01.001

Pachankis, J. E., Goldfried, M. R., & Ramrattan, M. E. (2008). Extension of the rejection sensitivity construct to the interpersonal functioning of gay men. *Journal of
Consulting and Clinical Psychology, 76,* 306–317. doi:10.1037/0022-006X.76.2.306

Pettijohn, T. F., II, & Walzer, A. (2008). Reducing racism, sexism, and homophobia
in college students by completing a psychology of prejudice course. *College Student Journal, 42,* 459–468.

Pilkington, N. W., & D'Augelli, A. R. (1995). Victimization of lesbian, gay, and bisexual youth in community settings. *Journal of Community Psychology, 23,* 34–56.
doi:10.1002/1520-6629(199501)23:1<34::AID-JCOP2290230105>3.0.CO;2-N

Poteat, V. P., & Espelage, D. (2007). Predicting psychosocial consequences of homophobic victimization in middle school students. *The Journal of Early Adolescence,
27,* 175–191. doi:10.1177/0272431606294839

Poteat, V. P., Espelage, D. L., & Koenig, B. W. (2009). Willingness to remain friends
and attend school with lesbian and gay peers: Relational expressions of preju-

dice among heterosexual youth. *Journal of Youth and Adolescence, 38,* 952–962. doi:10.1007/s10964-009-9416-x

Potoczniak, D. J., Aldea, M. A., & DeBlaere, C. (2007). Ego identity, social anxiety, social support, and self-concealment in lesbian, gay, and bisexual individuals. *Journal of Counseling Psychology, 54,* 447–457. doi:10.1037/0022-0167.54.4.447

Rankin, S. R. (2003). *Campus climate for gay, lesbian, bisexual, and transgender people: A national perspective.* New York, NY: The National Gay and Lesbian Task Force Institute. Retrieved from http://www.thetaskforce.org/downloads/reports/reports/CampusClimate.pdf

Rapaport, M. H., Clary, C., Fayyad, R., & Endicott, J. (2005). Quality-of-life impairment in depressive and anxiety disorders. *The American Journal of Psychiatry, 162,* 1171–1178. doi:10.1176/appi.ajp.162.6.1171

Remafedi, G. (1999). Sexual orientation and youth suicide. *JAMA, 282,* 1291–1292.

Remafedi, G. (2002). Suicidality in a venue-based sample of young men who have sex with men. *The Journal of Adolescent Health, 31,* 305–310. doi:10.1016/S1054-139X(02)00405-6

Remafedi, G., French, S., Story, M., Resnick, M. D., & Blum, R. (1998). The relationship between suicide risk and sexual orientation: Results of a population-based study. *American Journal of Public Health, 88,* 57–60. doi:10.2105/AJPH.88.1.57

Rivers, I., & D'Augelli, A. R. (2001). The victimization of lesbians, gay, and bisexual youths. In A. R. D'Augelli & C. J. Patterson (Eds.), *Lesbian, gay, and bisexual identities and youth: Psychological perspectives* (pp. 199–223). New York, NY: Oxford University Press.

Rogers, T. L., Emanuel, K., & Bradford, J. (2002). Sexual minorities seeking services: A retrospective study of the mental health concerns of lesbian and bisexual women. *Journal of Lesbian Studies, 7,* 127–146. doi:10.1300/J155v07n01_09

Roper, E. A., & Halloran, E. (2007). Attitudes toward gay men and lesbians among heterosexual male and female student-athletes. *Sex Roles, 57,* 919–928. doi:10.1007/s11199-007-9323-0

Rosario, M., Hunter, J., & Gwadz, M. (1997). Exploration of substance use among lesbian, gay, and bisexual youth: Prevalence and correlates. *Journal of Adolescent Research, 12,* 454–476. doi:10.1177/0743554897124003

Rosario, M., Schrimshaw, E. W., & Hunter, J. (2006). A model of sexual risk behaviors among young gay and bisexual men: Longitudinal associations of mental health, substance abuse, sexual abuse, and the coming-out process. *AIDS Education and Prevention, 18,* 444–460. doi:10.1521/aeap.2006.18.5.444

Rosario, M., Schrimshaw, E. W., & Hunter, J. (2008). Butch/femme differences in substance use and abuse among young lesbian and bisexual women: Examination and potential explanations. *Substance Use & Misuse, 43,* 1002–1015. doi:10.1080/10826080801914402

Rosario, M., Schrimshaw, E. W., Hunter, J., & Gwadz, M. (2002). Gay-related stress and emotional distress among gay, lesbian, and bisexual youths: A longitudinal examination. *Journal of Consulting and Clinical Psychology, 70,* 967–975. doi:10. 1037/0022-006X.70.4.967

Rotheram-Borus, M. J., Hunter, J., & Rosario, M. (1994). Suicidal behavior and gay-related stress among gay and bisexual male adolescents. *Journal of Adolescent Research, 9,* 498–508.

Rotherham-Borus, M. J., & Langabeer, K. A. (2001). Developmental trajectories of gay, lesbian, and bisexual youths. In A. R. D'Augelli & C. J. Patterson (Eds.), *Lesbian, gay, and bisexual identities and youth: Psychological perspectives* (pp. 97–128). New York, NY: Oxford University Press.

Rotheram-Borus, M. J., Rosario, M., Van Rossem, R., Reid, H., & Gillis, R. (1995). Prevalence, course, and predictors of multiple problem behaviors among gay and bisexual male adolescents. *Developmental Psychology, 31,* 75–85. doi:10.1037/ 0012-1649.31.1.75

Russell, S. T., Franz, B. T., & Driscoll, A. K. (2001). Same-sex romantic attraction and experiences of violence in adolescence. *American Journal of Public Health, 91,* 903–906. doi:10.2105/AJPH.91.6.903

Ryan, C., & Futterman, D. (1998). *Lesbian and gay youth: Care and counseling.* New York, NY: Columbia University Press.

Safren, S. A., & Heimberg, R. G. (1999). Depression, hopelessness, suicidality, and related factors in sexual minority and heterosexual adolescents. *Journal of Consulting and Clinical Psychology, 67,* 859–866. doi:10.1037/0022-006X. 67.6.859

Safren, S. A., Heimberg, R. G., Brown, E. J., & Holle, C. (1996). Quality of life in social phobia. *Depression and Anxiety, 4,* 126–133.

Safren, S. A., Hollander, G., Hart, T. A., & Heimberg, R. G. (2001). Cognitive-behavioral therapy with lesbian, gay, and bisexual youth. *Cognitive and Behavioral Practice, 8,* 215–223. doi:10.1016/S1077-7229(01)80056-0

Safren, S. A., & Pantalone, D. W. (2006). Social anxiety and barriers to resilience among lesbian, gay, and bisexual adolescents. In A. M. Omoto & H. Kurtzman (Eds.), *Sexual orientation and mental health: Examining identity and development in lesbian, gay, and bisexual people* (pp. 55–71). Washington, DC: American Psychological Association. doi:10.1037/11261-003

Safren, S. A., & Rogers, T. (2001). Cognitive-behavioral therapy with gay, lesbian, and bisexual clients. *Journal of Clinical Psychology, 57,* 629–643.

Sandfort, T. G. M., de Graaf, R., Bijl, R. V., & Schnabel, P. (2001). Same-sex sexual behavior and psychiatric disorders. *Archives of General Psychiatry, 58,* 85–91. doi:10.1001/archpsyc.58.1.85

Savin-Williams, R. C. (1994). Verbal and physical abuse as stressors in the lives of lesbian, gay male, and bisexual youths. *Journal of Consulting and Clinical Psychology, 62,* 261–269. doi:10.1037/0022-006X.62.2.261

Schellenberg, E. G., Hirt, J., & Sears, A. (1999). Attitudes toward homosexuals among students at a Canadian university. *Sex Roles, 40,* 139–152.

Schneier, F. R., Foose, T. E., Hasin, D. S., Heimberg, R. G., Liu, S. M., Grant, B. F., & Blanco, C. (2010). Social anxiety disorder and alcohol use disorder co-morbidity in the National Epidemiologic Survey on Alcohol and Related Conditions. *Psychological Medicine, 40,* 977–988.

Sharpe, S. (2002). It's just really hard to come to terms with: Young people's views on homosexuality. *Sex Education, 2,* 263–277. doi:10.1080/1468181022000025811

Saewyc, E., Skay, C. L., Richens, K., Reis, E., Poon, C., & Murphy, A. (2006). Sexual orientation, sexual abuse and HIV-risk behaviors among adolescents in the Pacific Northwest. *American Journal of Public Health, 96,* 1104–1110. doi:10.2105/AJPH.2005.065870

Silverman, A. B., Reinherz, H. Z., & Giaconia, R. M. (1996). The long term seque-lae of child and adolescent abuse: A longitudinal community study. *Child Abuse & Neglect, 20,* 709–723. doi:10.1016/0145-2134(96)00059-2

Swendeman, D., Rotheram-Borus, M. J., Comulada, S., Weiss, R., & Ramos, M. E. (2006). Predictors of HIV-related stigma among young people living with HIV. *Health Psychology, 25,* 501–509. doi:10.1037/0278-6133.25.4.501

Taylor, S. (1996). Meta-analysis of cognitive-behavioral treatments for social pho-bia. *Journal of Behavior Therapy and Experimental Psychiatry, 27,* 1–9.

Tomeo, M. E., Templer, D. I., Anderson, S., & Kotler, D. (2001). Comparative data of childhood and adolescence molestation in heterosexual and homosexual persons. *Archives of Sexual Behavior, 30,* 535–541.

Waldo, C. R., Hesson-McInnis, M. S., & D'Augelli, A. R. (1998). Antecedents and consequences of victimization of lesbian, gay, and bisexual young people: A structural model comparing rural university and urban samples. *American Journal of Community Psychology, 26,* 307–334. doi:10.1023/A:1022184704174

Weinrich, J. D., Atkinson, J. H., Jr., McCutchan, J. A., & Grant, I. (1995). Is gen-der dysphoria dysphoric? Elevated depression and anxiety in gender dysphoric and nondysphoric homosexual and bisexual men in an HIV sample. *Archives of Sexual Behavior, 24,* 55–72. doi:10.1007/BF01541989

10

SOCIAL ANXIETY IN ADOLESCENTS ON THE AUTISM SPECTRUM

SUSAN W. WHITE AND AMIE R. SCHRY

Autism spectrum disorders (ASDs), which include autistic disorder, Asperger's disorder, and pervasive developmental disorder not otherwise specified, are neurodevelopmental disorders that share a common underlying deficit in social interaction skills. Other diagnostic criteria, including delayed or unusual communication and repetitive behavior or restricted interests, vary across the ASD diagnostic subtypes. Individuals with Asperger's disorder, for instance, have no early language delay and often have a well-developed vocabulary and verbal communication skills. People with classic autistic disorder, on the other hand, typically have significant language delays in childhood, and many remain nonverbal. The U.S. Centers for Disease Control and Prevention (2007) reported that ASD may be as common as one in every 152 children, suggesting that these disorders pose "an urgent public health issue."

In addition to its core characteristics, individuals with ASD often exhibit co-occurring psychiatric problems. Anxiety-related concerns are among the most common presenting problems for school-age children and adolescents with ASD (Ghaziuddin, 2002). Though epidemiological studies on the co-occurrence of anxiety disorders in ASD do not exist, empirical reports from clinical samples report that between 11% and 84% of children with ASD experience impairing anxiety (White, Oswald, Ollendick, & Scahill, 2009). Social anxiety disorder (SAD) may be especially common among cognitively higher functioning adolescents with ASD; more than half (57.1%) of one ASD sample of children and adolescents 12 years and older and without intellectual disability reported clinically significant levels of social anxiety (Kuusikko et al., 2008). In another study, 49% of cognitively higher functioning adolescents with ASD self-reported clinically elevated levels of social anxiety (Bellini, 2004). Nonorthogonal diagnostic rubric alone does not explain the social anxiety often seen in youth with ASD (Kuusikko et al., 2008). An assessment of social anxiety through self-report and parent-report measures in a sample of youth (ages 8–15) with ASD indicated that youth with ASD were still more likely to experience social anxiety than same-age nonclinical control children.

On the basis of the common co-occurrence of these problems and disorders, in this chapter we examine both the distinct and overlapping features of SAD and ASD toward improving common diagnostic ambiguities. Key diagnostic criteria are specifically examined to help guide clinical understanding of both diagnoses. We also provide some specific distinctions in the social problems faced by both groups as a means of directing assessment as well as treatment practices. Finally, we examine and review assessment and treatment practices appropriate for adolescents and young adults with ASD.

SOCIAL ANXIETY IN ADOLESCENTS ON THE SPECTRUM

Although it is often assumed that youth with ASD prefer social isolation, many youth are intensely aware of their social disconnectedness and desire greater social interaction (Attwood, 2000). In a recent qualitative study, most young adults with high-functioning ASD reported that loneliness became more problematic as they got older (Müller, Schuler, & Yates, 2008). Although not a phenomenological characteristic, for many people there is a connection between problems with anxiety and the social impairment that characterizes ASD. The nature of this connection is not yet fully understood, and both physiological hyperarousal and social deficits are plausible hypotheses (Bellini, 2006). For example, Lopata, Volker, Putnam, Thomeer, and Nida (2008) found that higher functioning children with ASD had higher levels of cortisol, a stress regulation hormone, than typically developing children. Similarly, it is possible that anxiety stems from the core features of ASD, notably the need for sameness and consistency, fondness for rituals, rigidity in routines, and a high level of predictability (Church, Alisanski, & Amanullah, 2000; Gillott, Furniss, & Walter, 2001). In short, there are many plausible explanations that require further investigation, and a developmental approach to understanding how anxiety interacts with the core disabilities of ASD is important.

Cognitive awareness of one's own social difficulties and previous learning history (e.g., rejection from peers) also may contribute to the emergence of social anxiety and, in turn, exacerbate social deficits observed in ASD. Social avoidance may lead to fewer opportunities in which to practice appropriate social skills (Myles, Barnhill, Hagiwara, Griswold, & Simpson, 2001). As both social complexity and social demands rise during adolescence, youth with ASD often become even more aware of their social disabilities (Tantam, 2003). This awareness may contribute to the development of secondary mood and anxiety problems (Myles, 2003; Myles, Bock, & Simpson, 2001; Sukhodolsky et al., 2008; Tantam, 2003), a cycle especially likely for higher functioning individuals with ASD who are more cognizant of their social deficits (Tse, Strulovich, Tagalakis, Meng, & Fombonne, 2007).

AUTISM SPECTRUM DISORDERS AND SOCIAL ANXIETY DISORDER: SHARED AND DISTINCT FACTORS

An inability to interact with others fluidly and age appropriately represents the primary source of impairment in ASD, regardless of the person's cognitive or language ability (Carter, Davis, Klin, & Volkmar, 2005). Social skill deficits are also seen in teens who experience social anxiety and those with SAD (Interbitzen-Nolan, Anderson, & Johnson, 2007; Pine, Guyer, Goldwin, Towbin, & Leibenluft, 2008). Compared with SAD, however, there are two truisms of social disability in ASD. First, it is profound and pervasive, characteristic of all the spectrum disorders. Second, the deficit does not usually diminish with maturity. For higher functioning individuals, in fact, the social disability may be felt more acutely in adolescence (Tse et al., 2007). Nonetheless, it can be quite difficult to determine if specific social deficits are indicative of a co-occurring anxiety disorder or epiphenomena of ASD. Few same-age friends, limited involvement in extracurricular activities and apparent unease in social interactions may reflect either core social deficits or social anxiety.

The specific social skill deficits in people with ASD are diverse from person to person and vary in severity (Krasny, Williams, Provencal, & Ozonoff, 2003; Shaked & Yirmiya, 2003; Tager-Flusberg, 2003). A teen with ASD might launch into a conversation without providing sufficient contextual or background information or talk about a topic without consideration of the conversational partner's interest. He or she might do or say things when other youth would typically refrain, such as commenting negatively on someone's weight or hairstyle, or exhibit a general lack of appreciation for the unwritten rules of age-appropriate social behavior. Misperception of the emotional states, behaviors, and intentions of others is also common. The teen with Asperger's disorder might not recognize when he or she is the target of a joke or fail to pick up on aspects of communication such as subtle changes in vocal tone. This perception failure can lead to misunderstanding of the intended meaning of peers' nonliteral communication (e.g., irony).

Objective measures of social skills have also shown differences between adolescents with or without diagnoses of SAD. When children and young adolescents (ages 7–13) with SAD engaged in a role-play task with a same-aged peer, their interpersonal skills were rated lower than children without a psychiatric diagnosis (Beidel, Turner, & Morris, 1999). They also had significantly longer speech latencies. Adolescents with SAD also display social skill deficits (Inderbitzen-Nolan et al., 2007). On the basis of a 10-min speech given to a small audience and a 10-min conversation with a confederate, socially anxious adolescents were rated as less friendly, socially skilled, and assertive and more anxious and self-conscious than adolescents with no diagnosis.

There may be neurological and physiological differences in people with ASD that contribute to impaired social functioning. Sutton et al. (2005) compared possible psychophysiological differences in 23 high-functioning children with ASD, ages 9 to 14, and a control group consisting of typically developing children and children with learning disabilities. Participants with ASD and greater social anxiety displayed more left midfrontal activity on electroencephalograms. Control participants displayed the opposite pattern, greater right midfrontal activity. One possible explanation for this finding is that greater self-awareness of social difficulties contributed to the social anxiety of children with ASD. In fact, children with ASD who had more left frontal asymmetry reported more awareness of social difficulties and more fear of negative evaluation (Sutton et al., 2005). Such neurological and physiological differences have not been reported in children with SAD alone, suggesting that different mechanisms may lead to similar functional impairments.

In summary, for many adolescents there is considerable symptomatic overlap in terms of social skill deficits and social anxiety. In addition to anxiety and social skill deficits, the two conditions likely share some secondary or associated features. For instance, alexithymia, an inability to identify, interpret, and describe one's emotional states, is often found in individuals with ASD as well as in people with SAD (Evren & Evren, 2007). Being hypersensitive to certain stimuli (e.g., tactile, visual) and a tendency to become easily aroused or excited (e.g., Neal, Edelmann, & Glachan, 2002), combined with alexithymia, may predispose a person to experience anxiety (Liss, Mailloux, & Erchull, 2008). Further research on how such associated features may link SAD and ASD etiologically will inform the field and clinical practice.

Through a synthesis of the empirical research and clinical and anecdotal literature, there appears to be considerable overlap in the social deficiencies and anxiety symptoms among individuals with SAD without ASD and those with comorbid ASD and SAD. We propose that one distinction is in the area of social initiation. SAD may be more often characterized by a lack of social initiation and responsivity, whereas ASD (at least high-functioning ASD) is usually characterized by awkward, yet present, initiation skills. Observation of social interaction attempts may be very informative in this respect.

Yet another diagnostic distinction is in the global severity of the social deficit. Both groups display deficient social skills relative to nonanxious individuals, but people with ASD and social anxiety appear to be considerably more impaired socially, on the whole, than those with pure SAD. Further research is necessary to identify deficits that differentiate these two clinical groups. With respect to anxiety, individuals with ASD tend to have less insight and may rely on overt symptoms to describe their distress. Further, their symptoms may also not be typical of SAD. For example, teens with ASD may revert to a monologue on their special interest with heightened intensity when they experience social anxiety.

Table 10.1 provides a summary of some distinctions in social problems between adolescents with SAD versus ASD. These are general guidelines and do not apply to every child. For instance, a teen with ASD who has co-occurring SAD might be socially awkward and have few friends (typical of

TABLE 10. 1
Distinguishing Between Social Anxiety Disorder and
Autism Spectrum Disorder With Anxiety

Social anxiety disorder (without autism spectrum disorder)	Autism spectrum disorder and social anxiety
Social skill deficits may not have been a cause for concern in early childhood.	Social deficits have been present since very young, preceding emergence of symptoms of social anxiety.
Friendship with peers may be reciprocated but not intimate. The client may focus on receiving support from friend.	Few or no same-age friends. Friendships are often not reciprocated and often have an immature quality.
Youth avoids social initiation or other social evaluative situations because of anxiety.	Youth may initiate, but rendition is awkward, abrupt, and/or unskilled.
Less responsive to peers, less assertive.	May be socially responsive, but social behaviors are often intense, off topic, or unusual in some way.
Youth often reports feeling anxious or scared.	Youth does not self-identify feeling anxious. Anxiety may be expressed behaviorally (e.g., acting out, increase in stereotyped behaviors or rigid interests), yet the client does not label feelings of anxiety as such.

ASD) but have considerable insight into his symptoms of social anxiety (less typical of ASD).

EVALUATION AND DIAGNOSIS

The differential diagnosis of ASD and SAD can be quite complex because many of the same behaviors accurately describe both conditions. ASD is not a "rule-out" condition for SAD; the two disorders can be dually diagnosed. Anecdotally, however, even when a person with ASD meets criteria for SAD, the diagnosis is applied infrequently. To diagnose SAD in children, the child must have at least one age-appropriate social relationship with a peer. For a diagnosis of autistic disorder, on the other hand, a child must exhibit at least two symptoms of social impairment. One of the four key symptoms falling under this domain in the *Diagnostic and Statistical Manual of Mental Disorders* (4th ed., text rev.; *DSM–IV–TR*; American Psychiatric Association, 2000) is a "failure to develop peer relationships appropriate to developmental level" (p. 75). Hence, a critical determinant in diagnosis is evaluation of the teen's capacity for and achievement of age-appropriate peer relationships, a benchmark that requires a fair degree of subjective evaluation and judgment on the part of the evaluating clinician. Table 10.2 provides a summary of some of the key diagnostic criteria of ASD and how these behaviors and specific symptoms might also be conceptualized as features of SAD.

Many youngsters and young adults with ASD are socially naive and immature in their interests and behaviors. Moreover, they often have limited opportunities for engaging with same-age peers (e.g., because of their odd behaviors, educational placements) despite an often strong motivation to form friendships (Bauminger & Kasari, 2000; Müller et al., 2008; Turner-Brown, Perry, Dichter, Bodfish, & Penn, 2008). One may consider a 13-year-old boy referred for problems with social isolation who is the victim of severe and ongoing bullying at school. Does the teen demonstrate social knowledge and emotional insight yet feel unable to apply this knowledge in interactions with peers (more typical of SAD)? Or does he seem to have limited and/or inappropriate knowledge of how his peers interact or even how to determine who his friends might be (as in ASD)? Does he avoid social interactions and seclude himself, or does he exhibit unusual behaviors that bring unwanted attention and attempt social discourse with uninterested peers? Inquiries such as this, which assess the details of the client's social difficulties and anxiety, can yield important clinical information.

In addition to thoroughly exploring the nature of the social disability, age of symptom onset can sometimes aid appropriate diagnosis. Among individuals with SAD, 12.5 years is the median age of onset for this disorder (DeWit, Ogborne, Offord, & MacDonald, 1999; Grant et al., 2005). More

TABLE 10.2

Symptoms of Social Anxiety Disorder That Overlap With Diagnostic Criteria
for Autism Spectrum Disorder

DSM–IV–TR diagnostic criteria for autism spectrum disorder[a]	Seen as possible symptoms of social anxiety disorder
Qualitative impairment in social interaction is evidenced by at least two of the following: 1. obvious impairment in the practice of non-verbal behaviors (e.g., eye contact, facial expressions, body posture, and use of gestures); 2. a lack of peer relationships considered appropriate for developmental level; 3. failure to spontaneously seek to share enjoyment, interests, or achievements with others; and 4. lack of social or emotional reciprocity.	Possible social skill deficits, such as avoiding social interactions with peers, not knowing what to say in social interactions with peers, appearing less friendly, being less interpersonally skilled, and being less assertive
Qualitative impairment in communication[b] is evidenced by at least one of the following: 1. delay in, or total lack of, the development of spoken language (with no attempt to compensate with other modes of communication); 2. in individuals with sufficient spoken language, obvious impairment in the ability to start or maintain a conversation with others; 3. stereotyped and repetitive use of language or idiosyncratic language; and 4. lack of varied, spontaneous make-believe play or social imitative play considered appropriate for developmental level.	Possible impairment in ability to initiate or sustain conversations; lack of or reduced amount of interactive play and/or interaction with others in comparison with those of developmental level
Restricted repetitive and stereotyped patterns of behavior, interests, and activities[c] are evidenced by at least one of the following: 1. encompassing preoccupation with at least one stereotyped and restricted pattern of interest that is abnormal in either focus or intensity; 2. seemingly inflexible adherence to specific, nonfunctional routines or rituals; 3. stereotyped and repetitive motor mannerisms (such as hand or finger flapping or twisting or complex whole-body movements); and 4. persistent preoccupation with parts of objects.	Possible inflexible adherence to routines in order to avoid feeling anxious (e.g., by knowing the routine, the individual can predict whom he or she will come into contact with and can better prepare for the interaction or can avoid interaction)

[a] From the Diagnostic and Statistical Manual of Mental Disorders (4th ed., text rev.) by the American Psychiatric Association, 2000, Washington, DC: Author. [b] Required for a diagnosis of autistic disorder; may be present in pervasive developmental disorder not otherwise specified and not part of diagnostic criteria for Asperger's disorder. [c] May or may not be present in pervasive developmental disorder not otherwise specified.

than one half of older adults with a lifetime diagnosis of SAD reported that their symptoms were present before the age of 15, and another one fifth of participants reported that onset occurred between the ages of 15 and 19 (Cairney et al. 2007). Another study found that one half of adults with a lifetime diagnosis of SAD reported an age of onset before age 14, and 90% of people with SAD reported onset before the age of 23 (Kessler et al., 2005). Thus, whereas social impairment associated with SAD may not become apparent until the teenage years, youth with ASD commonly display social impairments from a much younger age.

Although there is variability across the spectrum disorders, symptoms of autism are, by definition, present in very early childhood and are often noticed during the first 3 years. The exception to this is pervasive developmental disorder not otherwise specified, which may have a later age of onset. The median age of diagnosis of childhood autistic disorder is 3.7 years (Williams, Thomas, Sidebotham, & Emond, 2008); individuals with Asperger's disorder are often diagnosed later, at 9.7 years on average (Williams et al., 2008). Even if never diagnosed, problems with social communication and interaction should be apparent (on the basis of caregiver history) from a very young age.

A third consideration is chronological course. For adolescents with both ASD and SAD (without ASD), symptoms of social anxiety become more prominent and more impairing during adolescence (e.g., Beidel & Turner, 2007; Farrugia & Hudson, 2006). Certain types of anxiety, for instance, social and evaluative anxiety and panic disorder, tend to emerge during adolescence in people with ASD, similar to youngsters without ASD (Bellini, 2004; Kuusikko et al., 2008). As previously discussed, this may be related to changing socioenvironmental demands and expectations and possibly to the youngster's experience of social failure. Greater social demands and more complex peer relationships coincide with very little explicit guidance on the "rules" for appropriate social behavior; an emphasis on fitting in among peers; and communication that is replete with slang, jargon, and sarcasm. Indeed, youngsters with ASD reported more social anxiety and behavioral avoidance as they approached adolescence, whereas typically developing nonclinical (i.e., without ASD or SAD) peers reported a decrease in symptoms of social anxiety and avoidance (Kuusikko et al., 2008).

Depending on the particular assessment practices used, certain behaviors and symptoms might be conceptualized as part of either SAD or an ASD. Consider the behaviors exhibited by a hypothetical adolescent (Table 10.3). Depending on the "lens" through which the clinician operates, which may be influenced by factors such as the referral questions, the clinician's area of expertise, and the type of setting in which the client is seen, exhibition of the same behavior can be conceptualized quite differently.

TABLE 10.3
Behaviors That Might Reflect Either Autism Spectrum Disorder or Social Anxiety Disorder in Adolescents

Observed behavior	Explained as autism spectrum disorder	Explained as social anxiety disorder
Refuses to eat in the cafeteria at school	Background noise level is overwhelming because of increased sensitivity to noise	Feelings of anxiety about eating in front of others
Becomes upset on learning that a pep rally will take place during school	Resistance to changes in schedule	Worry about being in crowded auditorium with other students
Breaks down in tears and sometimes yells when people get too close	Poor social skills, issues with personal space and boundaries	Poor social skills, anxiety about being around others, particularly strangers
Sits alone and reads while classmates are talking in a group nearby	Poor social skills, lack of knowledge of how to join a group, or low motivation to join	Poor social skills, anxiety about embarrassing oneself when attempting to join in

Several measures have been used to assess anxiety in young people with ASD. However, few measures have been developed explicitly to evaluate anxiety in people with ASD, and to date, very little research has evaluated the utility or validity of measures to assess anxiety in this population—much less specifically for social anxiety. In the sections that follow, we summarize the available research, emphasizing measures that have been used explicitly for assessment of social anxiety. This review is not exhaustive, as many measures have yet to be validated in people with ASD.

Parent- and Other-Report Measures

The Child and Adolescent Symptom Inventory—20 (CASI–20; Sukhodolsky et al., 2008) is a brief parent-report scale derived from a larger pool of anxiety items on the Child and Adolescent Symptom Inventory (Gadow & Sprafkin, 1994, 1997). Questions that relied heavily on language or reflected other conditions such as attention-deficit/hyperactivity disorder (e.g., motor restlessness) or ASD (e.g., repetitive behaviors) were excluded to create an anxiety severity scale unconfounded by symptoms core to ASD. In a well-characterized sample of youth with ASD, internal consistency was high ($\alpha = .85$), and scores were correlated with other indicators of impairment (Sukhodolsky et al., 2008). Each of the items on the CASI–20 is rated on a 0-to-3 scale and summed to yield a total anxiety score ranging from 0 to 60, with higher scores indicative of greater anxiety. The CASI–20 can also serve as a screen for specific anxiety disorders. On the basis of parent report, 42.7% of children in one sample met the cutoff on the screening scale for at least one anxiety disorder (Sukhodolsky et al., 2008). SAD was the second most common disorder in their ASD sample, with 31% scoring above the screening cutoff.

One measure of general stress developed specifically for assessing ASD is the Stress Survey Schedule for Persons With Autism and Developmental Disabilities (SSS; Groden et al., 2001). The SSS assesses stress reactions in children, teens, and adults with ASD and is completed by someone familiar with the individual, such as a parent or teacher. The SSS, which consists of 60 questions, yields scores for five separate stress dimensions (changes and social threats, ritual related, pleasant events, unpleasant events, and anticipation). Reliability across the five dimensions ranges from .57 to .91 (Goodwin, Groden, Velicer, & Diller, 2007). Although not developed for the assessment of social anxiety per se, the SSS may be useful in identifying those social dimensions most troublesome for persons with ASD.

Diagnostic Interviews, Observations, and Clinician Assessments

Many people with ASD have difficulty expressing their anxiety because of problems with expressive language, difficulties gauging level or degree of distress, and lack of emotional insight. To gauge anxiety accurately, clinicians often use alternative assessment formats including numerical ratings (e.g., a distress thermometer), multiple choice options rather than open-ended questions, or client's nonverbal responses (e.g., pointing; Attwood, 2006).

The Anxiety Disorders Interview Schedule for Children/Parents (ADIS–C/P; Silverman & Albano, 1996) is a well-known clinician-administered diagnostic interview of DSM–IV (American Psychiatric Association, 1994) disorders with established psychometric properties (Silverman, Saavedra, & Pena, 2001; Wood, Piacentini, Bergman, McCracken, & Barrios, 2002). Treatment studies of children and adolescents with ASD have begun using the ADIS–C/P to assess outcome (e.g., Chalfant, Rapee, & Carroll, 2007; White, Ollendick, Scahill, Oswald, & Albano, 2009), but there are few reliability and validity data for this population. Modifications of module content, including SAD, and administration may be needed to adequately distinguish social deficits of ASD from SAD. In our own experience, we have found it helpful to administer the ADIS–C/P to the parent and child together to address potentially problematic issues such as reduced emotional insight, restricted vocabulary and verbal self-expression, and difficulty accurately reporting historical events.

Self-Report Measures

Self-report questionnaires can aid screening and supplement diagnosis. The Multidimensional Anxiety Scale for Children (MASC; March, 1997) is a 39-item questionnaire that assesses anxiety across four separate subscales: physical symptoms, harm avoidance, social anxiety, and separation/panic. Bellini (2004) found that adolescents with ASD self-reported higher scores on the MASC, including in the domain of social anxiety, compared with the MASC's normative sample. However, White, Ollendick, et al. (2009) found that MASC scores were not elevated in a clinical sample of teens with ASD who were diagnosed with anxiety disorders on the basis of structured clinical interviews. Although the MASC has been used in studies with children and teens with ASD, further investigation of its utility with this population is needed. It is possible that some of the questions on the MASC are difficult for young people with ASD to understand, and as such, scores underestimate actual anxiety (White, Ollendick, et al., 2009).

Although not developed for children with ASD, the Social Phobia and Anxiety Inventory for Children (SPAI–C; Beidel, Turner, & Morris, 1995) has been used with and appears to be valid for this population (Kuusikko et al., 2008). These authors also revised the SPAI–C to exclude items that overlapped with symptoms of high-functioning autism and Asperger's disorder. Only the total score and Behavioral Avoidance scale were affected by the revision. The internal consistencies of the total score and the Behavioral Avoidance scale in the revised version were .96 and .32, respectively (Kuusikko et al., 2008). Melfsen, Walitza, and Warnke (2006) used the German version of the SPAI–C (Melfsen, Florin, & Warnke, 2001) in a sample of 341 clinically referred youth ages 7 to 18 years. In their study, participants diagnosed with ASD self-reported social anxiety scores above the clinical cutoff.

The Social Anxiety Scale for Children—Revised (SASC–R; La Greca & Stone, 1993) is a 22-item scale consisting of three subscales measuring fear of negative evaluation from peers, social avoidance and distress specific, and social avoidance and distress general and also appears reliable and valid for higher functioning children and adolescents with ASD (Kuusikko et al., 2008). The authors revised the measure to exclude items that are similar to diagnostic criteria of ASD. Using the SASC–R, individuals with ASD tend to report more symptoms of social anxiety compared with children with learning disabilities and typically developing children (Burnette et al., 2005; Kuusikko et al., 2008; Sutton et al., 2005). Bellini (2004) found nearly one half of one sample of adolescents with ASD to have clinically significant levels of social anxiety as measured on the self-reported Social Anxiety Scale for Adolescents (La Greca, 1999).

In summary, research on anxiety in ASD has for the most part used measures designed for non-ASD populations, and future research is needed to determine the measures' reliability and validity when used with adolescents who have ASD and to determine their ability to assess social anxiety that is separate from the social deficits of ASD. There is concern about poor reliability of self-report measures of anxiety (e.g., underreporting due to lack of insight) and misinterpretation from other-report measures due to variable expression of anxious symptoms in ASD. As such, multi-informant assessment tools should be used to screen for anxiety in adolescents with ASD.

TREATMENT CONSIDERATIONS

Few treatment programs have been developed explicitly for adolescents with ASD who struggle with social anxiety. Wood and colleagues have developed a cognitive behavioral treatment (CBT) program for children with ASD targeting disorder-specific deficits, including anxiety and social difficulties. In an initial waiting-list-controlled treatment study, Wood, Drahota, Sze, Har, et al. (2009) found a significant decrease in parent-reported anxiety but not child-reported anxiety following 16 weeks of CBT among children with Asperger's or pervasive developmental disorder not otherwise specified (ages 7–11 years).

In a smaller study that examined social outcomes more specifically, parent-reported improvements in social communication, social motivation, and social awareness were found following 16 weeks of treatment (Wood, Drahota, Sze, Van Dyke, et al., 2009). Although these findings await replication in adolescent samples, overall, outcome data are promising.

White, Ollendick, et al. (2009) recently reported results from a pilot study evaluating impact of a CBT program for teens with ASD and problems with anxiety, including social anxiety. Results from other CBT studies are promising as well (e.g., Chalfant et al., 2007; Reaven & Hepburn, 2003; Sofronoff, Attwood, & Hinton, 2005). Most researchers and clinicians agree that modifications to traditional CBT are usually necessary, such as including more frequent practice and exposure opportunities, increased parent involvement to promote skill use and generalization outside of treatment, and incorporation of visual aids especially when teaching abstract concepts (e.g., use of cartoons and thought bubbles to identify distorted thoughts). One goal of most treatment programs is increasing awareness of the anxiety. Many teens with ASD seem oblivious to their anxiety until it gets to the point of extreme behavioral reactions, such as tantrums, fleeing the situation, or other forms of emotional breakdown. Biofeedback helps youth learn to recognize indicators of increasing anxiety, such as physiological cues (e.g., sweating palms), cognitive signs (e.g., self-talk), and behaviors (e.g., avoidance; Attwood, 2006).

Given that social anxiety is related to feelings of loneliness in adolescents with ASD (White & Roberson-Nay, 2009), treatment should address self-perceptions and social isolation as well as monitor for possible depression. A behavioral approach in which specific triggers are identified and reduced or eliminated, along with teaching coping strategies, may be helpful. One critical aspect of intervention for teens with ASD and social anxiety is to focus on developing age-appropriate social skills. The social and evaluative anxiety experienced by teens and young adults with ASD is often reality based; they face harsh evaluation from peers and lack the requisite social skills. As such, incorporating strategies for increasing social competence (e.g., modeling, feedback) into treatment is important (White et al., 2010).

Treatment of SAD in adolescents with ASD may be enhanced by involving parents (or significant others) in the protocol through the provision of parent training. Generalization of skills can be particularly problematic, and parents can help assure generalization of learned skills to real-life situations (White, Ollendick, et al., 2009). Furthermore, parents may need to be educated on how their behaviors may influence their adolescent's anxiety and how they can modify these behaviors. In Multimodal Anxiety and Social Skills Intervention, a treatment curriculum for adolescents with ASD and anxiety disorders (White, Albano, et al., 2009; White, Ollendick, et al., 2009), parents learn about the skills discussed and practiced in that session. The adolescent is charged with summarizing the session for the parent. Parents are expected to remind their adolescents to use their new skills between sessions when out in the community and to model the skills being learned. Discussions with parents can also include education about the reinforcement of their adolescent's anxious behaviors, and parents can learn to stop the reinforcement of these behaviors.

Medications, including selective serotonin reuptake inhibitors, are sometimes used to treat anxiety in patients with ASD. In fact, between 21.6% and 32.1% of individuals with ASD are prescribed an antidepressant medication (Aman, Lam, & Collier-Crespin, 2003; Martin, Scahill, Klin, & Volkmar, 1999; Oswald & Sonenklar, 2007). Other medications such as tricyclic antidepressants and antipsychotics are also sometimes used, albeit less frequently (Martin et al., 1999). However, controlled treatment trials are limited, and evidence for changes in social anxiety and associated impairments following treatment is lacking. Further, because the efficacy and tolerability of these interventions are poorly understood at this time, behavioral therapies should be considered the first-line treatment for social problems in young people with ASD (Tsai, 2000).

CONCLUSION

Many adolescents and young adults with ASD are also socially anxious, and in some cases, this anxiety is reality based. As a result of their unusual behaviors and deficient social skills, there is always a high probability for unpleasant social interactions, social rejection, and alienation. As such, past social learning history and the social deficits core to ASD cannot be entirely separated from the experience of social anxiety. In addition, anxiety expression may be more variable. A teen with ASD might exhibit irritability, aggression, emotional dysregulation, increased rigidity, and repetitive behaviors or restricted interests as the primary indicators of rising anxiety while denying experiencing anxiety or worry.

In this chapter, we highlighted many unanswered questions. To date, there has been only one direct empirical comparison ($N = 12$) of the phenomenology of pure SAD and SAD comorbid with ASD (Cath et al., 2008), and more research with larger samples is needed. Also, the lack of research on the psychometric properties of social anxiety measures for ASD obfuscates clinical assessment and interpretation. Furthermore, development and refinement of more objective measures, such as physiological tools (e.g., resting heart rate) or technology-based assessment (e.g., eye tracking paradigms), may assist in the diagnostic process. Finally, given its frequency, further research on effective treatment options is of utmost importance.

REFERENCES

Aman, M. G., Lam, K. S. L., & Collier-Crespin, A. (2003). Prevalence and patterns of use of psychoactive medicines among individuals with autism in the Autism Society of Ohio. *Journal of Autism and Developmental Disorders, 33,* 527–534. doi:10.1023/A:1025883612879

American Psychiatric Association. (1994). *Diagnostic and statistical manual of mental disorders* (4th ed.). Washington, DC.

American Psychiatric Association. (2000). *Diagnostic and statistical manual of mental disorders* (4th ed., text rev.). Washington, DC: Author.

Attwood, T. (2000). Strategies for improving the social integration of children with Asperger syndrome. *Autism, 4,* 85–100. doi:10.1177/1362361300004001006

Attwood, T. (2006). Asperger's syndrome and problems related to stress. In M. G. Baron, J. Groden, G. Groden, & L. P. Lipsitt (Eds.), *Stress and coping in autism* (pp. 351–370). Oxford, England: Oxford University Press.

Bauminger, N., & Kasari, C. (2000). Loneliness and friendship in high-functioning children with autism. *Child Development, 71,* 447–456. doi:10.1111/1467-8624.00156

Beidel, D. C., & Turner, S. M. (2007). *Shy children, phobic adults: Nature and treatment of social anxiety disorder* (2nd ed.). Washington, DC: American Psychological Association. doi:10.1037/11533-000

Beidel, D. C., Turner, S. M., & Morris, T. L. (1995). A new inventory to assess childhood social anxiety and phobia: The social phobia and anxiety inventory for children. *Psychological Assessment, 7,* 73–79. doi:10.1037/1040-3590.7.1.73

Beidel, D. C., Turner, S. M., & Morris, T. L. (1999). Psychopathology of childhood social phobia. *Journal of the American Academy of Child and Adolescent Psychiatry, 38*, 643–650. doi:10.1097/00004583-199906000-00010

Bellini, S. (2004). Social skill deficits and anxiety in high-functioning adolescents with autism spectrum disorders. *Focus on Autism and Other Developmental Disabilities, 19*, 78–86. doi:10.1177/10883576040190020201

Bellini, S. (2006). The development of social anxiety in adolescents with autism spectrum disorders. *Focus on Autism and Other Developmental Disabilities, 21*, 138–145. doi: 10.1177/10883576060210030201

Burnette, C. P., Mundy, P. C., Meyer, J. A., Sutton, S. K., Vaughan, A. E., & Charak, D. (2005). Weak ventral coherence and its relations to theory of mind and anxiety in autism. *Journal of Autism and Developmental Disorders, 35*, 63–73. doi:10.1007/s10803-004-1035-5

Cairney, J., McCabe, L., Veldhuizen, S., Corna, L. M., Streiner, D., & Herrmann, N. (2007). Epidemiology of social phobia in later life. *The American Journal of Geriatric Psychiatry, 15*, 224–233. doi:10.1097/01.JGP.0000235702.77245.46

Carter, A., Davis, N., Klin, A., & Volkmar, F. (2005). Social development in autism. In F. R. Volkmar, R. Paul, A. Klin, & D. Cohen (Eds.), *Handbook of autism and pervasive developmental disorders* (3rd ed., pp. 312–334). Hoboken, NJ: Wiley.

Cath, D. C., Ran, N., Smit, J. H., van Balkom, A. J. L. M., & Comijs, H. C. (2008). Symptom overlap between autism spectrum disorder, generalized social anxiety disorder and obsessive-compulsive disorder in adults: A preliminary case-controlled study. *Psychopathology, 41*, 101–110. doi:10.1159/000111555

Chalfant, A. M., Rapee, R., & Carroll, L. (2007). Treating anxiety disorders in children with high functioning autism spectrum disorders: A controlled trial. *Journal of Autism and Developmental Disorders, 37*, 1842–1857. doi:10.1007/s10803-006-0318-4

Church, C., Alisanski, S., & Amanullah, S. (2000). The social, behavioral, and academic experiences of children with Asperger syndrome. *Focus on Autism and Other Developmental Disabilities, 15*, 12–20. doi:10.1177/108835760001500102

DeWit, D. J., Ogborne, A., Offord, D. R., & MacDonald, K. (1999). Antecedents of the risk of recovery from DSM–III–R social phobia. *Psychological Medicine, 29*, 569–582. doi:10.1017/S0033291799008399

Evren, B., & Evren, C. (2007). Relationship between alexithymia and social anxiety in female outpatients with dermatological disorder presenting for psychiatric consultation. *Journal of Clinical Psychology in Medical Settings, 14*, 258–265. doi:10.1007/s10880-007-9072-9

Farrugia, S., & Hudson, J. (2006). Anxiety in adolescents with Asperger syndrome: Negative thoughts, behavioral problems, and life interference. *Focus on Autism and Other Developmental Disabilities, 21*, 25–35. doi:10.1177/10883576060210010401

Gadow, K. D., & Sprafkin, J. (1994). *Child Symptom Inventory—4*. Stony Brook, NY: Checkmate Plus.

Gadow, K. D., & Sprafkin, J. (1997). *Adolescent Symptom Inventory—4 screening manual*. Stony Brook, NY: Checkmate Plus.

Ghaziuddin, M. (2002). Asperger syndrome: Associated psychiatric and medical conditions. *Focus on Autism and Other Developmental Disabilities, 17*, 138–144. doi:10.1177/10883576020170030301

Gillott, A., Furniss, F., & Walter, A. (2001). Anxiety in high-functioning children with autism. *Autism, 5*, 277–286. doi:10.1177/1362361301005003005

Goodwin, M. S., Groden, J., Velicer, W. F., & Diller, A. (2007). Brief report: Validating the stress survey schedule for persons with autism and other developmental disabilities. *Focus on Autism and Other Developmental Disabilities, 22*, 183–189. doi:10.1177/10883576070220030501

Grant, B. F., Hasin, D. S., Blanco, C., Stinson, F. S., Chous, S. P., Goldstein, R. B., . . . Huang, B. (2005). The epidemiology of social anxiety disorder in the United States: Results from the National Epidemiologic Survey on Alcohol and Related Conditions. *The Journal of Clinical Psychiatry, 66*, 1351–1361. doi:10.4088/JCP.v66n1102

Groden, J., Diller, A., Bausman, M., Velicer, W., Norman, G., & Cautella, J. (2001). The development of a stress survey schedule for persons with autism and other developmental disabilities. *Journal of Autism and Developmental Disorders, 31*, 207–217. doi:10.1023/A:1010755300436

Inderbitzen-Nolan, H. M., Anderson, E. R., & Johnson, H. S. (2007). Subjective versus objective behavioral ratings following two analogue tasks: A comparison of socially phobic and non-anxious adolescents. *Journal of Anxiety Disorders, 21*, 76–90. doi:10.1016/j.janxdis.2006.03.013

Kessler, R. C., Berglund, P., Demler, O., Jin, R., Merikangas, K. R., & Walters, E. E. (2005). Lifetime prevalence and age-of-onset distributions of DSM–IV disorders in the National Comorbidity Survey Replication. *Archives of General Psychiatry, 62*, 593–602. doi:10.1001/archpsyc.62.6.593

Krasny, L., Williams, B. J., Provencal, S., & Ozonoff, S. (2003). Social skills interventions for the autism spectrum: Essential ingredients and a model curriculum. *Child and Adolescent Psychiatric Clinics of North America, 12*, 107–122. doi:10.1016/S1056-4993(02)00051-2

Kuusikko, S., Pollock-Wurman, R., Jussila, K., Carter, A. S., Mattila, M., Ebieling, H., . . . Moilanen, I. (2008). Social anxiety in high-functioning children and adolescents with autism and Asperger syndrome. *Journal of Autism and Developmental Disorders, 38*, 1697–1709. doi: 10.1007/s10803-008-0555-9

La Greca, A. M. (1999). *Social Anxiety Scale for Children and Adolescents manual*. Miami, FL: University of Miami.

La Greca, A. M., & Stone, W. L. (1993). Social Anxiety Scale for Children— Revised: Factor structure and concurrent validity. *Journal of Clinical Child Psychology, 22*, 17–27. doi:10.1207/s15374424jccp2201_2

Liss, M., Mailloux, J., & Erchull, M. J. (2008). The relationships between sensory processing sensitivity, alexithymia, autism, depression, and anxiety. *Personality and Individual Differences, 45*, 255–259. doi:10.1016/j.paid.2008.04.009

Lopata, C., Volker, M. A., Putnam, S. K., Thomeer, M. L., & Nida, B. E. (2008). Effect of social familiarity on salivary cortisol and self-reports of social anxiety and stress in children with high functioning autism spectrum disorders. *Journal of Autism and Developmental Disorders, 38*, 1866–1877. doi:10.1007/s10803-008-0575-5

March, J. S. (1997). *Multidimensional Anxiety Scale for Children manual.* North Tonawanda, NY: Multi-Health Systems.

Martin, A., Scahill, L., Klin, A., & Volkmar, F. R. (1999). Higher-functioning pervasive developmental disorders: Rates and patterns of psychotropic drug use. *Journal of the American Academy of Child and Adolescent Psychiatry, 38*, 923–931. doi:10.1097/00004583-199907000-00024

Melfsen, S., Florin, I., & Warnke, A. (2001). *Das Sozialphobie und–angsinventar fur Kinder (SPAIK).* Gottengen, Germany: Hogrefe.

Melfsen, S., Walitza, S., & Warnke, A. (2006). The extent of social anxiety in combination with mental disorders. *European Child & Adolescent Psychiatry, 15*, 111–117. doi:10.1007/s00787-006-0510-2

Müller, E., Schuler, A., & Yates, G. B. (2008). Social challenges and supports from the perspective of individuals with Asperger syndrome and other autism spectrum disabilities. *Autism, 12*, 173–190. doi:10.1177/1362361307086664

Myles, B. S. (2003). Behavioral forms of stress management for individuals with Asperger syndrome. *Child and Adolescent Psychiatric Clinics of North America, 12*, 123–141. doi:10.1016/S1056-4993(02)00048-2

Myles, B. S., Barnhill, G., Hagiwara, T., Griswold, D., & Simpson, R. (2001). A synthesis of studies on the intellectual, academic, social/emotional and sensory characteristics of children with Asperger syndrome. *Education and Training in Mental Retardation and Developmental Disabilities, 36*, 304–311.

Myles, B. S., Bock, S., & Simpson, R. (2001). *Asperger syndrome diagnostic scale.* Austin, TX: Pro-Ed.

Neal, J. A., Edelmann, R. J., & Glachan, M. (2002). Behavioural inhibition and symptoms of anxiety and depression: Is there a specific relationship with social phobia? *The British Journal of Clinical Psychology, 41*, 361–374. doi:10.1348/014466502760387489

Oswald, D. P., & Sonenklar, N. A. (2007). Medication use among children with autism-spectrum disorders. *Journal of Child and Adolescent Psychopharmacology, 17*, 348–355. doi:10.1089/cap.2006.17303

Pine, D. S., Guyer, A. E., Goldwin, M., Towbin, K. A., & Leibenluft, E. (2008). Autism Spectrum Disorder Scale scores in pediatric mood and anxiety disorders. *Journal of the American Academy of Child and Adolescent Psychiatry, 47*, 652–661. doi:10.1097/CHI.0b013e31816bffa5

Reaven, J., & Hepburn, S. (2003). Cognitive-behavioral treatment of obsessive-compulsive disorder in a child with Asperger syndrome: A case report. *Autism, 7*, 145–164. doi:10.1177/1362361303007002003

Shaked, M., & Yirmiya, N. (2003). Understanding social difficulties. In M. Prior (Ed.), *Learning and behavior problems in Asperger syndrome* (pp. 104–125). New York, NY: Guilford Press.

Silverman, W. K., & Albano, A. M. (1996). *The Anxiety Disorders Interview Schedule for DSM–IV: Child and Parent Versions*. San Antonio, TX: Graywind.

Silverman, W. K., Saavedra, L. M., & Pena, A. A. (2001). Test–retest reliability of anxiety symptoms and diagnoses with the Anxiety Disorders Interview Schedule for DSM–IV: Child and Parent Versions. *Journal of the American Academy of Child and Adolescent Psychiatry, 40*, 937–944. doi:10.1097/00004583-200108000-00016

Sofronoff, K., Attwood, T., & Hinton, S. (2005). A randomized controlled trial of a CBT intervention for anxiety in children with Asperger syndrome. *Journal of Child Psychology and Psychiatry, and Allied Disciplines, 46*, 1152–1160. doi:10.1111/j.1469-7610.2005.00411.x

Sukhodolsky, D. G., Scahill, L., Gadow, K. D., Arnold, L. E., Aman, M. G., McDougle, C. J., . . . Vitiello, B. (2008). Parent-rated anxiety symptoms in children with pervasive developmental disorders: Frequency and association with core autism symptoms and cognitive functioning. *Journal of Abnormal Child Psychology, 36*, 117–128. doi:10.1007/s10802-007-9165-9

Sutton, S. K., Burnette, C. P., Mundy, P. C., Meyer, J., Vaughan, A., Sanders, C., & Yale, M. (2005). Resting cortical brain activity and social behavior in higher functioning children with autism. *Journal of Child Psychology and Psychiatry, and Allied Disciplines, 46*, 211–222. doi:10.1111/j.1469-7610.2004.00341.x

Tager-Flusberg, H. (2003). Effects of language and communicative deficits on learning and behavior. In M. Prior (Ed.), *Learning and behavior problems in Asperger syndrome* (pp. 85–103). New York, NY: Guilford Press.

Tantam, D. (2003). The challenge of adolescents and adults with Asperger syndrome. *Child and Adolescent Psychiatric Clinics of North America, 12*, 143–163. doi:10.1016/S1056-4993(02)00053-6

Tsai, L. (2000). Children with autism spectrum disorder: Medicine today and in the new millennium. *Focus on Autism and Other Developmental Disabilities, 15*, 138–145. doi:10.1177/108835760001500302

Tse, J., Strulovich, J., Tagalakis, V., Meng, L., & Fombonne, E. (2007). Social skills training for adolescents with Asperger syndrome and high-functioning autism. *Journal of Autism and Developmental Disorders, 37*, 1960–1968. doi:10.1007/s10803-006-0343-3

Turner-Brown, L. M., Perry, T. D., Dichter, G. S., Bodfish, J. W., & Penn, D. L. (2008). Brief report: Feasibility of social cognition and interaction training for adults with high functioning autism. *Journal of Autism and Developmental Disorders, 38*, 1777–1784. doi:10.1007/s10803-008-0545-y

U.S. Centers for Disease Control and Prevention. (2007). Prevalence of autism spectrum disorders: Autism and developmental disabilities monitoring network (No. SS-1). *Morbidity and Mortality Weekly Report, 56*, 1–40.

White, S. W., Albano, A., Johnson, C., Kasari, C., Ollendick, T., Klin, A., . . . Scahill, L. (2010). Development of a cognitive-behavioral intervention program to treat social anxiety and social deficits in teens with high functioning autism. *Clinical Child and Family Psychology Review, 13*, 77–90.

White, S. W., Ollendick, T., Scahill, L., Oswald, D., & Albano, A. (2009). Preliminary efficacy of a cognitive-behavioral treatment program for anxious youth with autism spectrum disorders. *Journal of Autism and Developmental Disorders* 39, 1652–1662.

White, S. W., Oswald, D., Ollendick, T., & Scahill, L. (2009). Anxiety in children and adolescents with autism spectrum disorders. *Clinical Psychology Review, 29,* 216–229. doi:10.1016/j.cpr.2009.01.003

White, S. W., & Roberson-Nay, R. (2009). Anxiety, social deficits, and loneliness in youth with autism spectrum disorders. *Journal of Autism and Developmental Disorders, 39,* 1006–1013. doi:10.1007/s10803-009-0713-8

Williams, E., Thomas, K., Sidebotham, H., & Emond, A. (2008). Prevalence and characteristics of autistic spectrum disorders in the ALSPAC cohort. *Developmental Medicine and Child Neurology, 50,* 672–677. doi:10.1111/j.1469-8749.2008.03042.x

Wood, J. J., Drahota, A., Sze, K., Har, K., Chiu, A., & Langer, D. A. (2009). Cognitive behavioral therapy for anxiety in children with autism spectrum disorders: A randomized, controlled trial. *Journal of Child Psychology and Psychiatry, and Allied Disciplines, 50,* 224–234. doi:10.1111/j.1469-7610.2008.01948.x

Wood, J. J., Drahota, A., Sze, K., Van Dyke, M., Decker, K., Fujii, C., . . . Spiker, M. (2009). Brief report: Effects of cognitive behavioral therapy on parent-reported autism symptoms in school-age children with high-functioning autism. *Journal of Autism and Developmental Disorders, 39,* 1608–1612. doi:10.1007/s10803-009-0791-7

Wood, J. J., Piacentini, J. C., Bergman, R. L., McCracken, J., & Barrios, V. (2002). Concurrent validity of the anxiety disorders section of the Anxiety Disorders Interview Schedule for *DSM–IV*: Child and Parent Versions. *Journal of Clinical Child and Adolescent Psychology, 31,* 335–342.

11

CULTURAL INFLUENCES ON SOCIAL ANXIETY IN AFRICAN AMERICAN, ASIAN AMERICAN, HISPANIC AND LATINO, AND NATIVE AMERICAN ADOLESCENTS AND YOUNG ADULTS

ARGERO A. ZERR, LINDSAY E. HOLLY, AND ARMANDO A. PINA

Although social anxiety disorder (SAD) is one of the most common psychiatric disorders in the population, research has focused primarily on Caucasians of European descent. However, cross-cultural research is beginning to emerge (e.g., Okazaki, 1997, 2002; Okazaki, Liu, Longworth, & Minn, 2002), revealing some notable variations in the experience and prevalence of the disorder across cultural groups. For example, *Taijin kyofusho* (TKS) is a culture-bound syndrome considered a form of SAD in Japan. The term's literal translation is disorder (*sho*) of fear (*kyofu*) of interpersonal relationships (*taijin*). Individuals with TKS believe they have socially inadequate bodily characteristics that offend others, leading them to avoid social situations and interpersonal relationships. Similar to those with SAD, they experience emotional distress such as shame, embarrassment, anxiety, and fear when faced with social situations. Different from SAD, however, TKS appears to be more prevalent in males than females (Kirmayer, 1991; Takahashi, 1989). Four subcategories of TKS are phobia of blushing (*sekimen-kyofu*), phobia of a deformed body (*shubo-kyofu*), phobia of eye contact (*jikoshisen-kyofu*), and phobia of having foul body odor (*jikoshu-kyofu*; Suzuki, Takei, Kawai, Minabe, & Mori, 2003). Data are relatively limited, but an epidemiological study reported a prevalence of 6.8% (Ono et al., 2001).

Although no other culture-bound syndrome with clinical phenomenology comparable to SAD is described in the literature, in this chapter, we present an overview of conceptual and methodological issues relevant for social anxiety research among four cultural and ethnic groups: Native Americans, African Americans, Asian Americans and Pacific Islanders, and Hispanics and Latinos. According to the most current U.S. Census Bureau population survey, there are about 4 million Native Americans (including Alaska Natives), 36 million African Americans, 12 million Asian Americans, and 35 million Hispanics and Latinos in the United States. Thus, each of these ethnic and cultural groups comprises a significant proportion of the U.S. population. Although these four broad groups are the focus of this chapter, it is important to note that there are within-group variations, and these groups should not be viewed as homogenous (Knight, Roosa, & Umaña-Taylor, 2009).

PREVALENCE OF SOCIAL ANXIETY AND SOCIAL ANXIETY DISORDER ACROSS ETHNIC AND CULTURAL GROUPS

Cross-ethnic and cross-cultural research shows both similarities and differences in the prevalence of SAD. Data from a large epidemiological study (Grant, Dawson, & Hasin, 2001) indicate a lifetime prevalence of 8.6% for SAD among Native Americans and a rate of 5.5% for Caucasians, who were significantly more likely to have SAD than African Americans (3.5%), Hispanics and Latinos (3.2%), and Asian Americans (3.3%; Grant et al., 2005). Using the National World Mental Health Composite International Diagnostic Interview (Kessler & Ustun, 2004), Himle, Baser, Taylor, Campbell, and Jackson (2009) reported a 12-month prevalence of 7.11% for SAD among Caucasians and 4.55% among African Americans, a statistically significant difference. For Mexican Americans and African Americans, prevalence of SAD has been reported to be more similar than different (about 4.5%; Vega, Scribney, Aguilar-Gaxiola, & Kolody, 2004).

Certain racial and ethnic groups also report high levels of social anxiety symptoms on the basis of rating scales. Adolescents from the Lumbee Native American tribe reported high levels of social anxiety (Newman, 2005) on the Social Anxiety Scale for Adolescents (La Greca, 1998). Using the Worry Inventory (Adolescent Health Program, 1987), D'Andrea (1994) found that Native American preadolescent and adolescent girls from the Lakota tribe endorsed more social worries than their male counterparts. On the basis of the Social Phobia and Anxiety Inventory for Children (Beidel, Turner, & Morris, 1995), African American youth had significantly lower social anxiety levels than Caucasians (Beidel, Turner, Hamlin, & Morris, 2000).

Similarities or differences in social anxiety across ethnic and cultural groups are interesting but need to be interpreted cautiously. In addition to typical study-to-study variation in the use of SAD diagnostic criteria (e.g., Beidel, Turner, & Trager, 1994; Cooley, Boyd, & Grados, 2004; Ginsburg & Drake, 2002; Tiwari & Wang, 2006) and the disadvantages of relying on retrospective reports (e.g., Angold et al., 2002; Heimberg, Stein, Hiripi, & Kessler, 2000; Ruscio et al., 2008), cross-cultural and cross-ethnic differences (or lack of) across groups may be artifactual if measures yield nonequivalent information. Even if the core features of SAD are the same across groups, the threshold at which the symptoms constitute a disorder may be different (Millsap, 1998). If so, studies might overestimate or underestimate prevalence and severity in one group versus another. Nonequivalent cross-ethnic information can arise from variations in respondents' values, attitudes, language, and worldviews (Okazaki & Sue, 1995). If one assumes the instruments are culturally robust, variations still require evaluation in the context of culturally ecological influencing factors. For example, using the Social Anxiety Scale for Adolescents (SAS–A; La Greca, 1998), Lau, Fung, Wang, and Kang (2009) found higher social anxiety for Asian Americans than for Caucasians. Also, ethnic differences in social anxiety symptoms were mediated by differences in "loss of face" concerns, a central cultural concept in Asian cultures involving one's awareness of one's social status, expectations of other individuals, and a motivation to prevent negative evaluations from others (Lau et al., 2009; Zane & Yeh, 2002).

MEASUREMENT OF SOCIAL ANXIETY

Overall, few structured measures have been used in studies with significant representation of ethnic minorities, and even fewer studies have reported reliability and validity data corresponding to minority samples. Pina and Silverman (2004) reported test–retest reliability for anxiety diagnoses derived using the Spanish versions of the Anxiety Disorders Interview Schedule for *DSM–IV*: Child and Parent Versions (Silverman & Albano, 1996) in the good to excellent range ($\kappa = .64–.96$). Similarly, the Social Interaction Anxiety Scale (Mattick & Clarke, 1998) showed strong reliability ($\alpha = .93$) and comparability of the Spanish versions with the well-established English version (Novy, Stanley, Averill, & Daza, 2001). Storch, Eisenberg, Roberti, and Barlas (2003) found support for the factor structure of the SAS (La Greca & Stone, 1993) in a Puerto Rican and Dominican youth sample. Among African Americans (Margolin, 2006), the SAS (La Greca, Dandes, Wick, Shaw, & Stone, 1988) yielded an alpha of .85, and the SAS–A showed strong reliability in samples of Native American youth (Newman, 2005, West & Newman, 2007). Studies with Asian American samples reported good reliability for the

SAS–A (Lau, Fung, Wang, & Kang, 2009; Zhou, Ingles, Hidalgo, & La Greca, 2008) and strong reliability for the Social Phobia and Anxiety Inventory (Hong & Woody, 2007; Lee, Ohazaki, & Yoo, 2006; Okazaki, 2002; Okazaki et al., 2002).

Although social anxiety research with minority samples is emerging, there are no cross-cultural measurement equivalence data for social anxiety measures. Consideration of measurement equivalence is critical because culturally biased measures of social anxiety may misrepresent symptoms across different groups. Misrepresentation of symptoms could lead to inconsistent research findings, erroneous reporting of mental health disparities, ineffective prevention and intervention efforts, and wasted resources (Knight et al., 2009; Knight & Zerr, 2010; Pina, Little, Knight, & Silverman, 2009; Vega, 1990). Measurement equivalence tests are needed not only to determine the cross-cultural validity of measures but also to determine the robustness of the social anxiety knowledge base published to date (Hui & Triandis, 1989; Knight & Hill, 1998; Vandenberg & Lance, 2000).

Measurement Equivalence

According to Hui and Triandis (1985), measurement equivalence includes item equivalence, functional equivalence, and scalar equivalence. Item equivalence indicates that items on a measure have the same meaning across groups. An example would be lack of eye contact as an indicator of social anxiety. In some Asian cultures maintaining eye contact with strangers is considered inappropriate or rude (Galanti, 2008; Iwamasa, 1997), suggesting that this behavioral indicator may have less predictive power toward deriving a SAD diagnosis in Asian Americans.

Linguistic equivalence also is relevant to item equivalence and includes comprehensive translational methods that evaluate internal validity of items across languages (Erkut, 2010). Without thorough translation techniques, such as back translation, multiple forward translations, and cross-cultural validity evaluations, symptoms may be misrepresented. For example, the Spanish word *pena* could refer to shyness (as in social anxiety) or may refer to sorrow (as in depression). For this reason, measures that use this word could easily misrepresent the item's intended meaning. In addition, for bilingual individuals it is important to consider the influence of native language. A Puerto Rican adolescent, for example, may interpret the word *nervous* as meaning *nervios*, which is semantically different (Baer et al., 2003; Guarnaccia, Lewis-Fernandez, & Marano, 2003; Salgado de Snyder, Diaz-Perez, & Ojeda, 2000). This is problematic because for Puerto Ricans the word *nervous* could refer to the culture-bound syndrome known as *ataque de nervios*, which is more characteristic of depression and trauma than of social anxiety (e.g.,

Guarnaccia, Rivera, Franco, & Neighbors, 1996; Hinton, Lewis-Fernandez, & Pollack, 2009).

Functional equivalence indicates that scores generated by a measure have similar antecedents, consequences, and correlates across groups. Social anxiety measures demonstrating cross-cultural functional equivalence would ideally show positive relations to measures of social withdrawal and negative relations to measures of social skills across cultural groups. If functional equivalence is lacking, then these relations may be interpreted as cultural differences instead of measurement artifact or vice versa (Mullen, 1995).

Last, scalar equivalence indicates that a given rating on a measure refers to the same degree, intensity, or magnitude of the construct across groups. Cultural research on scalar equivalence has found that less acculturated Latinos are more likely than acculturated Latinos and non-Latinos to endorse extreme anchors on response scales, which may lead to higher or lower total scores (Hui & Triandis, 1989; Marín, Gamba, & Marín, 1992) and affect clinical cutoff and impairment values. For example, symptoms of social anxiety may be more acceptable in Asian cultures (Chen, 2000; Heinrichs et al., 2006), so Asian individuals may not feel as impaired as Caucasians (Chen, Rubin, & Sun, 1992; Hsu & Alden, 2007; Okazaki et al., 2002). Examination of scalar equivalence may be the most important form of measurement equivalence for cross-cultural research because numeric ratings constitute the most fundamental level on which both research and clinical decisions are based.

Cultural Bias Across Assessment Methods

In addition to measurement equivalence, there also may be cultural (method) bias. Evaluation of method biases is important because the very nature of assessment involves confrontation of specific social fears, and the impact of assessment method may differ across cultures. Method biases such as differential social desirability, response styles, or stimulus familiarity can inappropriately appear as cultural differences (van de Vijver & Poortinga, 1997). Assessment formats may partially account for cross-cultural differences in social anxiety between Asian and European heritage adolescents (Hsu & Alden, 2007). For example, when interview-based assessment methods are used, Asian individuals score significantly lower on social anxiety than Caucasian individuals. When self-report questionnaires are used, Asian individuals score significantly higher on social anxiety than Caucasian individuals (Hwu, Yeh, & Chang, 1989; Lee et al., 1987; Okazaki, 1997, 2000; Somers, Goldner, Waraich & Hsu, 2006; Sue, Ino, & Sue, 1983; Wittchen & Fehm, 2001). Moreover, on self-report measures of social anxiety, Asian Americans score higher than Caucasians, but on peer-report and behavioral indices of social anxiety, Asian Americans score similar to Caucasians (Okazaki, 2002;

Okazaki et al., 2002). Furthermore, the discrepancy between self-report and peer-report measures appears to be greater for Asian Americans than Caucasians because peer reports underestimated social anxiety in Asian Americans (Okazaki, 2002). These examples of method-based differences may be due to Asian cultural values, which discourage display of emotions, especially to strangers (Matsumoto & Kupperbusch, 2001). Because many Asian cultures value emotional discretion, clinical interviews, peer reports, and behavioral indices may underestimate symptoms compared with self-reports.

BROAD CULTURAL AND ETHNIC FACTORS

In our review of the literature, two cultural factors emerged with regard to social anxiety. First, the transcultural research literature has focused on examining the impact of individualism and collectivism on the presentation of social anxiety. Second, the cultural-contextual research literature has focused on examining factors such as acculturation and immigration as influences on social anxiety. Both of these issues are discussed in the sections that follow.

Individualism, Collectivism, and Social Anxiety

Differences in societal values may partly explain cross-cultural differences in SAD, especially between Asian and Western cultures. Many Western societies value individualism, assertiveness, and independence, whereas Asian cultures adhere to more collectivistic values and connectedness with others (e.g., Chen, 2000; Markus & Kitayama, 1991). Individualism promotes independent self-construals in which individuals ideally strive for autonomy, personal achievement, and success. In contrast, collectivism promotes interdependent self-construals in which individuals value group harmony and stability over personal happiness. The link between individualism, collectivism, and social anxiety has been examined primarily in terms of cross-cultural group comparative research, within-person associations, and person-by-culture match studies.

Cross-cultural research from individualistic and collectivistic countries has shown group differences in the acceptability of certain social behaviors (e.g., fear of blushing; Heinrichs et al., 2006). For example, socially reserved and withdrawn behaviors are more acceptable in collectivistic countries (Heinrichs et al., 2006). Also, within-person associations among individualism, collectivism, and social anxiety have been examined by measuring individual-level orientations of perfectionism, self-esteem, and self-construal. Self-oriented perfectionism (i.e., high self-standards of performance) better predicts social anxiety for Caucasians, whereas socially prescribed perfectionism (i.e., high social standards of performance) better predicts social anxiety for Asians (Xie, Leong, & Feng, 2008). In addition, collective self-esteem (i.e., society-oriented self-esteem) is more robustly associated with anxiety among Asians than Caucasians (Xie et al., 2008). Asians tend to report interdependent self-construals, whereas Caucasians tend to report independent conceptualizations of the self (Okazaki, 1997). These differences in self-construals have been linked with cross-cultural differences in levels of social anxiety, particularly increased social anxiety in Asians (Lau et al., 2009; Okazaki, 1997; Xie et al., 2008). Socialization within collectivistic cultures also may emphasize emotional sensitivity to others yet limit opportunities to gain emotion recognition competencies. In fact, higher social anxiety symptoms among Asians were explained by emotion recognition skills (Lau et al., 2009). On the basis of these data, it appears that, at least to some extent, specific individual-level relations underlie cultural-level differences in social anxiety.

Third, person-by-culture match focuses on the interaction between individual values and societal values. When social orientation is inconsistent with societal values, people may be at risk for poor mental health. Among students residing in individualistic societies, collectivism scores were positively correlated with social anxiety and other mental health problems, whereas the inverse was found with individualism scores in their counterparts (Caldwell-Harris & Ayçiçegi, 2006). In contrast, for students residing in collectivistic societies, individualism was positively related to mental health problems, whereas collectivism was negatively related to mental health problems. These findings suggest that social anxiety may occur in individuals who emigrate to a culture where societal values contrast with individual values.

Immigration, Acculturation, and Social Anxiety

When individuals immigrate to a host culture, they typically bring their origin's cultural values. In addition to struggling to retain their native cultural values, immigrants face acculturation stressors that may influence the presentation of social anxiety. Illustratively, social anxiety and loneliness were significantly higher in immigrant Mexican American adolescents than their U.S.-born counterparts (Polo & López, 2009). Acculturation stress and English proficiency mediated the association between nativity and social anxiety. As such, social anxiety symptoms may be conceptualized as a direct effect of acculturation stressors, a direct effect of cultural values, or both (Weems & Pina, 2010).

Social Relations

Data on the association between social anxiety and interpersonal relationships, especially during adolescence, when peer relations become particularly influential, consistently show more cross-ethnic similarities than differences in regard to peer affiliation (Brown, 1990; Dolcini & Adler, 1994; Phillips, Hughes, & Wilkes, 1998) and romantic relationships (Collins, 2003; Kuttler & La Greca, 2004). In addition, associations among peer relations, social skills, and social anxiety tend to be similar across ethnic groups (e.g., Prinstein, Boergers, & Vernberg, 2001; Vernberg, Abwender, Ewell, & Beery, 1992). Positive friendships and peer affiliation (both high and low status) were negatively related to social anxiety in both Caucasian and Latino adolescents (La Greca & Harrison, 2005). Negative friendships were positively related to social anxiety in both ethnic groups. However, dating was negatively related to social anxiety in Latino but not Caucasian adolescents. In another study conducted with Asian Americans, Hispanics, African Americans, and Caucasians, dating competence and social assertion were negatively related to social anxiety, with no differences across groups (LeSure-Lester, 2001).

EVIDENCE-BASED TREATMENTS FOR SOCIAL ANXIETY DISORDER

Because SAD is among the most prevalent and impairing psychiatric disorders, significant efforts also have been made to develop, test, and disseminate evidence-based treatments. Although the research has focused primarily on Caucasian individuals of European descent, some notable exceptions exist (Ferrell, Beidel, & Turner, 2004; Ginsburg & Drake, 2002; Pina, Silverman, Fuentes, Kurtines, & Weems, 2003). Most likely, the lack of research is related to practical and cultural barriers in the recruitment and retention of minorities into psychotherapy and research studies (Cabassa, Zayas, & Hansen, 2006; Kouyoumdjian, Zamboanga, & Hansen, 2003; Miranda, Azocar, Organista, Muñoz, & Lieberman, 1996). Additionally, practical issues linked to acculturation, immigration, and socioeconomic status were some of the main barriers faced by Latino parents seeking treatment for their adolescents (Flores, Abreu, Olivar, & Kastner, 1998; Vega & López, 2001). Because of these barriers and cultural incongruencies, applying psychosocial treatments created for Caucasians to ethnocultural minorities has been contraindicated (see American Psychological Association, 1990a, 1990b, 2003; Constantine & Sue, 2005; Fouad & Arredondo, 2007), whereas adapting treatments for ethnocultural minorities has been advised (Malgady & Constantino, 1999; Wagner, 2003).

In a recent report on evidence-based treatments (Silverman, Pina, & Viswesvaran, 2008), no treatment was considered well established for SAD among children and adolescents, but several met criteria for probably efficacious. Huey and Polo (2008) evaluated research on evidence-based treatments for ethnic minority youth using criteria outlined by Chambless et al.

(1998; Chambless & Hollon, 1998). The review concluded that no well-established treatment exists. Huey and Polo (2008) rightfully concluded that "the literature is characterized by unrepresentative samples, Euro-centric outcome measures, inadequate sample sizes, and few direct tests of key theoretical assumptions" (p. 296).

In our review, we also found a scarcity of treatment research focusing on SAD among minority adolescents or young adults. Ferrell et al. (2004) examined treatment outcomes for African American and Caucasian youth with SAD participating in the Beidel, Turner, & Morris, (2000) randomized clinical trial of Social Effectiveness Therapy for Children and Adolescents (for a description, see Chapter 13, this volume). The sample included 19 African American and 39 Caucasian youth, and outcomes were not different for the two groups, either at posttreatment or 6-month follow-up (Ferrell et al., 2004). Although other investigations of treatment outcome among adolescents with SAD exist (Baer & Garland, 2005; Hayward et al., 2000; Masia, Klein, Storch, & Corda, 2001), ethnicity data were not reported.

For ethnic minorities, in general, lower rates of treatment participation are related to practical and cultural barriers (e.g., Cabassa et al., 2006; Kouyoumdjian et al., 2003; Miranda et al., 1996) and contribute to their underrepresentation in clinical trials (Adams-Campbell et al., 2004; Evelyn et al., 2001). As such, less is known about treatment efficacy for minorities. However, there seems to be a growing literature focused on evaluating cultural influences on the treatment of SAD, including barriers to treatment participation as well as efficacy of psychotherapeutic treatments (see Griner & Smith, 2006).

Treatment seeking and engagement may be particularly difficult for people with SAD because of their fear and nervousness when initiating social contact, making phone calls, and speaking to new people (Olfson et al., 2000). These social fears may be even more pronounced for ethnic minorities, especially those with relatively recent immigration histories. Specifically, retention of native cultural values or acculturation stressors may affect treatment participation. In terms of cultural values, lower treatment-seeking behavior was linked to stigma associated with mental illness (e.g., Alvidrez, 1999; Alvidrez & Azocar, 1999; Silva de Crane & Spielberger, 1981; Wynaden et al., 2005). This appears to be true for Hispanics and Latinos, Asian Americans, and African Americans who typically delay or avoid seeking mental health services (Cuffe et al., 1995; Lin, Inui, Kleinman, & Womack, 1982; Miranda et al., 1996; Vega & López, 2001). In addition, acculturation, immigration stressors, low English language proficiency, lack of insurance, and/or lack of transportation have been highlighted as factors that prevent minorities from seeking treatment (Flores et al., 1998; Pina, Villalta, & Zerr, 2009; Vega & López, 2001).

Adolescents and young adults who immigrate to the United States typically face an adjustment period (Berry, 2002) characterized by difficulty making new friends or attending social gatherings (Li, 2009). In addition, recently immigrated adolescents and young adults may face language barriers and deportation fears, exacerbating social isolation and loneliness, all of which may be synergistic with social anxiety (Ryder, Alden, & Paulhus, 2000). Reluctance to seek treatment may also stem from fear of institutionalization, mistrust, and perceived discrimination or racism, especially in the case of Native American and African American adolescents and young adults (Takeuchi, Bui, & Kim, 1993).

CONCLUSIONS AND RECOMMENDATIONS

In this chapter, we reviewed cross-cultural research relevant to SAD, with a focus on adolescents and young adults. A critical evaluation of cross-cultural comparison research focusing on social anxiety, risk factors, and intervention was presented. In addition, individual-level and cultural-level factors that may help explain cultural differences in the development and presentation of social anxiety were described. It is clear that there are several gaps in the research literature. First, there is a critical need for cross-cultural measurement equivalence data for SAD. Second, with evidence that social anxiety measures are culturally robust, tests of cross-cultural models of SAD development are needed to clarify the relations among transcultural risk and protective factors; resilience mechanisms; and the role cultural and contextual factors may play in the onset, development, and maintenance of SAD between and within cultures. Third, there is a critical need to test, refine, and disseminate evidence-based treatment and preventive interventions. As these data accumulate, greater progress can be made to improve the lives of adolescents and young adults with SAD.

REFERENCES

Adams-Campbell, L. L., Ahaghotu, C., Gaskins, M., Dawkins, F. W., Smoot, D., Polk, O. D., . . . DeWitty, R. L. et al. (2004). Enrollment of African Americans onto clinical treatment trials: Study design barriers. *Journal of Clinical Oncology, 22*, 730–734. doi:10.1200/JCO.2004.03.160

Adolescent Health Program. (1987). *The adolescent health survey.* St. Paul: University of Minnesota Press.

Alvidrez, J. (1999). Ethnic variations in mental health attitudes and service use among low-income African American, Latina, European American young women. *Community Mental Health Journal, 35*, 515–530. doi:10.1023/A:1018759201290

Alvidrez, J., & Azocar, F. (1999). Distressed women's clinic patients: Preferences for mental health treatments and perceived obstacles. *General Hospital Psychiatry, 21*, 340–347. doi:10.1016/S0163-8343(99)00038-9

American Psychological Association. (1990a). *General guidelines for providers of psychological services to ethnic, linguistic, and culturally diverse populations*. Washington, DC: Author.

American Psychological Association. (1990b). *Guidelines on multicultural education, training, research, practice, and organizational change for psychologists*. Washington, DC: Author.

American Psychological Association. (2003). Guidelines on multicultural education, training, research, practice, and organizational change for psychologists. *American Psychologist, 58*, 377–402. doi:10.1037/0003-066X.58.5.377

Angold, A., Erkanli, A., Farmer, E. M. Z., Fairbank, J. A., Burns, B. J., Keeler, G., & Costello, J. (2002). Psychiatric disorder, impairment, and service use in rural African American and White youth. *Archives of General Psychiatry, 59*, 893–901. doi:10.1001/archpsyc.59.10.893

Baer, R. D., Weller, S. C., de Alba Garcia, J. G., Glazer, M., Trotter, R., Pachter, L., & Klein, R. E. (2003). A cross-cultural approach to the study of the folk illness nervios. *Culture, Medicine and Psychiatry, 27*, 315–337. doi:10.1023/A:1025351231862

Baer, S., & Garland, J. E. (2005). Pilot study of community-based cognitive behavioral group therapy for adolescents with social phobia. *Journal of the American Academy of Child and Adolescent Psychiatry, 44*, 258–264. doi:10.1097/00004583-200503000-00010

Beidel, D. C., Turner, S. M., Hamlin, K., & Morris, T. L. (2000). The Social Phobia and Anxiety Inventory for Children (SPAI–C): External and discriminative validity. *Behavior Therapy, 31*, 75–87. doi:10.1016/S0005-7894(00)80005-2

Beidel, D. C., Turner, S. M., & Morris, T. L. (1995). A new inventory to assess childhood social anxiety and phobia: The Social Phobia and Anxiety Inventory for Children. *Psychological Assessment, 7*, 73–79. doi:10.1037/1040-3590.7.1.73

Beidel, D. C., Turner, S. M., & Morris, T. L. (2000). Behavioral treatment of childhood social phobia. *Journal of Consulting and Clinical Psychology, 68*, 1072–1080. doi:10.1037/0022-006X.68.6.1072

Beidel, D. C., Turner, S. M., & Trager, K. N. (1994). Test anxiety and childhood anxiety disorders in African American and White school children. *Journal of Anxiety Disorders, 8*, 169–179. doi:10.1016/0887-6185(94)90014-0

Berry, J. W. (2002). Conceptual approaches to acculturation. In K. M. Chun, P. Balls Organista, & G. Marín (Eds.), *Acculturation: Advances in theory, measurement, and applied research* (pp. 17–37). Washington, DC: American Psychological Association. doi:10.1037/10472-004

Brown, B. B. (1990). Peer groups and peer cultures. In S. S. Feldman & G. R. Elliott (Eds.), *At the threshold: The developing adolescent* (pp. 171–196). Cambridge, MA: Harvard University Press.

Cabassa, L. J., Zayas, L. H., & Hansen, M. C. (2006). Latino adults' access to mental health care: A review of epidemiological studies. *Administration and Policy in*

Mental Health and Mental Health Services Research, 33, 316–330. doi:10.1007/s10488-006-0040-8

Caldwell-Harris, C. L., & Ayçiçegi, A. (2006). When personality and culture clash: The psychological distress of allocentrics in an individualist culture and idiocentrics in a collectivist culture. *Transcultural Psychiatry, 43*, 331–361. doi:10.1177/1363461506066982

Chambless, D. L., Baker, M. J., Baucom, D. H., Beutler, L. E., Calhoun, K. S., Crits-Christoph, P., . . . Woody, S. R. (1998). Update on empirically validated therapies, II. *Clinical Psychologist, 51*, 3–16.

Chambless, D. L., & Hollon, S. D. (1998). Defining empirically supported therapies. *Journal of Consulting and Clinical Psychology, 66*, 7–18. doi:10.1037/0022-006X.66.1.7

Chen, X. (2000). Growing up in a collectivist culture: Socialization and socio-emotional development in Chinese children. In A. L. Comunian & U. P. Gielen (Eds.), *International perspectives on human development* (pp. 331–353). Lengerich, Germany: Pabst Science.

Chen, X., Rubin, K. H., & Sun, Y. (1992). Social reputation and peer relationships in Chinese and Canadian children: A cross-cultural study. *Child Development, 63*, 1336–1343. doi:10.2307/1131559

Collins, W. A. (2003). More than myth: The developmental significance of romantic relationships during adolescence. *Journal of Research on Adolescence, 13*, 1–24. doi:10.1111/1532-7795.1301001

Constantine, M. G., & Sue, D. W. (2005). The American Psychological Association's guidelines on multicultural education, training, research, practice, and organizational psychology: Initial development and summary. In M. Constantine & D. W. Sue (Eds.), *Strategies for building multicultural competence in mental health and educational settings* (pp. 3–15). Hoboken, NJ: Wiley.

Cooley, M. R., Boyd, R. C., & Grados, J. J. (2004). Feasibility of an anxiety preventive intervention for community violence exposed African American children. *The Journal of Primary Prevention, 25*, 105–123. doi:10.1023/B:JOPP.0000039941.85452.ea

Cuffe, S. P., Waller, J. L., Cuccaro, M. L., Pumariega, A. J., & Garrison, C. Z. (1995). Race and gender differences in the treatment of psychiatric disorders in youth adolescents. *Journal of the Academy of Child and Adolescent Psychiatry, 34*, 1536–1543. doi:10.1097/00004583-199511000-00021

D'Andrea, M. (1994). The concerns of Native American youth. *Journal of Multicultural Counseling and Development, 22*, 173–181.

Dolcini, M. M., & Adler, N. E. (1994). Perceived competencies, peer group affiliation, and risk behavior among early adolescents. *Health Psychology, 13*, 496–506. doi:10.1037/0278-6133.13.6.496

Erkut, S. (2010). Developing multiple language versions of instruments for intercultural research. *Child Development Perspectives, 4*, 19–24. doi:10.1111/j.1750-8606.2009.00111.x

Evelyn, B., Toigo, T., Banks, D., Pohl, D., Gray, K., Robins, B., & Ernat, J, (2001). Participation of racial/ethnic groups in clinical trials and race-related labeling: A review of new molecular entities approved 1995-1999. *Journal of the National Medical Association, 93*, 18S–24S.

Ferrell, C. B., Beidel, D. C., & Turner, S. M. (2004). Assessment and treatment of socially phobic children: A cross cultural comparison. *Journal of Clinical Child and Adolescent Psychology, 33*, 260–268. doi:10.1207/s15374424jccp3302_6

Flores, G., Abreu, M., Olivar, M. A., & Kastner, B. (1998). Access barriers to health care for Latino children. *Archives of Pediatrics & Adolescent Medicine, 152*, 1119–1125.

Fouad, N. A., & Arredondo, P. (2007). *Becoming culturally oriented: Practical advice for psychologists and educators.* Washington, DC: American Psychological Association. doi:10.1037/11483-000

Galanti, G. (2008). *Caring for patients from different cultures* (4th ed.). Baltimore, MD: University of Pennsylvania Press.

Ginsburg, G. S., & Drake, K. L. (2002). School-based treatment for anxious African-American adolescents: A controlled pilot study. *Journal of the American Academy of Child and Adolescent Psychiatry, 41*, 768–775. doi:10.1097/00004583-200207000-00007

Grant, B. F., Dawson, D. A., & Hasin, D. S. (2001). *The Alcohol Use Disorder and Associated Disabilities Interview Schedule—DSM–IV version.* Bethesda, MD: National Institute on Alcohol Abuse and Alcoholism.

Grant, B. F., Hasin, D. S., Blanco, C., Stinson, F. S., Chou, S. P., Goldstein, R. B., . . . Huang, B. (2005). The epidemiology of social anxiety disorder in the United States: Results from the national epidemiologic survey on alcohol and related conditions. *The Journal of Clinical Psychiatry, 66*, 1351–1361. doi:10.4088/JCP.v66n1102

Griner, D., & Smith, T. B. (2006). Culturally adapted mental health intervention: A meta-analytic review [Special issue]. *Psychotherapy Theory, Research, Practice, Training: Culture, Race, and Ethnicity in Psychotherapy, 43*, 531–548. doi:10.1037/0033-3204.43.4.531

Guarnaccia, P. J., Lewis-Fernandez, R., & Marano, M. R. (2003). Toward a Puerto Rican popular nosology: Nervios and ataque nervios. *Culture, Medicine and Psychiatry, 27*, 339–366. doi:10.1023/A:1025303315932

Guarnaccia, P. J., Rivera, M., Franco, F., & Neighbors, C. (1996). The experiences of *ataques de nervios*: Towards an anthropology of emotions in Puerto Rico. *Culture, Medicine and Psychiatry, 20*, 343–367. doi:10.1007/BF00113824

Hayward, C., Varady, S., Albano, A. M., Thienemann, M., Henderson, L., & Schatzberg, A. F. (2000). Cognitive-behavioral group therapy for social phobia in female adolescents: Results of a pilot study. *Journal of the American Academy of Child and Adolescent Psychiatry, 39*, 721–726. doi:10.1097/00004583-200006000-00010

Heimberg, R. G., Stein, M. B., Hiripi, E., & Kessler, R. C. (2000). Trends in the prevalence of social phobia in the United States: A synthetic cohort analysis of changes over four decades. *European Psychiatry, 15*, 29–37.

Heinrichs, N., Rapee, R. M., Alden, L. A., Bogels, S., Hofmann, S. G., Oh, K. J., & Sakano, Y. (2006). Cultural differences in perceived social norms and social anxiety. *Behaviour Research and Therapy, 44*, 1187–1197. doi:10.1016/j.brat.2005.09.006

Himle, J. A., Baser, R. E., Taylor, R. J., Campbell, R. D., & Jackson, J. S. (2009). Anxiety disorders among African Americans, Blacks of Caribbean descent, and non-Hispanic Whites in the United States. *Journal of Anxiety Disorders, 23*, 578–590. doi:10.1016/j.janxdis.2009.01.002

Hong, J. J., & Woody, S. R. (2007). Cultural mediators of self-reported social anxiety. *Behaviour Research and Therapy, 45*, 1779–1789. doi:10.1016/j.brat.2007.01.011

Hsu, L., & Alden, L. (2007). Social anxiety in Chinese- and European-heritage students: The effect of assessment format and judgments of impairment. *Behavior Therapy, 38*, 120–131. doi:10.1016/j.beth.2006.06.006

Huey, S. J., Jr., & Polo, A. J. (2008). Evidence-based psychosocial treatments for ethnic minority youth. *Journal of Clinical Child and Adolescent Psychology, 37*, 262–301. doi:10.1080/15374410701820174

Hui, H. C., & Triandis, H. C. (1985). The instability of response sets. *Public Opinion Quarterly, 49*, 253–260. doi:10.1086/268918

Hui, H. C., & Triandis, H. C. (1989). Effects of culture and response format on extreme response style. *Journal of Cross-Cultural Psychology, 20*, 296–309. doi:10.1177/0022022189203004

Hwu, H. G., Yeh, E., & Chang, L. (1989). Prevalence of psychiatric disorders in Taiwan defined by the Chinese Diagnostic Interview Schedule. *Acta Psychiatrica Scandinavica, 79*, 136–147. doi:10.1111/j.1600-0447.1989.tb08581.x

Iwamasa, G. Y. (1997). Asian Americans. In S. Friedman (Ed.), *Cultural issues in the treatment of anxiety* (pp. 99–129). New York, NY: Guilford Press.

Kessler, R. C., & Ustun, T. B. (2004). The World Mental Health (WMH) survey initiative version of the World Health Organization (WHO) Composite International Diagnostic Interview (CIDI). *International Journal of Methods in Psychiatric Research, 13*, 93–121. doi:10.1002/mpr.168

Kirmayer, L. J. (1991). The place of culture in psychiatric nosology: Taijin kyofusho and *DSM–III–R*. *Journal of Nervous and Mental Disease, 179*, 19–28. doi:10.1097/00005053-199101000-00005

Knight, G. P., & Hill, N. E. (1998). Measurement equivalence in research involving minority adolescents. In V. C. McLoyd & L. Steinberg (Eds.), *Studying minority adolescents: Conceptual, methodological, and theoretical issues* (pp. 183–210). Manwah, NJ: Erlbaum.

Knight, G. P., Roosa, M. W., & Umaña-Taylor, A. J. (2009). *Studying ethnic minority and economically disadvantaged populations: Methodological challenges and best practices*. Washington, DC: American Psychological Association. doi:10.1037/11887-000

Knight, G. P., & Zerr, A. A. (2010). Informed theory and measurement equivalence in child development research. *Child Development Perspectives*, *4*, 25–30. doi:10.1111/j.1750-8606.2009.00112.x

Kouyoumdjian, H., Zamboanga, B. L., & Hansen, D. J. (2003). Barriers to community mental health services for Latinos: Treatment considerations. *Clinical Psychology: Science and Practice*, *10*, 394–422. doi:10.1093/clipsy/bpg041

Kuttler, A. F., & La Greca, A. M. (2004). Linkages among adolescent girls' romantic relationships, best friendships, and peer networks. *Journal of Adolescence*, *27*, 395–414. doi:10.1016/j.adolescence.2004.05.002

La Greca, A. M. (1998). *Manual for the Social Anxiety Scales for Children and Adolescents*. Miami, FL: Author.

La Greca, A. M., Dandes, S. K., Wick, P., Shaw, K., & Stone, W. L. (1988). Development of the Social Anxiety Scale for Children: Reliability and concurrent validity. *Journal of Clinical Child Psychology*, *17*, 84–91. doi:10.1207/s15374424jccp1701_11

La Greca, A. M., & Harrison, H. M. (2005). Adolescent peer relations, friendships, and romantic relationships: Do they predict social anxiety and depression? *Journal of Clinical Child and Adolescent Psychology*, *34*, 49–61. doi:10.1207/s15374424jccp3401_5

La Greca, A. M., & Stone, W. L. (1993). Social Anxiety Scale for Children–Revised: Factor structure and concurrent validity. *Journal of Clinical Child Psychology*, *22*, 17–27.

Lau, A. S., Fung, J., Wang, S., & Kang, S. (2009). Explaining elevated social anxiety among Asian Americans: Emotional attunement and a cultural double bind. *Cultural Diversity & Ethnic Minority Psychology*, *15*, 77–85. doi:10.1037/a0012819

Lee, C. K., Kwak, Y. S., Rhee, H., Kim, Y. S., Han, J. H., Choi, J. O., & Lee, Y. H. (1987). The nationwide epidemiological study of mental disorders in Korea. *Journal of Korean Medical Science*, *2*, 19–34.

Lee, M. R., Ohazaki, S., & Yoo, H. C. (2006). Frequency and intensity of social anxiety in Asian Americans and European Americans. *Cultural Diversity & Ethnic Minority Psychology*, *12*, 291–305. doi:10.1037/1099-9809.12.2.291

LeSure-Lester, G. E. (2001). Dating competence, social assertion and social anxiety among college students. *College Student Journal*, *35*, 317–320.

Li, J. (2009). Forging the future between two different worlds: Recent Chinese immigrant adolescents tell their cross-cultural experiences. *Journal of Adolescent Research*, *24*, 477–504. doi:10.1177/0743558409336750

Lin, K. M., Inui, T. S., Kleinman, A. M., & Womack, W. M. (1982). Sociocultural determinants of the help-seeking behaviors of patients with mental illness. *Journal of Nervous and Mental Disease*, *170*, 78–85. doi:10.1097/00005053-19820 2000-00003

Malgady, R. G., & Constantino, G. (1999). Ethnicity and culture: Hispanic youth. In W. K. Silverman & T. H. Ollendick (Eds.), *Developmental issues in the clinical treatment of children* (pp. 231–238). Needham Heights, MA: Allyn & Bacon.

Margolin, S. (2006). African American youths with internalizing difficulties: Relation to social support and activity involvement. *Children & Schools, 28,* 135–144.

Marín, G., Gamba, R. J., & Marín, B. V. (1992). Extreme response style and acquiescence among Hispanics: The role of acculturation and education. *Journal of Cross-Cultural Psychology, 23,* 498–509. doi:10.1177/0022022192234006

Markus, H. R., & Kitayama, S. (1991). Culture and the self: Implications for cognition, emotion, and motivation. *Psychological Review, 98,* 224–253. doi:10.1037/0033-295X.98.2.224

Masia, C. L., Klein, R. G., Storch, E. A., & Corda, B. (2001). School-based behavioral treatment for SAD in adolescents: Results of a pilot study. *Journal of the American Academy of Child and Adolescent Psychiatry, 40,* 780–786. doi:10.1097/00004583-200107000-00012

Matsumoto, D., & Kupperbusch, C. (2001). Idiocentric and allocentric differences in emotional expression, experience, and the coherence between expression and experience. *Asian Journal of Social Psychology, 4,* 113–131. doi:10.1111/j.1467-839X.2001.00080.x

Mattick, R. P., & Clarke, J. C. (1998). Development and validation of measures of social phobia scrutiny fears and social interaction anxiety. *Behaviour Research and Therapy, 36,* 455–470.

Millsap, R. E. (1998). Group differences in regression intercepts: Implications for factorial invariance. *Multivariate Behavioral Research, 33,* 403–424. doi:10.1207/s15327906mbr3303_5

Miranda, J., Azocar, F., Organista, K. C., Muñoz, R. F., & Lieberman, A. (1996). Recruiting and retaining low-income Latinos in psychotherapy research. *Journal of Consulting and Clinical Psychology, 64,* 868–874. doi:10.1037/0022-006X.64.5.868

Mullen, M. R. (1995). Diagnosing measurement equivalence in cross-national research. *Journal of International Business Studies, 26,* 573–596. doi:10.1057/palgrave.jibs.8490187

Newman, D. L. (2005). Ego development and ethnic identity formation in rural American Indian adolescents. *Child Development, 76,* 734–746. doi:10.1111/j.1467-8624.2005.00874.x

Novy, D. M., Stanley, M. A., Averill, P., & Daza P. (2001). Psychometric comparability of English- and Spanish-language measures of anxiety and related affective symptoms. *Psychological Assessment, 13,* 347–355. doi:10.1037/1040-3590.13.3.347

Okazaki, S. (1997). Sources of ethnic differences between Asian American and White American college students on measures of depression and social anxiety. *Journal of Abnormal Psychology, 106,* 52–60. doi:10.1037/0021-843X.106.1.52

Okazaki, S. (2000). Asian American and White American differences on affective distress symptoms: Do symptom reports differ across reporting methods? *Journal of Cross-Cultural Psychology, 31,* 603–625.

Okazaki, S. (2002). Self–other agreement on affective distress scales in Asian Americans and White Americans. *Journal of Counseling Psychology, 49,* 428–437. doi:10.1037/0022-0167.49.4.428

Okazaki, S., Liu, J. F., Longworth, S. L., & Minn, J. Y. (2002). Asian American–White American difference in expressions of social anxiety: A replication and extension. *Cultural Diversity & Ethnic Minority Psychology, 8,* 234–247. doi:10.1037/1099-9809.8.3.234

Okazaki, S., & Sue, S. (1995). Methodological issues in assessment research with ethnic minorities. *Psychological Assessment, 7,* 367–375. doi:10.1037/1040-3590.7.3.367

Olfson, M., Guardino, M., Struening, E., Schneier, F. R., Hellman, F., & Klein, D. F. (2000). Barriers to treatment of social anxiety. *The American Journal of Psychiatry, 157,* 521–527. doi:10.1176/appi.ajp.157.4.521

Ono, Y., Yoshimura, K., Yamauchi, K., Asai, M., Young, J., Fujuhara, S., & Kitamura, T. (2001). Taijin kyofusho in a Japanese community population. *Transcultural Psychiatry, 38,* 506–514. doi:10.1177/136346150103800408

Phillips, L., Hughes, P., & Wilkes, K. (1998, February). Black students' peer crowds: An exploratory study. Paper presented at the Society for Research in Adolescence, San Diego, CA.

Pina, A. A., Little, M., Knight, G. P., & Silverman, W. K. (2009). Cross-ethnic measurement equivalence of the RCMAS in Latino and White youth with anxiety disorders. *Journal of Personality Assessment, 91,* 58–61. doi:10.1080/00223890802484183

Pina, A. A., & Silverman, W. K. (2004). Clinical phenomenology, somatic symptoms, and distress in Hispanic/Latino and European American youths with anxiety disorders. *Journal of Clinical Child and Adolescent Psychology, 33,* 227–236. doi:10.1207/s15374424jccp3302_3

Pina, A. A., Silverman, W. K., Fuentes, R. M., Kurtines, W. M., & Weems, C. F. (2003). Exposure-based cognitive-behavioral treatment for phobic and anxiety disorders: Treatment effects and maintenance for Hispanic/Latino relative to European-American Youths. *Journal of the American Academy of Child and Adolescent Psychology, 42,* 1179–1187. doi:10.1097/00004583-200310000-00008

Pina, A. A., Villalta, I. K., & Zerr, A. A. (2009). Exposure-based cognitive behavioral treatment of anxiety in youth: An emerging culturally-prescriptive framework. *Behavioral Psychology/Psicología Conductual, 17,* 111-135.

Polo, A. J., & López, S. R. (2009). Culture, context, and the internalizing distress of Mexican American youth. *Journal of Clinical Child and Adolescent Psychology, 38,* 273–285. doi:10.1080/15374410802698370

Prinstein, M. J., Boergers, J., & Vernberg, E. M. (2001). Overt and relational aggression in adolescents: Social–psychological adjustment of aggressors and victims. *Journal of Clinical Child Psychology, 30*, 479–491. doi:10.1207/S15374424JCCP3004_05

Ruscio, A. M., Brown, T. A., Chiu, W. T., Sareen, J., Stein, M. B., & Kessler, R. C. (2008). Social fears and social phobia in the United States: Results from the Nation Comorbidity Survey Replication. *Psychological Medicine, 38*, 15–28. doi:10.1017/S0033291707001699

Ryder, A. G., Alden, L. E., & Paulhus, D. L. (2000). Is acculturation unidimensional or bidimensional? A head-to-head comparison in the prediction of personality, self-identity, and adjustment. *Journal of Personality and Social Psychology, 79*, 49–65. doi:10.1037/0022-3514.79.1.49

Salgado de Synder, V. N., Diaz-Perez, M. J., & Ojeda, V. D. (2000). The prevalence of *nervios* and associated symptomatology among inhabitants of Mexican rural communities. *Culture, Medicine and Psychiatry, 24*, 453–470. doi:10.1023/A:1005655331794

Silva de Crane, R., & Spielberger, C. D. (1981). Attitudes of Hispanic, Black, and Caucasian university students toward mental illness. *Hispanic Journal of Behavioral Sciences, 3*, 241–255.

Silverman, W. K., & Albano, A. M. (1996). *The Anxiety Interview Schedule for Children (ADIS–C/P)*. San Antonio, TX: Psychological Corporation.

Silverman, W. K., Pina, A. A., & Viswesvaran, C. (2008). Evidence-based psychosocial treatments for phobic and anxiety disorders in children and adolescents. *Journal of Clinical Child and Adolescent Psychology, 37*, 105–130. doi:10.1080/15374410701817907

Somers, J. M., Goldner, E. M., Waraich, P., & Hsu, L. (2006). Prevalence and incidence studies of anxiety disorders: A systematic review of the literature. *Canadian Journal of Psychiatry, 51*, 100–113.

Storch, E. A., Eisenberg, P. S., Roberti, J. W., & Barlas, M. E. (2003). Reliability and validity of the Social Anxiety Scale for children. *Hispanic Journal of Behavioral Sciences, 25*, 410–422. doi:10.1177/0739986303256915

Sue, D., Ino, S., & Sue, D. M. (1983). Nonassertiveness of Asian Americans: An inaccurate assumption? *Journal of Counseling Psychology, 30*, 581–588. doi:10.1037/0022-0167.30.4.581

Suzuki, K., Takei, N., Kawai, M., Minabe, Y., & Mori, N. (2003). Is *taijin kyofusho* a culture-bound syndrome? [Letter to the editor]. *The American Journal of Psychiatry, 160*, 1358. doi:10.1176/appi.ajp.160.7.1358

Takahashi, T. (1989). Social phobia syndrome in Japan. *Comprehensive Psychiatry, 30*, 45–52. doi:10.1016/0010-440X(89)90117-X

Takeuchi, D. T., Bui, K. T., & Kim, L. (1993). The referral of minority adolescents to community health centers. *Journal of Health and Social Behavior, 34*, 153–164. doi:10.2307/2137241

Tiwari, S. K., & Wang, J. (2006). The epidemiology of mental and substance use-related disorders among White, Chinese, and other Asian populations in Canada. *Canadian Journal of Psychiatry, 51*, 904–912.

van de Vijver, F. J. R., & Poortinga, Y. H. (1997). Towards an integrated analysis of bias in cross-cultural assessment. *European Journal of Psychological Assessment, 13*, 29–37. doi:10.1027/1015-5759.13.1.29

Vandenberg, R. J., & Lance, C. E. (2000). A review and synthesis of the measurement invariance literature: Suggestions, practices, and recommendations of organization research. *Organizational Research Methods, 3*, 4–70. doi:10.1177/109442810031002

Vega, W. A. (1990). Hispanic families in the 1980s: A decade of research. *Journal of Marriage and the Family, 52*, 1015–1024. doi:10.2307/353316

Vega, W. A., & López, S. R. (2001). Priority issues in Latino mental health services research. *Mental Health Services Research, 3*, 189–200. doi:10.1023/A:1013125030718

Vega, W. A., Sribney, W. M., Aguilar-Gaxiola, S., & Kolody, B. (2004). 12-month prevalence of *DSM–III–R* psychiatric disorders among Mexican Americans: Nativity, social assimilation, and age determinants. *Journal of Nervous and Mental Disease, 192*, 532–541. doi:10.1097/01.nmd.0000135477.57357.b2

Vernberg, E. M., Abwender, D. A., Ewell, K. K., & Beery, S. H. (1992). Social anxiety and peer relationships in early adolescence: A prospective analysis. *Journal of Clinical Child Psychology, 21*, 189–196. doi:10.1207/s15374424jccp2102_11

Wagner, E. F. (2003). Conceptualizing alcohol treatment research for Hispanic/Latino adolescents. *Alcoholism, Clinical and Experimental Research, 27*, 1349–1352. doi:10.1097/01.ALC.0000080201.46747.D5

Weems, C. F., & Pina, A. A. (2010). The assessment of emotion regulation: Improving construct validity in research on psychopathology in youth—An introduction to the special section. *Journal of Psychopathology and Behavioral Assessment, 32*, 1–7.

West, A. E., & Newman, D. L. (2007). Childhood behavioral inhibition and the experience of social anxiety in American Indian adolescents. *Cultural Diversity and Ethnic Minority Psychology, 13*, 197–206.

Wittchen, H.-U., & Fehm, L. (2001). Epidemiology, patterns of comorbidity, and associated disabilities of social phobia [Special issue]. *The Psychiatric Clinics of North America, 24*, 617–641. doi:10.1016/S0193-953X(05)70254-9

Wynaden, D., Chapman, R., Orb, A., McGowan, S., Zeeman, Z., & Yeak, S. (2005). Factors that influence Asian communities' access to health care. *International Journal of Mental Health Nursing, 14*, 88–95. doi:10.1111/j.1440-0979.2005.00364.x

Xie, D., Leong, F. T. L., & Feng, S. Culture-specific personality correlates of anxiety among Chinese and Caucasian college students. *Asian Journal of Social Psychology, 11*, 163–174.

Zane, N., & Yeh, M. (2002). The use of culturally-based variables in assessment: Studies on loss of face. In K. S. Kurasaki, S. Okazaki, & S. Sue (Eds.), *Asian American mental health: assessment theories and methods* (pp. 123–138). New York, NY: Kluwer Academic/Plenum.

Zhou, X., Xu, Q., Ingles, C. J., Hidalgo, M. D., & La Greca, A. (2008). Reliability and validity of the Chinese version of the Social Anxiety Scale for Adolescents. *Child Psychiatry and Human Development, 39,* 185–200. doi:10.1007/s10578-007-0079-0

III

ASSESSMENT AND TREATMENT OF SOCIAL ANXIETY DISORDER

12

ASSESSMENT OF SOCIAL ANXIETY

ANDRES DE LOS REYES AND COURTNEY P. KEETON

A significant challenge in understanding social anxiety disorder (SAD) in adolescents and young adults involves developing reliable and valid strategies for assessing the disorder in this age group. Like any other psychiatric condition, no one strategy adequately quantifies SAD across all relevant symptom domains. Further, this period presents unique challenges to assessment and diagnosis. Adolescents' social worlds differ from those of younger children (e.g., greater involvement in activities and peer relationships outside of the home), and for the first time adolescents encounter social situations that are commonly experienced in adulthood (e.g., dating and romantic relationships, employment, automotive driving; see Lerner & Steinberg, 2009). Thus, successful identification of SAD requires developmentally sensitive assessment strategies that distinguish developmentally normal from developmentally atypical behaviors and experiences. Consistent with a developmental psychopathology framework, consideration of normative adolescent functioning serves as a gauge for clinically relevant concerns.

In this chapter, we focus specifically on evidence-based assessment strategies for SAD. At the same time, it is not uncommon for other anxiety- and non-anxiety-related problems to coexist. Common co-occurring conditions include other anxiety disorders, mood disorders, attention-deficit/hyperactivity

225

disorder, and substance abuse (Buckner et al., 2008; Ferdinand, de Nijs, van Lier, & Verhulst, 2005; Jarrett & Ollendick, 2008; Stein & Stein, 2008; Viana, Rabian, & Beidel, 2008). A comprehensive assessment, therefore, should consider symptoms beyond social anxiety to inform differential diagnosis, case conceptualization, and treatment planning.

AVAILABLE ASSESSMENT METHODS

Available methods for the assessment of SAD include clinical interviews in addition to standardized tools such as clinician-administered instruments, paper-and-pencil questionnaires, and behavioral and physiological methods. As mentioned, no single strategy reviewed in the sections that follow adequately quantifies social anxiety in its totality and across all relevant domains.

Clinical Interview

The goal of the clinical interview is to collect information about the quality and quantity of symptoms across the three response systems—behavioral, cognitive, physiological—in addition to global information such as past medical and psychiatric history. When assessing for SAD in particular, it is important to be attuned to symptoms and impairment that are not reported because of avoidant coping. Although avoidant behavior typically characterizes anxiety, some adolescents may not consider avoidance as impairing. Consider the following scenario: Teen A and Teen B are socially anxious, and they avoid the school homecoming dance because of worry about potential embarrassment or rejection on the dance floor. Teen A is disappointed to be missing out on the dance and wishes he could go. Teen B is relieved to be missing out on the dance and decides to use the time playing fantasy football at home. In this scenario, both teens are impaired; they experience distress associated with the dance, and they avoid the distressing situation. However, Teen B is less explicitly impaired because he values the adaptive function of his coping avoidance. As a result, adolescents like Teen B may be more difficult to assess.

A similar challenge arises when the youth and/or others accommodate anxiety symptoms in a way that reduces distress even in the face of continued worry. For example, a father who agrees to drive his socially anxious daughter rather than have her ride the school bus may perceive the arrangement as beneficial to both himself and his daughter because he enjoys their quality time together, experiences no disruption to his personal schedule, and sees that the arrangement makes his daughter happy. Therefore, careful questioning of an adolescent's daily routines may be necessary to unveil symptoms that are not automatically volunteered or perceived as impairing.

Additionally, one should consider the value of soliciting reports from multiple informants, as informants often disagree (De Los Reyes & Kazdin, 2005). Adolescents may be an important resource for understanding the relations between their physiological symptoms and their interpretations of the intensity of these symptoms (Anderson & Hope, 2009). Parents or other informants may often base their impressions on outwardly expressed behaviors and thus may have helpful insight around observed physical symptoms (fidgetiness) and avoidant behavior (refusal to talk on the phone with friends; see Kraemer et al., 2003). Finally, it is important to recognize that variability will exist in the degree of distress experienced within social and performance situations as well as in the number of situations in which these concerns exist. Presence of anxiety symptoms in some social situations and not others does not negate the seriousness of the disorder.

Standardized Assessment Methods

Commonly used standardized tools include clinician-administered instruments and questionnaires. Among the rating scales are ones developed specifically to assess social anxiety among children and adolescents, whereas others are multidimensional self-report instruments covering a broad range of anxiety symptoms. We have limited our review of broad-based questionnaires to those that include a subscale specific to social anxiety.

Clinician-Administered Scales and Interviews

The Liebowitz Social Anxiety Scale for Children and Adolescents is a reliable, 24-item clinician-administered scale that measures fear and avoidance of social situations over the past week (Masia, Klein, Storch, & Corda, 2001; Masia-Warner et al., 2003). The Liebowitz Social Anxiety Scale for Children and Adolescents consists of 11 items relating to social interaction and 13 items related to public performance. Each item is rated on two 4-point scales by a clinician. The first rating is a measure of fear and anxiety, and the second rating is a measure of avoidance. A total score is calculated by summing all of the fear and avoidance ratings. A total score of 30 discriminates clinically anxious youth from community controls, and a score of 60 discriminates those with generalized and nongeneralized SAD. A self-report version of the measure is available (e.g., Rytwinski et al., 2009). Evidence suggests that the clinician-administered and self-report versions are highly correlated and have similar cutoff scores (Rytwinski et al., 2009).

The Pediatric Anxiety Rating Scale (PARS) assesses the frequency, severity, and impairment of separation anxiety, social anxiety, and generalized anxiety symptoms in youth ages 6 to 17 (Research Unit on Pediatric Psychopharmacology Anxiety Study Group [RUPP], 2002). It consists of a 50-item symptom checklist of anxiety symptoms scored as present or absent (yes or no) during the past week. Endorsed symptoms are then collectively (i.e., integrating both child and parent information) rated by the clinician on the following seven dimensions of global severity: (a) number of symptoms, (b) frequency, (c) severity of distress associated with anxiety symptoms, (d) severity of physical symptoms, (e) avoidance, (f) interference at home, and (g) interference out of home.

The PARS was originally created to evaluate treatment response among anxious youth, and the measure has since been used in at least nine clinical trials, including serving as the primary scalar measure of efficacy in several trials (e.g., RUPP, 2001; Walkup et al., 2008). Unlike other clinician-rated instruments, the PARS accounts for the high rates of comorbidity between anxiety disorders and yields a global severity and impairment score across co-occurring anxiety symptoms. The PARS demonstrated acceptable internal consistency, test–retest reliability, and convergent and construct validity in a clinical sample of anxious children (RUPP, 2002). In addition, the PARS total score was sensitive to pharmacological treatment (RUPP, 2001, 2002).

The Anxiety Disorders Interview Schedule for *DSM–IV*: Child/Parent Version (ADIS–IV: C/P; Silverman & Albano, 1996) is a semistructured diagnostic interview for youth ages 6 to 17 and is considered the gold standard assessment of pediatric anxiety. The ADIS–IV is administered independently to the adolescent and the parent and assesses all *Diagnostic and Statistical Manual of Mental Disorders* (4th ed.; *DSM–IV*; American Psychiatric Association, 1994) anxiety disorders as well as mood and externalizing disorders. A clinician's severity rating is assigned to each diagnosis using a 0 (*none*) to 8 (*very disabling*) scale reflecting symptom severity and impairment. A minimum clinician's severity rating of 4 is required to make a diagnosis. The ADIS–IV: C/P is a reliable and valid measure of anxiety disorders in youth (Silverman & Eisen, 1992; Silverman & Rabian, 1995). Test–retest reliability on composite diagnoses was in the excellent range (Silverman, Saavedra, & Pina, 2001), as were interrater reliability estimates for diagnoses (Grills & Ollendick, 2003).

The Schedule for Affective Disorders and Schizophrenia for School-Age Children is a semistructured diagnostic interview for youth ages 6 to 18. There are three versions of this interview (see Ambrosini et al., 2000), and all provide similar diagnostic coverage, have parent and child versions, and have good rater reliability. Noteworthy differences among the three versions are the particular use of screening questions, skip-outs of questions, and the use of modules or syndrome-specific score sheets.

The National Institute of Mental Health Diagnostic Interview Schedule for Children—Version 4 (DISC–IV; Shaffer, Fisher, Lucas, Dulcan, & Schwab-Stone, 2000) is a structured diagnostic interview with parent and child versions. As a result of its structured design, the DISC–IV can be administered by lay interviewers or by telephone and is available in computerized and audio-computer-administered self-report versions. The DISC–IV inquires about the level of impairment associated with each diagnosis with regard to youth distress, school functioning, or relations with caretakers, family, friends, or teachers. It has been used in primary care and treatment outcome studies. The DISC has demonstrated good reliability and validity (Shaffer et al., 2000). The voice DISC possesses adequate reliability and demonstrates convergence with previous versions of the DISC (Wasserman, McReynolds, Lucas, Fisher, & Santos, 2002).

Broadband Anxiety Rating Scales

The Multidimensional Anxiety Scale for Children (MASC; March, 1998; March, Parker, Sullivan, Stallings, & Conners, 1997) is a 39-item measure for youth ages 8 to 19. The MASC has 4-point scoring and is available in self-report and parent-report format as well as an abbreviated 10-item version. Items were theoretically derived and factor analysis using community and clinical samples subsequently yielded the measure's four subscales: physical symptoms, social anxiety, separation anxiety, and harm avoidance. The social anxiety subscale comprises nine items (e.g., "laugh at me," "I look stupid") with a total range of 0 to 27 and has predictive utility for *DSM–IV* SAD (e.g., van Gastel & Ferdinand, 2008). Some data suggest a cutoff of 12.5 or 13.5 on the social anxiety subscale to differentiate socially anxious from non-socially-anxious youth (Anderson, Jordan, Smith, & Inderbitzen-Nolan, 2009; Wood, Piacentini, Bergman, McCracker, & Barrios, 2002) and a cutoff of 16.5 on the parent version (Wood et al., 2002). The MASC has shown good internal consistency, test–retest stability, concurrent validity, and discriminant validity, and psychometric properties are invariable across age and gender (Anderson et al., 2009; Grills-Taquechel, Ollendick, & Fisak, 2008; March et al., 1997; March et al., 1999; Wood et al., 2002). The MASC has been used in a number of treatment studies and is reasonably sensitive to treatment effects (e.g., Albano, 2009; RUPP, 2001).

The Screen for Child Anxiety and Related Disorders (SCARED; Birmaher et al., 1999; Birmaher, Khetarpal, Brent, & Cully, 1997) is a 41-item inventory for youth ages 9 to 19. It uses a 3-point scale and yields a total score and five factor scores, four of which correspond to *DSM–IV* anxiety diagnoses: somatic/panic, generalized anxiety, separation anxiety, social anxiety, and school phobia. A total score of 8 on the seven-item social anxiety scale is suggestive of a social anxiety diagnosis. The SCARED has parallel parent and child versions as well as an abbreviated five-item measure. One study showed that the single SCARED item "My child is shy" was a valid predictor of adolescent social anxiety (Gardner, Lucas, Kolko, & Campo, 2007). The SCARED has shown good psychometric properties in clinical and community samples and has been validated for use in primary care. It discriminates between anxiety and non-anxiety, anxiety and depression, and anxiety and disruptive disorders (Birmaher et al., 1999; Muris et al., 1998). The SCARED has been useful in many studies to demonstrate treatment effects (Albano, 2009; Birmaher et al., 2003; RUPP, 2001). Alternate versions of the SCARED have been created, including one with additional social anxiety items (Bodden, Bögels, & Muris, 2009).

The Spence Children's Anxiety Scale (SCAS; Spence, 1998) is a 44-item self-report questionnaire with a corresponding 38-item parent-report version (Nauta et al., 2004). Although it was originally developed with a sample of children ages 8 to 12, the reliability, concurrent validity, and factor structure have been confirmed with adolescent samples (Muris, Merckebach, Mayer, & Prins, 2000; Spence, Barrett, & Turner, 2003). The SCAS measures DSM-defined anxiety disorder symptoms with six anxiety subscales. Items are rated on a 4-point scale. The SCAS has adequate internal consistency and test–retest reliability and can differentiate between children with and without specific anxiety disorders (Spence, 1998). Most of the research on the SCAS has been conducted in other countries; however, one report confirmed the reliability and validity of the self- and parent-report in a North American sample of clinically anxious youth and normal controls (Whiteside & Brown, 2008).

The Revised Child Anxiety and Depression Scales (Chorpita, Yim, Moffitt, Umemoto, & Francis, 2000) is a 47-item self-report instrument for ages 8 to 18 adapted from the SCAS. The Revised Child Anxiety and Depression Scales assess DSM–IV symptoms of both anxiety disorders and depression. The social anxiety scale is similar to the SCARED social anxiety scale but includes a broader range of social situations. Psychometric properties have been demonstrated in both clinical and community samples (Chorpita, Moffitt, & Gray, 2005; Chorpita et al., 2000; Weems, Zakem, Costa, Cannon, & Watts, 2005).

Social-Anxiety-Specific Rating Scales

The Social Anxiety Scale for Adolescents (SAS–A; La Greca & Lopez, 1998; La Greca & Stone, 1993) is an 18-item self-report measure that assesses social fears in youth ages 12 to 18 years. The SAS–A yields both a total score and three subscales: fear of negative evaluation, social avoidance and distress in new situations, and social avoidance and distress in general situations. Items are rated on a 5-point scale, and higher total scores indicate higher levels of social anxiety, with a suggested cutoff score of 50 to reliably differentiate socially anxious and nonanxious adolescents (La Greca & Lopez, 1998). Adequate internal consistency, test–retest reliability, and discriminant validity of the SAS–A have been established (Ginsburg, La Greca, & Silverman; Inderbitzen-Nolan, Davies, & McKeon, 2004; Inderbitzen-Nolan & Walters, 2000; La Greca & Lopez, 1998; Storch, Masia-Warner, Dent, Roberti, & Fisher, P. H., 2004).

The Social Phobia and Anxiety Scale for Children (SPAI–C; Beidel, Turner, & Morris, 1995) is an empirically derived 26-item self-report measure that assesses somatic, cognitive, and behavioral symptoms associated with SAD. Although it was originally developed with children ages 8 to 13 years, data are now available to support its reliability and validity in adolescents up to age 17 (Bruzzese, Fisher, Lemp, & Warner, 2009; Storch et al., 2004). Scores range from 0 to 52 and load onto three factors: assertiveness and general conversation, traditional social encounters, and public performance. The recommended cutoff point suggesting clinically significant social anxiety is 18 (Beidel et al., 1995, 1999). Whereas the SAS–A measures general social distress, the SPAI–C assesses anxiety across a broader variety of social and performance situations as well as cognitive, physiological, and behavioral correlates. The SPAI–C has good reliability and validity estimates (Beidel et al., 1995; Silverman & Ollendick, 2005) and successfully discriminates SAD from other anxiety disorders (Morris & Masia, 1998).

The Social Phobia Inventory (Connor et al., 2000) is a self-administered questionnaire for estimating SAD across three symptom dimensions: fear in social situations, avoidance of performance or social situations, and physiological discomfort in social situations. Although it was originally designed and validated as a 17-item measure with support for both three-factor and five-factor structures, recent results suggest a 10-item three-factor solution for clinical samples (Carleton et al., 2010). Items are scored on the basis of frequency in the past week, with a range of 0–68 for the summed total score. One study established a cutoff score of 15 for adolescents in relation to an ADIS–IV diagnosis of SAD (Johnson, Davies, McKeon, & Inderbitzen-Nolan, 2002). The Social Phobia Inventory has demonstrated good psychometric properties when used with healthy adult volunteers and psychiatric patients (including older adolescents), and the total score has excellent internal consistency, test–retest reliability, convergent validity, and discriminant validity (Connor et al., 2000; Ranta, Kaltiala-Heino, Rantanen, Tuomisto, & Marttunen, 2007).

Observational, Performance-Based, and Physiological Measures

In addition to standardized instruments, observational, performance-based, and physiological methods for assessing social anxiety are available. These assessments include observing behavior in reaction to structured or prearranged scenarios (e.g., role-play situations, peer interactions) or computer-based stimuli (e.g., threat-valenced words or pictures of threatening stimuli such as faces). Measures also include assessments of adolescents' physiological reactions (e.g., heart rate, skin conductance) in relation to structured or observational tasks. Particular stimuli vary widely depending on age (Bierman & Welsh, 2000). Here, we focus on those tasks that incorporate stimuli most relevant to adolescents and young adults.

Observational and Performance-Based Methods

Behavioral coding systems (BCSs) assess specific behaviors when encountering situations set in naturalistic settings such as classrooms and conversational interactions (see Vasey & Lonigan, 2000). For example, Kendall and colleagues modified a BCS originally developed to assess preschool anxiety (Glennon & Weisz, 1978) to assess observed anxiety-related behaviors in older children and adolescents within controlled trials testing psychological treatments for anxiety (Kendall, 1994; Kendall et al., 1997). Specifically, the BCS was applied to coding observed behavior within a 5-min period during which the patient spoke about him- or herself in front of a video camera. Behavioral codes evidenced high interrater reliability.

Social competence tasks involve assessing social skills within various interactions between the adolescent patient and a same-age peer. Socially anxious individuals often have difficulties within interactions with same-age peers and others (e.g., adult authority figures). Thus, the goal of social competence tasks is to assess these interactions under standardized conditions. Specific behaviors of interest are adolescents' reactions to or initiations of interactions between themselves and the peer with whom they are interacting (e.g., speech quality, number of questions asked, quality of answers given; Beidel et al., 1999, 2000; Beidel et al., 2007; Beidel, Turner, & Young, 2006). The interactions observed include the patient starting conversations, offering help, giving compliments, and providing assertive responses. Social competence tasks are not designed to assess the presence of anxiety symptoms per se but the social skill strengths and deficits that commonly covary with an adolescent's level of social anxiety. At the same time, social competence tasks share commonalities with BCSs in that these tasks also demonstrate adequate psychometric properties and have been used to assess treatment effects within controlled trials (Beidel et al., 1999, 2000; Beidel et al., 2007; Beidel et al., 2006; Spence, Donovan, & Brechman-Toussaint, 2000).

Tasks assessing information-processing biases typically consist of (a) computer-based assessments of reactions to stimuli that vary in valence, (b) vignette-based assessments of adolescents' threat-based interpretations of ambiguous scenarios, or (c) vignette-based assessments of adolescents' reported coping responses in reaction to anxiety-provoking situations (Bar-Haim, Lamy,

Pergamin, Bakermans-Kranenberg, & van IJzendoorn, 2007; Vasey & Lonigan, 2000). Each of these assessments is grounded in the idea that anxious individuals, relative to nonanxious individuals, are attuned to a greater extent to threat-based cues in their environment (e.g., Mathews, 1990). For example, computer-based assessments often consist of dot-probe tasks in which an adolescent is presented with two stimuli beside each other, one threatening and one neutral (usually words or human faces). These stimuli are followed immediately by a small probe in the location in which one of the two stimuli was just presented. The adolescent is asked to respond to the probe as fast as possible. Here, evidence of greater attention to threat is revealed in faster reaction times to dot probes immediately preceded by threat-based stimuli.

A wealth of evidence supports the general observation that anxious people (both adults and children) evidence an attentional bias toward threat-based stimuli to a greater extent than nonanxious people (Bar-Haim et al., 2007). Additionally, recent work with adults meeting criteria for SAD suggests that modifications to the dot-probe paradigm can be used to train patients to reduce their attentional bias toward threat, with these reductions in attentional bias being accompanied by corresponding reductions in self-reported anxiety symptoms and independent rater judgments of performance on a public speaking task (Amir et al., 2009; Amir, Weber, Beard, Bomyea, & Taylor, 2008; Schmidt, Richey, Buckner, & Timpano, 2009). However, tests in adult samples of the psychometric properties of these paradigms suggest that they demonstrate poor internal consistency and poor test–retest reliability (Schmukle, 2005; Staugaard, 2007). Thus, the ability of these tasks to reliably capture individual differences in attentional bias to threat-based cues is unclear (MacLeod, Koster, & Fox, 2009).

Physiological Methods

Physiological measures include strategies that assess the electrocortical system (e.g., electroencephalograms, cortisol reactivity), the cardiovascular system (e.g., heart period, heart rate variability), electrodermal activity (e.g., skin conductance level), and muscle contraction activity (e.g., auditory startle reflex). These measures provide information about general arousal or indices of autonomic nervous system regulatory activities and have been related to individual differences in attention, cognition, and emotion in both child and adult populations (Fox, Schmidt, & Henderson, 2000). A major advantage of physiological measures is that they are unlikely to be affected by rater biases (e.g., halo effect) that may otherwise affect other methods. However, research on physiological methods, particularly with children and adolescents, is limited. The existing data have yielded equivocal results likely because of methodological limitations or inconsistent methodology. Also, although adult data do not necessarily generalize to adolescents, we review some of these data next.

Some studies have examined the stress hormone cortisol as a physiological marker of SAD, producing mixed results. Although one study found adolescent girls with SAD to exhibit increases in cortisol in anticipation of a socially stressful task (Martel et al., 1999), another study found a group of college students with SAD to exhibit comparably lower cortisol levels across anxiety-provoking situations relative to their nonanxious peers (Beaton et al., 2006). In explaining the contrary findings of the latter study, the authors speculated that individuals with chronic SAD may have adapted adrenocortical system responses to stress.

Interestingly, some studies have demonstrated that objective measures and subjective reports of physiological arousal are often discrepant. In one study, high and low socially anxious undergraduates were not different on physiological responses across all 12 measures; however, socially anxious individuals reported greater increases in perceived physiological activation in response to a speech task (Mauss, Wilhelm, & Gross, 2004). Similarly, another study of adolescents with and without SAD found no group differences on actual measures of heart rate and blood pressure during anxiety-provoking experimental conditions; however, the clinical group reported greater perceived increases in physiological arousal (Anderson & Hope, 2009). These data and others (e.g., Eley, Stirling, Ehlers, Gregory, & Clark, 2004) show that anxiety symptoms are associated with an enhanced ability to perceive internal physiological cues.

Other research has demonstrated that some measures are better than others in capturing responses. The auditory startle reflex assessed by the blink response shows no differences between anxious and nonanxious individuals, but an enlarged auditory startle reflex emerges in youth with anxiety disorders compared with nonanxious youth when assessed by the multiple-muscle response (Bakker, Tijssen, van der Meer, Koelman, & Boer, 2009). In this study, children and adolescents with anxiety disorders also demonstrated enlarged autonomic reactivity as assessed by the sympathetic skin response compared with normal controls. In another investigation (Schulz, Alpers, & Hofmann, 2008), the mediating role of negative self-focused cognitions on social anxiety in anticipation of a speech among a sample of college undergraduates was examined. The psychophysiological battery included skin conductance, heart rate, and startle eye blink. Increased self-reported anxiety during negative anticipation of the situation was matched by a significant decrease in high-frequency heart rate variability. Furthermore, higher levels of social anxiety predicted a stronger decrease of high-frequency heart rate variability. However, similar to earlier studies, evidence for physiological correlates of social anxiety was limited. This study exemplifies the current state of the research in adolescent social anxiety in that it is not clear what measures can reliably differentiate among degrees of social anxiety.

Another study measured heart rate, skin conductance level, respiratory sinus arrhythmia, and blushing as autonomic correlates of social anxiety and embarrassment in shy or nonshy college undergraduates (Hofmann, Moscovitch, & Kim, 2006). Social anxiety was significantly correlated with blushing during the experimental conditions, and blushing was the only autonomic measure that distinguished the two groups. Consistent with prior research, this study found no relationship between self-reported blushing propensity and actual blushing response, which points out the necessity of a multimodal approach. Overall, there is evidence to support the use of physiological measures in adolescent social phobia, but additional research is sorely needed.

RECOMMENDATIONS FOR FUTURE RESEARCH AND CLINICAL PRACTICE

There are a number of recommendations for future research and practice that can be drawn from the latest research on clinical instruments for social anxiety in adolescents.

Clinical Utility of Existing Measures

Overall, existing measures have a wealth of evidence with regard to standard psychometric properties and offer the major advantage of comparing samples by symptoms and severity across studies. However, a key limitation is that research on existing measures has not established their clinical utility (see Hunsley & Mash, 2007). That is, research has not delineated whether the very act of administering these measures (vs. not using them or using alternative instruments) enhances clinical decision making or patient outcomes. Do clinicians make better decisions if they use one structured interview (ADIS) versus another (DISC) or versus an informal interview? Can one improve the reliability of differential diagnoses when clinical interviews are augmented with a questionnaire measure that includes DSM–IV-specific anxiety subscales (SCAS) versus scales derived from factor analytic work (MASC)? In short, absent from this work is an evidence base for understanding the efficacy of the clinical use of measures previously described. To this end, we encourage future research to conduct randomized controlled trials testing the ability of these instruments to improve clinical decision making and patient outcomes.

Refinement of Measurement Process

A second area for future inquiry is how often reliable and valid measures should be administered during the course of treatment. Indeed, research to date largely justifies their use at a single time point during screening or diagnostic assessments or from pre- to posttreatment. Rarely are these measures tested for their ability to reliably assess changes over multiple assessment points. Further, several social anxiety screening measures adequately predict the presence of a diagnosis as assessed through reliable and valid structured interviews (e.g., ADIS). Presumably, one or more of these measures or a combination thereof might be used to predict the presence of a SAD diagnosis. If so, future research might test whether, once a clinician or research team has arrived at a pretreatment diagnosis through structured interviews, a battery of social anxiety screening measures can be administered at multiple time points during treatment to assess whether interviews provided an adequate prediction of a SAD diagnosis. If they did, this might suggest that measures traditionally used for screening purposes may be used over the course of treatment as proxy measures of diagnostic status. Such research might provide guidance for assessments in clinical practice for which it might not be clinically feasible to administer structured diagnostic interviews at multiple assessment points.

Toward Integrating Clinical Ratings, Behavioral Observations, and Physiological Indices

Finally, we previously reviewed the conceptual foundations underlying clinical assessments of SAD as consisting of behavioral, cognitive, and physiological components. Overall, standardized measures can assess aspects of each of these three domains. At the same time, they are all based on subjective report. This is astounding given that for two of these three domains (behavioral, physiological) more advanced technology has been available for many years. Indeed, recent physiological and behavioral work with adolescents has assessed physiological reactivity using heart rate monitors that are primarily marketed for athletic training and are substantially lower in cost relative to equipment marketed for research (Anderson & Hope, 2009). Perhaps the greatest limitation to build on with regard to the state of the art of evidence-based assessments for adolescents and young adults with SAD and anxiety in general is the idea that the construct's underlying concepts often do not translate into the measurements of social anxiety observed in research. Measurement batteries observed in basic and applied research on social anxiety in adolescents overemphasize use of subjective reports over and above behavioral indices of social anxiety, or sophisticated physiological assessments of social anxiety are administered at the expense of poor or limited use of subjective reports. Yet, recent advancements in objective assessments allow for low-cost and versatile administration of these methods. Further, researchers and practitioners can generally agree on the idea that the combination of subjective and objective reports for assessing a given clinical condition both capitalizes on the strengths and addresses the limitations of each of these methods (see Kazdin, 2003). Therefore, future research should seek to create and test standardized assessment protocols based on subjective, physiological, and behavioral assessment methodologies that reliably and validly measure the core domains of SAD.

REFERENCES

Albano, A. M. (2009, November). *The child/adolescent anxiety multimodal study: Secondary outcomes*. Paper presented at the meeting of the Association for Behavioral and Cognitive Therapies, New York, NY.

Ambrosini, P. J. (2000). Historical development and present status of the schedule for affective disorders and schizophrenia for school-age children (K-SADS). *Journal of the American Academy of Child and Adolescent Psychiatry, 39 ,* 49–58.

American Psychiatric Association. (1994) *Diagnostic and statistical manual of mental disorders* (4th ed.). Washington, DC: Author.

Amir, N., Beard, C., Taylor, C. T., Klumpp, H., Elias, J., Burns, M., & Chen, X. (2009). Attention training in individuals with generalized social phobia: A randomized controlled trial. *Journal of Consulting and Clinical Psychology, 77,* 961–973. doi:10.1037/a0016685

Amir, N., Weber, G., Beard, C., Bomyea, J., & Taylor, C. T. (2008). The effect of a single-session attention modification program on response to a public speaking challenge in socially anxious individuals. *Journal of Abnormal Psychology, 117,* 860–868. doi:10.1037/a0013445

Anderson, E. R., & Hope, D. A. (2009). The relationship among social phobia, objective and perceived physiological reactivity, and anxiety sensitivity in an adolescent population. *Journal of Anxiety Disorders, 23,* 18–26. doi:10.1016/j.janxdis.2008.03.011

Anderson, E. R., Jordan, J. A., Smith, A. J., Inderbitzen-Nolan, H. M. (2009). An examination of the MASC social anxiety scale in a non-referred sample of adolescents. *Journal of Anxiety Disorders, 23,* 1098–1105.

Bakker, M. J., Tijssen, M. J., van der Meer, J. N., Koelman, J. M., & Boer, F. (2009). Increased whole-body auditory startle reflex and autonomic reactivity in children with anxiety disorders. *Journal of Psychiatry & Neuroscience, 34,* 314–322.

Bar-Haim, Y., Lamy, D., Pergamin, L., Bakermans-Kranenberg, M. J., & van IJzendoorn, M. H. (2007). Threat-related attentional bias in anxious and nonanxious individuals: A meta-analytic study. *Psychological Bulletin, 133,* 1–24. doi:10.1037/0033-2909.133.1.1

Beaton, E. A., Schmidt, L. A., Ashbaugh, A. R., Santesso, D. L., Antony, M. M., McCabe, R. E., . . . Schulkin, J. (2006). Low salivary cortisol levels among socially anxious young adults: Preliminary evidence from a selected and a non-selected sample. *Personality and Individual Differences, 41,* 1217–1228. doi:10.1016/j.paid.2006.02.020

Beidel, D. C., Turner, S. M., & Morris, T. L. (1995). A new inventory to assess childhood social anxiety and phobia: The Social Phobia and Anxiety Inventory for Children. *Psychological Assessment, 7,* 73–79. doi:10.1037/1040-3590.7.1.73

Beidel, D. C., Turner, S. M., & Morris, T. L. (1999). Psychopathology of childhood social phobia. *Journal of the American Academy of Child and Adolescent Psychiatry, 38,* 643–650. doi:10.1097/00004583-199906000-00010

Beidel, D. C., Turner, S. M., & Morris, T. L. (2000). Behavioral treatment of childhood social phobia. *Journal of Consulting and Clinical Psychology, 68,* 1072–1080.

Beidel, D. C., Turner, S. M., Sallee, F. R., Ammerman, R. T., Crosby, L. A., & Pathak, S. (2007). SET–C versus fluoxetine in the treatment of childhood social phobia. *Journal of the American Academy of Child and Adolescent Psychiatry, 46,* 1622–1632. doi:10.1097/chi.0b013e318154bb57

Beidel, D. C., Turner, S. M., & Young, B. J. (2006). Social effectiveness therapy for children: Five years later. *Behavior Therapy, 37,* 416–425. doi:10.1016/j.beth.2006.06.002

Bierman, K. L., & Welsh, J. A. (2000). Assessing social dysfunction: The contributions of laboratory and performance-based measures. *Journal of Clinical Child Psychology, 29,* 526–539. doi:10.1207/S15374424JCCP2904_6

Birmaher, B., Axelson, D. A., Monk, K., Kalas, C., Clark, D. B., Ehmann, M., . . . Brent, D. A. (2003). Fluoxetine for the treatment of childhood anxiety disorders. *Journal of the American Academy of Child and Adolescent Psychiatry, 42,* 415–423.

Birmaher, B., Brent, D. A., Chiappetta, L., Bridge, J., Monga, S., & Baugher, M. (1999). Psychometric properties of the Screen for Child Anxiety Related Emotional Disorders (SCARED): A replication study. *Journal of the American Academy of Child and Adolescent Psychiatry, 38,* 1230–1236. doi:10.1097/00004583-199910000-00011

Birmaher, B., Khetarpal, S., Brent, D., & Cully, M. (1997). The Screen for Child Anxiety Related Emotional Disorders (SCARED): Scale construction and psychometric characteristics. *Journal of the American Academy of Child and Adolescent Psychiatry, 36,* 545–553. doi:10.1097/00004583-199704000-00018

Bodden, D. H. M., Bögels, S. M., & Muris, P. (2009). The diagnostic utility of the Screen for Child Anxiety Related Emotional Disorders—71 (SCARED–71). *Behaviour Research and Therapy, 47,* 418–425. doi:10.1016/j.brat.2009.01.015

Bruzzese, J.-M., Fisher, P. H., Lemp, N., & Warner, C. M. (2009). Asthma and social anxiety in adolescents. *The Journal of Pediatrics, 155,* 398–403. doi:10.1016/j.jpeds.2009.04.004

Buckner, J. D., Schmidt, N. B., Lang, A. R., Small, J. W., Schlauch, R. C., & Lewinsohn, P. M. (2008). Specificity of social anxiety disorder as a risk factor for alcohol and cannabis dependence. *Journal of Psychiatric Research, 42,* 230–239. doi:10.1016/j.jpsychires.2007.01.002

Carleton, R. N., Collimore, K. C., Asmundson, G. J. G., McCabe, R. E., Rowa, K., & Antony, M. M. (2010). SPINning factors: Factor analytic evaluation of the Social Phobia Inventory in clinical and nonclinical undergraduate samples. *Journal of Anxiety Disorders, 24,* 94–101.

Chorpita, B. F., Moffitt, C. E., & Gray, J. (2005). Psychometric properties of the Revised Child Anxiety and Depression Scale in a clinical sample. *Behaviour Research and Therapy, 43,* 309–322. doi:10.1016/j.brat.2004.02.004

Chorpita, B. F., Yim, L., Moffitt, C., Umemoto, L. A., & Francis, S. E. (2000). Assessment of symptoms of DSM–IV anxiety and depression in children: A revised child anxiety and depression scale. *Behaviour Research and Therapy, 38,* 835–855. doi:10.1016/S0005-7967(99)00130-8

Connor, K. M., Davidson, J. R. T., Churchill, L. E., Sherwood, A., Foa, E., & Weisler, R. H. (2000). Psychometric properties of the Social Phobia Inventory (SPIN): New self-rating scale. *The British Journal of Psychiatry, 176,* 379–386. doi:10.1192/bjp.176.4.379

De Los Reyes, A., & Kazdin, A. E. (2005). Informant discrepancies in the assessment of childhood psychopathology: A critical review, theoretical framework, and recommendations for further study. *Psychological Bulletin, 131,* 483–509. doi:10.1037/0033-2909.131.4.483

Eley, T. C., Stirling, L., Ehlers, A., Gregory, A. M., & Clark, D. M. (2004). Heart-beat perception, panic/somatic symptoms and anxiety sensitivity in children. *Behaviour Research and Therapy, 42,* 439–448. doi:10.1016/S0005-7967(03)00152-9

Ferdinand, R. F., de Nijs, P. F. A., van Lier, P., & Verhulst, F. C. (2005). Latent class analysis of anxiety and depressive symptoms in referred adolescents. *Journal of Affective Disorders, 88,* 299–306. doi:10.1016/j.jad.2005.08.004

Fox, N. A., Schmidt, L. A., & Henderson, H. A. (2000). Developmental psychophysiology: Conceptual and methodological perspectives. In J. T. Cacioppo, L. G. Tassinary, & G. Berntson (Eds.), *Handbook of psychophysiology* (2nd ed., pp. 665–686). New York, NY: Cambridge University Press.

Gardner, W., Lucas, A., Kolko, D. J., & Campo, J. V. (2007). Comparison of the PSC-17 and alternative mental health screens in an at-risk primary care sample. *Journal of the American Academy of Child and Adolescent Psychiatry, 46,* 611–618. doi:10.1097/chi.0b013e318032384b

Ginsburg, G. S., La Greca, A. M., & Silverman, W. K. (1998). Social anxiety in children with anxiety disorders: Relation with social and emotional functioning. *Journal of Abnormal Child Psychology, 26,* 175–185. doi:10.1023/A:1022668101048

Glennon, B., & Weisz, J. R. (1978). An observational approach to the assessment of anxiety in young children. *Journal of Consulting and Clinical Psychology, 46,* 1246–1257.

Grills, A. E., & Ollendick, T. H. (2003). Multiple informant agreement and the Anxiety Disorders Interview Schedule for Parents and Children. *Journal of the American Academy of Child and Adolescent Psychiatry, 42,* 30–40. doi:10.1097/00004583-200301000-00008

Grills-Taquechel, A. E., Ollendick, T. H., & Fisak, B. (2008). Reexamination of the MASC factor structure and discriminant ability in a mixed clinical outpatient sample. *Depression and Anxiety, 25*, 942–950. doi:10.1002/da.20401

Hofmann, S. G., Moscovitch, D. A., & Kim, H. (2006). Autonomic correlates of social anxiety and embarrassment in shy and non-shy individuals. *International Journal of Psychophysiology, 61*, 134–142. doi:10.1016/j.ijpsycho.2005.09.003

Hunsley, J., & Mash, E. J. (2007). Evidence-based assessment. *Annual Review of Clinical Psychology, 3*, 29–51. doi:10.1146/annurev.clinpsy.3.022806.091419

Inderbitzen-Nolan, H. M., Davies, C. A., & McKeon, N. D. (2004). Investigating the construct validity of the SPAI–C: Comparing the sensitivity and specificity of the SPAI–C and the SAS–A. *Journal of Anxiety Disorders, 18*, 547–560. doi:10.1016/S0887-6185(03)00042-2

Inderbitzen-Nolan, H. M., & Walters, K. (2000). Social Anxiety Scale for Adolescents: Normative data and further evidence of construct validity. *Journal of Clinical Child Psychology, 29*, 360–371. doi:10.1207/S15374424JCCP2903_7

Jarrett, M. A., & Ollendick, T. H. (2008). A conceptual review of the comorbidity of attention-deficit/hyperactivity disorder and anxiety: Implications for future research and practice. *Clinical Psychology Review, 28*, 1266–1280. doi:10.1016/j.cpr.2008.05.004

Johnson, H. S., Davies, C. A., McKeon, N. D., & Inderbitzen-Nolan, H. (2002, November). *New self-report measures for social anxiety: Investigating the sensitivity and specificity of the MASC and the SPIN in an adolescent population*. Poster session presented at the meeting of the Association for the Advancement of Behavioral Therapy, Reno, NV.

Kazdin, A. E. (2003). *Research design in clinical psychology* (4th ed.). Boston, MA: Allyn & Bacon.

Kendall, P. C. (1994). Treating anxiety disorders in children: Results of a randomized clinical trial. *Journal of Consulting and Clinical Psychology, 62*, 100–110. doi:10.1037/0022-006X.62.1.100

Kendall, P. C., Flannery-Schroeder, E., Panichelli-Mindel, S. M., Southam-Gerow, M., Henin, A., & Warman, M. (1997). Therapy for youths with anxiety disorders: A second randomized clinical trial. *Journal of Consulting and Clinical Psychology, 65*, 366–380. doi:10.1037/0022-006X.65.3.366

Kraemer, H. C., Measelle, J. R., Ablow, J. C., Essex, M. J., Boyce, W. T., & Kupfer, D. J. (2003). A new approach to integrating data from multiple informants in psychiatric assessment and research: Mixing and matching contexts and perspectives. *The American Journal of Psychiatry, 160*, 1566–1577. doi:10.1176/appi.ajp.160.9.1566

La Greca, A. M., & Lopez, N. (1998). Social anxiety among adolescents: Linkages with peer relations and friendships. *Journal of Abnormal Child Psychology, 26*, 83–94. doi:10.1023/A:1022684520514

La Greca, A. M., & Stone, W. L. (1993). Social Anxiety Scale for Children Revised: Factor structure and concurrent validity. *Journal of Clinical Child Psychology, 22*, 17–27. doi:10.1207/s15374424jccp2201_2

Lerner, R. M., & Steinberg, L. (Eds.). (2009). *Handbook of adolescent psychology* (3rd ed., Vols. 1 & 2). Hoboken, NJ: Wiley.

MacLeod, C., Koster, E. H. W., & Fox, E. (2009). Whither cognitive bias modification research? Commentary on special section articles. *Journal of Abnormal Psychology, 118*, 89–99. doi:10.1037/a0014878

March, J. S. (1998). *Manual for the Multidimensional Anxiety Scale for Children (MASC).* Toronto, Ontario, Canada: Multi-Health Systems.

March, J. S., Parker, J. D. A., Sullivan, K., Stallings, P., & Conners, K. (1997). The Multidimensional Anxiety Scale for Children (MASC): Factor structure, reliability and validity. *Journal of the American Academy of Child and Adolescent Psychiatry, 36*, 554–565. doi:10.1097/00004583-199704000-00019

Martel, F. L., Hayward, C., Lyons, D. M., Sanborn, K., Varady, S., & Schatzberg, A. F. (1999). Salivary cortisol levels in socially phobic adolescent girls. *Depression and Anxiety, 10*, 25–27. doi:10.1002/(SICI)1520-6394(1999)10:1<25::AID-DA4>3.0.CO;2-O

Masia, C. L., Klein, R. G., Storch, E. A., & Corda, B. (2001). School-based behavioral treatment for social anxiety disorder in adolescents: Results of a pilot study. *Journal of the American Academy Child Adolescence Psychiatry, 40*, 780–786.

Masia-Warner, C., Storch, E. A., Pincus, D. B., Klein, R. G., Heimberg, R. G., & Liebowitz, M. R. (2003). The Liebowitz Social Anxiety Scale for Children and Adolescents: An initial psychometric investigation. *Journal of the American Academy of Child and Adolescence Psychiatry, 42*, 9, 1076–1084.

Mathews, A. (1990). Why worry? The cognitive function of anxiety. *Behaviour Research and Therapy, 28*, 455–468. doi:10.1016/0005-7967(90)90132-3

Mauss, I. B., Wilhelm, F. H., & Gross, J. J. (2004). Is there less to social anxiety than meets the eye? Emotion experience, expression, and bodily responding. *Cognition and Emotion, 18*, 631–642. doi:10.1080/02699930341000112

Morris, T. L., & Masia, C. L. (1998). Psychometric evaluation of the Social Phobia and Anxiety Inventory for Children: Concurrent validity and normative data. *Journal of Clinical Child Psychology, 27*, 452–458. doi:10.1207/s15374424jccp2704_9

Muris, P., Merckelbach, H., Mayer, B., & Prins, E. (2000). How serious are common childhood fears? *Behaviour Research and Therapy, 38*, 217–228. doi:10.1016/S0005-7967(98)00204-6

Muris, P., Merckelbach, H., Mayer, B., van Brakel, A., Thissen, S., Moulaert, V., & Gadet, B. (1998). The Screen for Child Anxiety Related Emotional Disorders (SCARED) and traditional childhood anxiety measures. *Journal of Behavior Therapy and Experimental Psychiatry, 29*, 327–339. doi:10.1016/S0005-7916(98)00023-8

Ranta, R., Kaltiala-Heino, R., Rantanen, P., Tuomisto, M. T., & Marttunen, M. (2007). Screening social phobia in adolescents from general population: The validity of the Social Phobia Inventory (SPIN) against a clinical interview. *European Psychiatry, 22*, 244–251.

Research Unit on Pediatric Psychopharmacology Anxiety Study Group (RUPP). (2001). Fluvoxamine for the treatment of anxiety disorders in children and adolescents. *New England Journal of Medicine, 344,* 1279–1285.

Research Unit on Pediatric Psychopharmacology Anxiety Study Group (RUPP). (2002). The Pediatric Anxiety Rating Scale (PARS): Development and psychometric properties. *Journal of the American Academy of Child and Adolescent Psychiatry, 41,* 1061–1069.

Reynolds, C. R., & Paget, K. D. (1983). National normative and reliability data for the Revised Children's Manifest Anxiety Scale. *School Psychology Review, 12,* 324–336.

Rytwinski, N. K., Fresco, D. M., Heimberg, R. G., Coles, M. E., Liebowitz, M. R., Cissell, S., . . . Hofmann, S. G. (2009). Screening for social anxiety disorder with the self-report version of the Liebowitz Social Anxiety Scale. *Depression and Anxiety, 26,* 34–38. doi:10.1002/da.20503

Schmidt, N. B., Richey, J. A., Buckner, J. D., & Timpano, K. R. (2009). Attention training for generalized social anxiety disorder. *Journal of Abnormal Psychology, 118,* 5–14. doi:10.1037/a0013643

Schmukle, S. C. (2005). Unreliability of the dot probe task. *European Journal of Personality, 19,* 595–605. doi:10.1002/per.554

Schulz, S. M., Alpers, G. W., & Hofmann, S. G. (2008). Negative self-focused cognitions mediate the effect of trait social anxiety on state anxiety. *Behaviour Research and Therapy, 46,* 438–449. doi:10.1016/j.brat.2008.01.008

Shaffer, D., Fisher, P., Lucas, C., Dulcan, M. K., & Schwab-Stone, M. E. (2000). NIMH Diagnostic Interview Schedule for Children, Version IV (NIMH DISCIV): Description, differences from previous versions, and reliability of some common diagnoses. *Journal of the American Academy of Child and Adolescent Psychiatry, 39,* 28–38. doi:10.1097/00004583-200001000-00014

Silverman, W., & Albano, A. M. (1996). *The Anxiety Disorders Interview Schedule for Children (ADIS–C/P).* San Antonio, TX: Psychological Corporation.

Silverman, W., & Eisen, A. R. (1992). Age differences in the reliability of parent and child reports of child anxious symptomatology using a structure interview. *Journal of the American Academy of Child and Adolescent Psychiatry, 31,* 117–124. doi:10.1097/00004583-199201000-00018

Silverman, W. K., & Ollendick, T. H. (2005). Evidence-based assessment of anxiety and its disorders in children and adolescents. *Journal of Clinical Child and Adolescent Psychology, 34,* 380–411.

Silverman, W. K., & Rabian, B. (1995). Test–retest reliability of the *DSM–III–R* childhood anxiety disorders symptoms using the Anxiety Disorders Interview Schedule for Children. *Journal of Anxiety Disorders, 9,* 139–150. doi:10.1016/0887-6185(94)00032-8

Silverman, W., Saavedra, L., & Pina, A. (2001). Test–retest reliability of anxiety symptoms and disorders with the Anxiety Disorders Interview Schedule for

DSM–IV: Child and Parent Versions. *Journal of the American Academy of Child and Adolescent Psychiatry, 40,* 937–944. doi:10.1097/00004583-200108000-00016

Spence, S. H. (1998). A measure of anxiety symptoms among children. *Behaviour Research and Therapy, 36,* 545–566. doi:10.1016/S0005-7967(98)00034-5

Spence, S. H., Barrett, P. M., & Turner, C. M. (2003). Psychometric properties of the Spence Children's Anxiety Scale with young adolescents. *Journal of Anxiety Disorders, 17,* 605–625. doi:10.1016/S0887-6185(02)00236-0

Spence, S. H., Donovan, C., & Brechman-Toussaint, M. (2000). The treatment of childhood social phobia: The effectiveness of a social skills training-based, cognitive-behavioral intervention, with and without parental involvement. *Journal of Child Psychology and Psychiatry, 41,* 713–726.

Staugaard, S. R. (2007). Reliability of two versions of the dot-probe task using photographic faces. *Psychology Science Quarterly, 51,* 339–350.

Stein, M. B., & Stein, D. J. (2008). Social anxiety disorder. *The Lancet, 371,* 1115–1125. doi:10.1016/S0140-6736(08)60488-2

Storch, E. A., Masia-Warner, C., Dent, H. C., Roberti, J. W., & Fisher, P. H. (2004). Psychometric evaluation of the Social Anxiety Scale for Adolescents and the Social Phobia and Anxiety Inventory for Children: Construct validity and normative data. *Journal of Anxiety Disorders, 18,* 665–679. doi:10.1016/j.janxdis.2003.09.002

van Gastel, W., & Ferdinand, R. F. (2008). Screening capacity of the Multidimensional Anxiety Scale for Children (MASC) for *DSM–IV* anxiety disorders. *Depression and Anxiety, 25,* 1046–1052. doi:10.1002/da.20452

Vasey, M. W., & Lonigan, C. J. (2000). Considering the clinical utility of performance-based measures of childhood anxiety. *Journal of Clinical Child Psychology, 29,* 493–508. doi:10.1207/S15374424JCCP2904_4

Viana, A. G., Rabian, B., & Beidel, D. C. (2008). Self-report measures in the study of comorbidity in children and adolescents with social phobia: Research and clinical utility. *Journal of Anxiety Disorders, 22,* 781–792. doi:10.1016/j.janxdis.2007.08.005

Walkup, J. T., Albano, A. M., Piacentini, J. Birmhaer, B., Compton, S. W., Sherrill, J. T., . . . Kendall, P. C. (2008). Cognitive behavioral therapy, sertraline, or a combination in childhood anxiety. *New England Journal of Medicine, 359,* 2753–2766.

Wasserman, G. A., McReynolds, L. S., Lucas, C. P., Fisher, P., & Santos, L. (2002). The voice DISC-IV with incarcerated male youths: Prevalence of disorder. *Journal of the American Academy of Child & Adolescent Psychiatry, 41,* 314–321.

Weems, C. F., Zakem, A. H., Costa, N. M., Cannon, M. F., & Watts, S. E. (2005). Physiological response and childhood anxiety: Association with symptoms of anxiety disorders and cognitive bias. *Journal of Clinical Child and Adolescent Psychology, 34,* 712–723. doi:10.1207/s15374424jccp3404_13

Whiteside, S. P., & Brown, A. (2008). Exploring the utility of the Spence Children's Anxiety Scales parent- and child-report forms in a North American sample. *Journal of Anxiety Disorders, 22,* 1440–1446. doi:10.1016/j.janxdis.2008.02.006

Wood, J. J., Piacentini, J. C., Bergman, R. L., McCracken, J., & Barrios, V. (2002). Concurrent validity of the anxiety disorders section of the Anxiety Disorders Interview Schedule for *DSM–IV*: Child and Parent Versions. *Journal of Clinical Child and Adolescent Psychology, 31,* 335–342.

13

BEHAVIORAL AND COGNITIVE BEHAVIORAL TREATMENTS FOR SOCIAL ANXIETY DISORDER IN ADOLESCENTS AND YOUNG ADULTS

KERRI L. KIM, ADAIR F. PARR, AND CANDICE A. ALFANO

Prior to the fourth edition of the *Diagnostic and Statistical Manual of Mental Disorders* (4th ed.; *DSM–IV*; American Psychiatric Association, 1994), when developmentally sensitive descriptors for guiding the diagnosis were first included, social anxiety disorder (SAD) was given minimal attention in youth (Beidel, Turner, & Morris, 1999). Research was limited in part by the fact that previous versions of the *DSM* included two similar child-oriented diagnoses—specifically, avoidant and overanxious disorders of childhood—and by the common belief that most cases of "childhood shyness" represented variations of normal development that would remit with age and without intervention (Bruch, Giordano, & Pearl, 1986; Chorney, 2009; Mancini, Van Ameringen, Bennett, Patterson, & Watson, 2005). Although many youth do outgrow early shyness, it is also now clear that persistent shyness increases the risk of SAD and associated impairments in functioning (Hayward et al., 2000; Prior, Smart, Sanson, & Oberklaid, 2000).

With the increase in attention paid to the impairing symptomatology and high prevalence of SAD, treatment research has also increased. To date, numerous treatment studies indicate the efficacy of behavioral and cognitive behavioral interventions for socially anxious children, adolescents, and adults (Beidel & Turner, 2007; Cottraux, 2005; Powers, Sigmarsson, & Emmelkamp, 2008). Treatment outcome studies among adults with SAD, in particular, are extensive, and several efficacious treatment options are now available for this population.

In many ways, research among youth with SAD resembles the adult literature of 2 decades ago. First, only in recent years have controlled trials focusing exclusively on children and adolescents with SAD emerged (Beidel, Turner, & Morris, 2000; Beidel, Turner, Young, et al., 2007; Hayward et al., 2008; Spence, Donovan, & Brechman-Toussaint, 1999). A majority of treatment outcome studies continue to include children with other primary anxiety diagnoses in addition to SAD (Bodden et al., 2008; Hudson et al., 2009; Silverman, Kurtines, Jaccard & Pina, 2009; Walkup et al., 2008). Although all anxiety disorders share considerable overlap in symptomatology and rates of comorbidity, unique symptoms, impairments, and trajectories also exist. For example, compared with individuals with other anxiety disorders, individuals with SAD are more likely to exhibit social skill deficits, feelings of loneliness, stable anxiety symptoms from childhood through adulthood, and alcohol and substance abuse problems in adulthood (Beidel et al., 1999; Hale, Raaijmakers, Muris, van Hoof, & Meeus, 2008; Kushner, Sher, & Beitman, 1990; Spence et al., 1999; Turner, Beidel, & Larkin, 1986). Evidence for unique mediators of treatment response among youth with primary SAD also is beginning to emerge (Alfano et al., 2009). It is therefore becoming increasingly recognized that, similar to research in adults, treatment research in youth needs to focus on specific syndromes as opposed to broad models of psychopathology (Alfano et al., 2009; Ferdinand et al., 2006).

Of additional concern is the fact that a majority of the existing research base is focused on treatment among children and adolescents, with little to no differentiation between these two developmentally distinct periods. In support of this conceptualization, the symptoms and impairments observed in adolescents with SAD overlap to a large extent with those of younger children, including social isolation, skill deficits, and school avoidance (Beidel et al., 1999; Rao et al., 2007). Nonetheless, these observations do not ensure the appropriateness of childhood treatments for socially anxious teens and young adults.

The goal of this chapter is to provide a review of the relevant psychosocial treatment literature to guide the reader in considering the appropriateness of specific treatment strategies for adolescents and young adults with SAD. We begin with an overview of the most commonly used treatment components, followed by a review of specific treatment outcome studies using these strategies. Finally, we consider the clinical implications of these collective data.

INDIVIDUAL TREATMENT COMPONENTS

The components most commonly incorporated into the psychosocial treatment of SAD include systematic exposure, cognitive techniques, social skills training, peer experiences, and relaxation training.

Systematic Exposure

According to learning theory, avoidance serves to negatively reinforce anxiety levels through withdrawal from or removal of a feared stimulus (Lang, 1968). For individuals with SAD, avoidance is typically seen in the form of both macro (e.g., avoiding social events) and micro (e.g., avoiding eye contact in social settings) behaviors. Systematic exposure is the cornerstone of successful behavioral and cognitive behavioral interventions for SAD (Feske & Chambless, 1995; Mersch, 1995; Scholing & Emmelkamp, 1993). During exposure tasks, individuals face anxiety-provoking situations and stimuli that elicit symptoms of arousal, with the primary goal of *habituation*, defined as a progressive loss of physiological and behavioral responsivity to a stimulus as a result of repeated presentation. Secondary goals include increasing confidence that the feared situation can be faced with success and that anxiety symptoms, though uncomfortable, will eventually diminish. Habituation is most commonly determined by decreased ratings on a subjective scale of anxiety and distress, which uses Likert-type ratings. Physiological variables such as heart rate sometimes serve as a secondary channel by which to assess decreasing distress.

Exposure can be conducted in several formats. Most commonly, exposures are created in vivo (i.e., involving real-life situations and tasks), in a graduated fashion guided by a *fear hierarchy* created by the patient and therapist together. The fear hierarchy enumerates specific situations and tasks from least to most anxiety provoking. *Imaginal exposure* (sometimes called *imaginal flooding*), in which the patient imagines a distressing situation or event, also is commonly used in the treatment of SAD, particularly when a particular fear cannot be created in vivo. The therapist uses explicit information and details (provided by the patient) to create and describe a situation to be imagined in session, also with the goal of habituation. Decisions regarding the type of exposures to be used relate to both individual and practical issues. For instance, many feared social situations are difficult to either create or control in the clinical setting, necessitating the use of imaginal techniques. However, because younger patients sometimes demonstrate difficulty holding anxiety-provoking images in mind for extended periods, in vivo exposures are often necessary with younger patients.

Virtual reality (VR) offers a newer format for exposure and may serve as a bridge between the two former types. Specifically, the exposure material consists of a computer-generated environment intended to mimic reality. VR allows the environment to be precisely manipulated to target the nature and intensity of a patient's specific fears. VR also reduces problems of confidentiality that may arise from conducting in vivo social exposures. A disadvantage of VR is the high cost of equipment and software, although costs have decreased somewhat over the past decade with further development and expansion of this technique. On the whole, VR for the treatment of SAD is still a relatively new area of study, though emerging findings suggest positive treatment outcomes for young adults with fear of public speaking (Harris, Kemmerling, & North, 2002) and for adults with SAD (Klinger et al., 2005).

Cognitive Techniques

Individuals meeting criteria for SAD fear that they will "act in a way that will be humiliating or embarrassing" (*DSM–IV–TR*; American Psychiatric Association, 2000, p. 456). Thus, cognitive techniques are directed at identifying and altering negative self-perceptions. Commonly used treatment techniques in adults include helping to identify evidence that contradicts the patient's negative beliefs, modifying the patient's self-focus during social interactions, and reducing overestimations of negative social consequences (Foa, Franklin, Perry & Herbert, 1996; Rapee & Heimberg, 1997; Wells & Papageorgiou, 1998). A video-assisted cognitive technique also has been used to target negative thoughts and beliefs (e.g., Rapee & Hayman, 1996), allowing patients to view video recordings of their social performances as a means of challenging self-focused negative thoughts.

Despite their common use, cognitive techniques may not be critical for positive treatment outcomes. Numerous studies that have directly compared cognitive behavioral therapy with exposure therapy alone for adults with SAD have found both treatments to be equally effective (Butler, Cullington, Munby, Amies, & Gelder, 1984; Emmelkamp, Mersch, Vissia, & van der Helm, 1985; Gelernter et al., 1991; Hope, Heimberg, & Bruch, 1995; Mattick & Peters, 1988; Scholing & Emmelkamp, 1993). Other data indicate changes in cognition as a function of exposure therapy alone (Newman, Hofmann, Trabert, Roth, & Taylor, 1994; Hofmann, 2000). Additionally, although the inclusion of cognitive strategies is sometimes thought to help retain patients in treatment by providing a mechanism of coping with challenging exposure tasks, research indicates that both cognitive behavioral therapy and exposure alone produce similar treatment dropout rates (Taylor, 1996).

Although cognitive methods are commonly used among youth with SAD (e.g., Albano, Marten, Holt, Heimberg, & Barlow, 1995; Hayward et al.,

2000), description of specific treatment techniques is generally lacking. More important, because the cognitive features of SAD in this age group remain largely unexamined at this time, use of this specific treatment component represents little more than a downward extension of adult-based interventions. In one of the first studies to examine in-situation cognitions, no children and only 20% of adolescents with SAD reported the presence of negative thoughts during a social interaction task (Alfano, Beidel, & Turner, 2006). In a second study, adolescents with SAD reported more thoughts about their performance compared with nonanxious adolescents during a peer interaction (Alfano, Beidel, & Turner, 2008). However, performance-based thoughts consisted primarily of neutral observations rather than negative perceptions regarding the quality of performance. Although more research is needed at this time, these preliminary data suggest that many of the cognitive features of SAD in adults, including negative beliefs about one's performance and overestimations of negative social consequences, may represent long-term consequences of the disorder.

Social Skills Training

Substantial evidence exists for social skills deficits among individuals of all ages with SAD (Alfano et al., 2006; Beidel et al., 1999; Boone et al., 1999; Spence et al., 1999; Turner, Beidel, Dancu, & Keyes, 1986; Wenzel, Graff-Dolezal, Macho, & Brendle, 2005). Specific deficits vary but commonly pertain to voice volume, eye contact, speech length, social assertiveness, initiating and maintaining conversations, and listening skills. Thus, social skills training (SST) is a common component of various SAD treatment protocols. SST is generally conducted in a group format, though individual training may be used. Typically, areas of difficulty are discussed, followed by instruction and clinician modeling of specific skills. Patients are then provided opportunities to practice these new skills and receive feedback on their performance. In-session role plays and feedback are particularly important in shaping new skill development in that they allow for repeated practice in a structured, supportive environment.

Similar to exposure tasks, SST is tailored to the patient's specific difficulties and level of development because considerable differences exist in the skills required to make friends and gain social acceptance at different ages. So, for example, young children may require help in learning how to invite a schoolmate over to play; adolescents with SAD often struggle with negotiating their way into an established group of friends; and young adults often face the sociodevelopmental challenges of dating and job interviewing. Few systematic studies have examined social skills on the basis of unique periods of development, but Rao et al. (2007) found that children with SAD had significantly longer latencies to speak than adolescents during a structured role-play task with a peer. This finding likely reflects the fact that unstructured social situations tend to be more challenging for socially anxious teenagers (Beidel & Turner, 2005). Thus, SST programs designed primarily for either children or adults require some modification to possess relevance for adolescents with SAD.

Peer Experiences

The inclusion of peers as part of treatment for SAD is aimed at ensuring the generalization of newly acquired social skills to real-world settings. Social Effectiveness Therapy for Children and Adolescents (SET-C; Beidel, Turner, & Morris, 2003) is a treatment protocol that actively incorporates nonanxious peer helpers. Age-matched peers are recruited to interact with youth with SAD during weekly age-appropriate activities as part of SET-C. Because the social networks of children and adolescents with SAD are relatively limited, peer experiences provide these youth with real-world opportunities to practice social skills among a small group of outgoing, friendly peers. Structured and unstructured recreational activities are typically used, such as bowling, laser tag, and pizza parties where youth have the opportunity to interact with minimal therapist involvement. The Skills for Academic and Social Success (Masia-Warner et al., 2005), an adaptation of SET-C, is a school-based treatment program for adolescents with SAD that also incorporates peer activities with nonanxious youth to assist with skill generalization.

Treatment outcome data suggest that use of peer experiences during treatment is associated with significant increases in social skill and competence (e.g., Beidel, Turner, Sallee, et al., 2007), though some notable challenges also exist. Securing peers to help with activities can be time consuming, both in terms of recruitment activities and screening to ensure appropriateness. Additionally, confidentiality needs to be protected. Involving additional therapists and clinical assistants and arranging real-world social activities also add costs and logistical considerations.

Relaxation Training

Because socially anxious individuals experience distressing physiologic symptoms in anticipation of or in reaction to social situations, relaxation techniques are often incorporated into treatment. Progressive muscle relaxation instructs individuals to alternate between tensing and relaxing different muscle groups. Creating specific scripts for progressive muscle relaxation can be helpful in guiding patients through these techniques. Progressive muscle relaxation is also sometimes paired with controlled or deep breathing. Because anxiety results in accelerated heart and respiratory rates (hyperventilation), deep breathing attempts to slow down or reverse these uncomfortable physiological effects. Specific methods and techniques vary, but psychoeducation followed by correct modeling of techniques and instruction regarding practice are commonly used. Adult data on the efficacy of relaxation techniques specifically for SAD are mixed (Bogels, 2006; Heimberg, 2001; Jerremalm, Jansson & Öst, 1986). Controlled studies of applied relaxation in the treatment of childhood and adolescents SAD are absent from the empirical literature.

BEHAVIORAL AND COGNITIVE BEHAVIORAL TREATMENTS FOR SOCIAL ANXIETY DISORDER

Behavioral and cognitive behavioral treatments (CBT) for anxiety disorders, and for SAD specifically, have been classified as *evidence based* (Beidel & Turner, 2007; McLean & Woody, 2001; Silverman, Pina, & Viswesvaran, 2008) and defined by treatment outcome data from several well-designed studies (e.g., randomized controlled trials) that demonstrate significant effects for a particular intervention in comparison to other approaches (Kazdin & Weisz, 2003). Among adults, the vast majority of research includes broad age ranges (e.g., 18–65 years), thereby rendering it difficult to determine whether treatments are similarly effective across all ages. For this reason, only treatment findings with specific relevance for young adults with SAD are included in the discussion that follows. Regarding psychosocial treatments for youth, as Kashdan and Herbert (2001) highlighted, the existing evidence base is limited because (a) a majority of treatments evaluated are simply downward extensions of adult interventions; (b) most studies have evaluated treatment approaches for youth presenting with mixed anxiety disorders rather than SAD specifically; and (c) few studies have compared active treatments against alternative interventions, relying predominantly on comparison with waiting-list conditions. In recent years however, an increasing number of studies have used more rigorous methodological designs, including comparisons with active rather than nonactive control groups (Beidel et al., 2000; Beidel, Turner, Sallee, et al., 2007; Herbert et al., 2009; Masia-Warner et al., 2005). Behavioral treatments and CBT specifically developed for youth with SAD and demonstrating strong empirical support are reviewed in the sections that follow.

Treatment Studies Among Preadolescents and Adolescents With Social Anxiety Disorder

In one of the first studies to include exclusively adolescents with SAD (ages 13–16 years), Albano et al. (1995) evaluated cognitive behavioral group treatment for adolescents (CBGT-A), a 16-session program involving SST, problem solving, cognitive restructuring, and exposure. At 1 year following treatment, four of the five adolescents did not meet criteria for SAD. In another investigation, 35 adolescent girls (mean age 15.8 years) with SAD were randomly assigned to CBGT-A or a waiting-list condition (Hayward et al., 2000). Of the 11 girls who completed treatment, 45% treated with CBGT-A did not have a SAD diagnosis posttreatment compared with 4% of the waiting-list group. At 1-year follow-up, however, there were no significant group differences.

In a larger study including both children and adolescents with SAD, Spence and colleagues (1999) randomized youth with SAD ages 7 to 14 (mean age 10.9 years) to a CBT group, a CBT with parental involvement group, or a waiting-list condition. Both CBT conditions included SST, relaxation techniques, problem solving, positive self-instruction, cognitive challenging, and exposure. Given the wide age range of participants, groups were composed of either 7- to 11-year-olds or 12- to 14-year-olds to ensure the age appropriateness of treatment. The parental involvement group included parental reinforcement of newly learned skills and encouragement of participation in social activities. After 12 weeks of treatment, 58% of the CBT group, 87.5% of the CBT with parental involvement group, and 7% of the control group did not meet criteria for SAD. Both CBT conditions were superior to no treatment, but the two CBT conditions were not significantly different. No significant differences emerged among the three groups with respect to total number of peer interactions, social competence (based on parent report), or independent observer ratings of assertiveness, suggesting that treatment gains may not have included significant changes in overall functioning.

In the first randomized trial to use an active control condition, Beidel and colleagues (2000) compared SET-C with a nonspecific intervention called Testbusters among preadolescent children (ages 8–12 years). SET-C includes exposure, group SST, and peer generalization sessions. After 12 weeks of treatment, 67% of children treated with SET-C no longer met criteria for SAD, compared with 5% of the Testbusters group. Children treated with SET-C showed improvement across several domains including decreased anxiety, decreased avoidance of social situations, and increased observer-rated social skill. Treatment gains were maintained 5 years later (Beidel, Turner, & Young, 2006).

Using the same age group, Gallagher, Rabian, and McCloskey (2004) compared a three-session group CBT intervention for preadolescents with SAD with a waiting-list condition. Group CBT included psychoeducation, cognitive strategies, and exposure. At posttreatment, 37% in the CBT group and 0% in the waiting-list group were without a SAD diagnosis. However, although group CBT decreased children's general anxiety and depression, it did not result in significant reductions in social anxiety or improvements in social skill. The brief, three-session format of this intervention, coupled with the absence of SST may explain a lack of robust changes in social functioning, even among prepubescent children.

Baer and Garland (2005) incorporated SST, cognitive strategies, and exposure among adolescents with an average age of 15.5 years (range 13–18). At posttreatment, 36% of treated youth no longer met diagnostic criteria for SAD compared with 0% randomized to a waiting-list condition. Although results from this study were not as robust as those reported by Beidel et al. (2000), notable methodological differences of this study included a reduction in total treatment hours, the inclusion of participants already taking antianxiety medications, and the lack of inclusion of peer generalization experiences.

Herbert and colleagues (2009) randomly assigned 73 adolescents with SAD, ages 12 to 17 (mean age 15 years) to 12 sessions of individual CBT, group CBT, or psychoeducational supportive therapy (PST). Individual and group CBT included breathing retraining, cognitive restructuring, exposure, and SST and only differed in format. PST included group support and discussions of topics relevant to SAD but did not teach any specific skills. At posttreatment, recovery rates among the three groups were not significantly different (29% for CBT, 27% for CBGT, and 16% for PST). At 6 months follow-up however, the recovery rate for CBGT participants was 54%, which was significantly higher than both individual CBT (15%) and PST (19%). However, no significant differences were found between the conditions for self-reported social anxiety or observer-rated social skills at either time point.

Treatment Studies Among Young Adults With Social Anxiety Disorder

One of the best studied treatments for adult SAD is CBGT (Heimberg & Becker, 2002; Heimberg & Juster, 1994), a multicomponent treatment including coping skills training and exposure. CBGT is effective and produces lasting treatment effects (e.g., Brown, Heimberg, & Juster 1995; Heimberg, Becker, Goldfinger, & Vermilyea, 1985; Heimberg et al., 1990; Heimberg, Holt, Schneier, Spitzer, & Liebowitz, 1993; Hope et al., 1995; Leung & Heimberg, 1996). However, the efficacy of CBGT specifically for socially anxious young adults is unclear because most studies have been conducted among a wide age range of adults with a mean age of 35 to 40 years. Because middle-aged and older adults with SAD commonly differ from younger patients in terms of the types of social avoidance and impairments present, levels of familial and social support, and duration of their illness, generalizations that can be drawn may in some cases be limited.

Smits, Powers, Buxkamperb, and Telch (2006) published one of the few available controlled treatment studies among young adults with SAD. In an effort to understand the utility of individual treatment components, 77 young adults with SAD (mean age of approximately 21 years) were randomized to one of four treatment conditions: (a) exposure only, (b) exposure plus video feedback of social performance (in which the camera was focused on the participant during a speech), (c) exposure plus video feedback of audience responses (in which the camera was focused on the audience), or (d) an active placebo treatment (i.e., pulsed audio and photic stimulations described to participants as an effective means of reducing fear). The three-session treatment conditions were directly aimed at reducing anxiety about public speaking. Clinically significant changes in public speaking anxiety were observed for 61%, 50%, 35%, and 20% of the groups, respectively, at posttreatment. Comparisons between the exposure and exposure-plus-video-feedback conditions were nonsignificant, indicating a lack of advantage for the inclusion of video feedback over exposure alone. Also, although exposure was superior to the placebo condition on all measures at posttreatment, the magnitude of this effect was significantly reduced at 1-month follow-up, suggesting that three sessions of exposure may be inadequate to produce lasting changes in anxiety symptoms.

Comparative Treatment Studies Among Youth and Adults With Social Anxiety Disorder

There is limited evidence overall for the comparative effectiveness of behavioral treatment and CBT versus medication for children and adolescents with anxiety disorders. Recently, however, the first large multisite study to compare the effectiveness of CBT, sertraline (maximum dose 200 mg/day), the combination of CBT and sertraline, and pill placebo among 488 children and adolescents with social, separation, and generalized anxiety disorders was completed (Walkup et al., 2008). Overall results indicated the combination treatment to be superior to both CBT and sertraline, which did not differ from each other (80.7%, 59.7%, 54.9% rated as very much or much improved, respectively). All treatments were superior to placebo (23.7%). However, because approximately three quarters of participants were between 7 and 12 years old (mean of 10.2 years old) and outcomes based on primary disorder have not been examined to date, it is unclear how well these findings generalize to adolescents with primary SAD.

In a small treatment study that did not include a comparison control condition, Chavira and Stein (2002) examined the efficacy of 12 weeks of citalopram (maximum dose 40 mg/day) combined with eight brief counseling sessions (including psychoeducation, graduated exposure, basic social skills, cognitive challenging, and relapse prevention) among 12 youth with SAD (ages 8–17 years). At posttreatment, 10 of 12 children or youth (83.3%) were rated as improved, although significant SAD symptoms remained present.

Further, the fact that posttreatment assessments were conducted by treating clinicians rather than independent evaluators may have introduced bias into assessment procedures.

In the only randomized, placebo-controlled comparison trial for youth with primary SAD, Beidel, Turner, Sallee, and colleagues (2007) compared 12 weeks of treatment with SET-C, fluoxetine (maximum dose 40 mg/day), or pill placebo among 122 children and adolescents ages 7 to 17 years. Although both fluoxetine and SET-C were more effective than placebo (6.3%), a significantly greater number of SET-C participants were judged as treatment responders (79%) compared with the fluoxetine group (36.4%). Further, youth treated with SET-C demonstrated less behavioral avoidance, lower symptom severity, better social skills and competence, and higher overall general functioning at posttreatment. At 1-year follow-up, all (100%) youth treated with SET-C maintained their treatment responder status compared with 61% of the fluoxetine group. Thus, whereas both fluoxetine and SET-C are effective in decreasing social anxiety, SET-C resulted in changes in social avoidance and competence. A follow-up study found that age (child vs. adolescent) did not moderate treatment response to SET-C (Alfano et al., 2009). This lack of difference may be attributed to the fact that the content of individual and group SET-C sessions was modified as needed to be age appropriate for all participants.

A few studies have compared behavioral treatments or CBT to medications among adults with SAD. However, methodological designs generally parallel those found in the broader treatment literature in that age ranges for participants vary considerably, with an average age around 40 years. For example, in a comparison study by Davidson and colleagues (2004), 295 patients ranging in age from 18 to 65 (mean age 37.5 years) were randomly assigned to CBT, fluoxetine (maximum dose 60 mg/day), a combination of CBT plus fluoxetine, a combination of CBT plus placebo, or placebo. All active treatments were superior to placebo but did not differ from each other after 14 weeks of treatment. Clark et al. (2003) similarly found no evidence for greater benefit of combined treatment with fluoxetine over CBT alone. However, results from another large treatment trial, which included participants of the same age range (mean age 40.4 years), provide some evidence for the increased efficacy of combined sertraline (maximum dose of 150 mg/day) plus exposure for adults with SAD (Blomhoff et al., 2001).

Enhancement of Cognitive Behavioral Treatments for Social Anxiety Disorder

Because many socially anxious individuals do not seek treatment, drop out of treatment prematurely, or remain symptomatic after treatment ends, a recent paradigm shift includes the augmentation of CBT with various treatment enhancers. Buckner and Schmidt (2009) examined the efficacy of motivation enhancement therapy (MET) designed to increase CBT use among young adults with SAD (mean age 18.5 years). In their study, 27 college students who did not seek treatment were randomized to MET or a control condition. MET consisted of three sessions that provided feedback about social anxiety symptoms, explored the pros and cons of seeking CBT, and outlined short- and long-term goals. The control condition primarily controlled for the receipt of psychoeducation about SAD and CBT referrals. At 1 month after treatment, participants completed an online survey regarding treatment-seeking behaviors. Results indicated that 58.3% of MET participants had attended a CBT appointment, compared with 13.3% of control participants, a statistically significant difference. Further, 72.7% of participants in the MET condition indicated a desire to be contacted by a CBT therapist, compared with 33.3% of controls. Although results are promising, it will be important for future research to collect long-term follow-up data among SAD participants to assess the durability of findings.

Two recently published studies examined the efficacy of CBT augmented with the drug D-cycloserine (Guastella et al., 2008; Hofmann et al., 2006), and several additional trials are underway. D-cycloserine (DCS), a partial agonist at the N-methyl-D-aspartate receptor, has been approved by the U.S. Food and Drug Administration for the treatment of tuberculosis for over 20 years. In recent years, animal studies have shown both fear learning and extinction to be blocked by antagonists at the glutamatergic N-methyl-D-aspartate receptor and extinction of conditioned fears to be facilitated by administration of DCS prior to extinction (i.e., exposure therapy; Ledgerwood, Richardson, & Cranney, 2005). DCS augmentation of CBT has therefore been examined in the treatment of several anxiety disorders.

In a double-blind, placebo-controlled study of the efficacy of DCS (50 mg) for enhancing the effects of five sessions of CBT for public speaking anxiety, 27 adults with SAD (average age 30–35 years) were randomized to either DCS plus CBT or placebo plus CBT. The CBT component consisted of psychoeducation and exposure. The study drug (or placebo) was administered 1 hour before exposures. Participants who received DCS-augmented CBT demonstrated significantly greater reductions in social anxiety symptoms at posttreatment and 1-month follow-up. However, differences in clinician-rated severity scores did not reach statistical significance at either time point. The authors also reported that age did not significantly impact results. Using a similar treatment protocol, Guastella et al. (2008) randomized 56 adults with SAD (mean age 35 years, range 18–60 years) to the same two treatment groups. Results were similar to those reported by Hofmann and colleagues in that participants given DCS showed a greater reduction in social anxiety at posttreatment and 1-month follow-up. These findings are highly promising, though research establishing similar therapeutic benefits in youth is needed.

SUMMARY AND CLINICAL IMPLICATIONS

A preponderance of empirical evidence supports the efficacy of behavioral and cognitive behavioral interventions for individuals with SAD. However, treatment research in youth with SAD lags in comparison with adult findings. This discrepancy can be traced, in part, to the fact that a majority of controlled treatment studies continue to include children and adolescents with a range of anxiety diagnoses. However, just as evidence for unique symptoms and impairments exists, so do emerging findings for distinct etiologic factors and mediators of treatment response (Alfano et al., 2009; Ferdinand et al., 2006). For example, results from a recent investigation showed that youth-reported loneliness and social skill were significant predictors of changes in social anxiety and functioning following behavioral treatment (Alfano et al., 2009). Further, treatment-related changes in social anxiety were partially mediated by loneliness scores. These data suggest that for youth with SAD, attending to social functioning and peer relationships in addition to symptoms of social anxiety may be essential for optimal outcomes to occur.

Overall, behavioral and CBT protocols have been shown to be efficacious in several studies, yet it is not uncommon for social anxiety to decrease in the absence of significant changes in social competence and/or overall functioning (Baer & Garland, 2005; Herbert et al., 2009; Spence et al., 1999). The use of unstructured peer experiences represents one strategy used to help ensure the generalization of newly acquired skills to real-world settings. Several treatment studies incorporating the use of peers have reported improvements across several domains in addition to social anxiety, including decreased social avoidance and loneliness and increased social competence, with treatment gains documented up to 5 years later (Beidel et al., 2006; 2007). Future research might therefore focus on other methods by which to ensure the generalization of gains made in treatment to other relevant settings for youth. A final promising area of research includes efforts to enhance the effects of CBT. To date, both psychological (MET) and pharmacological (DCS) methods have been investigated among anxious adults with promising results. A necessary next step will be to extend this research to younger SAD patients on the basis of the use of developmentally appropriate methods.

REFERENCES

Albano, A. M., Marten, P. A., Holt, C. S., Heimberg, R. G., & Barlow, D. H. (1995). Cognitive-behavioral group treatment for social phobia in adolescents: A preliminary study. *Journal of Nervous and Mental Disease, 183,* 649–656. doi:10.1097/00005053-199510000-00006

Alfano, C. A., Beidel, D. C., & Turner, S. M. (2006). Cognitive correlates of social phobia among children and adolescents. *Journal of Abnormal Psychology, 34,* 189–201.

Alfano, C. A., Beidel, D. C., & Turner, S. M. (2008). Negative self-imagery among adolescents with social phobia: A test of an adult model of the disorder. *Journal of Clinical Child and Adolescent Psychology, 37,* 327–336. doi:10.1080/15374410801955870

Alfano, C. A., Pina, A. A., Villalta, I. K., Beidel, D. C., Ammerman, R. T., & Crosby, L. E. (2009). Mediators and moderators of outcome in the behavioral treatment of childhood social phobia. *Journal of the American Academy of Child and Adolescent Psychiatry, 48,* 945–953. doi:10.1097/CHI.0b013e3181af8216

American Psychiatric Association. (1994). *Diagnostic and statistical manual of mental disorders* (4th ed.). Washington, DC: Author.

American Psychiatric Association. (2000). *Diagnostic and statistical manual of mental disorders* (4th ed., text rev.). Washington, DC: Author.

Baer, S., & Garland, E. J. (2005). Pilot study of community-based cognitive behavioral group therapy for adolescents with social phobia. *Journal of the American Academy of Child and Adolescent Psychiatry, 44,* 258–264. doi:10.1097/00004583-200503000-00010

Beidel, D. C., & Turner, S. M. (2005). *Childhood anxiety disorders: A guide to research and treatment.* New York, NY: Routledge.

Beidel, D. C., & Turner, S. M. (2007). *Shy children, phobic adults: Nature and treatment of social anxiety disorder.* Washington, DC: American Psychological Association. doi:10.1037/11533-000

Beidel, D. C., Turner, S. M., & Morris, T. L. (1999). Psychopathology of childhood social phobia. *Journal of the American Academy of Child and Adolescent Psychiatry, 38,* 643–650. doi:10.1097/00004583-199906000-00010

Beidel, D. C., Turner, S. M., & Morris, T. L. (2000). Behavioral treatment of childhood social phobia. *Journal of the American Academy of Child and Adolescent Psychiatry, 68,* 1072–1080.

Beidel, D. C., Turner, S. M., & Morris, T. L. (2003). *Social effectiveness therapy for children and adolescents (SET-C): Therapist guide.* New York, NY: Multi-Health Systems.

Beidel, D. C., Turner, S. M., Sallee, R. F., Ammerman, R. T., Crosby, L., & Pathak, S. (2007). SET-C versus fluoxetine in the treatment of childhood social phobia. *Journal of the American Academy of Child and Adolescent Psychiatry, 46,* 1622–1632. doi:10.1097/chi.0b013e318154bb57

Beidel, D. C., Turner, S. M., & Young, B. J. (2006). Social effectiveness therapy for children: Five years later. *Behavior Therapy, 37,* 416–425. doi:10.1016/j.beth.2006.06.002

Beidel, D. C., Turner, S. M., Young, B. J., Ammerman, R. T., Sallee, R. F., & Crosby, L. (2007). Psychopathology of adolescent social phobia. *Journal of Psychopathology and Behavioral Assessment, 29,* 46–53. doi:10.1007/s10862-006-9021-1

Blomhoff, S., Haug, T. T., Hellstrom, K., Holme, I., Humble, M., Madsbu, H. P., & Wold, J. E. (2001). Randomised controlled general practice trial of sertraline, exposure therapy and combined treatment in generalised social phobia. *The British Journal of Psychiatry, 179,* 23–30. doi:10.1192/bjp.179.1.23

Bodden, D. H., Bögels, S. M., Nauta, M. H., De Haan, E., Ringrose, J., Appelboom, C., . . . Appelboom-Geerts, K. C. (2008). Child versus family cognitive-behavioral therapy in clinically anxious youth: An efficacy and partial effectiveness study. *Journal of the American Academy of Child and Adolescent Psychiatry, 47,* 1384–1394. doi:10.1097/CHI.0b013e318189148e

Bögels, S. M. (2006). Task concentration training versus applied relaxation, in combination with cognitive therapy, for social phobia patients with fear of blushing, trembling, and sweating. *Behaviour Research and Therapy, 44,* 1199–1210. doi:10.1016/j.brat.2005.08.010

Boone, M. L., McNeil, D. W., Masia, C. L., Turk, C. L., Carter, L. E., Ries, B. J., & Lewin, M. R. (1999). Multimodal comparisons of social phobia subtypes and avoidant personality disorder. *Journal of Anxiety Disorders, 13,* 271–292. doi:10.1016/S0887-6185(99)00004-3

Brown, E. J., Heimberg, R. G., & Juster, H. R. (1995). Social phobia subtype and avoidant personality disorder: Effect on severity of social phobia, impairment, and outcome of cognitive-behavioral treatment. *Behavior Therapy, 26,* 467–486. doi:10.1016/S0005-7894(05)80095-4

Bruch, M. A., Giordano, S., & Pearl, L. (1986). Differences between fearful and self-conscious shy subtypes in background and current adjustment. *Journal of Research in Personality, 20,* 172–186. doi:10.1016/0092-6566(86)90116-9

Buckner, J. D., & Schmidt, N. B. (2009). Understanding social anxiety as a risk factor for alcohol use disorders: Fear of scrutiny, not social interaction fears, prospectively predicts alcohol use disorders. *Journal of Psychiatric Research, 43,* 477–483. doi:10.1016/j.jpsychires.2008.04.012

Butler, G., Cullington, A., Munby, M., Amies, P., & Gelder, M. (1984). Exposure and anxiety management in the treatment of social phobia. *Journal of Consulting and Clinical Psychology, 52,* 642–650. doi:10.1037/0022-006X.52.4.642

Chavira, D. A., & Stein, M. B. (2002). Combined psychoeducation and treatment with selective serotonin reuptake inhibitors for youth with generalized social anxiety disorder. *Journal of Child and Adolescent Psychopharmacology, 12,* 47–54. doi:10.1089/10445460252943560

Chorney, D. B. (2009). Assessment of social anxiety in early childhood: Initial test construction and validation. *Dissertation Abstracts International: Section B: Sciences and Engineering, 69,* 5015.

Clark, D. M., Ehlers, A., McManus, F., Hackmann, A., Fennell, M., Campbell, H., . . . Louis, B. (2003). Cognitive therapy versus fluoxetine in generalized social phobia: A randomized placebo-controlled trial. *Journal of Consulting and Clinical Psychology, 71,* 1058–1067. doi:10.1037/0022-006X.71.6.1058

Cottraux, J. (2005). Recent developments in research and treatment of social phobia (social anxiety disorder). *Current Opinion in Psychiatry, 18*, 51–54.

Davidson, J. R., Foa, E. B., Huppert, J. D., Keefe, F. J., Franklin, M. E., Compton, J. S., . . . Gadde, K. M. (2004). Fluoxetine, comprehensive cognitive behavioral therapy and placebo in generalized social phobia. *Archives of General Psychiatry, 61*, 1005–1013. doi:10.1001/archpsyc.61.10.1005

Emmelkamp, P. M. G., Mersch, P. P., Vissia, E., & van der Helm, M. (1985). Social phobia: A comparative evaluation of cognitive and behavioral interventions. *Behaviour Research and Therapy, 23*, 365–369. doi:10.1016/0005-7967(85)90015-4

Ferdinand, R. F., Bongers, I. L., van der Ende, J., van Gastel, W., Tick, N., Utens, E., & Verhulst, F. C. (2006). Distinctions between separation anxiety and social anxiety in children and adolescents. *Behaviour Research and Therapy, 44*, 1523–1535. doi:10.1016/j.brat.2005.11.006

Feske, U., & Chambless, D. L. (1995). Cognitive behavioral versus exposure only treatment for social phobia: A meta-analysis. *Behavior Therapy, 26*, 695–720. doi:10.1016/S0005-7894(05)80040-1

Foa, E. B., Franklin, M. E., Perry, K. J., & Herbert, J. D. (1996). Cognitive biases in generalized social phobia. *Journal of Abnormal Psychology, 105*, 433–439. doi:10.1037/0021-843X.105.3.433

Gallagher, H. M., Rabian, B. A., & McCloskey, M. S. (2004). A brief group cognitive-behavioral intervention for social phobia in childhood. *Journal of Anxiety Disorders, 18*, 459–479. doi:10.1016/S0887-6185(03)00027-6

Gelernter, C. S., Uhde, T. W., Cimbolic, P., Arnkoff, D. B., Vittone, B. J., Tancer, M. E., & Bartko, J. J. (1991). Cognitive–behavioral and pharmacological treatments of social phobia. *Archives of General Psychiatry, 48*, 938–945.

Guastella, A. J., Richardson, R., Lovibond, P. F., Rapee, R. M., Gaston, J. E., Mitchell, P., & Dadds, M. R. (2008). A randomised controlled trial of D-cycloserine enhancement of exposure therapy for social anxiety disorder. *Biological Psychiatry, 63*, 544–549. doi:10.1016/j.biopsych.2007.11.011

Hale, W. W., Raaijmakers, Q., Muris, P., van Hoof, A., & Meeus, W. (2008). Developmental trajectories of adolescent anxiety disorder symptoms: A 5-year prospective community study. *Journal of the American Academy of Child and Adolescent Psychiatry, 47*, 556–564. doi:10.1097/CHI.0b013e3181676583

Harris, S., Kemmerling, R. L., & North, M. M. (2002). Brief virtual reality therapy for public speaking anxiety. *Cyberpsychology & Behavior, 5*, 543–550. doi:10.1089/109493102321018187

Hayward, C., Varady, S., Albano, A. M., Thienemann, M., Henderson, L., & Schatzberg, A. F. (2000). Cognitive-behavioral group therapy for social phobia in female adolescents: Results of a pilot study. *Journal of the American Academy of Child and Adolescent Psychiatry, 39*, 721–726. doi:10.1097/00004583-200006000-00010

Hayward, C., Wilson, K. A., Lagle, K., Kraemer, H. C., Killen, J. D., & Taylor, C. B. (2008). The developmental psychopathology of social anxiety in adolescents. *Depression and Anxiety, 25*, 200–206. doi:10.1002/da.20289

Heimberg, R. G. (2001). Current status of psychotherapeutic interventions for social phobia. *The Journal of Clinical Psychiatry, 62,* 36–42.

Heimberg, R. G., & Becker, R. E. (2002). *Cognitive-behavioral group therapy for social phobia: Basic mechanisms and clinical strategies.* New York, NY: Guilford Press.

Heimberg, R. G., Becker, R. E., Goldfinger, K., & Vermilyea, J. (1985). Treatment of social phobia by exposure, cognitive restructuring, and homework assignments. *Journal of Nervous and Mental Disease, 173,* 236–245. doi:10.1097/00005053-198504000-00006

Heimberg, R. G., Dodge, C. S., Hope, D. A., Kennedy, C. R., Zollo, L., & Becker, R. E. (1990). Cognitive behavioral group treatment of social phobia: Comparison to a credible placebo control. *Cognitive Therapy and Research, 14,* 1–23. doi:10.1007/BF01173521

Heimberg, R. G., Holt, C. S., Schneier, F. R., Spitzer, R. L., & Liebowitz, M. R. (1993). The issue of subtypes in the diagnosis of social phobia. *Journal of Anxiety Disorders, 7,* 249–269. doi:10.1016/0887-6185(93)90006-7

Heimberg, R. G., & Juster, H. R. (1994). Treatment of social phobia in cognitive-behavioral groups. *The Journal of Clinical Psychiatry, 55,* 38–46.

Herbert, J. D., Gaudino, B. A., Rheingold, A. A., Moitra, E., Myers, V. H., Dalrymple, K. L. & Brandsma, L. L. (2009). Cognitive behavior therapy for generalized social anxiety disorder in adolescents: A randomized controlled trial. *Journal of Anxiety Disorders, 23,* 167–177.

Hofmann, S. G. (2000). Self-focused attention before and after treatment of social phobia. *Behaviour Research and Therapy, 38,* 717–725. doi:10.1016/S0005-7967(99)00105-9

Hofmann, S. G., Meuret, A. E., Smits, J. A., Simon, N. M., Pollack, M. H., Eisenmenger, K., . . . Otto, M. W. (2006). Augmentation of exposure therapy with D-cycloserine for social anxiety disorder. *Archives of General Psychiatry, 63,* 298–304. doi:10.1001/archpsyc.63.3.298

Hope, D. A., Heimberg, R. G., & Bruch, M. A. (1995). Dismantling cognitive-behavioral group therapy for social phobia. *Behaviour Research and Therapy, 33,* 637–650. doi:10.1016/0005-7967(95)00013-N

Hudson, J. L., Rapee, R. M., Deveney, C., Schniering, C. A., Lyneham, H. J., & Bovopoulos, N. (2009). Cognitive-behavioral treatment versus an active control for children and adolescents with anxiety disorders: A randomized trial. *Journal of the American Academy of Child and Adolescent Psychiatry, 48,* 533–544. doi:10.1097/CHI.0b013e31819c2401

Jerremalm, A., Jansson, L., & Öst, L. (1986). Cognitive and physiological reactivity and the effects of different behavioral methods in the treatment of social phobia. *Behaviour Research and Therapy, 24,* 171–180. doi:10.1016/0005-7967(86)90088-4

Kashdan, T. B., & Herbert, J. D. (2001). Social anxiety disorder in childhood and adolescence: Current status and future directions. *Clinical Child and Family Psychology Review, 4,* 37–61. doi:10.1023/A:1009576610507

Kazdin, A. E., & Weisz, J. R. (2003). Introduction: Context and background of evidence-based psychotherapies for children and adolescents. In A. E. Kazdin & J. R. Weisz (Eds.), *Evidence-based psychotherapies for children and adolescents* (pp. 3–20). New York, NY: Guilford Press.

Klinger, E., Bouchard, S., Legeron, P., Roy, S., Lauer, F., Chemin, I., & Nugues, P. (2005). Virtual reality therapy versus cognitive behavior therapy for social phobia: A preliminary controlled study. *Cyberpsychology & Behavior, 8*, 76–88. doi:10.1089/cpb.2005.8.76

Kushner, M. G., Sher, K. J., & Beitman, B. D. (1990). The relation between alcohol problems and the anxiety disorders. *The American Journal of Psychiatry, 147*, 685–695.

Lang, P. J. (1968). Fear reduction and fear behavior: Problems in treating a construct. In J. M. Shlien (Ed.), *Research in psychotherapy* (Vol. 1, pp. 90–102). Washington, DC: American Psychological Association. doi:10.1037/10546-004

Ledgerwood, L., Richardson, R., & Cranney, J. (2005). D-cycloserine facilitates extinction of learned fear: Effects of reacquisition and generalized extinction. *Biological Psychiatry, 57*, 841–847. doi:10.1016/j.biopsych.2005.01.023

Leung, A. W., & Heimberg, R. G. (1996). Homework compliance, perceptions of control, and outcome of cognitive-behavioral treatment of social phobia. *Behaviour Research and Therapy, 34*, 423–432. doi:10.1016/0005-7967(96)00014-9

Mancini, C., Van Ameringen, M., Bennett, M., Patterson, B., & Watson, C. (2005). Emerging treatments for child and adolescent social phobia: A review. *Journal of Child and Adolescent Psychopharmacology, 15*, 589–607. doi:10.1089/cap.2005.15.589

Masia-Warner, C., Klein, R. G., Dent, H. C., Fisher, P. H., Alvir, J., Albano, A. M., & Guardino, M. (2005). School-based intervention for adolescents with social anxiety disorder: Results of a controlled study. *Journal of Abnormal Child Psychology, 33*, 707–722. doi:10.1007/s10802-005-7649-z

Mattick, R. P., & Peters, L. (1988). Treatment of severe social phobia: Effects of guided exposure with and without cognitive restructuring. *Journal of Consulting and Clinical Psychology, 56*, 251–260. doi:10.1037/0022-006X.56.2.251

McLean, P., & Woody, S. R. (2001). *Anxiety disorders in adults: An evidence-based approach to psychological treatment.* New York, NY: Oxford University Press.

Mersch, P. P. (1995). The treatment of social phobia: The differential effectiveness of exposure in vivo and an integration of exposure in vivo, rational emotive therapy and social skills training. *Behaviour Research and Therapy, 33*, 259–269. doi:10.1016/0005-7967(94)00038-L

Newman, M. G., Hofmann, S. G., Trabert, W., Roth, W. T., & Taylor, C. B. (1994). Does behavioral treatment of social phobia lead to cognitive changes? *Behavior Therapy, 25*, 503–517. doi:10.1016/S0005-7894(05)80160-1

Powers, M. B., Sigmarsson, S. R., & Emmelkamp, P. M. G. (2008). A meta-analytic review of psychological treatment for social anxiety disorder. *International Journal of Cognitive Therapy, 1*, 94–113. doi:10.1521/ijct.2008.1.2.94

Prior, M., Smart, D., Sanson, A., & Oberklaid, F. (2000). Does shy-inhibited temperament in childhood lead to anxiety problems in adolescence? *Journal of the American Academy of Child and Adolescent Psychiatry, 39*, 461–468. doi:10.1097/00004583-200004000-00015

Rao, P. A., Beidel, D. C., Turner, S. M., Ammerman, R. T., Crosby, L. E., & Sallee, F. R. (2007). Social anxiety disorder in childhood and adolescence: Descriptive psychopathology. *Behaviour Research and Therapy, 45*, 1181–1191. doi:10.1016/j.brat.2006.07.015

Rapee, R. M., & Hayman, K. (1996). The effects of video feedback on the self-evaluation of performance in socially anxious subjects. *Behaviour Research and Therapy, 34*, 315–322. doi:10.1016/0005-7967(96)00003-4

Rapee, R. M., & Heimberg, R. G. (1997). A cognitive-behavioral model of anxiety in social phobia. *Behaviour Research and Therapy, 35*, 741–756. doi:10.1016/S0005-7967(97)00022-3

Scholing, A., & Emmelkamp, P. M. G. (1993). Exposure with and without cognitive therapy for generalized social phobia: Effects of individual and group treatment. *Behaviour Research and Therapy, 31*, 667–681. doi:10.1016/0005-7967(93)90067-5

Silverman, W. K., Kurtines, W. M., Jaccard, J., & Pina, A. A. (2009). Directionality of change in youth anxiety treatment involving parents: An initial examination. *Journal of Consulting and Clinical Psychology, 77*, 474–485. doi:10.1037/a0015761

Silverman, W. K., Pina, A. A., & Viswesvaran, C. (2008). Evidence-based psychosocial treatments for phobic and anxiety disorders in children and adolescents. *Journal of Clinical Child and Adolescent Psychology, 37*, 105–130. doi:10.1080/15374410701817907

Smits, J. A., Powers, M. B., Buxkamperb, R., & Telch, M. J. (2006). The efficacy of videotape feedback for enhancing the effects of exposure-based treatment for social anxiety disorder: a controlled investigation. *Behaviour Research and Therapy, 44*, 1773–1785. doi:10.1016/j.brat.2006.01.001

Spence, S. H., Donovan, C., & Brechman-Toussaint, M. (1999). Social skills, social outcomes, and cognitive features of childhood social phobia. *Journal of Abnormal Psychology, 108*, 211–221. doi:10.1037/0021-843X.108.2.211

Taylor, S. (1996). Meta-analysis of cognitive-behavioral treatments for social phobia. *Journal of Behavior Therapy and Experimental Psychiatry, 27*, 1–9. doi:10.1016/0005-7916(95)00058-5

Turner, S. M., Beidel, D. C., Dancu, C. V., & Keys, D. J. (1986). Psychopathology of social phobia and comparison to avoidant personality disorder. *Journal of Abnormal Psychology, 95*, 389–394. doi:10.1037/0021-843X.95.4.389

Turner, S. M., Beidel, D. C., & Larkin, K. T. (1986). Situational determinants of social anxiety in clinic and nonclinic samples: Physiological and cognitive correlates. *Journal of Consulting and Clinical Psychology, 54*, 523–527. doi:10.1037/0022-006X.54.4.523

Walkup, J. T., Albano, A. M., Piacentini, J., Birmaher, B., Compton, S. N., Sherrill, J. T., . . . Kendall, P. C. (2008). Cognitive behavioral therapy, sertraline, or a combination in childhood anxiety. *The New England Journal of Medicine, 359,* 2753–2766. doi:10.1056/NEJMoa0804633

Wells, A., & Papageorgiou, C. (1998). Social phobia: Effects of external attention on anxiety, negative beliefs, and perspective taking. *Behavior Therapy, 29,* 357–370. doi:10.1016/S0005-7894(98)80037-3

Wenzel, A., Graff-Dolezal, J., Macho, M., & Brendle, J. R. (2005). Communication and social skills in socially anxious and nonanxious individuals in the context of romantic relationships. *Behaviour Research and Therapy, 43,* 505–519. doi:10.1016/j.brat.2004.03.010

14

PHARMACOTHERAPY FOR SOCIAL ANXIETY DISORDER IN ADOLESCENTS AND YOUNG ADULTS

L. N. RAVINDRAN AND M. B. STEIN

Social anxiety disorder (SAD) is characterized by persistent worry or concern about negative evaluation and embarrassment in social or performance situations. It is often associated with significant avoidance of these experiences, resulting in substantial impairment in relationships and overall functioning (Stein & Stein, 2008). Rates of comorbidity, particularly with depression and other forms of anxiety, are high, and the presence of secondary diagnoses compounds levels of impairment (Keller, 2003; Wittchen & Fehm, 2001). Given the extent of comorbidity and functional impairment in SAD, early diagnosis and intervention is imperative.

In contrast to the number of clinical trials investigating pharmacological interventions for SAD in adults, research in youth is lacking; for the most part, pharmacological treatment of this population takes its lead largely from findings in adults. In this chapter, we review the existing, albeit limited, evidence base for pharmacological interventions for SAD in adolescents and young adults. Given the overall paucity of controlled pharmacological treatment studies, both clinical trials and case reports that specifically target this population are included in this review.

In general, data are lacking on the treatment of SAD among young adults, specifically. Whereas young adults have been included in most adult (i.e., age 18 and older) pharmacotherapy clinical trials, to the best of our knowledge the data have never been parsed to look specifically at outcomes in young adults (e.g., ages 18–24). It is nonetheless the case that all of the pharmacological treatments that have been shown to be efficacious in adolescents with SAD are also useful in adults (Stein & Stein, 2008). It is therefore reasonable to infer, in the absence of direct evidence, that these medications would also be of benefit in young adults. It is also reasonable to infer that the same precautionary measures that apply to the use of these pharmacological agents in adolescents (described in the section that follows) would be equally applicable to young adults.

ANTIDEPRESSANTS

The vast majority of psychopharmacology trials for SAD in adolescents have investigated either selective serotonin reuptake inhibitors (SSRIs) or serotonin and norepinephrine reuptake inhibitors (SNRIs). The reasons for this are twofold. Although the term *social phobia* has been used for over 100 years after being coined by Pierre Janet in 1903, this disorder was only really accepted by the psychiatric community in 1980 with the *Diagnostic and Statistical Manual of Mental Disorders* (3rd ed.; *DSM–III*; American Psychiatric Association, 1980). Recognition of its existence in children and adolescents took even longer and coincided with the arrival of the newer generation antidepressants, mentioned here, onto the market. Further, these particular agents are also generally accepted to have improved tolerability and safety profiles compared with older generation antidepressants, which may also contribute to their investigation in younger populations.

Selective Serotonin Reuptake Inhibitors

Although weaker from an evidence-based-medicine perspective, positive case reports and case series of serotonergic antidepressants for youth with a primary diagnosis of SAD have been reported. Mancini, Van Ameringen, Oakman, and Farvolden (1999) reported on a series of seven children and adolescents with primary SAD treated with a variety of serotonergic agents. Five of the seven participants were adolescents, and five had comorbid diagnoses, which included obsessive–compulsive disorder, dysthmia, specific phobia, and major depression. The majority of participants ($n = 5$) were subsequently treated with paroxetine at a mean maximum dose of 40 mg/day and on average showed initial response at 5.6 weeks. The others were treated with sertraline or nefazodone (a 5-HT2 receptor antagonist and a weak inhibitor of serotonin and norepinephrine reuptake; Davis, Whittington, & Bryson, 1997) at maximum daily doses of 175 mg and 400 mg, respectively, with response seen at 4 weeks in both participants. All participants displayed significant improvement in SAD symptoms and generally tolerated these agents well. The authors noted that all participants experienced their symptoms for a number of years ($M = 8.4$ years) before seeking treatment, highlighting not only the persistence of this illness but also that treatment with a single agent could still effective despite chronicity. Finally, citalopram was used to treat generalized SAD in a 16-year-old boy (Kosieradzki, 2001). In this instance, citalopram 40 mg daily was both well tolerated and helpful in significantly improving social anxiety symptoms.

Following these reports, a number of open trials investigating SSRIs for primary SAD were conducted. Compton et al. (2001) reported results of an 8-week open trial of sertraline in 14 children and adolescents (ages 10–17 years, $M = 13.6$ years). Following a brief four-session cognitive behavioral therapy (CBT) lead-in, youth with no change in social anxiety symptoms were given flexibly dosed sertraline (50–200 mg daily). Overall, 64% to 71% of participants were deemed partial or full responders at study endpoint. Self-report measures reflected this improvement over time. The mean drug dose at endpoint was 123.2 mg and was generally well tolerated. The most commonly reported side effects were drowsiness, nausea, diarrhea, and feeling jittery, but there were no reports of suicidal ideation. One limitation addressed by the authors was the possibility of a carryover effect from the CBT lead-in, and in fact, when participants were asked about improvement at the end of the trial, several attributed improvement to the combination of treatment.

Chavira and Stein (2002) subsequently examined the effects of combining 12 weeks of open label citalopram (10–40 mg) treatment with eight brief CBT-oriented counseling sessions (15 min each) for children with SAD and their parents. Of the 12 participants, eight were adolescents and four were children (mean age 13.4 years). Following treatment, the rate of response as measured by the Clinical Global Impressions Scale—Improvement (CGI–I) was 83% ($n = 10$), with ratings completed by both children and parents reflecting this. Citalopram was generally well tolerated with a mean daily dose at endpoint of 35 mg. This study highlighted that even brief psychoeducational interventions provided along with medications can be useful in clinical management if access to more formal psychotherapeutic interventions is not available.

Most recently, Isolan et al. (2007) investigated the use of flexibly dosed escitalopram (5–20 mg) for SAD in a 12-week open label study. Of the 20 children and adolescents (mean age 15 years) enrolled, 65% were classified as treatment responders on the basis of levels of the CGI–I. Treatment with escitalopram resulted in significant improvements in quality of life in one of the only trials to evaluate this dimension in this particular population. However, in spite of these positive findings, a number of participants remained symptomatic at posttreatment on the basis of scores on the Social Phobia and Anxiety Inventory for Children (Beidel, Turner, & Morris, 1995). The authors speculated that a longer trial might have been helpful to demonstrate additional response. Overall, escitalopram was well tolerated at a mean endpoint dose of 13 +/- 4.1 mg daily; the most frequent side effects reported included sleep and appetite disturbance and flu symptoms. No participants developed emotional lability or suicidal ideation.

In an international multicenter trial, Wagner et al. (2004) randomized 322 children (8–11 years, $n = 91$) and adolescents (12–17 years, $n = 228$) to 16 weeks of flexibly dosed paroxetine (10–50 mg daily) or placebo. On both primary (CGI–I) and secondary efficacy measures (which included the Liebowitz Social Anxiety Scale for Children and Adolescents and the Kutcher Generalized Social Anxiety Disorder Scale for Adolescents), treatment with paroxetine was significantly superior to placebo, with 77.6% of all subjects treated with active medication achieving responder status compared with only 38.3% of placebo-treated subjects; differences were noted to be consistent across both age subgroups. Similarly, post hoc analysis of remission status significantly favored paroxetine treatment, with over 40% of paroxetine-treated adolescents achieving remission based on study criteria. The mean dose of paroxetine used by the adolescent group during the trial was 26.1 mg daily, and the overall mean dose for the entire study population was 24.8 mg daily. Dropout rates were slightly higher in the placebo group (33.3% vs. 23.9%) and appeared related to lack of efficacy. Overall, paroxetine was quite well tolerated, although the adolescent subgroup reported more issues with somnolence and insomnia compared with the younger population.

Although the previously discussed trials and reports have been focused on investigating SSRIs for youth with a predominant diagnosis of SAD, other trials have been conducted with these agents but in a more mixed anxiety population. Two open trials reported on the use of fluoxetine in populations of children and adolescents with mixed anxiety disorders that included SAD. Birmaher et al. (1994) provided one of earliest reports of an SSRI for this purpose. In their study population, all 21 patients (mean age 14 years, range 11–17 years) had overanxious disorder (now generalized anxiety disorder per the *DSM–IV*; American Psychiatric Association, 1994) with 10 patients having comorbid separation anxiety disorder or social phobia and five with all three conditions. Patients were treated with fluoxetine for a mean duration of 10 months with the average dose of fluoxetine being 25.7 mg daily. Overall, 81% of patients were rated as much or markedly improved following treatment, as measured by the CGI–I (score ≤ 2), with improvements mainly seen after 6 to 8 weeks of treatment. A strength of the study was that all patients had been unsuccessfully treated with at least one kind of psychotherapeutic intervention (e.g., CBT, individual dynamic psychotherapy), and 67% had previously failed an adequate trial of a tricyclic antidepressant. A major limitation of this study was that patients were identified through retrospective case review. Two of the authors then met to review the identified cases and come to consensus on diagnosis, severity of illness, and degree of improvement, rather than these measures having being identified in a truly prospective fashion, suggesting that this was really more of a retrospectively assessed case series than an open trial. Further, only a measure of global improvement assessed outcome, with no disorder-specific measures used. Thus, it is not possible to separate the differential effects of fluoxetine on SAD. Because most patients met criteria for overanxious disorder, one could argue that this study was more supportive of treatment for this condition rather than the other comorbid illnesses.

On the basis of earlier results (Black & Uhde, 1994) in which fluoxetine was found to be useful for children with selective mutism (considered an extreme childhood variant of SAD), Fairbanks et al. (1997) described a pilot study in which participants meeting criteria for at least one current anxiety disorder were treated with fluoxetine (5–80 mg daily) for up to 9 weeks. Five children (< 12 years old, mean age 9.4 years) and 11 adolescents (12–17 years, mean age 14.6 years) were enrolled in the trial, with 10 participants (nine adolescents) meeting criteria for social phobia. The mean daily dose of fluoxetine for adolescents was 40 +/− 18 mg. When results were analyzed by diagnosis, the authors noted that eight of the 10 youth with social phobia demonstrated improvement as measured by psychiatrist ratings on the CGI scale. However, in contrast to other studies, response was defined as a score of ≤ 3 at endpoint, as opposed to the more conventional definition of responders as those with scores ≤ 2. In this case, seven of the eight responders had final scores of 3 (improved), and only one had a score of 1 (completely recovered), although the authors did specify that for a score of 3 participants had to have demonstrated a significant reduction in symptoms. One other noteworthy finding from the study was that youths with a single anxiety disorder diagnosis were more likely to respond to lower doses of fluoxetine relative to those with comorbid anxiety disorders (0.49 +/− 0.14 mg/kg vs. 0.8 +/− 0.28 mg/kg). Limitations of this study included the heterogeneous nature of the population (inclusion of comorbidity) and the wide dose range of fluoxetine used in adolescents over a relative short time frame (up to 80 mg daily within 9 weeks), which may overestimate the actual dose required for improvement in this population.

Two randomized controlled trials have examined the use of SSRIs in mixed anxiety populations that included subjects with SAD. The Research Unit on Pediatric Psychopharmacology (Walkup et al., 2001) reported results of a multicenter double-blind randomized controlled trial of fluvoxamine in youth who met criteria for at least one of three anxiety disorders: SAD, separation anxiety disorder, or generalized anxiety disorder. Eligible subjects first underwent a 3-week course of open-label psychoeducational supportive therapy. The

128 nonresponders were then randomized to fluvoxamine (50–300 mg) or placebo for 8 weeks while continuing to receive supportive therapy. Of the enrolled subjects, the mean age was between 10.3 and 10.4 years for each treatment group, with only 33 (25.8%) subjects older than 13 years included overall. Fluvoxamine was well tolerated, with only five subjects withdrawing as a result of adverse effects of active medication, and was also more significantly associated with complaints of abdominal discomfort and increased motor activity compared with placebo. Following treatment, youth receiving active medication showed greater improvement in anxiety symptoms, with between-groups differences demonstrable as early as Week 3, and better clinical response (76% for those receiving medication vs. 29% for those receiving placebo). In contrast to several other studies, these authors used an 8-point scale of global improvement that defined responders as subjects with a score of ≤ 3 at the last study visit, which may have contributed to the relatively high response rate seen here. One other feature of this study was that subjects with three different anxiety disorders were included, 39 of whom met criteria at least for SAD. However, results were not examined by diagnosis, making it impossible to ascertain specific effects for youth with SAD.

More recently, Birmaher et al. (2003) randomized 74 individuals (mean age 11.8 +/– 2.8 years, range 7–17 years, $n = 31$ adolescents) to 12 weeks of treatment with fixed dose fluoxetine (20 mg) or placebo. Of the enrolled participants who had principal diagnoses of general anxiety disorder, SAD, and/or separation anxiety disorder, 54% met criteria for SAD. Overall, fluoxetine was associated with greater reduction of anxiety symptoms as well as greater treatment response with significant between-groups separations seen at Week 9. Interestingly, participants with a diagnosis of SAD and treated with fluoxetine were noted to have particular clinical improvement, as measured by the CGI–I, compared with participants with SAD treated with placebo (76% vs. 21%) and compared with those who were not diagnosed with SAD. These effects were either less robust or not seen in participants with diagnoses of general anxiety disorder or separation anxiety disorder. Similarly, improvements in functional outcome were also seen in participants with SAD treated with fluoxetine but not participants with SAD treated with placebo (45.5% vs. 10.5%) or in participants with other diagnoses, leading the authors to conclude that SAD appears to be a moderator of clinical and functional response.

Serotonin and Norepinephrine Reuptake Inhibitors

There are three SNRIs currently available on the U.S. market, venlafaxine, desvenlafaxine, and duloxetine. However, at this time, there is only one published trial of an SNRI for treatment of SAD in children and adolescents

(March, Entusah, Rynn, Albano, & Tourian, 2007). In this multisite double-blind randomized controlled trial, 293 youth (ages 8–17) meeting criteria for generalized SAD without significant comorbidity were randomized to either venlafaxine extended release (ER) or placebo for 16 weeks. Venlafaxine ER was initiated at 37.5 mg daily and flexibly titrated on the basis of subject weight. Primary efficacy assessments included the Social Anxiety Scale (child or adolescent version) and the CGI–I. Following treatment, there was a statistically significant benefit for venlafaxine ER ($p = .001$) with adjusted rates of response of 56% in the active treatment group and 37% in the placebo group. Overall, dropout rates were similar (venlafaxine ER, 35%; placebo, 27%), with lack of efficacy being the primary reason for withdrawal in both groups. Treatment-emergent side effects were generally mild to moderate in severity, with the venlafaxine ER group reporting higher rates of anorexia, weight loss, nervousness, nausea, and dizziness. Three of the venlafaxine-treated subjects did report suicidal ideation, but there were no reports of suicide attempts or completed suicides. The overall mean daily dose of venlafaxine ER at the study end was 155 +/– 39 mg. In contrast to the study by Wagner et al. (2004), no information was available on breakdown of results by age category (i.e., children vs. adolescents) other than a mention of mean daily doses of medication not being different between these two age populations.

Other

Mirtazapine is an antidepressant that appears to enhance both serotonergic and noradrenergic neurotransmission via antagonism of alpha-2 presynaptic receptor sites. Mrakotsky et al. (2008) reported findings of an 8-week open trial of flexibly dosed mirtazapine (15–45 mg daily) administered to 18 youths (ages 8–17 years, mean age 12.06 years) with a clinically predominant diagnosis of SAD. At the end of the study, 56% of patients were deemed responders and 39% of patients were deemed remitted. Among patients who improved, there was evidence of change not only in specific SAD symptoms but also with respect to general anxiety and depression. The most frequently reported side effects were sleepiness and irritability, which were mostly mild, but patients also reported significant weight gain ($M = 3.27$ kg). Of particular note, four patients (22%) dropped out because of adverse events, and an additional seven individuals dropped out for other reasons, although five of these were in the last 3 weeks of the trial. Overall, the authors cautioned against drawing definitive conclusions from the study on the basis of the tolerability issues, attrition rates, and lower rates of response compared with other similar pharmacological trials.

At this time, there do not appear to be any published reports of adolescents with a primary diagnosis of SAD treated with monoamine oxidase inhibitors, tricyclic antidepressants, or other antidepressant agents (e.g., bupropion).

BENZODIAZEPINES

Benzodiazepines were among the first agents investigated for childhood and adolescent anxiety disorders. In one trial, 12 subjects ages 8 to 16 years (mean age 11.5 years) diagnosed with either overanxious and/or avoidant disorder, now conceptualized as generalized anxiety disorder and SAD, respectively, received open-label alprazolam (0.5–1.5 mg daily) for 4 weeks with a 1-week up-titration and 1-week tapering period before and after treatment (Simeon & Ferguson, 1987). Overall, 58.3% of subjects displayed either moderate or marked improvement. Although adverse effects were generally uncommon or mild, there was significant weight gain (mean 0.87 kg) reported during treatment. On the basis of these promising results, the authors subsequently conducted a larger controlled trial in a similar population of children and adolescents with either primary overanxious disorder ($n = 21$) or avoidant disorder ($n = 9$; Simeon et al., 1992). Following a 1-week placebo lead-in, subjects (mean age 12.6 years) were assigned to 4 weeks of double-blind treatment with alprazolam (0.25–3.5 mg/day on the basis of body weight) or placebo. In contrast to the earlier positive findings for alprazolam, no statistical differences were found on clinical outcome between active treatment and placebo, even when results were examined by diagnosis. Reported side effects were mild and similar in both treatment groups.

OTHER AGENTS

Other pharmacological agents have been investigated for the treatment of SAD in adults. Certain anticonvulsants, including primarily pregabalin and gabapentin, and to a lesser extent topiramate have shown initial promise (Pande et al., 1999; Pande et al, 2004; Van Ameringen, Mancini, Pipe, Oakman, & Bennett, 2004). However, these agents have yet to be investigated in a youth population. Conflicting evidence exists for monotherapy with atypical antipsychotics to treat SAD in adults (Barnett, Kramer, Casat, Connor, & Davidson, 2002; Vaishnavi, Alamy, Zhang, Connor, & Davidson, 2007), but as mentioned previously, there are no trials of these agents for SAD in adolescents.

Although not substantiated by the literature, it is a relatively common practice to prescribe as needed beta-adrenergic blockers (e.g., propranolol, atenolol) for individuals with performance-related social anxiety. At this time, however, there are no published reports of beta-adrenergic blocker use for adolescents with SAD.

DISCUSSION

What is evident from a review of the literature is that there is a marked dearth of psychopharmacology trials for SAD in adolescents and young adults, with most of the existing literature supporting the use of serotonergic agents, such as SSRIs or SNRIs (with data in the latter category limited to venlafaxine ER). This deficit in the literature is a problem for patients who are unable to tolerate the typical first line agents or unable to access alternate effective therapies such as CBT. Further, the question of treatment resistance in this disorder has not been specifically addressed in any published studies within this population. As such, clinical management of this population is highly dependent on findings from adult research, resulting in frequent off-label use of psychotropic medications. What are the reasons for this? As pointed out earlier, the recognition of childhood anxiety disorders is a relatively recent concept in the history of psychiatry, which might explain why the bulk of psychopharmacological research of SAD in youth has been published in the last 10 years. However, several other potential issues have also been identified.

One putative factor has been the role of parental reluctance to medicate their child in spite of the impairment the child may be experiencing. Chavira, Stein, Bailey, and Stein (2003) assessed parental opinions regarding treatment for SAD in youth (8–17 years old). Medications were considered a less acceptable option than counseling, and parents were particularly concerned about possible medication-related side effects. Of note, severity of symptoms did not influence the acceptability of a given treatment. The authors speculated that this may be related to a child's anxiety-related distress being internalized in contrast to externalizing disorders, such as attention-deficit/hyperactivity disorder, in which severity may be more outwardly reflected. Also along these lines, Young et al. (2006) examined factors influencing attrition during the recruitment phase of a treatment study comparing behavior therapy, fluoxetine, and placebo for SAD in children and adolescents. The main identified reason for refusal to participate was parental concern about assignment to the medication arm, with other identified factors including child or teen refusal to participate, distance to study site, and concern about randomization to the placebo arm. When attitudes toward medication were specifically examined, risk of side effects and concern about dependency represented 66.7% of parental concerns about medication. Recent media attention focused on psychotropic medication in youth was also rated as a moderately influential factor in the decision not to participate.

Finally, in both studies described previously, Caucasian parents had more favorable attitudes toward medication compared with parents from ethnic minorities. The authors speculated that this could be explained by greater fears of unfavorable outcomes, cultural stigma associated with psychiatric diagnosis and treatment, and concern that therapies might not be culturally sensitive.

Another factor that may play a role in limiting the existing evidence base is youths' or adolescents' willingness to try psychotropic medication. Younger children are clearly required to have parental consent to have a trial of medications, so parental wishes play a much stronger role. However, this issue becomes more ambiguous with older adolescents. Developmentally, adolescents and young adults are in a unique situation—although still heavily influenced by familial attitudes toward treatment options, they are also increasingly trying to carve out a more independent persona. Further, decisions about intervention may now also be more heavily weighted by peer influences (Townsend, Floersch, & Findling, 2009), which in turn may have a bearing on not only the modality of treatment chosen but also adherence.

A better understanding of adolescent attitudes toward treatment, including psychological interventions, would be useful in designing clinical trials that address these concerns, as well as in improving recruitment, and would also provide clinicians meaningful information regarding different psychopharmacological strategies. For example, Jaycox et al. (2006) examined attitudes toward treatment in adolescents and young adults (13–21 years) screening positive for depression in a primary care setting. In general, adolescents, particularly girls, preferred active treatment to a wait-and-see approach, with a marked preference for counseling over medications. Predictors of those who preferred medications included past use of psychotropic medications, recent mental health care, and the presence of anxiety symptoms with depression. Overall, the adolescents in this sample were not particularly concerned about general stigma associated with depression, although close to 50% did report that relationships would suffer more if friends thought they had a recent history of depression or contact with a mental health specialist. Although these results were found in a depressive population, data collected among socially anxious teens may help inform clinical trials.

The use of antidepressants in adolescents and young adults has also come under great scrutiny recently. Following a finding submitted in 2003 that paroxetine-treated youth diagnosed mainly with major depressive disorder were at increased risk of suicidal ideation and behavior, the U.S. Food and Drug Administration (FDA) commissioned a report looking at similar effects in other antidepressant trials. In 2004, on the basis of findings presented by an advisory committee, the FDA implemented a black box warning that antidepressants, with the exception of fluoxetine, may increase the risk of suicidality in children and teenagers. In 2007, the warning was expanded to also include young adults ages 18 to 24 years. Evidence supporting the first black box warning was published in a 2006 (Hammad, Laughren, & Racoosin, 2006) meta-analysis that examined data from 24 short-term controlled clinical trials (4–16 weeks) of youth with different mood and anxiety disorders.

The warnings serve to raise awareness of the risks associated with younger individuals taking antidepressants; however, it is also important to remember that these medications are not actually contraindicated in adolescents and young adults but rather are to be used with caution by clinicians who carefully weigh the risks and benefits of pharmacological treatment against the potential long-lasting consequences of not receiving appropriate treatment for psychiatric disorders. When initiating use of an antidepressant, particularly close monitoring is warranted during the first 4 weeks of treatment, with patients and their families being advised to watch for symptoms of worsening depression or anxiety, irritability, hostility, sleep disturbance, agitation, restlessness, or other sudden changes in behavior. Although the findings of the meta-analysis were heavily weighted toward those with major depressive disorder and only a single trial of SAD was included, the significant comorbidity between SAD and other depressive or anxiety disorders would suggest that antidepressant agents still be used cautiously in adolescents and young adults with SAD.

One important remaining question is the optimal duration of medication. Unfortunately, no data to support an answer are available. There is a literature suggesting that childhood anxiety may herald later life psychiatric impairment, particularly depressive disorders, other anxiety disorders, or substance abuse (Keller, 2003; Schneier, Johnson, Hornig, Liebowitz, & Weissman, 1992; Wittchen & Fehm, 2001). To date, all published trials of adolescent SAD have focused on short-term pharmacological treatment, generally less than 16 weeks. As such, guidelines for duration of treatment again depend on adult data. There, relapse prevention studies suggest that medication responders be maintained on treatment for at least 6 months but up to 12 to 24 months (Baldwin et al., 2005; Blanco, Raza, Schneier, & Liebowitz, 2003; Swinson et al., 2006; Van Ameringen et al., 2003).

The existing evidence base has several limitations. Vast heterogeneity exists among published trials, including differences in how populations with SAD are recruited. Although not limited to adults when the term *social phobia* was first introduced, it was not diagnosed as frequently in children because of the symptom overlap between SAD and the alternative diagnosis of avoidant disorder of childhood. Further, only more recently have studies begun to differentiate between subtypes of SAD (generalized vs. nongeneralized) and to impose minimum severity guidelines for study inclusion, which may have affected the level of benefit observed in results. Several published trials have examined populations of "mixed" anxiety disorders in which subjects with at least one of three different primary diagnoses may have been included. Although as a group this might have lent power to the findings, the numbers of each subgroup were usually too small to form robust conclusions when results were stratified by diagnosis. Even when studies of primary SAD were conducted, there were differences in whether authors made the decision to keep the sample more "pure" or chose to permit comorbidities (e.g., concurrent depression), again rendering interpretation of results more complicated.

Finally, the majority of pharmacological trials published for SAD in the pediatric population have, by convention, permitted any individuals less than 18 years old to be included. At the other end of the age spectrum, subjects as young as 6 years old have also been included. Although only a span of 12 years, this age range includes extremely different developmental periods, which may play a role in severity and expression of illness and response to a particular kind of treatment. The focus of this volume is SAD in adolescents and young adults, but drawing conclusions about the efficacy of pharmacological agents in this particular subpopulation is challenging because only one study clearly reported results based on age stratifications.

Trial duration is also observed to be diverse, ranging from 4 to 16 weeks in controlled studies but up to 10 months in open investigations. Next, although the use of the CGI–I measure is fairly consistent across studies, use of measures to specifically assess SAD symptom severity and change is highly variable across studies, making it more difficult to compare degree of change between pharmacological agents. An additional challenge is the occasional use of different measures even within a study depending on subject age.

On the basis of the limitations identified here, future research might include greater numbers of controlled studies investigating the wide variety of psychotropic agents that currently exist and are used in adults with SAD. Long-term continuation and relapse prevention studies also are needed to provide improved direction for clinicians regarding optimal duration of treatment as well as a greater focus on augmentation and combination strategies in cases of treatment resistance. Within these areas, researchers would ideally design studies with more homogeneous populations and similar measures across trials, and provide results that are stratified by age group.

REFERENCES

American Psychiatric Association. (1980). *Diagnostic and statistical manual of mental disorders* (3rd ed.). Washington, DC: Author.

American Psychiatric Association. (1994). *Diagnostic and statistical manual of mental disorders* (4th ed.). Washington, DC: Author.

Baldwin, D. S., Anderson, I. M., Nutt, D. J., Bandelow, B., Bond, A., Davidson, J. R., . . . Wittchen, H.-U. (2005). Evidence-based guidelines for the pharmacological treatment of anxiety disorders: Recommendations from the British Association for Psychopharmacology. *Journal of Psychopharmacology, 19*, 567–596.

Barnett, S. D., Kramer, M. L., Casat, C. D., Connor, K. M., & Davidson, J. R. (2002). Efficacy of olanzapine in social anxiety disorder: A pilot study. *Journal of Psychopharmacology, 16*, 365–368. doi:10.1177/026988110201600412

Beidel, D. C., Turner, S. M., & Morris, T. L. (1995). A new inventory to assess childhood social anxiety and phobia: The Social Phobia and Anxiety Inventory for Children. *Psychological Assessment, 7*, 73–79. doi:10.1037/1040-3590.7.1.73

Birmaher, B., Axelson, D. A., Monk, K., Kalas, C., Clark, D. B., Ehmann, M., . . . Brent, D. (2003). Fluoxetine for the treatment of childhood anxiety disorders. *Journal of the American Academy of Child and Adolescent Psychiatry, 42*, 415–423.

Birmaher, B., Waterman, G. S., Ryan, N., Cully, M., Balach, L., Ingram, J., & Brodsky, M. (1994). Fluoxetine for childhood anxiety disorders. *Journal of the American Academy of Child and Adolescent Psychiatry, 33*, 993–999. doi:10.1097/00004583-199409000-00009

Black, B., & Uhde, T. W. (1994). Treatment of elective mutism with fluoxetine: A double-blind, placebo-controlled study. *Journal of the American Academy of Child and Adolescent Psychiatry, 33*, 1000–1006. doi:10.1097/00004583-199409000-00010

Blanco, C., Raza, M. S., Schneier, F. R., & Liebowitz, M. R. (2003). The evidence-based pharmacological treatment of social anxiety disorder. *The International Journal of Neuropsychopharmacology, 6*, 427–442.

Chavira, D. A., & Stein, M. B. (2002). Combined psychoeducation and treatment with selective serotonin reuptake inhibitors for youth with generalized social anxiety disorder. *Journal of Child and Adolescent Psychopharmacology, 12*, 47–54. doi:10.1089/10445460252943560

Chavira, D. A., Stein, M. B., Bailey, K., & Stein, M. T. (2003). Parental opinions regarding treatment for social anxiety disorder in youth. *Journal of Developmental and Behavioral Pediatrics: JDBP, 24*, 315–322. doi:10.1097/00004703-200310000-00002

Compton, S. N., Grant, P. J., Chrisman, A. K., Gammon, P. J., Brown, V. L., & March, J. S. (2001). Sertraline in children and adolescents with social anxiety disorder: An open trial. *Journal of the American Academy of Child and Adolescent Psychiatry, 40*, 564–571. doi:10.1097/00004583-200105000-00016

Davis, R., Whittington, R., & Bryson, H. M. (1997). Nefazodone. A review of its pharmacology and clinical efficacy in the management of major depression. *Drugs, 53*, 608–636. doi:10.2165/00003495-199753040-00006

Fairbanks, J. M., Pine, D. S., Tancer, N. K., Dummit, E. S., III, Kentgen, L. M., Martin, J., . . . Klein, R. G. (1997). Open fluoxetine treatment of mixed anxiety disorders in children and adolescents. *Journal of Child and Adolescent Psychopharmacology, 7*, 17–29. doi:10.1089/cap.1997.7.17

Hammad, T. A., Laughren, T., & Racoosin, J. (2006). Suicidality in pediatric patients treated with antidepressant drugs. *Archives of General Psychiatry, 63,* 332–339. doi:10.1001/archpsyc.63.3.332

Isolan, L., Pheula, G., Salum, G. A., Jr., Oswald, S., Rohde, L. A., & Manfro, G. G. (2007). An open-label trial of escitalopram in children and adolescents with social anxiety disorder. *Journal of Child and Adolescent Psychopharmacology, 17,* 751–759. doi:10.1089/cap.2007.0007

Janet, P. (1903). *Les obsessions et la psychasthénie* [Obsessions and psychasthenia]. Paris, France: Alcan.

Jaycox, L. H., Asarnow, J. R., Sherbourne, C. D., Rea, M. M., LaBorde, A. P., & Wells, K. B. (2006). Adolescent primary care patients' preferences for depression treatment. *Administration and Policy in Mental Health, 33,* 198–207. doi:10.1007/s10488-006-0033-7

Keller, M. B. (2003). The lifelong course of social anxiety disorder: A clinical perspective. *Acta Psychiatrica Scandinavica, 108,* 85–94. doi:10.1034/j.1600-0447.108.s417.6.x

Kosieradzki, P. H. (2001). Citalopram in social phobia. *Journal of the American Academy of Child and Adolescent Psychiatry, 40,* 1126–1127. doi:10.1097/00004583-200110000-00006

Mancini, C., Van Ameringen, M., Oakman, J. M., & Farvolden, P. (1999). Serotonergic agents in the treatment of social phobia in children and adolescents: A case series. *Depression and Anxiety, 10,* 33–39. doi:10.1002/(SICI)1520-6394(1999)10:1<33::AID-DA6>3.0.CO;2-H

March, J. S., Entusah, A. R., Rynn, M., Albano, A. M., & Tourian, K. A. (2007). A randomized controlled trial of venlafaxine ER versus placebo in pediatric social anxiety disorder. *Biological Psychiatry, 62,* 1149–1154. doi:10.1016/j.biopsych.2007.02.025

Mrakotsky, C., Masek, B., Biederman, J., Raches, D., Hsin, O., Forbes, P., . . . Gonzalez-Heydrich, J. (2008). Prospective open-label pilot trial of mirtazapine in children and adolescents with social phobia. *Journal of Anxiety Disorders, 22,* 88–97. doi:10.1016/j.janxdis.2007.01.005

Pande, A. C., Davidson, J. R., Jefferson, J. W., Janney, C. A., Katzelnick, D. J., Weisler, R. H., . . . Sutherland, S. M. (1999). Treatment of social phobia with gabapentin: A placebo-controlled study. *Journal of Clinical Psychopharmacology, 19,* 341–348. doi:10.1097/00004714-199908000-00010

Pande, A. C., Feltner, D. E., Jefferson, J. W., Davidson, J. R., Pollack, M., Stein, M. B., . . . Werth, J. L. (2004). Efficacy of the novel anxiolytic pregabalin in social anxiety disorder: A placebo-controlled, multicenter study. *Journal of Clinical Psychopharmacology, 24,* 141–149. doi:10.1097/01.jcp.0000117423.05703.e7

Schneier, F. R., Johnson, J., Hornig, C. D., Liebowitz, M. R., & Weissman, M. M. (1992). Social phobia: Comorbidity and morbidity in an epidemiologic sample. *Archives of General Psychiatry, 49,* 282–288.

Simeon, J. G., & Ferguson, H. B. (1987). Alprazolam effects in children with anxiety disorders. *Canadian Journal of Psychiatry, 32,* 570–574.

Simeon, J. G., Ferguson, H. B., Knott, V., Roberts, N., Gauthier, B., Dubois, C. & Wiggins, D. (1992). Clinical, cognitive, and neurophysiological effects of alprazolam in children and adolescents with overanxious and avoidant disorders. *Journal of the American Academy of Child and Adolescent Psychiatry, 31,* 29–33. doi:10.1097/00004583-199201000-00006

Stein, M. B., & Stein, D. J. (2008). Social anxiety disorder. *The Lancet, 371,* 1115–1125. doi:10.1016/S0140-6736(08)60488-2

Swinson, R. P., Antony, M. M., Bleau, P., Chokka, P., Craven, M., Fallu, A., . . . Walker, J. R. (2006). Clinical practice guidelines: Management of anxiety disorders. *Canadian Journal of Psychiatry, 51*(Suppl. 2), 1–92.

Townsend, L., Floersch, J., & Findling, R. L. (2009). Adolescent attitudes toward psychiatric medication: The utility of the drug attitude inventory. *Journal of Child Psychology and Psychiatry, and Allied Disciplines, 50,* 1523–1531,

Vaishnavi, S., Alamy, S., Zhang, W., Connor, K. M., & Davidson, J. R. (2007). Quetiapine as monotherapy for social anxiety disorder: A placebo-controlled study. *Progress in Neuro-Psychopharmacology & Biological Psychiatry, 31,* 1464–1469.

Van Ameringen, M., Mancini, C., Pipe, B., Oakman, J., & Bennett, M. (2004). An open trial of topiramate in the treatment of generalized social phobia. *The Journal of Clinical Psychiatry, 65,* 1674–1678. doi:10.4088/JCP.v65n1213

Van Ameringen, M., Allgulander, C., Bandelow, B., Greist, J. H., Hollander, E., Montgomery, S. A., . . . Swinson, R. P. (2003). WCA recommendations for the long-term treatment of social phobia. *CNS Spectrums, 8*(Suppl. 1), 40–52.

Wagner, K. D., Berard, R., Stein, M. B., Wetherhold, E., Carpenter, D. J., Perera, P., . . . Machin, A. (2004). A multicenter, randomized, double-blind, placebo-controlled trial of paroxetine in children and adolescents with social anxiety disorder. *Archives of General Psychiatry, 61,* 1153–1162.

Walkup, J. T., Labellarte, M. J., Riddle, M. A., Pine, D. S., Greenhill, L., Klein, R., . . . Roper, M. (2001). Fluvoxamine for the treatment of anxiety disorders in children and adolescents. *The New England Journal of Medicine, 344,* 1279–1285.

Wittchen, H.-U., & Fehm, L. (2001). Epidemiology, patterns of comorbidity, and associated disabilities of social phobia. *The Psychiatric Clinics of North America, 24,* 617–641. doi:10.1016/S0193-953X(05)70254-9

Young, B. J., Beidel, D. C., Turner, S. M., Ammerman, R. T., McGraw, K., & Coaston, S. C. (2006). Pretreatment attrition and childhood social phobia: Parental concerns about medication. *Journal of Anxiety Disorders, 20,* 1133–1147. doi:10.1016/j.janxdis.2006.03.007

15

ADAPTING TREATMENT OF SOCIAL ANXIETY DISORDER FOR DELIVERY IN SCHOOLS: A SCHOOL-BASED INTERVENTION FOR ADOLESCENTS

CARRIE MASIA-WARNER, PAIGE H. FISHER, KRISTY A. LUDWIG, REBECCA RIALON, AND JULIE L. RYAN

The high prevalence and serious nature of social anxiety disorder (SAD) in adolescence have been thoroughly covered in the preceding chapters. Despite this disorder's substantial detrimental impact and the availability of efficacious psychological and pharmacological treatments (reviewed in Chapters 13 and 14, this volume), socially anxious adolescents remain highly unlikely to receive services (Essau, Conradt, & Petermann, 1999; Kashdan & Herbert, 2001; Masia-Warner, Fisher, Shrout, Rathor, & Klein, 2007; Wittchen, Stein, & Kessler, 1999). Considering the prevalence, chronicity, and long-term disability associated with SAD, treatment underutilization is particularly alarming.

This problem is consistent with a larger literature documenting that the majority of affected children in the community do not receive mental health services (Burns et al., 1995; Farmer, Stangl, Burns, Costello, & Angold, 1999; Flisher et al., 1997; Leaf et al., 1996; Offord et al., 1987; Verhulst & Van der Ende, 1997). Many children and families have difficulties accessing adequate mental health care (Essau et al., 1999; Wittchen et al., 1999), and fewer than 20% of those who do seek treatment receive empirically based treatments like cognitive behavioral therapy (CBT; Collins, Westra, Dozois, & Burns, 2004; Labellarte, Ginsburg, Walkup, & Riddle, 1999). Thus, schools play an important role in addressing the unmet mental health needs of youth by potentially increasing access to care in a cost-effective manner. This setting provides unparalleled access to youth (Adelman & Taylor, 1999; Weist, 1997), and represents a single location through which the majority of children can be reached (Anglin, 2003).

School-based intervention provides particular benefits for adolescents with SAD for several reasons. First, because of the social nature of the disorder, group treatment can be particularly valuable. Whereas forming groups in clinical settings can be challenging because of variability in client diagnoses and scheduling, schools are conducive to conducting groups. Second, despite the high prevalence of (Verhulst, van der Ende, Ferdinand, & Kasius, 1997; Wittchen et al., 1999) and impairment associated with SAD, these adolescents are rarely identified (Kashdan & Herbert, 2001) and are unlikely to receive treatment (Essau et al., 1999; Wittchen et al., 1999). Teachers and parents often overlook teenagers with social anxiety, most likely because of their quiet, compliant manner (Masia, Klein, Storch, & Corda, 2001). Such behaviors are less noticeable to adults than the disruptive conduct associated with external-izing disorders (Wu et al., 1999). In addition, even when parents and teachers notice that teenagers are extremely shy or nervous, they typically underestimate their difficulties (Kashdan & Herbert, 2001) and believe that they will "grow out" of the anxiety (Masia et al., 2001). Partnering with schools creates opportunities to facilitate identification and treatment of SAD by educating teachers and parents about its symptoms and potential consequences and providing support for appropriate treatment referrals.

In addition, adolescents are often reluctant to pursue mental health services because of concerns about stigma and being labeled "abnormal" (Hoganbruen, Clauss-Ehlers, Nelson, & Faenza, 2003). Such worries can be particularly intense for individuals with social anxiety because of their sensitivity to embarrassment and humiliation. Offering services in a familiar setting like schools may make treatment more acceptable (Catron & Weiss, 1994; Weist, 1999) because many students already receive school-based services for nonmental health concerns.

Finally, because socially anxious adolescents incur the greatest disadvantage at school (Hofmann et al., 1999), intervention implemented within this setting allows for a real-world treatment approach. That is, the school environment provides opportunities for real-life exposures to commonly avoided situations (e.g., answering questions in class, eating in the cafeteria, speaking with office personnel, initiating conversations with unfamiliar peers) and for practicing skills in realistic contexts and with various individuals (e.g., teachers, staff, peers). In addition, peers and teachers with whom socially anxious students routinely associate can be enlisted to support students' progress. In this way, treatment delivered in school reduces the division between the treatment setting and natural environment and may enhance the effectiveness of school interventions for SAD relative to clinic-based treatment (Evans, Langberg, & Williams, 2003).

On the basis of these potential advantages, Masia and colleagues (1999) sought to develop a treatment program that would draw from empirically supported techniques and could be feasibly implemented in schools. They primarily derived their school-based program, Skills for Academic and Social Success (SASS; Masia et al., 1999), from Social Effectiveness Therapy for Children (SET-C; Beidel, Turner, & Morris, 1998), a clinic-based treatment that consists of 12 individual sessions of behavioral exposures and 12 group sessions of social skills training followed by unstructured peer generalization exercises in which treated children practice socializing with nonanxious peers. The SET-C program was selected on the basis of documentation of social skills deficits in socially anxious youth (Beidel, Turner, & Morris 1999; Spence, Donovan, & Brechman-Toussaint, 1999) and the demonstrated efficacy of SET-C compared with an attention control condition (Beidel, Turner, & Morris, 2000; Beidel, Turner, Young, & Paulson, 2005). Additionally, the SET-C emphasis on using peers to assist with generalization fit well with the natural availability of same-aged peers in the school environment.

Implementing intervention with adolescents and in the school setting necessitated significant modifications. Given evidence that negative self-talk is more common among teenagers than among children with SAD (Alfano, Beidel, & Turner, 2006), we added training in realistic thinking. In addition, social skills sessions were revised to be more developmentally appropriate for adolescents. The number, length, and pace of sessions were substantially decreased to avoid interrupting academic courses and to correspond to the school calendar. In addition, the school environment was incorporated through the participation of teachers, parents, and school peers as well as by conducting exposures and practicing skills in various school and community locations.

In the remainder of this chapter, we describe the SASS program and its treatment outcome data. We also discuss challenges involved in delivering this intervention in schools and offer suggestions for addressing these issues.

SKILLS FOR ACADEMIC AND SOCIAL SUCCESS OVERVIEW

The SASS intervention consists of 12 weekly group school sessions, two group booster sessions to address relapse and remaining obstacles, and two brief individual meetings (15 min). Additionally, four weekend social events (90 min) that include prosocial peers, called *peer assistants* (described in the discussion that follows) provide real-world exposures and skills generalization. Parents attend two group meetings (45 min) during which they receive psychoeducation regarding social anxiety and learn techniques to address their child's anxiety. Teachers can participate in two meetings in which they learn about social anxiety and the program and receive instruction to help students practice classroom exposures. The program is designed to be flexible to accommodate school calendars (e.g., vacations and exams) and typically spans about 3 months.

TREATMENT COMPONENTS

All treatment components are discussed in detail in the sections that follow.

School Group Sessions

Treatment groups are small, consisting of up to six students, and can be facilitated by one or two group leaders (i.e., psychologists or school counselors). The group sessions cover five core components: (a) psychoeducation, (b) realistic thinking, (c) social skills training, (d) exposure, and (e) relapse prevention.

Psychoeducation

In the first session, group leaders provide a description of the cognitive, somatic, and behavioral symptoms of social anxiety. Students are encouraged to identify their own anxiety symptoms and to examine how social anxiety is maintained through the interaction of negative thoughts, physical sensations, and avoidance. Commonly feared social situations and associated difficulties are reviewed.

Realistic Thinking

The second group session focuses on realistic thinking, primarily adapted from Ronald Rapee's (1998) book *Overcoming Shyness and Social Phobia*. Group leaders highlight the relationships among thoughts, feelings, and behavior. They explain that teenagers with social anxiety tend to overestimate the likelihood of negative outcomes and exaggerate the consequences. For example, socially anxious adolescents are likely to assume that they will give the wrong answer when called on in class, and that they will be viewed as unintelligent. Students are taught to identify such negative expectations and to use specific questions to evaluate them more realistically (e.g., Am I exaggerating? How many times has this happened in the past? How do I feel when I see others in similar situations?). This is the only session focused exclusively on helping group members identify and challenge negative thinking; however, these strategies are practiced and emphasized throughout the program.

Social Skills Training

Enhancing social skills is an essential treatment component because the development of these key social behaviors is likely to have been impeded by the adolescent's history of inadequate socialization experiences (Beidel & Turner, 1998; Kearney, 2005). The four social skills sessions include (a) initiating conversations, (b) maintaining conversations and establishing friendships, (c) listening and remembering, and (d) assertiveness. For each skill, group leaders introduce the concept and rationale and then facilitate group discussions. The leaders demonstrate skills through brief role plays, choosing situations relevant to adolescent experiences (e.g., being paired with another student to work on a project. meeting new people through friends). Each student participates in at least two role plays. Both group leaders and members provide feedback, praise positive aspects of role-play performance, and provide suggestions for improvement, such as speaking more clearly or increasing eye contact. Students are asked to practice learned skills outside of sessions.

Certain techniques are particularly relevant for teaching the nuances of social skills to adolescents with social anxiety. First, because socially anxious individuals can become dependent on certain types of conversational questions or statements, flexibility is specifically trained. Through repeated practice, students are asked to generate different statements to the same role-play scenarios. If students have difficulty with these exercises, observing group members are encouraged to provide support by calling out alternative suggestions. Second, shy students often look unfriendly or unapproachable because of nonverbal behaviors, such as frowning or avoiding eye contact. To address this, all skills groups emphasize teaching students to become aware of their unintended nonverbal messages to others and reinforce more "friendly" and confident behaviors (i.e., smiling, eye contact, speech volume, intonation, and relaxed and engaged body posture). Finally, socially anxious individuals often have difficulty maintaining natural dialogues, which is partly due to their tendency to change topics abruptly as well as to their difficulty attending to the conversation content. Often, such impairments are related to interfering negative cognitions focusing on evaluative concerns (e.g., "I sound boring," "I don't know what to say next"). Therefore, conversational skills practice requires students to remain on a topic until group leaders give permission to switch. Depending on a student's progress, group leaders might adjust the level of task difficulty by providing a shorter or longer time span. In addition, through two attentional exercises, students are taught to attend to personal details (e.g., name, hobbies, personal facts) that others have shared and to practice initiating conversations based on this information. Tailoring the skills training to meet the specific needs of socially anxious adolescents seems to enhance the value of these sessions.

Facing Your Fear

SASS includes five exposure sessions, referred to as *facing-your-fear* sessions, which alternate with the social skills sessions. Group leaders present the rationale and procedure for exposure while emphasizing the role of avoidance in maintaining anxiety and the expectation that anxiety will diminish with increased exposure. Students develop a fear hierarchy, or ladder, that rank orders 10 anxiety-provoking situations, beginning with the least feared situation. Group leaders assist students in identifying specific contexts that make a situation more or less comfortable, such as speaking with males versus females or friends versus family members. In composing hierarchies, it is particularly important to tap the *core fears* surrounding humiliation, rejection, and being negatively evaluated. Therefore, we include items that target these specific concerns, such as giving the wrong answer in class, making social mistakes, and inviting school peers to get together. We also incorporate exposure situations that can be feasibly integrated into the school environment (e.g., talking to school personnel, approaching a peer in the cafeteria).

Each exposure session includes practice of anxiety-provoking situations chosen by students and group leaders that are conducted in session or around the school. Students are asked to provide subjective units of distress ratings from 1 to 100 (1 = *completely calm*, 100 = *absolutely terrified*), which are expected to decrease by at least 50% by the end of the exposure. If a student is reluctant, negative thoughts about the student's expectations are explored, and the feared outcome is compared with the actual outcome after exposure. Following exposure exercises, students discuss their experience, and the group provides feedback. Students are given practice exposures between sessions, which are reviewed at the beginning of each session.

Conducting exposure at school provides a meaningful opportunity to capitalize on the school environment by creating a realistic context for encouraging new and challenging behaviors. Exposure tasks implemented during sessions involve other group members. An example of an in-session group exposure is speed chatting, based on speed dating. This exercise allows conversations with several different people in a short period of time. Group members sit in two rows facing each other, engage in conversation with the person opposite them, and rotate positions every 5 min to start a dialogue with a new partner. Because group participants are also school peers, they are also seen outside of sessions in school or community settings where conversations can be continued.

Exposure sessions also utilize various school locations. Some common exposures include sending students to the cafeteria to initiate conversations with peers or to purchase and return food, asking questions to the librarian, or visiting the main office to speak to administrative staff. Student pairs might be sent to various locations and return to group to discuss their experiences.

Conducting treatment in school also provides the opportunity to enlist the assistance of school personnel. Because many students experience anxiety talking to authority figures, some exposures involve interaction with administrators. For example, students may schedule meetings to converse or to make suggestions or complaints. Group leaders ask several school administrators (e.g., principal, dean, assistant principal) to be available for these meetings. In addition, group members might deliver the morning school announcements. Teachers may participate in classroom exposures involving students arriving unprepared or late to class, being reprimanded in front of others, assigning leadership roles in group activities, answering questions, or asking for clarification of educational material. Finally, group members might approach club advisors and coaches to discuss joining clubs or teams.

When treating adolescents with SAD, it is common to experience resistance to engaging in exposures with higher potential for negative evaluation or rejection (e.g., inviting peers to get together, attending a school function). Unlike traditional clinical settings where patients return to their natural environment to attempt challenging behaviors on their own, integrating treatment into school allows for social risk taking in a more controlled environment. Group leaders and supportive peers are present in the natural setting to encourage and assist students to overcome the anticipatory anxiety involved in attempting more challenging behaviors. This enhances the likelihood that initial attempts will be successful, thus reinforcing future independent action. For example, students might be encouraged to invite school peers to get together; these peers, who have been previously identified by group leaders, are known to be likely to accept the invitation. In addition, group participants may initially attend a school club or activity in pairs. To encourage social mistakes, students may be prepared in group to leave with messy hair or arrive late to their next class. Exposure conducted in this way capitalizes on the school environment, which provides a rich and unique context to optimize implementation of this technique.

Relapse Prevention

The final group focuses on maintenance of gains and relapse prevention. Each group member gives a speech about their experience in the program, focusing on what they have learned, their accomplishments, and areas for continued improvement. Following presentations, group leaders discuss maintaining gains, strategies for continuing progress, and how to handle potential setbacks. The warning signs of emerging symptoms and strategies for reversing them are discussed.

Individual Sessions

Students attend two 15-min individual sessions to discuss treatment goals and any issues that may be interfering with progress that they are not comfortable discussing during the groups. In addition, these meetings may be used for tailored cognitive restructuring, review of specific social skills, or individual exposures (i.e., calling to invite someone to get together). The meetings also provide opportunities to strengthen rapport between the student and group leader and to identify stressors other than social anxiety (e.g., being bullied, parental divorce) that may be impacting group participation or the student's ability to practice and change behaviors.

Booster Sessions

Group booster sessions are conducted monthly for 2 months after termination. Their purpose is to monitor progress, evaluate and discuss any obstacles to continued improvement, and highlight additional ways to practice skills and establish relationships. Additional exposures may be enacted during group booster sessions.

Social Events

The four weekend social events are considered an essential component of the program and are attended by group leaders, participants, and peer assistants from the students' high schools (see the next section). Activities may consist of bowling, laser tag, going to the mall, playing billiards, miniature golf, or a picnic. The activities provide group members the opportunity to practice social skills and allow for exposure to several commonly avoided situations (e.g., attending a social event without friends or with unfamiliar peers, initiating conversations, performing in front of others). These activities also offer a unique opportunity for group leaders to observe students' functioning in realistic social situations.

Peer Assistants

Peer assistants are helpful, friendly, and kind students identified by school personnel to assist with the SASS program. Ideally, peer assistants are students who have previously completed the SASS program. Their primary role is to create a positive experience for group members at social events. Peer assistants "grease the wheels" by bringing enthusiasm and energy to the events and ensuring that all students are engaged in conversation and integrated into the group activities. Peer assistants also facilitate peer support within the school environment through assisting with exposures and skill practice such as bringing a group member to join a school club or having conversations in the cafeteria or hallways.

Parent Meetings

Two parent meetings are conducted during the intervention. These meetings are essential because many parents have a limited understanding of the symptoms and impairment associated with social anxiety. Parents may interpret socially anxious behavior as part of their child's personality, something their child will "grow out of" or "unfriendly behavior." In addition, parents are often frustrated and overwhelmed by their children's avoidance behaviors (e.g., refusing to order food in restaurants) and fail to understand the extent of what they are experiencing. Therefore, two group meetings are conducted to teach parents about social anxiety and the SASS program and to provide them with support and suggestions from group leaders and other parents.

In the first parent meeting, parents or caregivers learn about the symptoms and maintenance of social anxiety. Psychoeducation helps parents to better understand their child's experience and the anxiety underlying avoidance behavior. It is very common for parents to ask about the causes of social anxiety and express concerns that they have caused these difficulties. Therefore, we have found it important to help parents understand the multifaceted etiology of social anxiety and to discuss how parental behavior plays a role in the development and maintenance of anxiety in a nonjudgmental way (e.g., it is a natural instinct for parents to remove their children from distressing situations or to assist them when they are struggling). The parent session concludes by explaining the SASS program structure and rationale.

During the second parent meeting, common parental reactions to their children's anxiety are reviewed. Through a facilitated discussion, parents identify their overprotective behaviors and are encouraged to implement more developmentally appropriate limits. Group leaders advise parents that increased autonomy leads to more effective coping and problem-solving skills, which are essential for nurturing independent individuals capable of making a successful transition to young adulthood. Therefore, parents are encouraged to discontinue providing excessive reassurance, being overly directive, and allowing avoidance of social interactions. Parents are instead instructed to encourage independence and positive coping, to provide reinforcement for nonanxious behavior, to prevent avoidance, to communicate empathy, and to model nonanxious behavior.

Teacher Meetings

Teacher education and collaboration are important benefits of school-based intervention. Teachers are often eager for information about how to assist shy students. Group leaders meet with teachers to educate them about social anxiety and the goals of SASS. Teachers identify areas of social difficulty for participants, and potential classroom exposures are discussed. Throughout the program, group leaders work with teachers to develop appropriate gradual exposures. For instance, if a student fears answering questions in class, the teacher may initially provide the student with the answer to a question prior to class, followed by providing the student with the question but not the answer, until eventually the student practices answering questions more spontaneously. Teachers provide feedback about students' progress and identify additional areas to be targeted.

IMPLEMENTATION CHALLENGES

Although the advantages are evident, there are a number of challenges to implementing school-based intervention.

School Culture

Successful entry of any novel program into the school system requires an awareness of the school culture and attitudes about school-based mental health. Because academic instruction is the primary mission of schools, it is important to minimize interference with class instruction. However, conducting groups after school is difficult because of extracurricular school programs, transportation schedules, and students' desire to leave school at the end of the day. Therefore, it is recommended that groups occur during school hours, but because of competing school demands (e.g., field trips, exams, teacher reluctance to release students from class), flexibility in implementation is essential. Intervention sessions can be rotated weekly to ensure that students do not miss the same class repeatedly; occasional missed group sessions can be conducted individually; and meetings with teachers can facilitate a better understanding of the value of the program.

Identification of Social Anxiety

Unfortunately, SAD is often unrecognized in clinical settings, and a substantial portion of patients are not referred for treatment services (e.g., Weiller, Bisserbe, Boyer, Lepine, & Lecrubier, 1996). Therefore, any school-based treatment for SAD also has to involve methods for identification of cases. Social anxiety self-report inventories can be incorporated into standard school screenings conducted by the guidance or counseling department. Other options for identifying anxious students may include sending letters with screening tools to parents, observation of students in various school settings, and teacher and counselor nominations. The accuracy of referrals by school personnel may be enhanced by psychoeducation and in-service trainings about social anxiety and the benefits of intervention (Weissman, Antinoro, & Chu, 2008).

Confidentiality

Although providing treatment in schools can reduce stigma associated with seeking mental health services in traditional clinic settings, it may also increase student sensitivity about confidentiality, given the presence of peers and school personnel. There are many ways to address concerns regarding privacy in the school setting. First, the program is named Skills for Academic and Social Success, which prevents it from sounding too "therapy oriented," and intentionally obscures the nature of the program. Second, school personnel are informed about the general purpose of the program and about which students are participating but are not provided with detailed information about students' difficulties or concerns. Third, students are fully informed about confidentiality limits and the role of teachers and peer assistants in SASS. In addition, group leaders discuss confidentiality in the first session, and participating students sign a confidentiality agreement to maintain the privacy of others. Similarly, the importance of confidentiality is discussed with peer assistants, and group leaders review how to handle interacting with group members outside of scheduled program activities. Last, program meetings should be conducted in a private room in an area with minimal student traffic, and guidance passes can be used to inform students of the time and location of intervention sessions while maintaining their anonymity.

SKILLS FOR ACADEMIC AND SOCIAL
SUCCESS OUTCOME STUDIES

SASS has been evaluated in a small open trial (Masia et al., 2001), a waiting-list control trial (Masia-Warner et al., 2005), and an attention control trial (Masia-Warner et al., 2007). In the waiting-list control trial, 35 adolescents, ages 14 to 16 years, from two urban parochial schools were randomized to either SASS or a waiting list. Treatment was conducted by a clinical psychologist trained in the intervention. The SASS intervention was superior to a waiting list in reducing social anxiety and avoidance and enhancing functioning, as noted by blinded evaluator, parent, and adolescent ratings. Of the SASS group,

94% were classified as responders compared with only 12% of waiting-list participants. In addition, 67% of SASS participants, versus 6% in the waiting-list group, no longer met diagnostic criteria for social phobia at postassessment. Clinical gains were maintained 9 months following treatment termination. This initial study demonstrated that adolescents participating in SASS improved over time in comparison with students who received no treatment and that SASS could be feasibly implemented in school settings.

The second controlled investigation compared SASS with a credible attention control in 36 adolescents ages 14 to 16 with SAD (Masia-Warner et al., 2007). The attention control omitted any therapeutic elements considered specific to reversing social anxiety but was matched on other relevant therapy variables. It was designed to match SASS in overall structure with the inclusion of the four social events conducted without the outgoing school peers. The content consisted of psychoeducation about social anxiety, relaxation techniques, and support. Credibility, as perceived by students and their parents, was assessed and was equivalent across interventions. At posttreatment, SASS was superior to the attention control in reducing social anxiety and improving overall functioning. Only 7% in the attention control, versus 82% in SASS, were treatment responders. In addition, 59% of the SASS group no longer qualified for a diagnosis of social phobia versus 0% of the attention control. SASS was also superior to the attention control 6 months beyond the cessation of treatment. Overall, this study supported the specific efficacy of SASS and provided further justification for its dissemination to schools.

These two studies have particular significance because schools provide the opportunity to enhance recognition of social anxiety through education of school personnel and parents and to intervene with impaired teenagers who otherwise would not receive treatment. Only a minority of adolescents had ever sought treatment for social anxiety (Masia-Warner et al., 2005, 2007) in spite of the student samples being from middle-class backgrounds. The participating adolescents were comparable to clinic-based samples in severity, self-reported social anxiety, and comorbidity, demonstrating the clinical significance of identifying and intervening with nonreferred community youth.

SUMMARY

Schools play an important role in addressing the unmet mental health needs of adolescents and can provide a cost-effective setting for service delivery. School-based intervention may be particularly relevant to adolescents with SAD because they are unlikely to receive treatment, and their impairments are social in nature and often related to the school environment. On the basis of the positive features of addressing SAD in schools, SASS was developed specifically for school delivery. Although considerably shorter than other treatment programs, efficacy was demonstrated on multiple outcomes. Intervening in school may optimize benefits by providing a real-world setting in which to implement exposure and to facilitate generalization. It enables enrollment of school staff to tailor exposures (e.g., asking questions to the librarian, speaking to the principal) and of school peers to practice social interaction. Finally, the fact that treated adolescents and peer assistants are in school together facilitates social risk taking and generalization to the natural environment. This central treatment goal is difficult to accomplish in traditional clinic settings.

FUTURE DIRECTIONS

Thus far, the clinical trials examining the efficacy of SASS have used doctoral-level clinical psychologists as group leaders. Relying on highly trained professionals may limit the impact and value of school-based intervention. A logical next step toward dissemination and sustainability is to determine if school counselors can implement SASS effectively. We are currently conducting a large federally funded clinical trial to evaluate the clinical utility of SASS delivered by school counselors. This study will also provide information on the value of training frontline school professionals to deliver evidence-based programs. It will be important to explore the type and level of training necessary for school personnel as well as ways to ensure treatment integrity such as using innovative technologies for intervention training and implementation. If successful, this approach could vastly increase the availability of effective treatments for youth with social anxiety as well as other underserved children and adolescents.

REFERENCES

Adelman, H. S., & Taylor, L. (1999). Mental health in schools and system restructuring. Clinical Psychology Review, 19, 137–163. doi:10.1016/S0272-7358(98)00071-3

Alfano, C. A., Beidel, D. C., & Turner, S. M. (2006). Cognitive correlates of social phobia among children and adolescents. Journal of Abnormal Child Psychology, 34, 182–194. doi:10.1007/s10802-005-9012-9

Anglin, T. M. (2003). Mental health in schools: Programs of the federal government. In M. D. Weist, S. W. Evans, & N. A. Lever (Eds.), Handbook of school mental health: Advancing practice and research (pp. 89–106). New York, NY: Kluwer Academic/Plenum.

Beidel, D. C., & Turner, S. M. (1998). Shy children, phobic adults: The nature and treatment of social phobia. Washington, DC: American Psychological Association. doi:10.1037/10285-000

Beidel, D. C., Turner, S. M., & Morris, T. L. (1998). *Social effectiveness therapy for children: A treatment manual.* Charleston: Medical University of South Carolina.

Beidel, D. C., Turner, S. M., & Morris, T. L. (1999). Psychopathology of childhood social phobia. *Journal of the American Academy of Child and Adolescent Psychiatry, 38,* 643–650. doi:10.1097/00004583-199906000-00010

Beidel, D. C., Turner, S. M., & Morris, T. L. (2000). Behavioral treatment of childhood social phobia. *Journal of Consulting and Clinical Psychology, 68,* 1072–1080. doi:10.1037/0022-006X.68.6.1072

Beidel, D. C., Turner, S. M., Young, B., & Paulson, A. (2005). Social Effectiveness Therapy for children: Three-year follow-up. *Journal of Consulting and Clinical Psychology, 73,* 721–725. doi:10.1037/0022-006X.73.4.721

Burns, B. J., Costello, E. J., Angold, A., Tweed, D., Stangl, D., Farmer, E. M., & Erkanli, A. (1995). Children's mental health service use across service sectors. *Health Affairs, 14,* 147–159. doi:10.1377/hlthaff.14.3.147

Catron, T., & Weiss, B. (1994). The Vanderbilt School-Based Counseling Program: An interagency, primary-care model of mental health services. *Journal of Emotional and Behavioral Disorders, 2,* 247–253. doi:10.1177/106342669400200407

Collins, K. A., Westra, H. A., Dozois, D. J. A., & Burns, D. D. (2004). Gaps in accessing treatment for anxiety and depression: Challenges for the delivery of care. *Clinical Psychology Review, 24,* 583–616. doi:10.1016/j.cpr.2004.06.001

Essau, C. A., Conradt, J., & Petermann, F. (1999). Frequency and comorbidity of social phobia and social fears in adolescents. *Behaviour Research and Therapy, 37,* 831–843. doi:10.1016/S0005-7967(98)00179-X

Evans, S. W., Langberg, J., & Williams, J. (2003). Achieving generalization in school-based mental health. In M. D. Weist, S. W. Evans, & N. A. Lever (Eds.), *Handbook of school mental health: Advancing practice and research* (pp. 335–348). New York, NY: Kluwer Academic/Plenum Publishers.

Farmer, E. M., Stangl, D. K., Burns, B. J., Costello, E., & Angold, A. (1999). Use, persistence, and intensity: Patterns of care for children's mental health across one year. *Community Mental Health Journal, 35,* 31–46. doi:10.1023/A:1018743908617

Flisher, A. J., Kramer, R., Grosser, R., Alegria, M., Bird, H., Bourdon, K., . . . Hoven, C. W. (1997). Correlates of unmet need for mental health services by children and adolescents. *Psychological Medicine, 27,* 1145–1154. doi:10.1017/S0033291797005412

Hofmann, S. G., Albano, A. M., Heimberg, R. G., Tracey, S., Chorpita, B. F., & Barlow, D. H. (1999). Subtypes of social phobia in adolescents. *Depression and Anxiety, 9,* 15–18. doi:10.1002/(SICI)1520-6394(1999)9:1<15::AID-DA2>3.0.CO;2-6

Hoganbruen, K., Clauss-Ehlers, C., Nelson, D., & Faenza, M. M. (2003). Effective advocacy for school-based mental health programs. In M. D. Weist, S. W. Evans, & N. A. Lever (Eds.), *Handbook of school mental health advancing practice and research* (pp. 45–59). New York, NY: Kluwer Academic/Plenum.

Kashdan, T. B., & Herbert, J. D. (2001). Social anxiety disorder in childhood and adolescence: Current status and future directions. *Clinical Child and Family Psychology Review, 4*, 37–61. doi:10.1023/A:1009576610507

Kearney, C. A. (2005). *Social anxiety and social phobia in youth: Characteristics, assessment, and psychological treatment.* New York, NY: Springer.

Labellarte, M. J., Ginsburg, G. S., Walkup, J. T., & Riddle, M. A. (1999). The treatment of anxiety disorders in children and adolescents. *Biological Psychiatry, 46*, 1567–1578. doi:10.1016/S0006-3223(99)00248-6

Leaf, P. J., Alegria, M., Cohen, P., Goodman, S. H., Horowitz, S. M., Hoven, C. W., . . . Regier, D. A. (1996). Mental health service use in the community and schools: Results from the four-community MECA study. *Journal of the American Academy of Child and Adolescent Psychiatry, 35*, 889–897. doi:10.1097/00004583-199607000-00014

Masia, C. L., Beidel, D. C., Albano, A. M., Rapee, R. M., Turner, S. M., Morris, T. L., & Klein, R. G. (1999). *Skills for academic and social success.* Unpublished manuscript, New York University School of Medicine, Child Study Center.

Masia, C. L., Klein, R. G., Storch, E. A., & Corda, B. (2001). School-based behavioral treatment for social anxiety disorder in adolescents: Results of a pilot study. *Journal of the American Academy of Child and Adolescent Psychiatry, 40*, 780–786. doi:10.1097/00004583-200107000-00012

Masia-Warner, C., Fisher, P. F., Shrout, P. E., Rathor, S., & Klein, R. G. (2007). Treating adolescents with social anxiety disorder in school: An attention control trial. *Journal of Child Psychology and Psychiatry, 48*, 676–686.

Masia-Warner, C., Klein, R. G., Dent, H. C., Fisher, P. H., Alvir, J., Albano, A. M., & Guardino, M. (2005). School-based intervention for adolescents with social anxiety disorder: Results of a controlled study. *Journal of Abnormal Child Psychology, 33*, 707–722. doi:10.1007/s10802-005-7649-z

Offord, D. R., Boyle, M. H., Szatmari, P., Rae-Grant, N. I., Links, P. S., Cadman, D. T., . . . Woodward, C. A. (1987). Ontario Child Health Study: II. Six-month prevalence of disorder and rates of service utilization. *Archives of General Psychiatry, 44*, 832–836.

Rapee, R. M. (1998). *Overcoming shyness and social phobia: A step-by-step guide.* Northvale, NJ: Aronson.

Spence, S. H., Donovan, C., & Brechman-Toussaint, M. (1999). Social skills, social outcomes, and cognitive features of childhood social phobia. *Journal of Abnormal Psychology, 108*, 211–221. doi:10.1037/0021-843X.108.2.211

Verhulst, F. C., & Van der Ende, J. (1997). Factors associated with child mental health service use in the community. *Journal of the American Academy of Child and Adolescent Psychiatry, 36*, 901–909. doi:10.1097/00004583-199707000-00011

Verhulst, F. C., van der Ende, J., Ferdinand, R. F., & Kasius, M. C. (1997). The prevalence of *DSM–III–R* diagnoses in a national sample of Dutch adolescents. *Archives of General Psychiatry, 54*, 329–336.

Weiller, E., Bisserbe, J. C., Boyer, P., Lepine, J. P., & Lecrubier, Y. (1996). Social phobia in general health care: An unrecognized undertreated disabling disorder. *The British Journal of Psychiatry, 168,* 169–174. doi:10.1192/bjp.168.2.169

Weissman, A. S., Antinoro, D., & Chu, B. C. (2008). Cognitive-behavioral therapy for anxiety in school settings: Advances and challenges. In M. Mayer, R. Van Acker, J. E. Lochman, & F. M. Gresham (Eds.), *Cognitive-behavioral interventions for students with emotional/behavioral disorders* (pp. 173–203). New York, NY: Guilford Press.

Weist, M. D. (1997). Expanded school mental health services: A national movement in progress. In T. H. Ollendick & R. J. Prinz (Eds.), *Advances in clinical child psychology* (Vol. 19, pp. 319–352). New York, NY: Plenum Press.

Weist, M. D. (1999). Challenges and opportunities in expanded school mental health. *Clinical Psychology Review, 19,* 131–135. doi:10.1016/S0272-7358(98)00068-3

Wittchen, H.-U., Stein, M., & Kessler, R. (1999). Social fears and social phobia in a community sample of adolescents and young adults: Prevalence, risk factors and comorbidity. *Psychological Medicine, 29,* 309–323. doi:10.1017/S0033291798008174

Wu, P., Hoven, C. W., Bird, H. R., Moore, R. E., Cohen, P., Alegria, M., . . . Bostic, J. Q. (1999). Depressive and disruptive disorders and mental health service utilization in children and adolescents. *Journal of the American Academy of Child and Adolescent Psychiatry, 38,* 1081–1089. doi:10.1097/00004583-199909000-00010

INDEX

Avoidance , *continued*
    as response option, 154
    of social situations, 15–17
    strategies of, 151
    Axis I disorders, 21

Baer, S., 253
Baker-Morissette, S. L., 116
Barlas, M. E., 205
Barlow, D. H., 30, 116
Barriers
    to participation in clinical trials,
        211
    to treatment, 18, 282
    to treatment of minorities, 210–212
Baser, R. E., 204
Battaglia, M., 34
BCSs (behavioral coding systems), 232
Beck, J. G., 76
Behavioral and cognitive behavioral
        treatments, 245–257
    for autism spectrum disorders, 194
    components of, 247–251
    enhanced with pharmacotherapy,
        256
    evidence-based, 251–256
    for LGBT youth, 172
    medication vs., 254–255
    with pharmacotherapy, 267
    for school refusal behavior, 132–133
Behavioral avoidance, 15–16
Behavioral Avoidance scale (of
        SPAI–C), 193
Behavioral coding systems (BCSs), 232
Behavioral inhibition (BI), 34–35,
        81–82
Behavioral observations, 236–237
Beidel, D. C., 11, 13, 15, 18–29, 32, 39,
        128, 211, 252, 253, 255, 283, 285
Bellini, S., 193
Benzodiazepines, 272
Berndt, T. J., 145
Beta-adrenergic blockers, 272–273
Beta-adrenergic system, 12
BI (behavioral inhibition), 34–35,
        81–82
Biases
    cognitive, 40–41
    cultural, 207–208
    in information processing, 232–233

Biederman, J., 35
Bierman, K. L., 150
Birmaher, B., 268, 270
Bisexual youth. *See* Lesbian, gay, bisex-
        ual, and transgender youth
Blair, K., 61
Blood pressure, 12–13
Blushing, 235
Bohlin, G., 36
Bolton, D., 33
Booster sessions, 288
Booth-LaForce, C., 144–145, 153
Bourland, S., 37
Boys
    brain development in, 55
    dating and romantic relationships of,
        95
    depression and SAD rates in, 82–83
Brain development, 54–55
Brain structures, 55–58
Broadwin, I. T., 126
Buckner, J. D., 115, 256
Bukowski, W. M., 150
Burgess, K. B., 144–145, 153
Burke, R. S., 112
Buxkamperb, R., 253–254

Cambron, S., 37
Campbell, R. D., 204
Cannabis use disorder (CUD), 114–115
Carrigan, M. H., 111, 112
Cartwright-Hatton, S., 32
Caucasian youth, 207–208, 210, 274
Causal direction, 40, 97
Causal factors, 116–117, 162–167,
        169–170
Causal risk factors, 37
CBGT-A (cognitive behavioral group
        treatment for adolescents), 252,
        253
Centers for Disease Control and Pre-
        vention, 183
Chambless, D. L., 210
Chavira, D. A., 254, 267
Child and Adolescent Symptom Inven-
        tory–20, 191–192
Childhood abuse, 166–167
Chronological course, 190
Cigarette smokers, 116
Citalopram, 254–255, 267

Clark, D. M., 30, 255
Clinical interviews, 226–227
Clinical trials, 211, 265–266, 275–276
Clinician-administered scales and interviews, 227–229
Cognitive behavioral group treatment for adolescents (CBGT-A), 252, 253
Cognitive behavioral therapy (CBT). *See* Behavioral and cognitive behavioral treatments
Cognitive biases, 40–41
Cognitive factors, 77–78
Cognitive measures, 236–237
Cognitive processes, 78
Cognitive symptoms, 13–15
Cognitive techniques, 248–249
Collaboration, 133–134
Collectivism, 208–209
College students, 165
Communication, nonverbal, 285
Communication technology, 98–100
Comorbid disorders. *See also specific headings*
    research on, 20–22
    and temperament, 81–82
    timing of symptoms with, 76
Comparative studies, 254–255
Compton, S. N., 267
Computer-based assessments, 233
Conceptualization, 190–191
Conditioning experiences, 38–39
Conduct disorder, 125
Confidentiality, 291
Conflict, family, 134
Conger, J. J., 109
Conradt, J., 75
Contexts, 95–96, 286–287
Conversational skills, 285
Co-occuring conditions, 225–226
Cook, M., 39
Cooper, M. L., 113
Corcoran, K. J., 112
Core fears, 286–287
Cortisol levels, 234
Cost-effectiveness, 282, 292
Costello, E. J., 126–127
Counseling, 274
Counselors, school, 293
Crick, N. R., 153

Cross-ethnic and cross-cultural research, 204–205, 208–209
CUD (cannabis use disorder), 114–115
Cultural biases, 207–208
Cultural influences, 203–212
    broad factors in, 208–210
    and evidence-based treatments, 210–212
    in measurement of social anxiety, 205–208
    on social anxiety prevalence, 204–205
Culture, school, 290
Culture-bound syndromes, 203–204

Dahl, R. E., 4
Daleiden, E. L., 32
D'Andrea, M., 204
Dating and romantic relationships, 93–101. *See also* Lesbian, gay, bisexual, and transgender youth
    contexts for, 95–96
    developmental and qualitative aspects of, 94–95
    gender and ethnicity in, 95
    and social and dating anxiety, 96–98
    and technological advancements, 98–100
Dating anxiety, 96–98
Dating violence, 99–100
Davila, J., 76
D-cycloserine (DCS), 256
Dependence, 114
Depression, 75–84
    with autism spectrum disorders, 195
    as comorbid disorder, 20–22
    in LGBT youth, 169
    pharmacological treatment of, 274
    sex differences in, 82–83
    timing of comorbid symptoms of, 76
    unique and shared features with SAD, 77–82
Detrimental effects, 17–18
Developmental psychopathology framework, 5–6, 29–30
Developmental stage(s). *See also* Neurodevelopmental aspects
    adolescence as, 4–5, 42
    assessment strategies for, 225

Developmental stage(s), *continued*
   dating and romantic relationships at, 94–95
   medication decisions at, 274
   peer relations at, 149–151
   in SAD research, 11
   social skills at, 19
   variance in SAD, 246
Deviant peers, 134
Diagnosis
   with autism spectrum disorders, 188–194
   of social anxiety disorder, 245
   structured interviews for, 129, 229
Diagnostic and Statistical Manual of Mental Disorders (DSM–III), 110
Diagnostic and Statistical Manual of Mental Disorders (DSM–IV), 110, 245
Diagnostic interviews, 129, 192
Diagnostic Interview Schedule for Children–Version 4 (DISC–IV), 229
Direct conditioning, 38–39
DISC–IV (Diagnostic Interview Schedule for Children-Version 4), 229
Dizygotic (DZ) twins, 33
Dodge, K. A., 153
Dopaminergic dysregulation, 34
Dot probe task, 59–60
Doyle, J., 117
Drahota, A., 194
Drinking motives, 112–113
Drink refusal self-efficacy, 112
Drug use. *See* Alcohol and drug use
DSM–III (Diagnostic and Statistical Manual of Mental Disorders), 110
DSM–IV (Diagnostic and Statistical Manual of Mental Disorders), 110, 245
Dyadic relationships, 94
DZ (dizygotic) twins, 33

Early onset, 17–18, 150
Early risks, 146–148
Early timing hypothesis, 150
Eaves, L. J., 33
Egger, H. L., 126–127
Ego identity, 168–169
Eisenberg, M. E., 169
Eisenberg, P. S., 205
Eley, T. C., 33

Emotions
   in dating and romantic relationships, 93, 97
   facial gestures related to, 59–60
   negative, 81, 97
   neurobiological experience of, 55–56
   positive, 81
   processing of, 61
   regulation of, 77
Encoding, 153
Eng, W., 36
Environments, natural, 282–283
Epidemiology, 16–17
Essau, C. A., 75
Ethnicity, 95, 274. *See also specific headings*
Etiology, 29–42
   in developmental psychopathology framework, 29–30
   maintaining factors, 39–41
   models of, 30–32
   precipitating factors, 37–39
   predisposing factors, 32–37
   of substance use disorders, 107–108
Evaluation, 188–194
Evidence-based treatment
   behavioral and cognitive behavioral, 251–256
   in cultural contexts, 210–212
   limitations of pharmacological trials, 275–276
Exosystem interventions, 135
Expectancies, 111–112, 115
Exposure therapy
   and cognitive behavioral therapy, 248
   imaginal, 247
   in school-based interventions, 286–287
   systematic, 247–248
   treatment studies on, 253–254

Facial cues, 58–59, 61–62
Fairbanks, J. M., 269
Family. *See also* Parents
   abusive and negative experiences with, 166–167
   conflict in, 79, 134
   as factor in SAD and depression, 79–80
Farrow, S. M., 76

Farvolden, P., 266
FDA (Food and Drug Administration), 274
Fear circuit, 56
Fear hierarchy, 247, 286–287
Fears, 17, 286–287
Feeling different, 165–166
Ferrell, C. B., 211
Flexibility, 285
Fluoxetine, 255, 268–270
Fluvoxamine, 269
FMRI (functional magnetic resonance imaging), 55
Food and Drug Administration (FDA), 274
Formal observations, 131
Fraternal twins, 33
Fresco, D. M., 112
Friendships
    in adolescence, 144–145
    developmental trajectory of, 15–16
    as protective factor, 148–149
    shifts in, 150–151
    as stressor, 80–81
Functional equivalence, 207
Functional impairment, 18
Functional magnetic resonance imaging (fMRI), 55
Fung, J., 205

Gallagher, H. M., 252
Garland, E. J., 253
Gay youth. See Lesbian, gay, bisexual, and transgender youth
Gender
    in dating and romantic relationships, 95
    nonconformity with roles of, 162–163
    in peer relations, 83
Gender identities. See Lesbian, gay, bisexual, and transgender youth
Generalized subtypes, 21
Genetic vulnerabilities, 33–34
Giedd, J. N., 54
Gilles, D. M., 112
Girls
    brain development of, 55
    dating and romantic relationships of, 95

depression and SAD rates in, 82–83
    puberty maturation of, 149–150
    risk of dating violence for, 99–100
Gladstone, G. L., 82
GM (gray matter), 54
Goals, for treatment, 131
Gonzales, N. A., 133
Grant, D. M., 76
Gray matter (GM), 54
Greca, A. M., 145
Greco, L. A., 152
Group acceptance, 145, 148, 152
Group treatments, 282, 284–287
Gulliver, S. B., 116

Habituation, 247
Hagekull, B., 36
Ham, L. S., 111
Har, K., 194
Harada, Y., 128
Hardy, C. L., 150
Hart, T. A., 36
Heart rate, 12–13
Heath, A. C., 33
Heimberg, R., 32, 36
Hemodynamics, 55
Herbert, J. D., 251, 253
Heritability, 33–34
Heterosexual adolescents. See Dating and romantic relationships
Heterosocial situations, 96, 98
Higa, C. K., 32
Himle, J. A., 204
Hirshfeld-Becker, D. R., 35
Hispanic youth, 95. See also Cultural influences
HIV (human immunodeficiency virus), 162, 164
Homophobia, 163, 164
Hope, D. A., 32
Hudson, J. L., 37
Huey, S. J., Jr., 210–211
Hugadahl, K., 39
Hui, H. C., 206
Human immunodeficiency virus (HIV), 162, 164

Identical twins, 33
Imaginal exposure, 247
Imaginal flooding, 247

Immigration, 209, 211–212
Implementation, 290–291
Impression management, 117
Indirect conditioning, 39
Individualism, 208–209
Individualized education plans, 135
Individual sessions, 288
Informal observations, 131
Information processing, 153–154,
    232–233
Inhibited temperament, 147–148
Insecure attachment, 35–36
Integrative models, 169–170
Intercourse, sexual, 94
Intergenerational transmission, 79
Internalized homophobia, 164
Internet, 98–100
Interpersonal relationships, 78–81,
    209–210
Interpretation, of social cues, 153–154
Interviews, 129, 192, 226–229
Intimacy, 152
Isolan, L., 267

Jackson, J. S., 204
Janet, P., 266
Jaycox, L. H., 274

Kagan, J., 35
Kaltiala-Heino, R., 80
Kang, S., 205
Kashdan, T. B., 97, 251
Kearney, C. A., 127
Kendall, P. C., 151, 232
Kendler, K. S., 33, 39
Kennedy, W. A., 126
Kessler, R. C., 33, 75
Kushner, M. G., 109–110, 112

Latino youth, 95, 207, 210. See also Cul-
    tural influences
Lau, A. S., 205
Learning theory, 247
Length of treatment, 275
Lesbian, gay, bisexual, and transgender
    (LGBT) youth, 161–173
    causal factors for, 162–167
    effects of social anxiety on, 167–172
LGBT. See Lesbian, gay, bisexual, and
    transgender youth

Liebowitz, M. R., 34, 36
Liebowitz Social Anxiety Scale for
    Children and Adolescents, 227
Lindstrom, K. M., 59, 60
Linguistic equivalence, 206–207
Loneliness, 194–195
Lopata, C., 184
"Loss of face," 205

Magee, W. J., 38
Magnetic resonance imaging (MRI), 55
Maintaining factors, 31, 39–41, 289
Mancini, C., 266
Markon, K. E., 81
Marttunen, M., 80
MASC (Multidimensional Anxiety
    Scale for Children), 193, 229
Masia, C. L., 283
Maturation, 23, 149–150
McCloskey, M. S., 252
Mcshane, G., 126, 128
Measurement
    cultural influences on, 205–208
    equivalence of, 205–207
    process of, 235–236
    of social skills with ASD, 186
Measures
    clinical utility of, 235
    cognitive, 236–237
    observational, 231–233
    other-report, 192
    parent-report, 191–192
    for parents, 129–130, 191–192
    performance-based, 231–233
    physiological, 231–237
    self-report, 129–130, 193–194
Medication. See Pharmacotherapy
Medina, K. L., 109–110
Mental health care, 281–282
Merikangas, K. R., 108
MET (motivation enhancement ther-
    apy), 256
Methods, 226–235
Milham, M. P., 64
Mineka, S., 39
Mirtazapine, 271
Moak, D. H., 111
Monk, C. S., 59
Monoamines, 57
Monozygotic (MZ) twins, 33

Risk factors
    for alcohol or drug dependence, 107
    causal, 37
    for dating violence, 99–100
    in early life, 146–148
    in pharmacological treatment, 275
Risk-taking behaviors, 4
Risky sexual behaviors, 100, 168
Roberti, J. W., 205
Rofey, D. L., 112
ROIs (regions of interest), 63, 64
Romantic relationships. *See* Dating and
    romantic relationships
Rose, A. J., 83
Rose-Kasnor, L., 144–145
Rose-Krasnor, L., 153
Rubin, K. H., 144–145, 153
Rudolph, K. D., 83
Rumination, 77–78
Rydell, A., 36

SAD. *See* Social anxiety disorder
Saitoh, K., T., 128
Sallee, R. F., 255
SAS–A (Social Anxiety Scale for Ado-
    lescents), 205–206, 230–231
SASC–R (Social Anxiety Scale for
    Children–Revised), 193
Scalar equivalence, 207
Scales. *See also specific headings*
    clinician-administered, 227–229
    for rating anxiety, 229–231
SCARED (Screen for Child Anxiety
    and Related Disorders), 229–230
SCAS (Spence Children's Anxiety
    Scale), 230
Schedule for Affective Disorders and
    Schizophrenia for School-Age
    Children, 228–229
Schemas, 153–154
Schilder, Paul, 3
Schmidt, N. B., 256
Schneier, F. R., 34, 36
School-based interventions, 281–293
    benefits of, 281–283
    implementation of, 290–291
    outcome studies on, 291–292
    Skills for Academic and Social Suc-
        cess program, 283–284
    treatment components, 284–290

School counselors, 293
School culture, 290
School records, 131
School Refusal Assessment
    Scale–Revised (SRAS–R), 130
School refusal behavior. *See* Opposi-
    tional and school refusal behavior
School settings, 171–172
School transitions, 150–151
Screen for Child Anxiety and Related
    Disorders (SCARED), 229–230
Seiffge-Krenke, I., 98
Selective mutism, 269
Selective serotonin reuptake inhibitors
    (SSRIs), 195, 266–270
Self-efficacy, 112
Self-focused attention, 14–15, 31, 153
Self-medication, 107–110
Self-perceptions, 248
Self-report measures, 129–130,
    193–194
Separation anxiety disorder, 22
Serotonergic functioning, 34, 273
Serotonin and norepinephrine reuptake
    inhibitors (SNRIs), 266
Sertraline, 254
SET-C. *See* Social Effectiveness Ther-
    apy for Children and Adolescents
Sex differences, 82–83
Sexual abuse, 166–167
Sexual behaviors, risky, 100, 168
Sexual intercourse, 94
Sexual orientation. *See* Lesbian, gay,
    bisexual, and transgender youth
Sexual orientation victimization
    (SOV), 162, 165
Shared environments, 33
Shyness
    as predictor, 147
    as related condition, 19–20
    and SAD diagnosis, 245
    with social withdrawal, 148–149
Silverman, W. K., 205
Sippola, K., 150
Situational cues, 153
Skills for Academic and Social Success
    (SASS), 250, 283. *See also*
    School-based interventions
Smith, J. P., 112
Smits, J. A., 253–254

ABOUT THE EDITORS

Candice A. Alfano, PhD, received her doctorate in clinical psychology in 2005 from the University of Maryland, College Park. After completing a postdoctoral research fellowship at the Johns Hopkins University School of Medicine, she joined the faculty at Children's National Medical Center in Washington, DC. Dr. Alfano is an assistant professor of psychology and pediatrics at the George Washington University School of Medicine. She founded and directs the Child and Adolescent Anxiety Program at Children's National Medical Center, providing comprehensive clinical services for anxious youth and training for psychology interns and child psychiatry fellows. Dr. Alfano has received several awards for her research, including awards from the Anxiety Disorders Association of America, Division 53 (Society of Clinical Child and Adolescent Psychology) of the American Psychological Association (APA), and a 2008 New Investigator Award cosponsored by the National Institute of Mental Health and the American Society for Clinical Psychopharmacology. She received awards in 2009 and 2010 for Outstanding Teaching at Children's National Medical Center. Dr. Alfano serves on the editorial board of several scientific journals, including the *Journal of Anxiety Disorders*, and has authored numerous peer-reviewed articles and chapters. She is coauthor (with Deborah C. Beidel) of the book *Childhood Anxiety Disorders: A Guide to Research and*

Treatment. Her primary academic, research, and clinical interests focus on the early etiology, pathogenesis, and treatment of anxiety disorders, including the role of childhood sleep abnormalities. Dr. Alfano is the recipient of a 5-year Mentored Career Development Award from the National Institute of Mental Health to study sleep disturbances in children with anxiety disorders, including potential targets for psychosocial intervention.

Deborah C. Beidel, PhD, received her doctorate in 1986 from the University of Pittsburgh. After serving as faculty at the University of Pittsburgh; the Medical University of South Carolina; the University of Maryland, College Park; and Pennsylvania State College of Medicine, she joined the doctoral program in clinical psychology at the University of Central Florida in 2007. In addition to her appointment as professor of psychology, she is director of the doctoral program in clinical psychology and director of the University of Central Florida Anxiety Disorders Clinic. She was the 1990 recipient of the Association for Advancement of Behavior Therapy's New Researcher Award, the 1995 Distinguished Educator Award from the Association of Medical School Psychologists, and the 2005 recipient of the Samuel M. Turner Clinical Research Award from Division 12 (Society for Clinical Psychology) Section III (Society for a Science of Clinical Psychology) of the American Psychological Association (APA). Dr. Beidel is the American Board of Professional Psychology diplomate in clinical psychology and behavioral psychology and is a fellow of the APA and the Association for Psychological Science. Her academic, research, and clinical interests focus on child and adult anxiety disorders, including their etiology, psychopathology, and behavioral treatment. She is associate editor of the *Journal of Anxiety Disorders*. In addition to several professional books, Dr. Beidel is the author (with Cynthia Bulik, and Melinda Stanley) of the undergraduate textbook *Abnormal Psychology: A Scientist-Practitioner Approach*. She has been the recipient of numerous National Institute of Mental Health grants addressing the development and efficacy of behavioral interventions for adults and children with anxiety disorders.